CAMBRIDGE LIBRARY

Books of enduring scholar

Classics

From the Renaissance to the nineteenth century, Latin and Greek were compulsory subjects in almost all European universities, and most early modern scholars published their research and conducted international correspondence in Latin. Latin had continued in use in Western Europe long after the fall of the Roman empire as the lingua franca of the educated classes and of law, diplomacy, religion and university teaching. The flight of Greek scholars to the West after the fall of Constantinople in 1453 gave impetus to the study of ancient Greek literature and the Greek New Testament. Eventually, just as nineteenth-century reforms of university curricula were beginning to erode this ascendancy, developments in textual criticism and linguistic analysis, and new ways of studying ancient societies, especially archaeology, led to renewed enthusiasm for the Classics. This collection offers works of criticism, interpretation and synthesis by the outstanding scholars of the nineteenth century.

The Golden Bough: The Third Edition

This work by Sir James Frazer (1854–1941) is widely considered to be one of the most important early texts in the fields of psychology and anthropology. At the same time, by applying modern methods of comparative ethnography to the classical world, and revealing the superstition and irrationality beneath the surface of the classical culture which had for so long been a model for Western civilisation, it was extremely controversial. Frazer was greatly influenced by E.B. Tylor's *Primitive Culture* (also reissued in this series), and by the work of the biblical scholar William Robertson Smith, to whom the first edition is dedicated. The twelve-volume third edition, reissued here, was greatly revised and enlarged, and published between 1911 and 1915; the two-volume first edition (1890) is also available in this series. Volume 5 (1914) considers the oriental roots of the Greek myths of Adonis and Attis.

The Golden Bough
The Third Edition

VOLUME 5: ADONIS ATTIS OSIRIS:
STUDIES IN THE HISTORY
OF ORIENTAL RELIGION 1

J.G. FRAZER

CAMBRIDGE
UNIVERSITY PRESS

CAMBRIDGE UNIVERSITY PRESS

Cambridge, New York, Melbourne, Madrid, Cape Town,
Singapore, São Paolo, Delhi, Mexico City

Published in the United States of America by Cambridge University Press, New York

www.cambridge.org
Information on this title: www.cambridge.org/9781108047340

© in this compilation Cambridge University Press 2012

This edition first published 1914
This digitally printed version 2012

ISBN 978-1-108-04734-0 Paperback

THE GOLDEN BOUGH

A STUDY IN MAGIC AND RELIGION

THIRD EDITION

PART IV

ADONIS ATTIS OSIRIS

VOL. I

MACMILLAN AND CO., Limited
LONDON · BOMBAY · CALCUTTA
MELBOURNE

THE MACMILLAN COMPANY
NEW YORK · BOSTON · CHICAGO
DALLAS · SAN FRANCISCO

THE MACMILLAN CO. OF CANADA, Ltd.
TORONTO

ADONIS ATTIS OSIRIS

STUDIES IN THE HISTORY OF ORIENTAL RELIGION

BY

J. G. FRAZER, D.C.L., LL.D., Litt.D.

FELLOW OF TRINITY COLLEGE, CAMBRIDGE
PROFESSOR OF SOCIAL ANTHROPOLOGY IN THE UNIVERSITY OF LIVERPOOL

THIRD EDITION, REVISED AND ENLARGED

IN TWO VOLUMES
VOL. I

MACMILLAN AND CO., LIMITED
ST. MARTIN'S STREET, LONDON
1914

PREFACE TO THE FIRST EDITION

THESE studies are an expansion of the corresponding sections in my book *The Golden Bough*, and they will form part of the third edition of that work, on the preparation of which I have been engaged for some time. By far the greater portion of them is new, and they make by themselves a fairly complete and, I hope, intelligible whole. I shall be glad if criticisms passed on the essays in their present shape should enable me to correct and improve them when I come to incorporate them in my larger work.

In studying afresh these three Oriental worships, akin to each other in character, I have paid more attention than formerly to the natural features of the countries in which they arose, because I am more than ever persuaded that religion, like all other institutions, has been profoundly influenced by physical environment, and cannot be understood without some appreciation of those aspects of external nature which stamp themselves indelibly on the thoughts, the habits, the whole life of a people. It is a matter of great regret to me that I have never visited the East, and so cannot describe from personal knowledge the native lands of Adonis, Attis, and Osiris. But I have sought to remedy the defect by comparing the descriptions of eye-witnesses, and painting from them what may be called composite pictures of some of the scenes on which I have been led to touch in the course of this volume. I shall not have wholly failed if I have caught from my authorities and conveyed to my readers some notion, however dim, of the scenery, the atmosphere, the gorgeous colouring of the East.

J. G. FRAZER.

TRINITY COLLEGE, CAMBRIDGE,
    22*nd July* 1906.

PREFACE TO THE SECOND EDITION

IN this second edition some minor corrections have been
made and some fresh matter added. Where my views
appear to have been misunderstood, I have endeavoured to
state them more clearly ; where they have been disputed, I
have carefully reconsidered the evidence and given my reasons
for adhering to my former opinions. Most of the additions
thus made to the volume are comprised in a new chapter
(" Sacred Men and Women "), a new section (" Influence
of Mother-kin on Religion "), and three new appendices
(" Moloch the King," " The Widowed Flamen," and " Some
Customs of the Pelew Islanders "). Among the friends and
correspondents who have kindly helped me with information
and criticisms of various sorts I wish to thank particularly
Mr. W. Crooke, Professor W. M. Flinders Petrie, Mr. G. F.
Hill of the British Museum, the Reverend J. Roscoe of the
Church Missionary Society, and Mr. W. Wyse. Above all
I owe much to my teacher the Reverend Professor R. H.
Kennett, who, besides initiating me into the charms of the
Hebrew language and giving me a clearer insight into the
course of Hebrew history, has contributed several valuable
suggestions to the book and enhanced the kindness by
reading and criticizing some of the proofs.

J. G. FRAZER.

TRINITY COLLEGE, CAMBRIDGE,
22nd September 1907.

PREFACE TO THE THIRD EDITION

IN revising the book for this third edition I have made use of several important works which have appeared since the last edition was published. Among these I would name particularly the learned treatises of Count Baudissin on Adonis, of Dr. E. A. Wallis Budge on Osiris, and of my colleague Professor J. Garstang on the civilization of the Hittites, that still mysterious people, who begin to loom a little more distinctly from the mists of the past. Following the example of Dr. Wallis Budge, I have indicated certain analogies which may be traced between the worship of Osiris and the worship of the dead, especially of dead kings, among the modern tribes of Africa. The conclusion to which these analogies appear to point is that under the mythical pall of the glorified Osiris, the god who died and rose again from the dead, there once lay the body of a dead man. Whether that was so or not, I will not venture to say. The longer I occupy myself with questions of ancient mythology the more diffident I become of success in dealing with them, and I am apt to think that we who spend our years in searching for solutions of these insoluble problems are like Sisyphus perpetually rolling his stone up hill only to see it revolve again into the valley, or like the daughters of Danaus doomed for ever to pour water into broken jars that can hold no water. If we are taxed with wasting life in seeking to know what can never be known, and what, if it could be discovered, would not be worth knowing, what can we plead in our defence? I fear, very little. Such pursuits can hardly be defended on the ground of pure reason. We can only say that something, we know not what, drives us to attack the great enemy Ignorance wherever we see him, and that if we fail, as we probably shall, in our attack on his entrenchments, it may be useless but it is not inglorious to fall in leading a Forlorn Hope.

J. G. FRAZER.

CAMBRIDGE,
16*th January* 1914.

CONTENTS

BOOK FIRST

ADONIS . . . Pp. 1-259

CHAPTER I.—THE MYTH OF ADONIS . . Pp. 3-12

Changes of the seasons explained by the life and death of gods, p. 3 ; magical ceremonies to revive the divine energies, 4 *sq.*; prevalence of these ceremonies in Western Asia and Egypt, 5 *sq.*; Tammuz or Adonis in Babylon, 6-10 ; Adonis in Greek mythology, 10-12.

CHAPTER II.—ADONIS IN SYRIA . . . Pp. 13-30

Adonis and Astarte worshipped at Byblus, the kingdom of Cinyras, 13 *sq.*; divinity of Semitic kings, 15 *sqq.*; kings named Adonis, 16 *sq.*; "sacred men," 17 *sq.*; divinity of Hebrew kings, 18 *sqq.*; the Baal and Baalath the sources of fertility, 26 *sq.*; personation of the Baal by the king, 27 ; Cinyras, king of Byblus, 27 *sq.*; Aphaca and the vale of the Adonis, 28 *sqq.*

CHAPTER III.—ADONIS IN CYPRUS . . Pp. 31-56

Phoenician colonies in Cyprus, 31 *sq.*; kingdom of Paphos, 32 *sq.*; sanctuary of Aphrodite at Paphos, 33 *sq.*; the Aphrodite of Paphos a Phoenician or aboriginal deity, 34 ; her conical image, 34 *sqq.*; sacred prostitution in the worship of the Paphian Aphrodite and of other Asiatic goddesses, 36 *sqq.*; the Asiatic Mother Goddess a personification of all the reproductive energies of nature, 39 ; her worship reflects a period of sexual communism, 40 *sq.*; the daughters of Cinyras, 40 ; the Paphian dynasty of the Cinyrads, 41-43 ; incest of Cinyras with his daughter Myrrha and birth of Adonis, 43 ; suggested explanation of legends of royal incest, 43 *sq.*; the Flamen Dialis and his Flaminica at Rome, 45 *sq.*; Indian

parallels, 46-48 ; Cinyras beloved by Aphrodite, 48 *sq.*; Pygmalion and
Aphrodite, 49 ; the Phoenician kings of Cyprus and their sons the hereditary lovers of the goddess, 49 *sqq.*; the father and mother of a god, 51
sq.; Cinyras as a musician, 52 ; the uses of music in religion, 52 *sqq.*;
traditions as to the death of Cinyras, 55 *sq.*

CHAPTER IV.—SACRED MEN AND WOMEN   Pp. 57-109

§ 1. *An Alternative Theory*, pp. 57-61.— Theory of the secular origin of sacred
prostitution in Western Asia, p. 57 ; it fails to account for the facts, 57 *sqq.*

§ 2. *Sacred Women in India*, pp. 61-65.—The dancing-girls of Southern India
are at once prostitutes and wives of the god, 61 *sqq.*

§ 3. *Sacred Men and Women in West Africa*, pp. 65-70.— Among the Ewe
peoples the sacred prostitutes are regarded as the wives of the god, 65 *sqq.*;
human wives of serpent gods, 66-68 ; sacred men and women in West
Africa supposed to be possessed by the deity, 68 *sqq.*

§ 4. *Sacred Women in Western Asia*, pp. 70-72.—Sacred prostitutes of Western
Asia probably viewed as possessed by the deity and married to him, 70 *sq.*;
wives of the god in Babylon and Egypt, 71 *sq.*

§ 5. *Sacred Men in Western Asia*, pp. 72-78.—The sacred men (*kedeshim*) of
Western Asia may have been regarded as possessed by the deity and re-
presenting him, 72 *sq.*; the prophets, 74 *sqq.*; "holy men" in modern
Syria, 77 *sq.*

§ 6. *Sons of God*, pp. 78-82.—Belief that men and women may be the sons and
daughters of a god, 78 *sq.*; sons of the serpent-god, 80 *sqq.*

§ 7. *Reincarnation of the Dead*, pp. 82-107.—Belief that the dead come to life
as serpents, 82 *sqq.*; reincarnation of the dead in America, Africa, and
India, 91 *sqq.*; belief in the Virgin Birth among the savages of New
Guinea, Melanesia, and Australia, 96-107.

§ 8. *Sacred Stocks and Stones among the Semites*, pp. 107-109.—Procreative
virtue apparently ascribed to sacred stocks and stones among the Semites,
107 *sq.*; the excavations at Gezer, 108 *sq.*

CHAPTER V.—THE BURNING OF MELCARTH   Pp. 110-116

Semitic custom of sacrificing a member of the royal family, 110 ; the burning of
Melcarth at Tyre, 110 *sqq.*; the burning of Melcarth at Gades, 112 *sq.*;
the burning of a god or goddess at Carthage, 113 *sq.*; the fire-walk at
Tyre and at Castabala, 114 *sq.*; burnt sacrifice of King Hamilcar, 115 *sq.*;
the death of Hercules a Greek version of the burning of Melcarth, 116.

Chapter VI.—The Burning of Sandan Pp. 117-171

§ 1. *The Baal of Tarsus*, pp. 117-119.—The Tyrian Melcarth in Cyprus, 117 ; the lion-slaying god, 117 *sq.*; the Baal of Tarsus an Oriental god of corn and grapes, 118 *sq.*

§ 2. *The God of Ibreez*, pp. 119-123.—Counterpart of the Baal of Tarsus at Ibreez in Cappadocia, 119 *sq.*; the god of Ibreez a god of corn and grapes, 120 *sq.*; fertility of Ibreez, 122 *sq.*; the horned god, 123.

§ 3. *Sandan of Tarsus*, pp. 124-127.—The god of Ibreez a Hittite deity, 124 *sq.*; the burning of Sandan or Hercules at Tarsus, 125 *sq.*; Sandan of Tarsus an Asiatic god with the symbols of the lion and double axe, 127.

§ 4. *The Gods of Boghaz-Keui*, pp. 128-142.—Boghaz-Keui the ancient capital of a Hittite kingdom in Cappadocia, 128 *sq.*; the rock-sculptures in the sanctuary at Boghaz-Keui, the two processions, 129 *sqq.*; the lion-god, 131 ; the god and his priest, 131 *sq.*; the great Asiatic goddess and her consort, 133 *sqq.*; the Father God of the thundering sky, 134-136 ; the Mother Goddess, 137 ; the divine Son and lover of the goddess, 137 *sq.*; the mystery of the lion-god, 139 *sq.*; the Sacred Marriage of the god and goddess, 140 *sq.*; traces of mother-kin among the Hittites, 141 *sq.*

§ 5. *Sandan and Baal at Tarsus*, pp. 142 *sq.*—Sandan at Tarsus apparently a son of Baal, as Hercules of Zeus, 142 *sq.*

§ 6. *Priestly Kings of Olba*, pp. 143-152.—Priests of Sandan or Hercules at Tarsus, 143 *sq.*; kings of Cilicia related to Sandan, 144 ; priestly kings of Olba bearing the names of Teucer and Ajax, 144 *sq.*; the Teucrids of Salamis in Cyprus, 145 ; burnt sacrifices of human victims at Salamis and traces of a similar custom elsewhere, 145-147 ; the priestly Teucers of Olba perhaps representatives of a native god Tark, 147 *sq.*; Western or Rugged Cilicia, 148 *sq.*; the Cilician pirates, 149 *sq.*; the gorges of Cilicia, 150 ; the site and ruins of Olba, 151 *sq.*; the temple of Olbian Zeus, 151.

§ 7. *The God of the Corycian Cave*, pp. 152-161.—Limestone caverns of Western Cilicia, 152 *sq.*; the city of Corycus, 153 ; the Corycian cave, 153 *sq.*; the priests of Corycian Zeus, 155 ; the cave of the giant Typhon, 155 *sq.*; battle of Zeus and Typhon, 156 *sq.*; fossil bones of extinct animals a source of tales of giants, 157 *sq.*; chasm of Olbian Zeus at Kanytelideis, 158 *sq.*; the god of these chasms called Zeus by the Greeks, but probably a native god of fertility, 159 *sq.*; analogy of these caverns to Ibreez and the vale of the Adonis, 160 ; the two gods of Olba perhaps a father and son, 160 *sq.*

§ 8. *Cilician Goddesses*, pp. 161-170.—Goddesses less prominent than gods in Cilician religion, 161 ; the goddess 'Atheh the partner of Baal at Tarsus, 162 *sq.*; the lion-goddess and the bull-god, 162-164 ; the old goddess in later times the Fortune of the City, 164 *sq.*; the Phoenician god El and his wife at Mallus, 165 *sq.*; assimilation of native Oriental deities to Greek divinities, 166 *sq.*; Sarpedonian Artemis, 167 ; the goddess Perasia at Hieropolis-Castabala, 167 *sqq.*; the fire-walk in the worship of Perasia, 168 *sq.*; insensibility to pain a mark of inspiration, 169 *sq.*

§ 9. *The Burning of Cilician Gods*, pp. 170 *sq.*—Interpretation of the fiery rites of Sandan and Perasia, 170 *sq.*

CHAPTER VII.—SARDANAPALUS AND HER-
CULES . . . . . . Pp. 172-187

§ 1. *The Burning of Sardanapalus*, pp. 172-174.—Tarsus said to have been founded by Sardanapalus, 172 *sq.* ; his legendary death in the fire, 173 ; historical foundation of the legend, 173 *sq.*

§ 2. *The Burning of Croesus*, pp. 174-179.—Improbability of the story that Cyrus intended to burn Croesus, 174 *sq.* ; older and truer tradition that Croesus attempted to burn himself, 175 *sq.* ; death of Semiramis in the fire, 176 *sq.* ; "great burnings" for Jewish kings, 177 *sqq.*

§ 3. *Purification by Fire*, pp. 179-181.—Death by fire a mode of apotheosis, 179 *sq.* ; fire supposed to purge away the mortal parts of men, leaving the immortal, 180 *sq.*

§ 4. *The Divinity of Lydian Kings*, pp. 182-185.—Descent of Lydian kings from Hercules, the god of the double axe and the lion, 182 *sq.* ; Lydian kings held responsible for the weather and crops, 183 ; the lion-god of Lydia, 184 ; identity of the Lydian and Cilician Hercules, 184 *sq.*

§ 5. *Hittite Gods at Tarsus and Sardes*, p. 185.—The Cilician and Lydian Hercules (Sandan or Sandon) apparently a Hittite deity, 185.

§ 6. *The Resurrection of Tylon*, pp. 186-187.—Death and resurrection of the Lydian hero Tylon, 186 ; feast of the Golden Flower at Sardes, 187.

CHAPTER VIII.—VOLCANIC RELIGION Pp. 188-222

§ 1. *The Burning of a God*, pp. 188 *sq.*—The custom of burning a god perhaps intended to recruit his divine energies, 188 *sq.*

§ 2. *The Volcanic Region of Cappadocia*, pp. 189-191.—The custom of burning a god perhaps related to volcanic phenomena, 189 *sq.* ; the great extinct volcano Mount Argaeus in Cappadocia, 190 *sq.*

§ 3. *Fire-Worship in Cappadocia*, pp. 191-193.—Persian fire-worship in Cappadocia, 191 ; worship of natural fires which burn perpetually, 192 *sq.*

§ 4. *The Burnt Land of Lydia*, pp. 193-194.—The Burnt Land of Lydia, 193 *sq.* ; its soil favourable to the cultivation of the vine, 194.

§ 5. *The Earthquake God*, pp. 194-203.—Earthquakes in Asia Minor, 194 *sq.* ; worship of Poseidon, the earthquake god, 195 *sq.* ; Spartan propitiation of Poseidon during an earthquake, 196 ; East Indian and other modes of stopping an earthquake, 197-201 ; religious and moral effects of earthquakes, 201 *sq.* ; the god of the sea and of the earthquake naturally conceived as the same, 202 *sq.*

§ 6. *The Worship of Mephitic Vapours,* pp. 203-206.—Poisonous mephitic vapours, 203 *sq.* ; places of Pluto or Charon, 204 ; the valley of Amsanctus, 204 *sq.* ; sanctuaries of Charon or Pluto in Caria and Lydia or Phrygia, 206 *sq.*

§ 7. *The Worship of Hot Springs,* pp. 206-216.—The hot springs and petrified cascades of Hierapolis, 206-208 ; Hercules the patron of hot springs, 209 *sq.* ; hot springs of Hercules at Thermopylae and Aedepsus, 210-212 ; reasons for the association of Hercules with hot springs, 213 ; the hot springs of Callirrhoe in Moab, 214-216.

§ S. *The Worship of Volcanoes in other Lands,* pp. 216-222.—The worship of the great volcano Kirauea in Hawaii, 216-219 ; sacrifices to volcanoes in America, Java, and Sicily, 219-221 ; no evidence that the kings and gods burnt in Asia were sacrificed to volcanoes, 221 *sq.*

CHAPTER IX.—THE RITUAL OF ADONIS . Pp. 223-235

Results of the preceding inquiry, 223 ; festivals of the death and resurrection of Adonis, 224 *sq.* ; the festival at Alexandria, 224 *sq.* ; the festival at Byblus, 225 *sq.* ; the anemone and the red rose the flowers of Adonis, 225 *sq.* ; festivals of Adonis at Athens and Antioch, 226 *sq.* ; resemblance of these rites to Indian and European ceremonies, 227 ; the death and resurrection of Adonis a myth of the decay and revival of vegetation, 227 *sqq.* ; Tammuz or Adonis as a corn-spirit bruised and ground in a mill, 230 *sq.* ; the mourning for Adonis interpreted as a harvest rite, 231 *sq.* ; Adonis probably a spirit of wild fruits before he became a spirit of the cultivated corn, 232 *sq.* ; propitiation of the corn-spirit perhaps fused with the worship of the dead, 233 *sq.* ; the festival of the dead a festival of flowers, 234 *sq.*

CHAPTER X.—THE GARDENS OF ADONIS . Pp. 236-259

Pots of corn, herbs, and flowers called the Gardens of Adonis, 236 ; these " gardens " charms to promote the growth of vegetation, 236 *sq.* ; the throwing of the " gardens " into water a rain-charm, 236 ; parallel customs of wetting the corn at harvest or sowing, 237-239 ; "gardens of Adonis " in India, 239-243 ; "gardens of Adonis " on St. John's Day in Sardinia and Sicily, 244 *sqq.* ; St. John perhaps a substitute for Adonis, 246 ; custom of bathing on the Eve or Day of St. John (Midsummer Eve or Midsummer Day), 246-249 ; heathen origin of the custom, 249 ; Midsummer festival of St. John formed perhaps by the union of Oriental and northern elements, 249 *sq.* ; midsummer fires and midsummer pairs,

250 *sq.*; divination by plants at midsummer, 252 *sq.*; in Sicily "gardens of Adonis" sown in spring as well as at midsummer, 253 *sq.*; resemblance of Easter ceremonies to rites of Adonis, 254-256; the Christian festival of Easter perhaps grafted on a festival of Adonis, 256 *sq.*; worship of Adonis at Bethlehem and Antioch, 257 *sq.*; the Star of Salvation, 258 *sq.*

BOOK SECOND

ATTIS . . . Pp. 261-317

CHAPTER I.—THE MYTH AND RITUAL OF ATTIS . . . . . . Pp. 263-276

Attis the Phrygian counterpart of Adonis, 263; his relation to Cybele, 263; his miraculous birth, 263 *sq.*; his death, 264 *sq.*; Cybele and Attis at Rome, 265 *sq.*; their spring festival, 266 *sqq.*; the Day of Blood, 268 *sq.*; eunuch priests in the service of Asiatic goddesses, 269 *sq.*; the sacrifice of virility, 271; the mourning for Attis, 272; his resurrection, 272 *sq.*; his mysteries, the sacrament and the baptism of blood, 274 *sq.*; diffusion of his religion from the Vatican, 275 *sq.*

CHAPTER II.—ATTIS AS A GOD OF VEGETATION . . . . . . Pp. 277-280

Sanctity of the pine-tree in the worship of Attis, 277 *sq.*; Attis as a corn-god, 279; Cybele a goddess of fertility, 279 *sq.*; the bath in the river, 280.

CHAPTER III.—ATTIS AS THE FATHER GOD Pp. 281-284

Meaning of the name Attis, 281; relation of Attis to the Mother Goddess, 281 *sq.*; Attis as a sky-god or Heavenly Father, 282 *sqq.*; the emasculation of the sky-god, 283 *sq.*

CHAPTER IV.—HUMAN REPRESENTATIVES OF ATTIS . . . . . . Pp. 285-287

Personation of Attis by his high priest, 285 *sq.*; name of Attis in the royal families of Phrygia and Lydia, 286 *sq.*

CHAPTER V.—THE HANGED GOD . . Pp. 288-297

Death of Marsyas on the tree, 288 *sq.*; Marsyas apparently a double of Attis, 289; the hanging of Odin on the gallows-tree, 290; the hanging of human victims among the Bagobos, 290 *sq.* ; the hanging of Artemis, 291 *sq.* ; the hanging of animal victims, 292 ; skins of human victims used to effect the resurrection, 293 ; skins of men and horses set up at graves, 293 *sq.* ; skulls employed in Borneo to ensure the fertility of the ground and of women, 294-296 ; skin of the human representative of the god in Phrygia perhaps used for like purposes, 296 *sq.*

CHAPTER VI.—ORIENTAL RELIGIONS IN THE WEST. . . . . . Pp. 298-312

Popularity of the worship of Cybele and Attis in the Roman empire, 298 *sq.* ; effect of Oriental religions in undermining the civilization of Greece and Rome, 299-301 ; popularity of the worship of Mithra, its rivalry with Christianity, 301 *sq.* ; the festival of Christmas borrowed by the Church from the Mithraic religion, 302-305 ; the festival of Easter apparently adapted to the spring festival of Attis, 305-310 ; compromise of Christianity with paganism, parallel with Buddhism, 310-312.

CHAPTER VII.—HYACINTH . . . Pp. 313-317

Hyacinth interpreted as the vegetation which blooms and withers, 313 *sq.* ; tomb of Hyacinth at Amyclae, 314 *sq.* ; Hyacinth an aboriginal deity, perhaps a dead king, 315 *sq.* ; his sister Polyboea perhaps originally his spouse, 316 *sq.*

BOOK FIRST

ADONIS

CHAPTER I

THE MYTH OF ADONIS

THE spectacle of the great changes which annually pass over the face of the earth has powerfully impressed the minds of men in all ages, and stirred them to meditate on the causes of transformations so vast and wonderful. Their curiosity has not been purely disinterested ; for even the savage cannot fail to perceive how intimately his own life is bound up with the life of nature, and how the same processes which freeze the stream and strip the earth of vegetation menace him with extinction. At a certain stage of development men seem to have imagined that the means of averting the threatened calamity were in their own hands, and that they could hasten or retard the flight of the seasons by magic art. Accordingly they performed ceremonies and recited spells to make the rain to fall, the sun to shine, animals to multiply, and the fruits of the earth to grow. In course of time the slow advance of knowledge, which has dispelled so many cherished illusions, convinced at least the more thoughtful portion of mankind that the alternations of summer and winter, of spring and autumn, were not merely the result of their own magical rites, but that some deeper cause, some mightier power, was at work behind the shifting scenes of nature. They now pictured to themselves the growth and decay of vegetation, the birth and death of living creatures, as effects of the waxing or waning strength of divine beings, of gods and goddesses, who were born and died, who married and begot children, on the pattern of human life.

3

Magical
ceremonies
to revive
the failing
energies of
the gods.

Thus the old magical theory of the seasons was displaced, or rather supplemented, by a religious theory. For although men now attributed the annual cycle of change primarily to corresponding changes in their deities, they still thought that by performing certain magical rites they could aid the god, who was the principle of life, in his struggle with the opposing principle of death. They imagined that they could recruit his failing energies and even raise him from the dead. The ceremonies which they observed for this purpose were in substance a dramatic representation of the natural processes which they wished to facilitate ; for it is a familiar tenet of magic that you can produce any desired effect by merely imitating it. And as they now explained the fluctuations of growth and decay, of reproduction and dissolution, by the marriage, the death, and the rebirth or revival of the gods, their religious or rather magical dramas turned in great measure on these themes. They set forth the fruitful union of the powers of fertility, the sad death of one at least of the divine partners, and his joyful resurrection. Thus a religious theory was blended with a magical practice. The combination is familiar in history. Indeed, few religions have ever succeeded in wholly extricating themselves from the old trammels of magic. The inconsistency of acting on two opposite principles, however it may vex the soul of the philosopher, rarely troubles the common man ; indeed he is seldom even aware of it. His affair is to act, not to analyse the motives of his action. If mankind had always been logical and wise, history would not be a long chronicle of folly and crime.[1]

---

[1] As in the present volume I am concerned with the beliefs and practices of Orientals I may quote the following passage from one who has lived long in the East and knows it well : " The Oriental mind is free from the trammels of logic. It is a literal fact that the Oriental mind can accept and believe two opposite things at the same time. We find fully qualified and even learned Indian doctors practising Greek medicine, as well as English medicine, and enforcing sanitary restrictions to which their own houses and families are entirely strangers. We find astronomers who can predict eclipses, and yet who believe that eclipses are caused by a dragon swallowing the sun. We find holy men who are credited with miraculous powers and with close communion with the Deity, who live in drunkenness and immorality, and who are capable of elaborate frauds on others. To the Oriental mind, a thing must be incredible to command a ready belief " (" Riots and Unrest in the Punjab, from a corre-

Of the changes which the seasons bring with them, the most striking within the temperate zone are those which affect vegetation. The influence of the seasons on animals, though great, is not nearly so manifest. Hence it is natural that in the magical dramas designed to dispel winter and bring back spring the emphasis should be laid on vegetation, and that trees and plants should figure in them more prominently than beasts and birds. Yet the two sides of life, the vegetable and the animal, were not dissociated in the minds of those who observed the ceremonies. Indeed they commonly believed that the tie between the animal and the vegetable world was even closer than it really is ; hence they often combined the dramatic representation of reviving plants with a real or a dramatic union of the sexes for the purpose of furthering at the same time and by the same act the multiplication of fruits, of animals, and of men. To them the principle of life and fertility, whether animal or vegetable, was one and indivisible. To live and to cause to live, to eat food and to beget children, these were the primary wants of men in the past, and they will be the primary wants of men in the future so long as the world lasts. Other things may be added to enrich and beautify human life, but unless these wants are first satisfied, humanity itself must cease to exist. These two things, therefore, food and children, were what men chiefly sought to procure by the performance of magical rites for the regulation of the seasons.

Nowhere, apparently, have these rites been more widely

The principles of animal and of vegetable life confused in these ceremonies.

---

spondent," *The Times Weekly Edition*, May 24, 1907, p. 326). Again, speaking of the people of the Lower Congo, an experienced missionary describes their religious ideas as " chaotic in the extreme and impossible to reduce to any systematic order. The same person will tell you at different times that the departed spirit goes to the nether regions, or to a dark forest, or to the moon, or to the sun. There is no coherence in their beliefs, and their ideas about cosmogony and the future are very nebulous. Although they believe in punishment after death their faith is so hazy that it has lost all its deterrent force. If in the following pages a lack of logical unity is observed, it must be put to the debit of the native mind, as that lack of logical unity really represents the mistiness of their views." See Rev. John H. Weeks, " Notes on some Customs of the Lower Congo People," *Folk-lore*, xx. (1909) pp. 54 *sq.* Unless we allow for this innate capacity of the human mind to entertain contradictory beliefs at the same time, we shall in vain attempt to understand the history of thought in general and of religion in particular.

Prevalence
of these
rites in
Western
Asia and
Egypt.
and solemnly celebrated than in the lands which border the Eastern Mediterranean.   Under the names of Osiris, Tammuz, Adonis, and Attis, the peoples of Egypt and Western Asia represented the yearly decay and revival of life, especially of vegetable life, which they personified as a god who annually died and rose again from the dead.   In name and detail the rites varied from place to place : in substance they were the same.   The supposed death and resurrection of this oriental deity, a god of many names but of essentially one nature, is the subject of the present inquiry. We begin with Tammuz or Adonis.[1]

Tammuz
or Adonis
in Baby-
lonia.
The worship of Adonis was practised by the Semitic peoples of Babylonia and Syria, and the Greeks borrowed it from them as early as the seventh century before Christ.[2] The true name of the deity was Tammuz : the appellation of Adonis is merely the Semitic Adon, " lord," a title of honour by which his worshippers addressed him.[3]   In the Hebrew text of the Old Testament the same name Adonai,

---

[1] The equivalence of Tammuz and Adonis has been doubted or denied by some scholars, as by Renan (Mission de Phénicie, Paris, 1864, pp. 216, 235) and by Chwolsohn (Die Ssabier und der Ssabismus, St. Petersburg, 1856, ii. 510).   But the two gods are identified by Origen (Selecta in Ezechielem, Migne's Patrologia Graeca, xiii. 797), Jerome (Epist. lviii. 3 and Commentar. in Ezechielem, viii. 13, 14, Migne's Patrologia Latina, xxii. 581, xxv. 82), Cyril of Alexandria (In Isaiam, lib. ii. tomus. iii., and Comment. on Hosea, iv. 15, Migne's Patrologia Graeca, lxx. 441, lxxi. 136), Theodoretus (In Ezechielis cap. viii., Migne's Patrologia Graeca, lxxxi. 885), the author of the Paschal Chronicle (Migne's Patrologia Graeca, xcii. 329) and Melito (in W. Cureton's Spicilegium Syriacum, London, 1855, p. 44) ; and accordingly, we may fairly conclude that, whatever their remote origin may have been, Tammuz and Adonis were in the later period of antiquity practically equivalent to each other.   Compare W. W. Graf Baudissin, Studien zur semitischen Religionsgeschichte (Leipsic, 1876–1878), i. 299 ; id., in Realency-

clopädie für protestantische Theologie und Kirchengeschichte,[3] s.v. "Tammuz"; id., Adonis und Esmun (Leipsic, 1911), pp. 94 sqq. ; W. Mannhardt, Antike Wald- und Feldkulte (Berlin, 1877), pp. 273 sqq.; Ch. Vellay, "Le dieu Thammuz," Revue de l'Histoire des Religions, xlix. (1904) pp. 154-162. Baudissin holds that Tammuz and Adonis were two different gods sprung from a common root (Adonis und Esmun, p. 368).   An Assyrian origin of the cult of Adonis was long ago affirmed by Macrobius (Sat. i. 21. 1). On Adonis and his worship in general see also F. C. Movers, Die Phoenizier, i. (Bonn, 1841) pp. 191 sqq.; W. H. Engel, Kypros (Berlin, 1841), ii. 536 sqq.; Ch. Vellay, Le culte et les fêtes d'Adonis - Thammouz dans l'Orient antique (Paris, 1904).

[2] The mourning for Adonis is mentioned by Sappho, who flourished about 600 B.C. See Th. Bergk's Poetae Lyrici Graeci,[3] iii. (Leipsic, 1867) p. 897 ; Pausanias, ix. 29. 8.

[3] Ed. Meyer, Geschichte des Altertums,[2] i. 2 (Berlin, 1909), pp. 394 sq.; W. W. Graf Baudissin, Adonis und Esmun, pp. 65 sqq.

originally perhaps Adoni, "my lord," is often applied to Jehovah.[1] But the Greeks through a misunderstanding converted the title of honour into a proper name. While Tammuz or his equivalent Adonis enjoyed a wide and lasting popularity among peoples of the Semitic stock, there are grounds for thinking that his worship originated with a race of other blood and other speech, the Sumerians, who in the dawn of history inhabited the flat alluvial plain at the head of the Persian Gulf and created the civilization which was afterwards called Babylonian. The origin and affinities of this people are unknown; in physical type and language they differed from all their neighbours, and their isolated position, wedged in between alien races, presents to the student of mankind problems of the same sort as the isolation of the Basques and Etruscans among the Aryan peoples of Europe. An ingenious, but unproved, hypothesis would represent them as immigrants driven from central Asia by that gradual desiccation which for ages seems to have been converting once fruitful lands into a waste and burying the seats of ancient civilization under a sea of shifting sand. Whatever their place of origin may have been, it is certain that in Southern Babylonia the Sumerians attained at a very early period to a considerable pitch of civilization; for they tilled the soil, reared cattle, built cities, dug canals, and even invented a system of writing, which their Semitic neighbours in time borrowed from them.[2] In the pantheon

His worship seems to have originated with the Sumerians.

---

[1] *Encyclopaedia Biblica*, ed. T. K. Cheyne and J. S. Black, iii. 3327. In the Old Testament the title *Adoni,* "my lord," is frequently given to men. See, for example, Genesis xxxiii. 8, 13, 14, 15, xlii. 10, xliii. 20, xliv. 5, 7, 9, 16, 18, 19, 20, 22, 24.

[2] C. P. Tiele, *Geschichte der Religion im Altertum* (Gotha, 1896–1903), i. 134 *sqq.*; G. Maspero, *Histoire Ancienne des Peuples de l'Orient Classique, les Origines* (Paris, 1895), pp. 550 *sq.*; L. W. King, *Babylonian Religion and Mythology* (London, 1899), pp. 1 *sqq.*; *id., A History of Sumer and Akkad* (London, 1910), pp. 1 *sqq.*, 40 *sqq.*; H. Winckler, in E. Schrader's *Die Keilinschriften und das alte Testament*[3] (Berlin, 1902),

pp. 10 *sq.*, 349; Fr. Hommel, *Grundriss der Geographie und Geschichte des alten Orients* (Munich, 1904), pp. 18 *sqq.*; Ed. Meyer, *Geschichte des Altertums,*[2] i. 2 (Berlin, 1909), pp. 401 *sqq.* As to the hypothesis that the Sumerians were immigrants from Central Asia, see L. W. King, *History of Sumer and Akkad,* pp. 351 *sqq.* The gradual desiccation of Central Asia, which is conjectured to have caused the Sumerian migration, has been similarly invoked to explain the downfall of the Roman empire; for by rendering great regions uninhabitable it is supposed to have driven hordes of fierce barbarians to find new homes in Europe. See Professor J. W. Gregory's lecture "Is the earth drying up?"

of this ancient people Tammuz appears to have been one of the oldest, though certainly not one of the most important figures.[1] His name consists of a Sumerian phrase meaning "true son" or, in a fuller form, "true son of the deep water,"[2] and among the inscribed Sumerian texts which have survived the wreck of empires are a number of hymns in his honour, which were written down not later than about two thousand years before our era but were almost certainly composed at a much earlier time.[3]

Tammuz the lover of Ishtar.

Descent of Ishtar to the nether world to recover Tammuz.

In the religious literature of Babylonia Tammuz appears as the youthful spouse or lover of Ishtar, the great mother goddess, the embodiment of the reproductive energies of nature. The references to their connexion with each other in myth and ritual are both fragmentary and obscure, but we gather from them that every year Tammuz was believed to die, passing away from the cheerful earth to the gloomy subterranean world, and that every year his divine mistress journeyed in quest of him "to the land from which there is no returning, to the house of darkness, where dust lies on door and bolt." During her absence the passion of love ceased to operate : men and beasts alike forgot to reproduce their kinds : all life was threatened with extinction. So

---

delivered before the Royal Geographical Society and reported in *The Times*, December 9th, 1913. It is held by Prof. Hommel (*op. cit.* pp. 19 *sqq.*) that the Sumerian language belongs to the Ural-altaic family, but the better opinion seems to be that its linguistic affinities are unknown. The view, once ardently advocated, that Sumerian was not a language but merely a cabalistic mode of writing Semitic, is now generally exploded.

[1] H. Zimmern, "Der babylonische Gott Tamūz," *Abhandlungen der philologisch- historischen Klasse der Königl. Sächsischen Gesellschaft der Wissenschaften*, xxvii. No. xx. (Leipsic, 1909) pp. 701, 722.

[2] *Dumu-zi*, or in fuller form *Dumu-zi-abzu*. See P. Jensen, *Assyrisch-Babylonische Mythen und Epen* (Berlin, 1900), p. 560; H. Zimmern, *op. cit.* pp. 703 *sqq.*; *id.*, in E. Schrader's

Die Keilinschriften und das Alte Testament[3] (Berlin, 1902), p. 397; P. Dhorme, *La Religion Assyro - Babylonienne* (Paris, 1910), p. 105; W. W. Graf Baudissin, *Adonis und Esmun* (Leipsic, 1911), p. 104.

[3] H. Zimmern, "Der babylonische Gott Tamūz," *Abhandl. d. Kön. Sächs. Gesellschaft der Wissenschaften*, xxvii. No. xx. (Leipsic, 1909) p. 723. For the text and translation of the hymns, see H. Zimmern, "Sumerisch-babylonische Tamūzlieder," *Berichte über die Verhandlungen der Königlich Sächsischen Gesellschaft der Wissenschaften zu Leipzig, Philologisch - historische Klasse*, lix. (1907) pp. 201-252. Compare H. Gressmann, *Altorientalische Texte und Bilder* (Tübingen, 1909), i. 93 *sqq.*; W. W. Graf Baudissin, *Adonis und Esmun* (Leipsic, 1911), pp. 99 *sq.*; R. W. Rogers, *Cuneiform Parallels to the Old Testament* (Oxford, N.D.), pp. 179-185.

intimately bound up with the goddess were the sexual functions of the whole animal kingdom that without her presence they could not be discharged. A messenger of the great god Ea was accordingly despatched to rescue the goddess on whom so much depended. The stern queen of the infernal regions, Allatu or Eresh-Kigal by name, reluctantly allowed Ishtar to be sprinkled with the Water of Life and to depart, in company probably with her lover Tammuz, that the two might return together to the upper world, and that with their return all nature might revive.

Laments for the departed Tammuz are contained in several Babylonian hymns, which liken him to plants that quickly fade. He is

" A tamarisk that in the garden has drunk no water,
  Whose crown in the field has brought forth no blossom.
A willow that rejoiced not by the watercourse,
  A willow whose roots were torn up.
A herb that in the garden had drunk no water."

His death appears to have been annually mourned, to the shrill music of flutes, by men and women about midsummer in the month named after him, the month of Tammuz. The dirges were seemingly chanted over an effigy of the dead god, which was washed with pure water, anointed with oil, and clad in a red robe, while the fumes of incense rose into the air, as if to stir his dormant senses by their pungent fragrance and wake him from the sleep of death. In one of these dirges, inscribed *Lament of the Flutes for Tammuz*, we seem still to hear the voices of the singers chanting the sad refrain and to catch, like far-away music, the wailing notes of the flutes :—

" At his vanishing away she lifts up a lament,
  ' Oh my child !' at his vanishing away she lifts up a lament;
' My Damu !' at his vanishing away she lifts up a lament.
  ' My enchanter and priest !' at his vanishing away she lifts up a
    lament,
At the shining cedar, rooted in a spacious place,
  In Eanna, above and below, she lifts up a lament.
Like the lament that a house lifts up for its master, lifts she up a
    lament,
  Like the lament that a city lifts up for its lord, lifts she up a
    lament.

Laments for Tammuz. (margin note)

Her lament is the lament for a herb that grows not in the bed,
Her lament is the lament for the corn that grows not in the ear.
Her chamber is a possession that brings not forth a possession,
A weary woman, a weary child, forspent.
Her lament is for a great river, where no willows grow,
Her lament is for a field, where corn and herbs grow not.
Her lament is for a pool, where fishes grow not.
Her lament is for a thicket of reeds, where no reeds grow.
Her lament is for woods, where tamarisks grow not.
Her lament is for a wilderness where no cypresses (?) grow.
Her lament is for the depth of a garden of trees, where honey and wine
grow not.
Her lament is for meadows, where no plants grow.
Her lament is for a palace, where length of life grows not." [1]

Adonis
in Greek
mythology
merely a

The tragical story and the melancholy rites of Adonis are better known to us from the descriptions of Greek writers than from the fragments of Babylonian literature or

[1] A. Jeremias, *Die babylonisch-assyrischen Vorstellungen vom Leben nach dem Tode* (Leipsic, 1887), pp. 4 *sqq.*; *id.*, in W. H. Roscher's *Lexikon der griech. und röm. Mythologie*, ii. 808, iii. 258 *sqq.*; M. Jastrow, *The Religion of Babylonia and Assyria* (Boston, 1898), pp. 565-576, 584, 682 *sq.*; W. L. King, *Babylonian Religion and Mythology*, pp. 178-183; P. Jensen, *Assyrisch-babylonische Mythen und Epen*, pp. 81 *sqq.*, 95 *sqq.*, 169; R. F. Harper, *Assyrian and Babylonian Literature* (New York, 1901), pp. 316 *sq.*, 338, 408 *sqq.*; H. Zimmern, in E. Schrader's *Die Keilinschriften und das Alte Testament*,[3] pp. 397 *sqq.*, 561 *sqq.*; *id.*, "Sumerisch - babylonische Tamūzlieder," *Berichte über die Verhandlungen der Königlich Sächsischen Gesellschaft der Wissenschaften zu Leipzig, Philologisch-historische Klasse*, lix. (1907) pp. 220, 232, 236 *sq.*; *id.*, "Der babylonische Gott Tamūz," *Abhandlungen der philologisch-historischen Klasse der Königl. Sächsischen Gesellschaft der Wissenschaften*, xxvii. No. xx. (Leipsic, 1909) pp. 725 *sq.*, 729-735; H. Gressmann, *Altorientalische Texte und Bilder zum Alten Testamente* (Tübingen, 1909), i. 65-69; R. W. Rogers, *Cuneiform Parallels to the Old Testament* (Oxford, N.D.), pp. 121-131; W. W. Graf Baudissin, *Adonis und Esmun* (Leipsic, 1911), pp. 99 *sqq.*, 353 *sqq.* According to Jerome (on Ezekiel viii. 14) the month of Tammuz was June; but according to modern scholars it corresponded rather to July, or to part of June and part of July. See F. C. Movers, *Die Phoenizier*, i. 210; F. Lenormant, "Il mito di Adone-Tammuz nei documenti cuneiformi," *Atti del IV. Congresso Internazionale degli Orientalisti* (Florence, 1880), i. 144 *sq.*; W. Mannhardt, *Antike Wald- und Feldkulte*, p. 275; *Encyclopaedia Biblica*, *s.v.* "Months," iii. 3194. My friend W. Robertson Smith informed me that owing to the variations of the local Syrian calendars the month of Tammuz fell in different places at different times, from midsummer to autumn, or from June to September. According to Prof. M. Jastrow, the festival of Tammuz was celebrated just before the summer solstice (*The Religion of Babylonia and Assyria*, pp. 547, 682). He observes that "the calendar of the Jewish Church still marks the 17th day of Tammuz as a fast, and Houtsma has shown that the association of the day with the capture of Jerusalem by the Romans represents merely the attempt to give an ancient festival a worthier interpretation."

the brief reference of the prophet Ezekiel, who saw the reflection of the Oriental Tammuz. women of Jerusalem weeping for Tammuz at the north gate of the temple.[1] Mirrored in the glass of Greek mythology, the oriental deity appears as a comely youth beloved by Aphrodite. In his infancy the goddess hid him in a chest, which she gave in charge to Persephone, queen of the nether world. But when Persephone opened the chest and beheld the beauty of the babe, she refused to give him back to Aphrodite, though the goddess of love went down herself to hell to ransom her dear one from the power of the grave. The dispute between the two goddesses of love and death was settled by Zeus, who decreed that Adonis should abide with Persephone in the under world for one part of the year, and with Aphrodite in the upper world for another part. At last the fair youth was killed in hunting by a wild boar, or by the jealous Ares, who turned himself into the likeness of a boar in order to compass the death of his rival. Bitterly did Aphrodite lament her loved and lost Adonis.[2] The strife between the divine rivals for the possession of Adonis appears to be depicted on an Etruscan mirror. The two goddesses, identified by inscriptions, are stationed on either side of Jupiter, who occupies the seat of judgment and lifts an admonitory finger as he looks sternly towards Persephone. Overcome with grief the goddess of love buries her face in her mantle, while her pertinacious rival, grasping a branch in one hand, points with the other at a closed coffer, which probably contains the youthful Adonis.[3] In

---

[1] Ezekiel viii. 14.

[2] Apollodorus, *Bibliotheca*, iii. 14. 4 ; Bion, *Idyl*, i. ; J. Tzetzes, *Schol. on Lycophron*, 831 ; Ovid, *Metam.* x. 503 *sqq.* ; Aristides, *Apology*, edited by J. Rendel Harris (Cambridge, 1891), pp. 44, 106 *sq.* In Babylonian texts relating to Tammuz no reference has yet been found to death by a boar. See H. Zimmern, "Sumerisch-babylonische Tamūzlieder," p. 451 ; *id.*, "Der babylonische Gott Tamūz," p. 731. Baudissin inclines to think that the incident of the boar is a late importation into the myth of Adonis. See his *Adonis und Esmun*, pp. 142 *sqq.* As to the relation of the boar to the

kindred gods Adonis, Attis, and Osiris see *Spirits of the Corn and of the Wild*, ii. 22 *sqq.*, where I have suggested that the idea of the boar as the foe of the god may be based on the terrible ravages which wild pigs notoriously commit in fields of corn.

[3] W. W. Graf Baudissin, *Adonis und Esmun* (Leipsic, 1911), pp. 152 *sq.*, with plate iv. As to the representation of the myth of Adonis on Etruscan mirrors and late works of Roman art, especially sarcophaguses and wall-paintings, see Otto Jahn, *Archäologische Beiträge* (Berlin, 1847), pp. 45-51.

this form of the myth, the contest between Aphrodite and Persephone for the possession of Adonis clearly reflects the struggle between Ishtar and Allatu in the land of the dead, while the decision of Zeus that Adonis is to spend one part of the year under ground and another part above ground is merely a Greek version of the annual disappearance and reappearance of Tammuz.

CHAPTER II

ADONIS IN SYRIA

THE myth of Adonis was localized and his rites celebrated with much solemnity at two places in Western Asia. One of these was Byblus on the coast of Syria, the other was Paphos in Cyprus. Both were great seats of the worship of Aphrodite, or rather of her Semitic counterpart, Astarte ;[1] and of both, if we accept the legends, Cinyras, the father of Adonis, was king.[2] Of the two cities Byblus was the more ancient ; indeed it claimed to be the oldest city in Phoenicia, and to have been founded in the early ages of the world by the great god El, whom Greeks and Romans identified with Cronus and Saturn respectively.[3] However that may have been, in historical times it ranked as a holy place, the religious capital of the country, the Mecca or Jerusalem of the Phoenicians.[4] The city stood on a height beside the sea,[5] and contained a great sanctuary of Astarte,[6] where

---

[1] The ancients were aware that the Syrian and Cyprian Aphrodite, the mistress of Adonis, was no other than Astarte. See Cicero, *De natura deorum*, iii. 23. 59 ; Joannes Lydus, *De mensibus*, iv. 44. On Adonis in Phoenicia see W. W. Graf Baudissin, *Adonis und Esmun* (Leipsic, 1911), pp. 71 *sqq.*

[2] As to Cinyras, see F. C. Movers, *Die Phoenizier*, i. 238 *sqq.*, ii. 2. 226-231 ; W. H. Engel, *Kypros* (Berlin, 1841), i. 168-173, ii. 94-136 ; Stoll, *s.v.* "Kinyras," in W. H. Roscher's *Lexikon der griech. und röm. Mythologie*, ii. 1189 *sqq.* Melito calls the father of Adonis by the name of Cuthar, and represents him as king of the Phoenicians with his capital at Gebal

(Byblus). See Melito, "Oration to Antoninus Caesar," in W. Cureton's *Spicilegium Syriacum* (London, 1855), p. 44.

[3] Philo of Byblus, quoted by Eusebius, *Praeparatio Evangelii*, i. 10 ; *Fragmenta Historicorum Graecorum*, ed. C. Müller, iii. 568 ; Stephanus Byzantius, *s.v.* Βύβλος. Byblus is a Greek corruption of the Semitic Gebal (גבל), the name which the place still retains. See E. Renan, *Mission de Phénicie* (Paris, 1864), p. 155.

[4] R. Pietschmann, *Geschichte der Phoenizier* (Berlin, 1889), p. 139. On the coins it is designated " Holy Byblus."

[5] Strabo, xvi. 1. 18, p. 755.

[6] Lucian, *De dea Syria*, 6.

13

in the midst of a spacious open court, surrounded by cloisters and approached from below by staircases, rose a tall cone or obelisk, the holy image of the goddess.[1] In this sanctuary the rites of Adonis were celebrated.[2] Indeed the whole city was sacred to him,[3] and the river Nahr Ibrahim, which falls into the sea a little to the south of Byblus, bore in antiquity the name of Adonis.[4] This was the kingdom of Cinyras.[5] From the earliest to the latest times the city appears to have been ruled by kings, assisted perhaps by a senate or council of elders.[6] The first of the kings of whom we have historical evidence was a certain Zekar-baal. He reigned about a century before Solomon; yet from that dim past his figure stands out strangely fresh and lifelike in the journal of an Egyptian merchant or official named Wen-Ammon, which has fortunately been preserved in a papyrus. This man spent some time with the king at Byblus, and received from him, in return for rich presents, a supply of timber felled in the forests of Lebanon.[7] Another king of Byblus, who bore the name of Sibitti-baal, paid tribute to Tiglath-pileser III., king of Assyria, about the year 739 B.C.[8] Further, from an inscription of the fifth or fourth century before our era we learn that a king of Byblus, by name Yehaw-melech, son of Yehar-baal, and grandson of Adom-melech or Uri-melech, dedicated a pillared portico with a carved work of gold and a bronze altar to the goddess, whom he worshipped under the name of Baalath Gebal, that is, the female Baal of Byblus.[9]

The kings of Byblus.

[1] The sanctuary and image are figured on coins of Byblus. See T. L. Donaldson, *Architectura Numismatica* (London, 1859), pp. 105 *sq.*; E. Renan, *Mission de Phénicie*, p. 177; G. Perrot et Ch. Chipiez, *Histoire de l'Art dans l'Antiquité*, iii. (Paris, 1885) p. 60; R. Pietschmann, *Geschichte der Phoenizier*, p. 202; G. Maspero, *Histoire Ancienne des Peuples de l'Orient Classique*, ii. (Paris, 1897) p. 173. Renan excavated a massive square pedestal built of colossal stones, which he thought may have supported the sacred obelisk (*op. cit.* pp. 174-178).

[2] Lucian, *De dea Syria*, 6.

[3] Strabo, xvi. 1. 18, p. 755.

[4] Lucian, *De dea Syria*, 8; Pliny, *Nat. Hist.* v. 78; E. Renan, *Mission de Phénicie*, pp. 282 *sqq.*

[5] Eustathius, *Commentary on Dionysius Periegetes*, 912 (*Geographi Graeci Minores*, ed. C. Müller, ii. 376); Melito, in W. Cureton's *Spicilegium Syriacum*, p. 44.

[6] Ezekiel xxvii. 9. As to the name Gebal see above, p. 13, note [1].

[7] L. B. Paton, *The Early History of Syria and Palestine* (London, 1902), pp. 169-171. See below, pp. 75 *sq.*

[8] L. B. Paton, *op. cit.* p. 235; R. F. Harper, *Assyrian and Babylonian Literature*, p. 57 (the Nimrud inscription of Tiglath-pileser III.).

[9] The inscription was discovered by Renan. See Ch. Vellay, *Le culte et*

The names of these kings suggest that they claimed Divinity of Semitic kings. affinity with their god Baal or Moloch, for Moloch is only a corruption of *melech*, that is, "king." Such a claim at all events appears to have been put forward by many other Semitic kings.[1] The early monarchs of Babylon were worshipped as gods in their lifetime.[2] Mesha, king of Moab, perhaps called himself the son of his god Kemosh.[3] Among the Aramean sovereigns of Damascus, mentioned in the Bible, we find more than one Ben-hadad, that is, "son of the god Hadad," the chief male deity of the Syrians ;[4] and Josephus tells us that down to his own time, in the first century of our era, Ben-hadad I., whom he calls simply Adad, and his successor, Hazael, continued to be worshipped as gods by the people of Damascus, who held processions daily in their honour.[5] Some of the kings of Edom seem to have gone a step farther and identified themselves with the god in their lifetime ; at all events they bore his name Hadad without any qualification.[6] King Bar-rekub, who

les fêtes d'Adonis - Thammouz dans l'Orient antique (Paris, 1904), pp. 38 *sq.* ; G. A. Cooke, *Text-book of North-Semitic Inscriptions* (Oxford 1903), No. 3, pp. 18 *sq.* In the time of Alexander the Great the king of Byblus was a certain Enylus (Arrian, *Anabasis*, ii. 20), whose name appears on a coin of the city (F. C. Movers, *Die Phoenizier*, ii. 1, p. 103, note 81).

[1] On the divinity of Semitic kings and the kingship of Semitic gods see W. R. Smith, *Religion of the Semites*[2] (London, 1894), pp. 44 *sq.*, 66 *sqq.*

[2] H. Radau, *Early Babylonian History* (New York and London, 1900), pp. 307-317 ; P. Dhorme, *La Religion Assyro-Babylonienne* (Paris, 1910), pp. 168 *sqq.*

[3] The evidence for this is the Moabite stone, but the reading of the inscription is doubtful. See S. R. Driver, in *Encyclopaedia Biblica*, *s.v.* "Mesha," vol. iii. 3041 *sqq.* ; *id.*, *Notes on the Hebrew Text and the Topography of the Books of Samuel*, Second Edition (Oxford, 1913), pp. lxxxv., lxxxvi., lxxxviii. *sq.* ; G. A. Cooke, *Text-book of North-Semitic Inscriptions*, No. 1, pp. 1 *sq.*, 6.

[4] 2 Kings viii. 7, 9, xiii. 24 *sq.* ; Jeremiah xlix. 27. As to the god Hadad see Macrobius, *Saturn.* i. 23. 17-19 (where, as so often in late writers, the Syrians are called Assyrians) ; Philo of Byblus, in *Fragmenta Historicorum Graecorum*, ed. C. Müller, iii. 569 ; F. Baethgen, *Beiträge zur semitischen Religionsgeschichte* (Berlin, 1888), pp. 66-68 ; G. A. Cooke, *Text-book of North-Semitic Inscriptions*, Nos. 61, 62, pp. 161 *sq.*, 164, 173, 175 ; M. J. Lagrange, *Études sur les Religions Sémitiques*[2] (Paris, 1905), pp. 93, 493, 496 *sq.* The prophet Zechariah speaks (xii. 11) of a great mourning of or for Hadadrimmon in the plain of Megiddon. This has been taken to refer to a lament for Hadad - Rimmon, the Syrian god of rain, storm, and thunder, like the lament for Adonis. See S. R. Driver's note on the passage (*The Minor Prophets*, pp. 266 *sq.*, Century Bible) ; W. W. Graf Baudissin, *Adonis und Esmun*, p. 92.

[5] Josephus, *Antiquit. Jud.* ix. 4. 6.

[6] Genesis xxxvi. 35 *sq.* ; 1 Kings xi. 14-22 ; 1 Chronicles i. 50 *sq.* Of the eight kings of Edom mentioned in Genesis (xxxvi. 31-39) and in 1 Chron-

reigned over Samal in North-Western Syria in the time of Tiglath-pileser (745–727 B.C.) appears from his name to have reckoned himself a son of Rekub-el, the god to whose favour he deemed himself indebted for the kingdom.[1] The kings of Tyre traced their descent from Baal,[2] and apparently professed to be gods in their own person.[3] Several of them bore names which are partly composed of the names of Baal and Astarte ; one of them bore the name of Baal pure and simple.[4] The Baal whom they personated was no doubt Melcarth, "the king of the city," as his name signifies, the great god whom the Greeks identified with Hercules ; for the equivalence of the Baal of Tyre both to Melcarth and to Hercules is placed beyond the reach of doubt by a bilingual inscription, in Phoenician and Greek, which was found in Malta.[5]

In like manner the kings of Byblus may have assumed the style of Adonis ; for Adonis was simply the divine Adon

---

icles (i. 43-50) not one was the son of his predecessor. This seems to indicate that in Edom, as elsewhere, the blood royal was traced in the female line, and that the kings were men of other families, or even foreigners, who succeeded to the throne by marrying the hereditary princesses. See *The Magic Art and the Evolution of Kings*, ii. 268 *sqq.* The Israelites were forbidden to have a foreigner for a king (Deuteronomy xvii. 15 with S. R. Driver's note), which seems to imply that the custom was known among their neighbours. It is significant that some of the names of the kings of Edom seem to be those of divinities, as Prof. A. H. Sayce observed long ago (*Lectures on the Religion of the Ancient Babylonians*, London and Edinburgh, 1887, p. 54).

[1] G. A. Cooke, *op. cit.* Nos. 62, 63, pp. 163, 165, 173 *sqq.*, 181 *sqq.* ; M. J. Lagrange, *op. cit.* pp. 496 *sqq.* The god Rekub-el is mentioned along with the gods Hadad, El, Reshef, and Shamash in an inscription of King Bar-rekub's mortal father, King Panammu (G. A. Cooke, *op. cit.* No. 61, p. 161).

[2] Virgil, *Aen.* i. 729 *sq.*, with

Servius's note ; Silius Italicus, *Punica*, i. 86 *sqq.*

[3] Ezekiel xxviii. 2, 9.

[4] Menander of Ephesus, quoted by Josephus, *Contra Apionem*, i. 18 and 21 ; *Fragmenta Historicorum Graecorum*, ed. C. Müller, iv. 446 *sq.* According to the text of Josephus, as edited by B. Niese, the names of the kings in question were Abibal, Balbazer, Abdastart, Methusastart, son of Leastart, Ithobal, Balezor, Baal, Balator, Merbal. The passage of Menander is quoted also by Eusebius, *Chronic.* i. pp. 118, 120, ed. A. Schoene.

[5] G. A. Cooke, *Text-book of North-Semitic Inscriptions*, No. 36, p. 102. As to Melcarth, the Tyrian Hercules, see Ed. Meyer, *s.v.* "Melqart," in W. H. Roscher's *Lexikon d. griech. u. röm. Mythologie*, ii. 2650 *sqq.* One of the Tyrian kings seems to have been called Abi-milk (Abi-melech), that is, "father of a king" or "father of Moloch," that is, of Melcarth. A letter of his to the king of Egypt is preserved in the Tel-el-Amarna correspondence. See R. F. Harper, *Assyrian and Babylonian Literature*, p. 237. As to a title which implies that the bearer of it was the father of a god, see below, pp. 51 *sq.*

or "lord" of the city, a title which hardly differs in sense Divinity of the Phoenician
from Baal ("master") and Melech ("king"). This conjecture
would be confirmed if one of the kings of Byblus actually kings of
bore, as Renan believed, the name of Adom-melech, that is, Byblus and the
Adonis Melech, the Lord King. But, unfortunately, the read- Canaanite kings of
ing of the inscription in which the name occurs is doubtful.[1] Jerusalem.
Some of the old Canaanite kings of Jerusalem appear to have
played the part of Adonis in their lifetime, if we may judge
from their names, Adoni-bezek and Adoni-zedek,[2] which are
divine rather than human titles. Adoni-zedek means "lord
of righteousness," and is therefore equivalent to Melchizedek,
that is, "king of righteousness," the title of that mysterious
king of Salem and priest of God Most High, who seems to
have been neither more nor less than one of these same
Canaanitish kings of Jerusalem.[3] Thus if the old priestly
kings of Jerusalem regularly played the part of Adonis, we
need not wonder that in later times the women of Jerusalem
used to weep for Tammuz, that is, for Adonis, at the north
gate of the temple.[4] In doing so they may only have been
continuing a custom which had been observed in the same
place by the Canaanites long before the Hebrews invaded
the land. Perhaps the "sacred men," as they were called, The
who lodged within the walls of the temple at Jerusalem "sacred men" at
down almost to the end of the Jewish kingdom,[5] may have Jerusalem.
acted the part of the living Adonis to the living Astarte of
the women. At all events we know that in the cells of

---

[1] E. Renan, quoted by Ch. Vellay, *Le culte et les fêtes d'Adonis-Thammouz*, p. 39. Mr. Cooke reads ארמלך (Uri-milk) instead of אדמלך (Adon-milk) (G. A. Cooke, *Text-book of North-Semitic Inscriptions*, No. 3, p. 18).

[2] Judges i. 4-7 ; Joshua x. 1 *sqq.*

[3] Genesis xiv. 18-20, with Prof. S. R. Driver's commentary ; *Encyclopaedia Biblica, s.vv.* "Adoni-bezek," "Adoni-zedek," "Melchizedek." It is to be observed that names compounded with Adoni- were occasionally borne by private persons. Such names are Adoni-kam (Ezra ii. 13) and Adoni-ram (1 Kings iv. 6), not to mention Adoni-jah (1 Kings i. 5 *sqq.*), who was a prince and aspired to the

throne of his father David. These names are commonly interpreted as sentences expressive of the nature of the god whom the bearer of the name worshipped. See Prof. Th. Nöldeke, in *Encyclopaedia Biblica, s.v.* "Names," iii. 3286. It is quite possible that names which once implied divinity were afterwards degraded by application to common men.

[4] Ezekiel viii. 14.

[5] They were banished from the temple by King Josiah, who came to the throne in 637 B.C. Jerusalem fell just fifty-one years later. See 2 Kings xxiii. 7. As to these "sacred men" (*kedēshīm*), see below, pp. 72 *sqq.*

these strange clergy women wove garments for the *asherim*,[1] the sacred poles which stood beside the altar and which appear to have been by some regarded as embodiments of Astarte.[2]   Certainly these "sacred men" must have discharged some function which was deemed religious in the temple at Jerusalem ; and we can hardly doubt that the prohibition to bring the wages of prostitution into the house of God, which was published at the very same time that the men were expelled from the temple,[3] was directed against an existing practice.   In Palestine as in other Semitic lands the hire of sacred prostitutes was probably dedicated to the deity as one of his regular dues : he took tribute of men and women as of flocks and herds, of fields and vineyards and oliveyards.

David as heir of the old sacred kings of Jerusalem.

But if Jerusalem had been from of old the seat of a dynasty of spiritual potentates or Grand Lamas, who held the keys of heaven and were revered far and wide as kings and gods in one, we can easily understand why the upstart David chose it for the capital of the new kingdom which he had won for himself at the point of the sword.   The central position and the natural strength of the virgin fortress need not have been the only or the principal inducements which

---

[1] 2 Kings xxiii. 7, where, following the Septuagint, we must apparently read בָּתִּים for the בָּתִּים of the Massoretic Text. So R. Kittel and J. Skinner.

[2] The *asherah* (singular of *asherim*) was certainly of wood (Judges vi. 26) : it seems to have been a tree stripped of its branches and planted in the ground beside an altar, whether of Jehovah or of other gods (Deuteronomy xvi. 21 ; Jeremiah xvii. 2). That the *asherah* was regarded as a goddess, the female partner of Baal, appears from 1 Kings xviii. 19 ; 2 Kings xxi. 3, xxiii. 4 ; and that this goddess was identified with Ashtoreth (Astarte) may be inferred from a comparison of Judges ii. 13 with Judges iii. 7.   Yet on the other hand the pole or tree seems by others to have been viewed as a male power (Jeremiah ii. 27 ; see below, pp. 107 *sqq.*), and the identification of the *asherah* with Astarte has been doubted or disputed by some eminent modern

scholars. See on this subject W. Robertson Smith, *Religion of the Semites*,[2] pp. 187 *sqq.*; S. R. Driver, on Deuteronomy xvi. 21 ; J. Skinner, on 1 Kings xiv. 23 ; M. J. Lagrange, *Études sur les religions Sémitiques*,[2] pp. 173 *sqq.*; G. F. Moore, in *Encyclopaedia Biblica*, vol. i. 330 *sqq.*, *s.v.* "Asherah."

[3] Deuteronomy xxiii. 17 *sq.* (in Hebrew 18 *sq.*). The code of Deuteronomy was published in 621 B.C. in the reign of King Josiah, whose reforms, including the ejection of the *kedeshim* from the temple, were based upon it. See W. Robertson Smith, *The Old Testament in the Jewish Church*[2] (London and Edinburgh, 1892), pp. 256 *sqq.*, 353 *sqq.* ; S. R. Driver, *Critical and Exegetical Commentary on Deuteronomy*[3] (Edinburgh, 1902), pp. xliv. *sqq.* ; K. Budde, *Geschichte der althebräischen Litteratur* (Leipsic, 1906), pp. 105 *sqq.*

decided the politic monarch to transfer his throne from Hebron to Jerusalem.[1] By serving himself heir to the ancient kings of the city he might reasonably hope to inherit their ghostly repute along with their broad acres, to wear their nimbus as well as their crown.[2] So at a later time when he had conquered Ammon and captured the royal city of Rabbah, he took the heavy gold crown of the Ammonite god Milcom and placed it on his own brows, thus posing as the deity in person.[3] It can hardly, therefore, be unreasonable to suppose that he pursued precisely the same policy at the conquest of Jerusalem. And on the other side the calm confidence with which the Jebusite inhabitants of that city awaited his attack, jeering at the besiegers from the battlements,[4] may well have been born of a firm trust in the local deity rather than in the height and thickness of their grim old walls. Certainly the obstinacy

---

[1] He reigned seven years in Hebron and thirty-three in Jerusalem (2 Samuel v. 5 ; 1 Kings ii. 11 ; 1 Chronicles xxix. 27).

[2] Professor A. H. Sayce has argued that David's original name was Elhanan (2 Samuel xxi. 19 compared with xxiii. 24), and that the name David, which he took at a later time, should be written Dod or Dodo, "the Beloved One," which according to Prof. Sayce was a name for Tammuz (Adonis) in Southern Canaan, and was in particular bestowed by the Jebusites of Jerusalem on their supreme deity. See A. H. Sayce, *Lectures on the Religion of the Ancient Babylonians* (London and Edinburgh, 1887), pp. 52-57. If he is right, his conclusions would accord perfectly with those which I had reached independently, and it would become probable that David only assumed the name of David (Dod, Dodo) after the conquest of Jerusalem, and for the purpose of identifying himself with the god of the city, who had borne the same title from time immemorial. But on the whole it seems more likely, as Professor Kennett points out to me, that in the original story Elhanah, a totally different person from David, was the slayer of Goliath, and that the part of the giant-killer was thrust

on David at a later time when the brightness of his fame had eclipsed that of many lesser heroes.

[3] 2 Samuel xii. 26-31 ; 1 Chronicles xx. 1-3. Critics seem generally to agree that in these passages the word מלכם must be pointed *Milcom*, not *malcham* "their king," as the Massoretic text, followed by the English version, has it. The reading *Milcom*, which involves no change of the original Hebrew text, is supported by the reading of the Septuagint Μολχὸμ τοῦ βασιλέως αὐτῶν, where the three last words are probably a gloss on Μολχόμ. See S. R. Driver, *Notes on the Hebrew Text and the Topography of the Books of Samuel*, Second Edition (Oxford, 1913), p. 294 ; Dean Kirkpatrick, in his note on 2 Samuel xii. 30 (*Cambridge Bible for Schools and Colleges*) ; *Encyclopaedia Biblica*, iii. 3085 ; R. Kittel, *Biblia Hebraica*, i. 433 ; Brown, Driver, and Briggs, *Hebrew and English Lexicon of the Old Testament* (Oxford, 1906), pp. 575 *sq*. David's son and successor adopted the worship of Milcom and made a high place for him outside Jerusalem. See 1 Kings xi. 5 ; 2 Kings xxiii. 13.

[4] 2 Samuel v. 6-10 ; 1 Chronicles xi. 4-9.

with which in after ages the Jews defended the same place
against the armies of Assyria and Rome sprang in large
measure from a similar faith in the God of Zion.

Be that as it may, the history of the Hebrew kings
presents some features which may perhaps, without straining
them too far, be interpreted as traces or relics of a time
when they or their predecessors played the part of a
divinity, and particularly of Adonis, the divine lord of the
land. In life the Hebrew king was regularly addressed
as *Adoni-ham-melech*, "My Lord the King,"[1] and after
death he was lamented with cries of *Hoi ahi! Hoi Adon!*
"Alas my brother! alas Lord!"[2] These exclamations of
grief uttered for the death of a king of Judah were, we
can hardly doubt, the very same cries which the weeping
women of Jerusalem uttered in the north porch of the
temple for the dead Tammuz.[3] However, little stress can
be laid on such forms of address, since *Adon* in Hebrew,
like "lord" in English, was a secular as well as a
religious title. But whether identified with Adonis or
not, the Hebrew kings certainly seem to have been
regarded as in a sense divine, as representing and to

---

[1] See for example 1 Samuel xxiv.
8; 2 Samuel xiv. 9, 12, 15, 17, 18,
19, 22, xv. 15, 21, xvi. 4, 9, xviii.
28, 31, 32; 1 Kings i. 2, 13, 18, 20,
21, 24, 27; 1 Chronicles xxi. 3, 23.

[2] Jeremiah xxii. 18, xxxiv. 5. In
the former passage, according to the
Massoretic text, the full formula of
mourning was, "Alas my brother!
alas sister! alas lord! alas his glory!"
Who was the lamented sister? Professor T. K. Cheyne supposes that
she was Astarte, and by a very slight
change (דדה for חרה) he would read
"Dodah" for "his glory," thus restoring the balance between the clauses;
for "Dodah" would then answer to
"Adon" (lord) as "sister" answers
to "brother." I have to thank Professor Cheyne for kindly communicating
this conjecture to me by letter. He
writes that Dodah "is a title of Ishtar,
just as Dôd is a title of Tamûz," and
for evidence he refers me to the Dodah
of the Moabite Stone, where, however,
the reading Dodah is not free from

doubt. See G. A. Cooke, *Text-book of
North-Semitic Inscriptions*, No. 1, pp.
1, 3, 11; *Encyclopaedia Biblica*, ii. 3045;
S. R. Driver, *Notes on the Hebrew
Text and the Topography of the Books
of Samuel*, Second Edition (Oxford,
1913), pp. lxxxv., lxxxvi., xc.; F.
Baethgen, *Beiträge zur semitischen
Religionsgeschichte* (Berlin, 1888), p.
234; H. Winckler, *Geschichte Israels*
(Leipsic, 1895-1900), ii. 258. As to
Hebrew names formed from the root
dôd in the sense of "beloved," see
Brown, Driver, and Briggs, *Hebrew
and English Lexicon of the Old Testament*, pp. 187 *sq.*; G. B. Gray, *Studies
in Hebrew Proper Names* (London,
1896), pp. 60 *sqq.*

[3] This was perceived by Renan
(*Histoire du peuple d'Israel*, iii. 273),
and Prof. T. K. Cheyne writes to me:
"The formulae of public mourning
were derived from the ceremonies of
the Adonia; this Lenormant saw long
ago."

some extent embodying Jehovah on earth. For the king's throne was called the throne of Jehovah;[1] and the application of the holy oil to his head was believed to impart to him directly a portion of the divine spirit.[2] Hence he bore the title of Messiah, which with its Greek equivalent Christ means no more than "the Anointed One." Thus when David had cut off the skirt of Saul's robe in the darkness of a cave where he was in hiding, his heart smote him for having laid sacrilegious hands upon *Adoni Messiah Jehovah*, "my Lord the Anointed of Jehovah."[3]

Like other divine or semi-divine rulers the Hebrew kings were apparently held answerable for famine and pestilence. When a dearth, caused perhaps by a failure of the winter rains, had visited the land for three years, King David inquired of the oracle, which discreetly laid the blame not on him but on his predecessor Saul. The dead king was indeed beyond the reach of punishment, but his sons were

The Hebrew kings seem to have been held responsible for drought and famine.

---

[1] 1 Chronicles xxix. 23; 2 Chronicles ix. 8.

[2] 1 Samuel xvi. 13, 14, compare *id.*, x. 1 and 20. The oil was poured on the king's head (1 Samuel x. 1; 2 Kings ix. 3, 6). For the conveyance of the divine spirit by means of oil, see also Isaiah lx. 1. The kings of Egypt appear to have consecrated their vassal Syrian kings by pouring oil on their heads. See the Tell-el-Amarna letters, No. 37 (H. Winckler, *Die Thontafeln von Tell-el-Amarna*, p. 99). Some West African priests are consecrated by a similar ceremony. See below, p. 68. The natives of Buru, an East Indian island, imagine that they can keep off demons by smearing their bodies with coco-nut oil, but the oil must be prepared by young unmarried girls. See G. A. Wilken, "Bijdrage tot de kennis der Alfoeren van het eiland Boeroe," *Verhandelingen van het Bataviaasch Genootschap van Kunsten en Wetenschappen*, xxxviii. (Batavia, 1875) p. 30; *id.*, *Verspreide Geschriften* (The Hague, 1912), i. 61. In some tribes of North-West America hunters habitually anointed their hair with decoctions of certain plants and deer's brains before they set out to hunt. The practice was probably a charm to secure success in the hunt. See C. Hill-Tout, *The Home of the Salish and Déné* (London, 1907), p. 72.

[3] 1 Samuel xxiv. 6. Messiah in Hebrew is *Mashiah* (מָשִׁיחַ). The English form Messiah is derived from the Aramaic through the Greek. See T. K. Cheyne, in *Encyclopaedia Biblica*, s.v. "Messiah," vol. iii. 3057 *sqq.* Why hair oil should be considered a vehicle of inspiration is by no means clear. It would have been intelligible if the olive had been with the Hebrews, as it was with the Athenians, a sacred tree under the immediate protection of a deity; for then a portion of the divine essence might be thought to reside in the oil. W. Robertson Smith supposed that the unction was originally performed with the fat of a sacrificial victim, for which vegetable oil was a later substitute (*Religion of the Semites*,[2] pp. 383 *sq.*). On the whole subject see J. Wellhausen, "Zwei Rechtsriten bei den Hebräern," *Archiv für Religionswissenschaft*, vii. (1904) pp. 33-39; H. Weinel, "משׁח und seine Derivate," *Zeitschrift für die alttestamentliche Wissenschaft*, xviii. (1898) pp. 1-82.

not. So David had seven of them sought out, and they were hanged before the Lord at the beginning of barley harvest in spring : and all the long summer the mother of two of the dead men sat under the gallows-tree, keeping off the jackals by night and the vultures by day, till with the autumn the blessed rain came at last to wet their dangling bodies and fertilize the barren earth once more. Then the bones of the dead were taken down from the gibbet and buried in the sepulchre of their fathers.[1] The season when these princes were put to death, at the beginning of barley harvest, and the length of time they hung on the gallows, seem to show that their execution was not a mere punishment, but that it partook of the nature of a rain-charm. For it is a common belief that rain can be procured by magical ceremonies performed with dead men's bones,[2] and it would be natural to ascribe a special virtue in this respect to the bones of princes, who are often expected to give rain in their life. When the Israelites demanded of Samuel that he should give them a king, the indignant prophet, loth to be superseded by the upstart Saul, called on the Lord to send thunder and rain, and the Lord did so at once, though the season was early summer and the reapers were at work in the wheat-fields, a time when in common years no rain falls from the cloudless Syrian sky.[3] The pious historian who records the miracle seems to have regarded it as a mere token of the wrath of the deity, whose voice was heard in the roll of thunder ; but we may surmise that in giving this impressive proof of his control of the weather Samuel meant to hint gently at the naughtiness of asking for a king to do for the fertility of the land what could be done quite as well and far more cheaply by a prophet.

In Israel the excess as well as the deficiency of rain seems to have been set down to the wrath of the

---

[1] 2 Samuel xxi. 1-14, with Dean Kirkpatrick's notes on 1 and 10.

[2] *The Magic Art and the Evolution of Kings*, i. 284 *sq.*

[3] 1 Samuel xii. 17 *sq.* Similarly, Moses stretched forth his rod toward heaven and the Lord sent thunder and rain (Exodus ix. 23). The word for thunder in both these passages is "voices" (נִלֹּק). The Hebrews heard in the clap of thunder the voice of Jehovah, just as the Greeks heard in it the voice of Zeus and the Romans the voice of Jupiter.

deity.[1]   When the Jews returned to Jerusalem from the great captivity and assembled for the first time in the square before the ruined temple, it happened that the weather was very wet, and as the people sat shelterless and drenched in the piazza they trembled at their sin and at the rain.[2]   In all ages it has been the strength or the weakness of Israel to read the hand of God in the changing aspects of nature, and we need not wonder that at such a time and in so dismal a scene, with a lowering sky overhead, the blackened ruins of the temple before their eyes, and the steady drip of the rain over all, the returned exiles should have been oppressed with a double sense of their own guilt and of the divine anger.   Perhaps, though they hardly knew it, memories of the bright sun, fat fields, and broad willow-fringed rivers of Babylon,[3] which had been so long their home, lent a deeper shade of sadness to the austerity of the Judean landscape, with its gaunt grey hills stretching away, range beyond range, to the horizon, or dipping eastward to the far line of sombre blue which marks the sullen waters of the Dead Sea.[4]

Excessive rain set down to the wrath of the deity.

In the days of the Hebrew monarchy the king was apparently credited with the power of making sick and making whole.   Thus the king of Syria sent a leper to the king of Israel to be healed by him, just as scrofulous patients

Hebrew kings apparently supposed to heal disease and stop epidemics.

---

[1] Ezekiel xiii. 11, 13, xxxviii. 22; Jeremiah iii. 2 *sq.*   The Hebrews looked to Jehovah for rain (Leviticus xxvi. 3-5; Jeremiah v. 24) just as the Greeks looked to Zeus and the Romans to Jupiter.

[2] Ezra x. 9-14.   The special sin which they laid to heart on this occasion was their marriage with Gentile women.   It is implied, though not expressly said, that they traced the inclemency of the weather to these unfortunate alliances.   Similarly, " during the rainy season, when the sun is hidden behind great masses of dark clouds, the Indians set up a wailing for their sins, believing that the sun is angry and may never shine on them again."   See Francis C. Nicholas, " The Aborigines of Santa Maria, Colombia," *American Anthropologist*, N.S., iii. (New York, 1901)

p. 641.   The Indians in question are the Aurohuacas of Colombia, in South America.

[3] Psalm cxxxvii.   The willows beside the rivers of Babylon are mentioned in the laments for Tammuz. See above, pp. 9, 10.

[4] The line of the Dead Sea, lying in its deep trough, is visible from the Mount of Olives; indeed, so clear is the atmosphere that the blue water seems quite near the eye, though in fact it is more than fifteen miles off and nearly four thousand feet below the spectator.   See K. Baedeker, *Palestine and Syria*[4] (Leipsic, 1906), p. 77.   When the sun shines on it, the lake is of a brilliant blue (G. A. Smith, *Historical Geography of the Holy Land*, London, 1894, pp. 501 *sq.*); but its brilliancy is naturally dimmed under clouded skies.

used to fancy that they could be cured by the touch of a French or English king. However, the Hebrew monarch, with more sense than has been shown by his royal brothers in modern times, professed himself unable to work any such miracle. "Am I God," he asked, "to kill and to make alive, that this man doth send unto me to recover a man of his leprosy?" [1] On another occasion, when pestilence ravaged the country and the excited fancy of the plague-stricken people saw in the clouds the figure of the Destroying Angel with his sword stretched out over Jerusalem, they laid the blame on King David, who had offended the touchy and irascible deity by taking a census. The prudent monarch bowed to the popular storm, acknowledged his guilt, and appeased the angry god by offering burnt sacrifices on the threshing-floor of Araunah, one of the old Jebusite inhabitants of Jerusalem. Then the angel sheathed his flashing sword, and the shrieks of the dying and the lamentations for the dead no longer resounded in the streets.[2]

The rarity of references to the divinity of Hebrew kings in the historical books may be ex- To this theory of the sanctity, nay the divinity of the Hebrew kings it may be objected that few traces of it survive in the historical books of the Bible. But the force of the objection is weakened by a consideration of the time and the circumstances in which these books assumed their final shape. The great prophets of the eighth and the

---

[1] 2 Kings v. 5-7.

[2] 2 Samuel xxiv. ; 1 Chronicles xxi. In this passage, contrary to his usual practice, the Chronicler has enlivened the dull tenor of his history with some picturesque touches which we miss in the corresponding passage of Kings. It is to him that we owe the vision of the Angel of the Plague first stretching out his sword over Jerusalem and then returning it to the scabbard. From him Defoe seems to have taken a hint in his account of the prodigies, real or imaginary, which heralded the outbreak of the Great Plague in London. "One time before the plague was begun, otherwise than as I have said in St. Giles's, I think it was in March, seeing a crowd of people in the street, I joined with them to satisfy my curiosity, and found them all staring up into the air to see what a woman told them appeared plain to her, which was an angel clothed in white with a fiery sword in his hand, waving it or brandishing it over his head. . . . One saw one thing and one another. I looked as earnestly as the rest, but, perhaps, not with so much willingness to be imposed upon ; and I said, indeed, that I could see nothing but a white cloud, bright on one side, by the shining of the sun upon the other part." See Daniel Defoe, *History of the Plague in London* (Edinburgh, 1810, pp. 33 *sq.*). It is the more likely that Defoe had here the Chronicler in mind, because a few pages earlier he introduces the prophet Jonah and a man out of Josephus with very good effect.

seventh centuries by the spiritual ideals and the ethical fervour of their teaching had wrought a religious and moral reform perhaps unparalleled in history.   Under their influence an austere monotheism had replaced the old sensuous worship of the natural powers : a stern Puritanical spirit, an unbending rigour of mind, had succeeded to the old easy supple temper with its weak compliances, its wax-like impressionability, its proclivities to the sins of the flesh. And the moral lessons which the prophets inculcated were driven home by the political events of the time, above all by the ever-growing pressure of the great Assyrian empire on the petty states of Palestine.   The long agony of the siege of Samaria [1] must have been followed with trembling anxiety by the inhabitants of Judea, for the danger was at their door.   They had only to lift up their eyes and look north to see the blue hills of Ephraim, at whose foot lay the beleaguered city.   Its final fall and the destruction of the northern kingdom could not fail to fill every thoughtful mind in the sister realm with sad forebodings.   It was as if the sky had lowered and thunder muttered over Jerusalem. Thenceforth to the close of the Jewish monarchy, about a century and a half later, the cloud never passed away, though once for a little it seemed to lift, when Sennacherib raised the siege of Jerusalem [2] and the watchers on the walls beheld the last of the long line of spears and standards disappearing, the last squadron of the blue-coated Assyrian cavalry sweeping, in a cloud of dust, out of sight.[3]

It was in this period of national gloom and despondency that the two great reformations of Israel's religion were accomplished, the first by king Hezekiah, the second a century later by king Josiah.[4]   We need not wonder then

---

[1] 2 Kings xvii. 5 *sq.*, xviii. 9 *sq.*

[2] 2 Kings xix. 32-36.

[3] We owe to Ezekiel (xxiii. 5 *sq.*, 12) the picture of the handsome Assyrian cavalrymen in their blue uniforms and gorgeous trappings.   The prophet writes as if in his exile by the waters of Babylon he had seen the blue regiments filing past, in all the pomp of war, on their way to the front.

[4] Samaria fell in 722 B.C., during

or just before the reign of Hezekiah : the Book of Deuteronomy, the cornerstone of king Josiah's reformation, was produced in 621 B.C. ; and Jerusalem fell in 586 B.C.   The date of Hezekiah's accession is a much-disputed point in the chronology of Judah.   See the Introduction to Kings and Isaiah i.-xxxix. by J. Skinner and O. C. Whitehouse respectively, in *The Century Bible.*

influence of the prophetic reformation.

that the reformers who in that and subsequent ages composed or edited the annals of their nation should have looked as sourly on the old unreformed paganism of their forefathers as the fierce zealots of the Commonwealth looked on the far more innocent pastimes of Merry England; and that in their zeal for the glory of God they should have blotted many pages of history lest they should perpetuate the memory of practices to which they traced the calamities of their country. All the historical books passed through the office of the Puritan censor,[1] and we can hardly doubt that they emerged from it stript of many gay feathers which they had flaunted when they went in. Among the shed plumage may well have been the passages which invested human beings, whether kings or commoners, with the attributes of deity. Certainly no pages could seem to the censor more rankly blasphemous; on none, therefore, was he likely to press more firmly the official sponge.

The Baal and his female Baalath the sources of all fertility.

But if Semitic kings in general and the kings of Byblus in particular often assumed the style of Baal or Adonis, it follows that they may have mated with the goddess, the Baalath or Astarte of the city. Certainly we hear of kings of Tyre and Sidon who were priests of Astarte.[2] Now to the agricultural Semites the Baal or god of a land was the author of all its fertility; he it was who produced the corn, the wine, the figs, the oil, and the flax, by means of his quickening waters, which in the arid parts of the Semitic world are oftener springs, streams, and underground flow than the rains of heaven.[3] Further, "the life-giving power of the god was not limited to vegetative nature, but to him also was ascribed the increase of animal life, the

---

[1] Or the Deuteronomic redactor, as the critics call him. See W. Robertson Smith, *The Old Testament in the Jewish Church*[2] (London and Edinburgh, 1892), pp. 395 *sq.*, 425; *Encyclopaedia Biblica*, ii. 2078 *sqq.*, 2633 *sqq.*, iv. 4273 *sqq.*; K. Budde, *Geschichte der althebräischen Litteratur* (Leipsic, 1906), pp. 99, 121 *sqq.*, 127 *sqq.*, 132; Principal J. Skinner, in his introduction to Kings (in *The Century Bible*), pp. 10 *sqq.*

[2] Menander of Ephesus, quoted by Josephus, *Contra Apionem*, i. 18 (*Fragmenta Historicorum Graecorum*, ed. C. Müller, iv. 446); G. A. Cooke, *Text-book of North-Semitic Inscriptions*, No. 4, p. 26. According to Justin, however, the priest of Hercules, that is, of Melcarth, at Tyre, was distinct from the king and second to him in dignity. See Justin, xviii. 4. 5.

[3] Hosea ii. 5 *sqq.*; W. Robertson Smith, *Religion of the Semites*[2] (London, 1894), pp. 95-107.

multiplication of flocks and herds, and, not least, of the human inhabitants of the land.   For the increase of animate nature is obviously conditioned, in the last resort, by the fertility of the soil, and primitive races, which have not learned to differentiate the various kinds of life with precision, think of animate as well as vegetable life as rooted in the earth and sprung from it.   The earth is the great mother of all things in most mythological philosophies, and the comparison of the life of mankind, or of a stock of men, with the life of a tree, which is so common in Semitic as in other primitive poetry, is not in its origin a mere figure.   Thus where the growth of vegetation is ascribed to a particular divine power, the same power receives the thanks and homage of his worshippers for the increase of cattle and of men.   Firstlings as well as first-fruits were offered at the shrines of the Baalim, and one of the commonest classes of personal names given by parents to their sons or daughters designates the child as the gift of the god."   In short, "the Baal was conceived as the male principle of reproduction, the husband of the land which he fertilised."[1]   So far, therefore, as the Semite personified the reproductive energies of nature as male and female, as a Baal and a Baalath, he appears to have identified the male power especially with water and the female especially with earth.   On this view plants and trees, animals and men, are the offspring or children of the Baal and Baalath.

If, then, at Byblus and elsewhere, the Semitic king was allowed, or rather required, to personate the god and marry the goddess, the intention of the custom can only have been to ensure the fertility of the land and the increase of men and cattle by means of homoeopathic magic.   There is reason to think that a similar custom was observed from a similar motive in other parts of the ancient world, and particularly at Nemi, where both the male and the female powers, the Dianus and Diana, were in one aspect of their nature personifications of the life-giving waters.[2] *Persona-tion of the Baal by the king.*

The last king of Byblus bore the ancient name of Cinyras, and was beheaded by Pompey the Great for his *Cinyras, king of Byblus.*

[1] W. Robertson Smith, *Religion of the Semites*,[2] pp. 107 *sq.*

[2] *The Magic Art and the Evolution of Kings*, ii. 120 *sqq.*, 376 *sqq.*

tyrannous excesses.[1]   His legendary namesake Cinyras is
said to have founded a sanctuary of Aphrodite, that is, of
Astarte, at a place on Mount Lebanon, distant a day's
journey from the capital.[2]   The spot was probably Aphaca,
at the source of the river Adonis, half-way between Byblus
and Baalbec ; for at Aphaca there was a famous grove
and sanctuary of Astarte which Constantine destroyed on
account of the flagitious character of the worship.[3]   The site
of the temple has been discovered by modern travellers near
the miserable village which still bears the name of Afka at
the head of the wild, romantic, wooded gorge of the Adonis.
The hamlet stands among groves of noble walnut-trees on
the brink of the lyn.   A little way off the river rushes
from a cavern at the foot of a mighty amphitheatre of
towering cliffs to plunge in a series of cascades into the
awful depths of the glen.   The deeper it descends, the
ranker and denser grows the vegetation, which, sprouting
from the crannies and fissures of the rocks, spreads a
green veil over the roaring or murmuring stream in the
tremendous chasm below.   There is something delicious,
almost intoxicating, in the freshness of these tumbling
waters, in the sweetness and purity of the mountain air, in
the vivid green of the vegetation.   The temple, of which
some massive hewn blocks and a fine column of Syenite
granite still mark the site, occupied a terrace facing the
source of the river and commanding a magnificent prospect.
Across the foam and the roar of the waterfalls you look
up to the cavern and away to the top of the sublime
precipices above.   So lofty is the cliff that the goats
which creep along its ledges to browse on the bushes
appear like ants to the spectator hundreds of feet below.
Seaward the view is especially impressive when the sun
floods the profound gorge with golden light, revealing all
the fantastic buttresses and rounded towers of its mountain rampart, and falling softly on the varied green of the
woods which clothe its depths.[4]   It was here that, according

*Aphaca
and the
vale of the
Adonis.*

---

[1] Strabo, xvi. 1. 18, p. 755.

[2] Lucian, *De dea Syria*, 9.

[3] Eusebius, *Vita Constantini*, iii. 55 ;
Sozomenus, *Historia Ecclesiastica*, ii. 5 ;
Socrates, *Historia Ecclesiastica*, i. 18 ;

Zosimus, i. 58.

[4] On the valley of the Nahr Ibrahim,
its scenery and monuments, see Edward
Robinson, *Biblical Researches in Palestine*[3] (London, 1867), iii. 603-609 ;

to the legend, Adonis met Aphrodite for the first or the last time,[1] and here his mangled body was buried.[2]   A fairer scene could hardly be imagined for a story of tragic love and death.   Yet, sequestered as the valley is and must always have been, it is not wholly deserted.   A convent or a village may be observed here and there standing out against the sky on the top of some beetling crag, or clinging to the face of a nearly perpendicular cliff high above the foam and the din of the river ; and at evening the lights that twinkle through the gloom betray the presence of human habitations on slopes which might seem inaccessible to man.   In antiquity the whole of the lovely vale appears to have been dedicated to Adonis, and to this day it is haunted by his memory ; for the heights which shut it in are crested at various points by ruined monuments of his worship, some of them overhanging dreadful abysses, down which it turns the head dizzy to look and see the eagles wheeling about their nests far below.   One such monument exists at Ghineh.   The face of a great rock, above a roughly hewn recess, is here carved with figures of Adonis and Aphrodite.   He is portrayed with spear in rest, awaiting the attack of a bear, while she is seated in an attitude of sorrow.[3]   Her grief-stricken figure may well be the mourning

Monuments of Adonis.

W. M. Thomson, *The Land and the Book, Lebanon, Damascus, and beyond Jordan* (London, 1886), pp. 239-246 ; E. Renan, *Mission de Phénicie*, pp. 282 *sqq.*; G. Maspero, *Histoire Ancienne des Peuples de l'Orient Classique*, ii. (Paris, 1897) pp. 175-179 ; Sir Charles Wilson, *Picturesque Palestine* (London, N.D.), iii. 16, 17, 27.   Among the trees which line the valley are oak, sycamore, bay, plane, orange, and mulberry (W. M. Thomson, *op. cit.* p. 245).   Travellers are unanimous in testifying to the extraordinary beauty of the vale of the Adonis.   Thus Robinson writes : "There is no spot in all my wanderings on which memory lingers with greater delight than on the sequestered retreat and exceeding loveliness of Afka."   Renan says that the landscape is one of the most beautiful in the world.   My friend the late Sir Francis Galton wrote to me (20th

September 1906) : "I have no good map of Palestine, but strongly suspect that my wanderings there, quite sixty years ago, took me to the place you mention, above the gorge of the river Adonis.   Be that as it may, I have constantly asserted that the view I then had of a deep ravine and blue sea seen through the cliffs that bounded it, was the most beautiful I had ever set eyes on."

[1] *Etymologicum Magnum*, *s.v.* Ἄφακα, p. 175.

[2] Melito, "Oration to Antoninus Caesar," in W. Cureton's *Spicilegium Syriacum* (London, 1855), p. 44.

[3] E. Renan, *Mission de Phénicie*, pp. 292-294.   The writer seems to have no doubt that the beast attacking Adonis is a bear, not a boar.   Views of the monument are given by A. Jeremias, *Das Alte Testament im Lichte des Alten Orients*[2] (Leipsic, 1906), p.

Aphrodite of the Lebanon described by Macrobius,[1] and the recess in the rock is perhaps her lover's tomb.   Every year, in the belief of his worshippers, Adonis was wounded to death on the mountains, and every year the face of nature itself was dyed with his sacred blood.   So year by year the Syrian damsels lamented his untimely fate,[2] while the red anemone, his flower, bloomed among the cedars of Lebanon, and the river ran red to the sea, fringing the winding shores of the blue Mediterranean, whenever the wind set inshore, with a sinuous band of crimson.

90, and by Baudissin, *Adonis und Esmun*, plates i. and ii., with his discussion, pp. 78 *sqq.*

[1] Macrobius, *Saturn.* i. 21. 5.

[2] Lucian, *De dea Syria*, 8.

CHAPTER III

ADONIS IN CYPRUS

THE island of Cyprus lies but one day's sail from the coast of Syria. Indeed, on fine summer evenings its mountains may be descried looming low and dark against the red fires of sunset.[1] With its rich mines of copper and its forests of firs and stately cedars, the island naturally attracted a commercial and maritime people like the Phoenicians; while the abundance of its corn, its wine, and its oil must have rendered it in their eyes a Land of Promise by comparison with the niggardly nature of their own rugged coast, hemmed in between the mountains and the sea.[2] Accordingly they settled in Cyprus at a very early date and remained there long after the Greeks had also established themselves on its shores; for we know from inscriptions and coins that Phoenician kings reigned at Citium, the Chittim of the Hebrews, down to the time of Alexander the Great.[3]

---

[1] F. C. Movers, *Die Phoenizier*, ii. 2, p. 224; G. Maspero, *Histoire Ancienne des Peuples de l'Orient Classique*, ii. 199; G. A. Smith, *Historical Geography of the Holy Land* (London, 1894), p. 135.

[2] On the natural wealth of Cyprus see Strabo, xiv. 6. 5; W. H. Engel, *Kypros*, i. 40-71; F. C. Movers, *Die Phoenizier*, ii. 2, pp. 224 *sq.*; G. Maspero, *Histoire Ancienne des Peuples de l'Orient Classique*, ii. 200 *sq.*; E. Oberhummer, *Die Insel Cypern*, i. (Munich, 1903) pp. 175 *sqq.*, 243 *sqq.* As to the firs and cedars of Cyprus see Theophrastus, *Historia Plantarum*, v. 7. 1, v. 9. 1. The Cyprians boasted that they could build

and rig a ship complete, from her keel to her topsails, with the native products of their island (Ammianus Marcellinus, xiv. 8. 14).

[3] G. A. Cooke, *Text-Book of North-Semitic Inscriptions*, Nos. 12-25, pp. 55-76, 347-349; P. Gardner, *New Chapters in Greek History* (London, 1892), pp. 179, 185. It has been held that the name of Citium is etymologically identical with Hittite. If that was so, it would seem that the town was built and inhabited by a non-Semitic people before the arrival of the Phoenicians. See *Encyclopaedia Biblica, s.v.* "Kittim." Other traces of this older race, akin to the primitive stock of Asia Minor, have been detected in Cyprus;

Naturally the Semitic colonists brought their gods with them from the mother-land. They worshipped Baal of the Lebanon,[1] who may well have been Adonis, and at Amathus on the south coast they instituted the rites of Adonis and Aphrodite, or rather Astarte.[2] Here, as at Byblus, these rites resembled the Egyptian worship of Osiris so closely that some people even identified the Adonis of Amathus with Osiris.[3] The Tyrian Melcarth or Moloch was also worshipped at Amathus,[4] and the tombs discovered in the neighbourhood prove that the city remained Phoenician to a late period.[5]

Kingdom of Paphos.

But the great seat of the worship of Aphrodite and Adonis in Cyprus was Paphos on the south-western side of the island. Among the petty kingdoms into which Cyprus was divided from the earliest times until the end of the fourth century before our era Paphos must have ranked with the best. It is a land of hills and billowy ridges, diversified by fields and vineyards and intersected by rivers, which in the course of ages have carved for themselves beds of such tremendous depth that travelling in the interior is difficult and tedious. The lofty range of Mount Olympus (the modern Troodos), capped with snow the greater part of the year, screens Paphos from the northerly and easterly winds and cuts it off from the rest of the island. On the slopes of the range the last pine-woods of Cyprus linger, sheltering here and there monasteries

amongst them the most obvious is the Cyprian syllabary, the characters of which are neither Phoenician nor Greek in origin. See P. Gardner, *op. cit.* pp. 154, 173-175, 178 *sq.*

[1] G. A. Cooke, *Text-Book of North-Semitic Inscriptions*, No. 11, p. 52.

[2] Stephanus Byzantius, *s.v.* Ἀμαθοῦς; Pausanias, ix. 41. 2 *sq.* According to Pausanias, there was a remarkable necklace of green stones and gold in the sanctuary of Adonis and Aphrodite at Amathus. The Greeks commonly identified it with the necklace of Harmonia or Eriphyle. A terra-cotta statuette of Astarte, found at Amathus (?), represents her wearing a necklace which she touches with one hand. See L. P. di Cesnola,

Cyprus (London, 1877), p. 275. The scanty ruins of Amathus occupy an isolated hill beside the sea. Among them is an enormous stone jar, half buried in the earth, of which the four handles are adorned with figures of bulls. It is probably of Phoenician manufacture. See L. Ross, *Reisen nach Kos, Halikarnassos, Rhodes und der Insel Cypern* (Halle, 1852), pp. 168 *sqq.*

[3] Stephanus Byzantius, *s.v.* Ἀμαθοῦς. For the relation of Adonis to Osiris at Byblus see below, vol. ii. pp. 9 *sq.*, 22 *sq.*, 127.

[4] Hesychius, *s.v.* Μάλικα.

[5] L. P. di Cesnola, *Cyprus*, pp. 254-283; G. Perrot et Ch. Chipiez, *Histoire de l'Art dans l'Antiquité*, iii. (Paris, 1885) pp. 216-222.

in scenery not unworthy of the Apennines.   The old city of
Paphos occupied the summit of a hill about a mile from the
sea ; the newer city sprang up at the harbour some ten miles
off.[1]   The sanctuary of Aphrodite at Old Paphos (the Sanctuary of Aphrodite at Paphos.
modern Kuklia) was one of the most celebrated shrines in
the ancient world.   From the earliest to the latest times it
would seem to have preserved its essential features unchanged.   For the sanctuary is represented on coins of the
Imperial age,[2] and these representations agree closely with
little golden models of a shrine which were found in two of
the royal graves at Mycenae.[3]   Both on the coins and in
the models we see a façade surmounted by a pair of doves
and divided into three compartments or chapels, of which
the central one is crowned by a lofty superstructure.   In
the golden models each chapel contains a pillar standing in
a pair of horns : the central superstructure is crowned by
two pairs of horns, one within the other ; and the two side
chapels are in like manner crowned each with a pair of horns
and a single dove perched on the outer horn of each pair.
On the coins each of the side chapels contains a pillar or
candelabra-like object : the central chapel contains a cone
and is flanked by two high columns, each terminating in a
pair of ball-topped pinnacles, with a star and crescent
appearing between the tops of the columns.   The doves are
doubtless the sacred doves of Aphrodite or Astarte,[4] and the

---

[1] D. G. Hogarth, *Devia Cypria* (London, 1889), pp. 1-3 ; *Encyclopaedia Britannica*,[9] vi. 747 ; Élisée Reclus, *Nouvelle Géographie Universelle* (Paris, 1879–1894), ix. 668.

[2] T. L. Donaldson, *Architectura Numismatica* (London, 1859), pp. 107-109, with fig. 31 ; *Journal of Hellenic Studies*, ix. (1888) pp. 210-213 ; G. F. Hill, *Catalogue of the Greek Coins of Cyprus* (London, 1904), pp. cxxvii-cxxxiv, with plates xiv. 2, 3, 6-8, xv. 1-4, 7, xvi. 2, 4, 6-9, xvii. 4-6, 8, 9, xxvi. 3, 6-16 ; George Macdonald, *Catalogue of Greek Coins in the Hunterian Collection* (Glasgow, 1899–1905), ii. 566, with pl. lxi. 19. As to the existing remains of the temple, which were excavated by an English expedition in 1887-1888, see " Excavations in Cyprus, 1887-1888," *Journal of Hel-*

lenic Studies, ix. (1888) pp. 193 *sqq.* Previous accounts of the temple are inaccurate and untrustworthy.

[3] C. Schuchhardt, *Schliemann's Ausgrabungen*[2] (Leipsic, 1891), pp. 231-233 ; G. Perrot et Ch. Chipiez, *Histoire de l'Art dans l'Antiquité*, vi. (Paris, 1894) pp. 336 *sq.*, 652-654 ; *Journal of Hellenic Studies*, ix. (1888) pp. 213 *sq.* ; P. Gardner, *New Chapters in Greek History*, p. 181.

[4] J. Selden, *De dis Syris* (Leipsic, 1668), pp. 274 *sqq.* ; S. Bochart, *Hierozoicon*, Editio Tertia (Leyden, 1692), ii. 4 *sqq.* Compare the statue of a priest with a dove in his hand, which was found in Cyprus (Perrot et Chipiez, *Histoire de l'Art dans l'Antiquité*, iii. Paris, 1885, p. 510), with fig. 349.

horns and pillars remind us of the similar religious emblems which have been found in the great prehistoric palace of Cnossus in Crete, as well as on many monuments of the Mycenaean or Minoan age of Greece.[1] If antiquaries are right in regarding the golden models as copies of the Paphian shrine, that shrine must have suffered little outward change for more than a thousand years ; for the royal graves at Mycenae, in which the models were found, can hardly be of later date than the twelfth century before our era.

The Aphrodite of Paphos a Phoenician or aboriginal deity.

Thus the sanctuary of Aphrodite at Paphos was apparently of great antiquity.[2] According to Herodotus, it was founded by Phoenician colonists from Ascalon ;[3] but it is possible that a native goddess of fertility was worshipped on the spot before the arrival of the Phoenicians, and that the newcomers identified her with their own Baalath or Astarte, whom she may have closely resembled. If two deities were thus fused in one, we may suppose that they were both varieties of that great goddess of motherhood and fertility whose worship appears to have been spread all over Western Asia from a very early time. The supposition is confirmed as well by the archaic shape of her image as by the licentious character of her rites ; for both that shape and those rites were shared by her with other Asiatic deities. Her image was simply a white cone or pyramid.[4]

Her conical image.

---

[1] A. J. Evans, "Mycenaean Tree and Pillar Cult," *Journal of Hellenic Studies*, xxi. (1901) pp. 99 *sqq.*

[2] Tacitus, *Annals*, iii. 62.

[3] Herodotus, i. 105 ; compare Pausanias, i. 14. 7. Herodotus only speaks of the sanctuary of Aphrodite in Cyprus, but he must refer to the great one at Paphos. At Ascalon a goddess was worshipped in mermaid-shape under the name of Derceto, and fish and doves were sacred to her (Diodorus Siculus, ii. 4 ; compare Lucian, *De dea Syria*, 14). The name Derceto, like the much more correct Atargatis, is a Greek corruption of 'Attâr, the Aramaic form of *Astarte*, but the two goddesses Atargatis and Astarte, in spite of the affinity of their names, appear to have been historically distinct. See Ed. Meyer, *Geschichte des Altertums*,[2] i. 2 (Stuttgart and Berlin, 1909), pp. 605, 650 *sq.* ; F. Baethgen, *Beiträge zur Semitischen Religionsgeschichte* (Berlin, 1888), pp. 68 *sqq.* ; F. Cumont, *s.vv.* "Atargatis" and "Dea Syria," in Pauly-Wissowa's *Real-Encyclopädie der classischen Altertumswissenschaft* ; René Dussaud, *Notes de Mythologie Syrienne* (Paris, 1903), pp. 82 *sqq.* ; R. A. Stewart Macalister, *The Philistines, their History and Civilization* (London, 1913), pp. 94 *sqq.*

[4] It is. described by ancient writers and figured on coins. See Tacitus, *Hist.* ii. 3 ; Maximus Tyrius, *Dissert.* viii. 8 ; Servius on Virgil, *Aen.* i. 720 ; T. L. Donaldson, *Architectura Numismatica*, p. 107, with fig. 31 ; *Journal of Hellenic Studies*, ix. (1888) pp. 210-

In like manner, a cone was the emblem of Astarte at Byblus,[1] of the native goddess whom the Greeks called Artemis at Perga in Pamphylia,[2] and of the sun-god Heliogabalus at Emesa in Syria.[3] Conical stones, which apparently served as idols, have also been found at Golgi in Cyprus, and in the Phoenician temples of Malta;[4] and cones of sandstone came to light at the shrine of the "Mistress of Torquoise" among the barren hills and frowning precipices of Sinai.[5] The precise significance of such

---

212. According to Maximus Tyrius, the material of the pyramid was unknown. Probably it was a stone. The English archaeologists found several fragments of white cones on the site of the temple at Paphos : one which still remains in its original position in the central chamber was of limestone and of somewhat larger size (*Journal of Hellenic Studies*, ix. (1888) p. 180).

[1] See above, p. 14.

[2] On coins of Perga the sacred cone is represented as richly decorated and standing in a temple between sphinxes. See B. V. Head, *Historia Numorum* (Oxford, 1887), p. 585 ; P. Gardner, *Types of Greek Coins* (Cambridge, 1883), pl. xv. No. 3 ; G. F. Hill, *Catalogue of the Greek Coins of Lycia, Pamphylia, and Pisidia* (London, 1897), pl. xxiv. 12, 15, 16. However, Mr. G. F. Hill writes to me : "Is the stone at Perga really a cone ? I have always thought it was a cube or something of that kind. On the coins the upper, sloping portion is apparently an elaborate veil or headdress. The head attached to the stone is seen in the middle of this, surmounted by a tall *kalathos*." The sanctuary stood on a height, and a festival was held there annually (Strabo, xiv. 4. 2, p. 667). The native title of the goddess was *Anassa*, that is, "Queen." See B. V. Head, *l.c.*; Wernicke, *s.v.* "Artemis," in Pauly-Wissowa, *Real-Encyclopädie der classischen Altertumswissenschaft*, ii. 1, col. 1397. Aphrodite at Paphos bore the same title. See below, p. 42, note [6]. The worship of Pergaean Artemis at Halicarnassus was cared for by a priestess,

who held office for life and had to make intercession for the city at every new moon. See G. Dittenberger, *Sylloge Inscriptionum Graecarum*[2] (Leipsic, 1898-1901), vol. ii. p. 373, No. 601.

[3] Herodian, v. 3. 5. This cone was of black stone, with some small knobs on it, like the stone of Cybele at Pessinus. It is figured on coins of Emesa. See B. V. Head, *Historia Numorum* (Oxford, 1887), p. 659 ; P. Gardner, *Types of Greek Coins*, pl. xv. No. 1. The sacred stone of Cybele, which the Romans brought from Pessinus to Rome during the Second Punic War, was small, black, and rugged, but we are not told that it was of conical shape. See Arnobius, *Adversus Nationes*, vii. 49; Livy, xxix. 11. 7. According to one reading, Servius (on Virgil, *Aen.* vii. 188) speaks of the stone of Cybele as a needle (*acus*), which would point to a conical shape. But the reading appears to be without manuscript authority, and other emendations have been suggested.

[4] G. Perrot et Ch. Chipiez, *Histoire de l'Art dans l'Antiquité*, iii. 273, 298 *sq.*, 304 *sq.* The sanctuary of Aphrodite, or rather Astarte, at Golgi is said to have been even more ancient than her sanctuary at Paphos (Pausanias, viii. 5. 2).

[5] W. M. Flinders Petrie, *Researches in Sinai* (London, 1906), pp. 135 *sq.*, 189. Votive cones made of clay have been found in large numbers in Babylonia, particularly at Lagash and Nippur. See M. Jastrow, *The Religion of Babylonia and Assyria* (Boston, U.S.A., 1898), pp. 672-674.

an emblem remains as obscure as it was in the time of
Tacitus.[1]　It appears to have been customary to anoint the
sacred cone with olive oil at a solemn festival, in which
people from Lycia and Caria participated.[2]　The custom of
anointing a holy stone has been observed in many parts of
the world; for example, in the sanctuary of Apollo at Delphi.[3]
To this day the old custom appears to survive at Paphos, for
" in honour of the Maid of Bethlehem the peasants of Kuklia
anointed lately, and probably still anoint each year, the
great corner-stones of the ruined Temple of the Paphian
Goddess.　As Aphrodite was supplicated once with cryptic
rites, so is Mary entreated still by Moslems as well as
Christians, with incantations and passings through perforated
stones, to remove the curse of barrenness from Cypriote
women, or increase the manhood of Cypriote men." [4]　Thus
the ancient worship of the goddess of fertility is continued
under a different name.　Even the name of the old goddess
is retained in some parts of the island ; for in more than
one chapel the Cypriote peasants adore the mother of Christ
under the title of Panaghia Aphroditessa.[5]

Sacred
prostitu-
tion in the
worship
of the
Paphian
Aphrodite
and of
other
Asiatic
goddesses.

In Cyprus it appears that before marriage all women
were formerly obliged by custom to prostitute themselves to
strangers at the sanctuary of the goddess, whether she went
by the name of Aphrodite, Astarte, or what not.[6]　Similar
customs prevailed in many parts of Western Asia.　Whatever its motive, the practice was clearly regarded, not as an
orgy of lust, but as a solemn religious duty performed in
the service of that great Mother Goddess of Western Asia
whose name varied, while her type remained constant, from
place to place.　Thus at Babylon every woman, whether
rich or poor, had once in her life to submit to the embraces
of a stranger at the temple of Mylitta, that is, of Ishtar or

---

[1] Tacitus, *Hist.* ii. 3.

[2] We learn this from an inscription
found at Paphos.　See *Journal of
Hellenic Studies*, ix. (1888) pp. 188,
231.

[3] Pausanias, x. 24. 6, with my note.

[4] D. G. Hogarth, *A Wandering
Scholar in the Levant* (London, 1896),
pp. 179 *sq.*　Women used to creep
through a holed stone to obtain children
at a place on the Dee in Aberdeen-

shire.　See *Balder the Beautiful*, ii.
187.

[5] G. Perrot et Ch. Chipiez, *Histoire
de l'Art dans l'Antiquité*, iii. 628.

[6] Herodotus, i. 199; Athenaeus,
xii. 11, p. 516 A; Justin, xviii. 5. 4;
Lactantius, *Divin. Inst.* i. 17 ; W. H.
Engel, *Kypros*, ii. 142 *sqq.*　Asiatic
customs of this sort have been rightly
explained by W. Mannhardt (*Antike
Wald- und Feldkulte*, pp. 283 *sqq.*).

Astarte, and to dedicate to the goddess the wages earned by this sanctified harlotry. The sacred precinct was crowded with women waiting to observe the custom. Some of them had to wait there for years.[1] At Heliopolis or Baalbec in Syria, famous for the imposing grandeur of its ruined temples, the custom of the country required that every maiden should prostitute herself to a stranger at the temple of Astarte, and matrons as well as maids testified their devotion to the goddess in the same manner. The emperor Constantine abolished the custom, destroyed the temple, and built a church in its stead.[2] In Phoenician temples women prostituted themselves for hire in the service of religion, believing that by this conduct they propitiated the goddess and won her favour.[3] " It was a law of the Amorites, that

[1] Herodotus, i. 199; Strabo, xvi. 1. 20, p. 745. As to the identity of Mylitta with Astarte see H. Zimmern in E. Schrader's *Die Keilinschriften und das alte Testament*,[3] pp. 423, note[7], 428, note[4]. According to him, the name Mylitta comes from *Mu 'allidtu*, " she who helps women in travail." In this character Ishtar would answer to the Greek Artemis and the Latin Diana. As to sacred prostitution in the worship of Ishtar see M. Jastrow, *The Religion of Babylonia and Assyria*, pp. 475 *sq.*, 484 *sq.*; P. Dhorme, *La Religion Assyro-Babylonienne* (Paris, 1910), pp. 86, 300 *sq.*

[2] Eusebius, *Vita Constantini*, iii. 58; Socrates, *Historia Ecclesiastica*, i. 18. 7-9; Sozomenus, *Historia Ecclesiastica*, v. 10. 7. Socrates says that at Heliopolis local custom obliged the women to be held in common, so that paternity was unknown, " for there was no distinction of parents and children, and the people prostituted their daughters to the strangers who visited them " (τοῖς παριοῦσι ξένοις). The prostitution of matrons as well as of maids is mentioned by Eusebius. As he was born and spent his life in Syria, and was a contemporary of the practices he describes, the bishop of Caesarea had the best opportunity of informing himself as to them, and we ought not, as Prof. M. P. Nilsson does (*Griechische Feste*, Leipsic, 1906, p. 366 n.[2]), to allow his

positive testimony on this point to be outweighed by the silence of the later historian Sozomenus, who wrote long after the custom had been abolished. Eusebius had good reason to know the heathenish customs which were kept up in his diocese ; for he was sharply taken to task by Constantine for allowing sacrifices to be offered on altars under the sacred oak or terebinth at Mamre ; and in obedience to the imperial commands he caused the altars to be destroyed and an oratory to be built instead under the tree. So in Ireland the ancient heathen sanctuaries under the sacred oaks were converted by Christian missionaries into churches and monasteries. See Socrates, *Historia Ecclesiastica*, i. 18 ; *The Magic Art and the Evolution of Kings*, ii. 242 *sq.*

[3] Athanasius, *Oratio contra Gentes*, 26 (Migne's *Patrologia Graeca*, xxv. 52), γυναῖκες γοῦν ἐν εἰδωλείοις τῆς Φοινίκης πάλαι προεκαθέζοντο, ἀπαρχόμεναι τοῖς ἐκεῖ θέοις ἑαυτῶν τὴν τοῦ σώματος αὐτῶν μισθαρνίαν, νομίζουσαι τῇ πορνείᾳ τὴν θέον ἑαυτῶν ἱλάσκεσθαι καὶ εἰς εὐμενείαν ἄγειν αὐτὴν διὰ τούτων. The account of the Phoenician custom which is given by H. Ploss (*Das Weib*,[2] i. 302) and repeated after him by Fr. Schwally (*Semitische Kriegsaltertümer*, Leipsic, 1901, pp. 76 *sq.*) may rest only on a misapprehension of this passage of Athanasius. But if it is correct,

she who was about to marry should sit in fornication seven days by the gate."[1]   At Byblus the people shaved their heads in the annual mourning for Adonis.   Women who refused to sacrifice their hair had to give themselves up to strangers on a certain day of the festival, and the money which they thus earned was devoted to the goddess.[2]   This custom may have been a mitigation of an older rule which at Byblus as elsewhere formerly compelled every woman without exception to sacrifice her virtue in the service of religion.   I have already suggested a reason why the offering of a woman's hair was accepted as an equivalent for the surrender of her person.[3]   We are told that in Lydia all girls were obliged to prostitute themselves in order to earn a dowry;[4] but we may suspect that the real motive of the custom was devotion rather than economy.   The suspicion is confirmed by a Greek inscription found at Tralles in Lydia, which proves that the practice of religious prostitution survived in that country as late as the second century of our era.   It records of a certain woman, Aurelia Aemilia by name, not only that she herself served the god in the capacity of a harlot at his express command, but that her mother and other female ancestors had done the same before her; and the publicity of the record, engraved on a marble column which supported a votive offering, shows that no stain attached to such a life and such a parentage.[5]   In Armenia the noblest families dedicated their daughters to the service of the goddess Anaitis in her temple at Acilisena, where the damsels acted as prostitutes for a long time before they were given in marriage.   Nobody scrupled to take one of these girls to wife when her period of service was over.[6]

---

we may conjecture that the slaves who deflowered the virgins were the sacred slaves of the temples, the *kedeshim*, and that they discharged this office as the living representatives of the god. As to these *kedeshim*, or "sacred men," see above, pp. 17 *sq.*, and below, pp. 72 *sqq.*

[1] *The Testaments of the Twelve Patriarchs*, translated and edited by R. H. Charles (London, 1908), chapter xii. p. 81.

[2] Lucian, *De dea Syria*, 6. The writer is careful to indicate that none

but strangers were allowed to enjoy the women (ἡ δὲ ἀγορὴ μούνοισι ξείνοισι παρακέεται).

[3] *The Magic Art and the Evolution of Kings*, i. 30 *sq.*

[4] Herodotus, i. 93 *sq.*; Athenaeus, xii. 11, pp. 515 *sq.*

[5] W. M. Ramsay, "Unedited Inscriptions of Asia Minor," *Bulletin de Correspondance Hellénique*, vii. (1883) p. 276; *id.*, *Cities and Bishoprics of Phrygia*, i. (Oxford, 1895) pp. 94 *sq.*, 115.

[6] Strabo, xi. 14. 16, p. 532.

Again, the goddess Ma was served by a multitude of sacred harlots at Comana in Pontus, and crowds of men and women flocked to her sanctuary from the neighbouring cities and country to attend the biennial festivals or to pay their vows to the goddess.[1]

If we survey the whole of the evidence on this subject, some of which has still to be laid before the reader, we may conclude that a great Mother Goddess, the personification of all the reproductive energies of nature, was worshipped under different names but with a substantial similarity of myth and ritual by many peoples of Western Asia ; that associated with her was a lover, or rather series of lovers, divine yet mortal, with whom she mated year by year, their commerce being deemed essential to the propagation of animals and plants, each in their several kind ;[2] and further, that the fabulous union of the divine pair was simulated and, as it were, multiplied on earth by the real, though temporary, union of the human sexes at the sanctuary of the goddess for the sake of thereby ensuring the fruitfulness of the ground and the increase of man and beast.[3] And if the

The Asiatic Mother Goddess a personification of all the reproductive energies of nature.

---

[1] Strabo, xii. 3. 32, 34 and 36, pp. 557-559 ; compare xii. 2. 3, p. 535. Other sanctuaries in Pontus, Cappadocia, and Phrygia swarmed with sacred slaves, and we may conjecture, though we are not told, that many of these slaves were prostitutes. See Strabo, xi. 8. 4, xii. 2. 3 and 6, xii. 3. 31 and 37, xii. 8. 14.

[2] On this great Asiatic goddess and her lovers see especially Sir W. M. Ramsay, *Cities and Bishoprics of Phrygia,* i. 87 *sqq.*

[3] Compare W. Mannhardt, *Antike Wald- und Feldkulte,* pp. 284 *sq.* ; W. Robertson Smith, *The Prophets of Israel,* New Edition (London, 1902), pp. 171-174. Similarly in Camul, formerly a province of the Chinese Empire, the men used to place their wives at the disposal of any foreigners who came to lodge with them, and deemed it an honour if the guests made use of their opportunities. The emperor, hearing of the custom, forbade the people to observe it. For three years they obeyed, then, finding that their lands

were no longer fruitful and that many mishaps befell them, they prayed the emperor to allow them to retain the custom, "for it was by reason of this usage that their gods bestowed upon them all the good things that they possessed, and without it they saw not how they could continue to exist." See *The Book of Ser Marco Polo,* translated and edited by Colonel Henry Yule, Second Edition (London, 1875), i. 212 *sq.* Here apparently the fertility of the soil was deemed to depend on the intercourse of the women with strangers, not with their husbands. Similarly, among the Oulad Abdi, an Arab tribe of Morocco, "the women often seek a divorce and engage in prostitution in the intervals between their marriages ; during that time they continue to dwell in their families, and their relations regard their conduct as very natural. The administrative authority having bestirred itself and attempted to regulate this prostitution, the whole population opposed the attempt, alleging that such a measure

Her
worship
perhaps
reflects a
period of
sexual
commun-
ism.

conception of such a Mother Goddess dates, as seems probable, from a time when the institution of marriage was either unknown or at most barely tolerated as an immoral infringement of old communal rights, we can understand both why the goddess herself was regularly supposed to be at once unmarried and unchaste, and why her worshippers were obliged to imitate her more or less completely in these respects. For had she been a divine wife united to a divine husband, the natural counterpart of their union would have been the lawful marriage of men and women, and there would have been no need to resort to a system of prostitution or promiscuity in order to effect those purposes which, on the principles of homoeopathic magic, might in that case have been as well or better attained by the legitimate intercourse of the sexes in matrimony. Formerly, perhaps, every woman was obliged to submit at least once in her life to the exercise of those marital rights which at a still earlier period had theoretically belonged in permanence to all the males of the tribe. But in course of time, as the institution of individual marriage grew in favour, and the old communism fell more and more into discredit, the revival of the ancient practice even for a single occasion in a woman's life became ever more repugnant to the moral sense of the people, and accordingly they resorted to various expedients for evading in practice the obligation which they still acknowledged in theory. One of these evasions was to let the woman offer her hair instead of her person ; another apparently was to substitute an obscene symbol for the obscene act.[1] But while the majority of women thus contrived to observe the forms of religion without sacrificing their virtue, it was still thought necessary to the general welfare that a certain number of them should discharge the old obligation in the old way. These became prostitutes either for life or for a term of years at one of the temples : dedicated to the service of religion, they were invested with

---

would impair the abundance of the crops." See Edmond Doutté, *Magie et Religion dans l'Afrique du Nord* (Algiers, 1908), pp. 560 *sq.*

[1] Clement of Alexandria, *Protrept.*

ii. 14, p. 13, ed. Potter ; Arnobius, *Adversus Nationes*, v. 19 ; compare Firmicus Maternus, *De errore profanarum religionum*, 10.

a sacred character,[1] and their vocation, far from being deemed infamous, was probably long regarded by the laity as an exercise of more than common virtue, and rewarded with a tribute of mixed wonder, reverence, and pity, not unlike that which in some parts of the world is still paid to women who seek to honour their Creator in a different way by renouncing the natural functions of their sex and the tenderest relations of humanity. It is thus that the folly of mankind finds vent in opposite extremes alike harmful and deplorable.

At Paphos the custom of religious prostitution is said to have been instituted by King Cinyras,[2] and to have been practised by his daughters, the sisters of Adonis, who, having incurred the wrath of Aphrodite, mated with strangers and ended their days in Egypt.[3] In this form of the tradition the wrath of Aphrodite is probably a feature added by a later authority, who could only regard conduct which shocked his own moral sense as a punishment inflicted by the goddess instead of as a sacrifice regularly enjoined by her on all her devotees. At all events the story indicates that the princesses of Paphos had to conform to the custom as well as women of humble birth. *The daughters of Cinyras.*

The legendary history of the royal and priestly family of the Cinyrads is instructive. We are told that a Syrian man, by name Sandacus, migrated to Cilicia, married Pharnace, daughter of Megassares, king of Hyria, and founded the city of Celenderis. His wife bore him a son, Cinyras, who in time crossed the sea with a company of people to Cyprus, wedded Metharme, daughter of Pygmalion, king of the island, and founded Paphos.[4] These legends *The Paphian dynasty of the Cinyrads.*

---

[1] In Hebrew a temple harlot was regularly called "a sacred woman" (*kĕdēsha*). See *Encyclopaedia Biblica*, *s.v.* "Harlot"; S. R. Driver, on Genesis xxxviii. 21. As to such "sacred women" see below, pp. 70 *sqq.*

[2] Clement of Alexandria, *Protrept.* ii. 13, p. 12, ed. Potter : Arnobius, *Adversus Nationes*, v. 19 ; Firmicus Maternus, *De errore profanarum religionum*, 10.

[3] Apollodorus, *Bibliotheca*, iii. 14. 3.

[4] Apollodorus, *Bibliotheca*, iii. 14. 3. I follow the text of R. Wagner's edition in reading Μεγασσάρου τοῦ

Τριέων βασιλέως. As to Hyria in Isauria see Stephanus Byzantius, *s.v.* Τρία. The city of Celenderis, on the south coast of Cilicia, possessed a small harbour protected by a fortified peninsula. Many ancient tombs survived till recent times, but have now mostly disappeared. It was the port from which the Turkish couriers from Constantinople used to embark for Cyprus. As to the situation and remains see F. Beaufort, *Karmania* (London, 1817), p. 201 ; W. M. Leake, *Journal of a Tour in Asia Minor* (London, 1824), pp. 114-118 ; R. Heberdey und A.

seem to contain reminiscences of kingdoms in Cilicia and Cyprus which passed in the female line, and were held by men, sometimes foreigners, who married the hereditary princesses. There are some indications that Cinyras was not in fact the founder of the temple at Paphos. An older tradition ascribed the foundation to a certain Aerias, whom some regarded as a king, and others as the goddess herself.[1] Moreover, Cinyras or his descendants at Paphos had to reckon with rivals. These were the Tamirads, a family of diviners who traced their descent from Tamiras, a Cilician augur. At first it was arranged that both families should preside at the ceremonies, but afterwards the Tamirads gave way to the Cinyrads.[2] Many tales were told of Cinyras, the founder of the dynasty. He was a priest of Aphrodite as well as a king,[3] and his riches passed into a proverb.[4] To his descendants, the Cinyrads, he appears to have bequeathed his wealth and his dignities ; at all events, they reigned as kings of Paphos and served the goddess as priests. Their dead bodies, with that of Cinyras himself, were buried in the sanctuary.[5] But by the fourth century before our era the family had declined and become nearly extinct. When Alexander the Great expelled a king of Paphos for injustice and wickedness, his envoys made search for a member of the ancient house to set on the throne of his fathers. At last they found one of

Wilhelm, " Reisen in Kilikien," *Denkschriften der kais. Akademie der Wissenschaften, Philosoph.-historische Classe*, xliv. (1896) No. vi. p. 94. The statement that the sanctuary of Aphrodite at Paphos was founded by the Arcadian Agapenor, who planted a colony in Cyprus after the Trojan war (Pausanias, viii. 5. 2), may safely be disregarded.

[1] Tacitus, *Hist.* ii. 3 ; *Annals*, iii. 62.

[2] Tacitus, *Hist.* ii. 3 ; Hesychius, *s.v.* Ταμιράδαι.

[3] Pindar, *Pyth.* ii. 13-17.

[4] Tyrtaeus, xii. 6 (*Poetae Lyrici Graeci*, ed. Th. Bergk,³ Leipsic, 1866–1867, ii. 404) ; Pindar, *Pyth.* viii. 18 ; Plato, *Laws*, ii. 6, p. 660 E ; Clement of Alexandria, *Paedag.* iii. 6, p. 274, ed. Potter ; Dio Chrysostom, *Orat.*

viii. (vol. i. p. 149, ed. L. Dindorf); Julian, *Epist.* lix. p. 574, ed. F. C. Hertlein ; Diogenianus, viii. 53 ; Suidas, *s.v.* Καταγηράσαις.

[5] Schol. on Pindar, *Pyth.* ii. 15 (27) ; Hesychius, *s.v.* Κινυράδαι ; Clement of Alexandria, *Protrept.* iii. 45, p. 40, ed. Potter ; Arnobius, *Adversus Nationes*, vi. 6. That the kings of Paphos were also priests of the goddess is proved, apart from the testimony of ancient writers, by inscriptions found on the spot. See H. Collitz, *Sammlung der griechischen Dialektinschriften*, i. (Göttingen, 1884) p. 22, Nos. 38, 39, 40. The title of the goddess in these inscriptions is Queen or Mistress (Ϝαναϭ(ϭ)ας). It is perhaps a translation of the Semitic Baalath.

them living in obscurity and earning his bread as a market gardener. He was in the very act of watering his beds when the king's messengers carried him off, much to his astonishment, to receive the crown at the hands of their master.[1] Yet if the dynasty decayed, the shrine of the goddess, enriched by the offerings of kings and private persons, maintained its reputation for wealth down to Roman times.[2] When Ptolemy Auletes, king of Egypt, was expelled by his people in 57 B.C., Cato offered him the priesthood of Paphos as a sufficient consolation in money and dignity for the loss of a throne.[3]

Among the stories which were told of Cinyras, the ancestor of these priestly kings and the father of Adonis, there are some that deserve our attention. In the first place, he is said to have begotten his son Adonis in incestuous intercourse with his daughter Myrrha at a festival of the corn-goddess, at which women robed in white were wont to offer corn-wreaths as first-fruits of the harvest and to observe strict chastity for nine days.[4] Similar cases of incest with

Incest of Cinyras with his daughter Myrrha, and birth of Adonis.

[1] Plutarch, *De Alexandri Magni fortuna aut virtute*, ii. 8. The name of the gardener-king was Alynomus. That the Cinyrads existed as a family down to Macedonian times is further proved by a Greek inscription found at Old Paphos, which records that a certain Democrates, son of Ptolemy, head of the Cinyrads, and his wife Eunice, dedicated a statue of their daughter to the Paphian Aphrodite. See L. Ross, "Inschriften von Cypern," *Rheinisches Museum*, N.F. vii. (1850) pp. 520 sq. It seems to have been a common practice of parents to dedicate statues of their sons or daughters to the goddess at Paphos. The inscribed pedestals of many such statues were found by the English archaeologists. See *Journal of Hellenic Studies*, ix. (1888) pp. 228, 235, 236, 237, 241, 244, 246, 255.

[2] Tacitus, *Hist.* ii. 4; Pausanias, viii. 24. 6.

[3] Plutarch, *Cato the Younger*, 35.

[4] Ovid, *Metam.* x. 298 sqq.; Hyginus, *Fab.* 58, 64; Fulgentius, *Mythol.* iii. 8; Lactantius Placidius, *Narrat. Fabul.* x. 9; Servius on Virgil, *Ecl.* x. 18, and *Aen.* v. 72;

Plutarch, *Parallela*, 22; Schol. on Theocritus, i. 107. It is Ovid who describes (*Metam.* x. 431 sqq.) the festival of Ceres, at which the incest was committed. His source was probably the *Metamorphoses* of the Greek writer Theodorus, which Plutarch (*l.c.*) refers to as his authority for the story. The festival in question was perhaps the Thesmophoria, at which women were bound to remain chaste (Schol. on Theocritus, iv. 25; Schol. on Nicander, *Ther.* 70 sq.; Pliny, *Nat. Hist.* xxiv. 59; Dioscorides, *De Materia Medica*, i. 134 (135); compare Aelian, *De natura animalium*, ix. 26). Compare E. Fehrle, *Die kultische Keuschheit im Altertum* (Giessen, 1910), pp. 103 sqq., 121 sq., 151 sqq. The corn and bread of Cyprus were famous in antiquity. See Aeschylus, *Suppliants*, 549 (555); Hipponax, cited by Strabo, viii. 3. 8, p. 340; Eubulus, cited by Athenaeus, iii. 78, p. 112 F; E. Oberhummer, *Die Insel Cypern*, i. (Munich, 1903) pp. 274 sqq. According to another account, Adonis was the fruit of the incestuous intercourse of Theias, a Syrian

Legends
of royal
incest—a
suggested
explana-
tion.

a daughter are reported of many ancient kings.[1] It seems unlikely that such reports are without foundation, and perhaps equally improbable that they refer to mere fortuitous outbursts of unnatural lust. We may suspect that they are based on a practice actually observed for a definite reason in certain special circumstances. Now in countries where the royal blood was traced through women only, and where consequently the king held office merely in virtue of his marriage with an hereditary princess, who was the real sovereign, it appears to have often happened that a prince married his own sister, the princess royal, in order to obtain with her hand the crown which otherwise would have gone to another man, perhaps to a stranger.[2] May not the same rule of descent have furnished a motive for incest with a daughter? For it seems a natural corollary from such a rule that the king was bound to vacate the throne on the death of his wife, the queen, since he occupied it only by virtue of his marriage with her. When that marriage terminated, his right to the throne terminated with it and passed at once to his daughter's husband. Hence if the king desired to reign after his wife's death, the only way in which he could legitimately continue to do so was by marrying his daughter, and thus prolonging through her the title which had formerly been his through her mother.

king, with his daughter Myrrha. See Apollodorus, *Bibliotheca*, iii. 14. 4 (who cites Panyasis as his authority); J. Tzetzes, *Schol. on Lycophron*, 829; Antoninus Liberalis, *Transform*. 34 (who lays the scene of the story on Mount Lebanon). With the corn - wreaths mentioned in the text we may compare the wreaths which the Roman Arval Brethren wore at their sacred functions, and with which they seem to have crowned the images of the goddesses. See G. Henzen, *Acta Fratrum Arvalium* (Berlin, 1874), pp. 24-27, 33 *sq*. Compare Pausanias, vii. 20. 1. *sq*.

[1] A list of these cases is given by Hyginus, *Fab*. 253. It includes the incest of Clymenus, king of Arcadia, with his daughter Harpalyce (compare Hyginus, *Fab*. 206); that of Oenomaus, king of Pisa, with his daughter Hippodamia (compare J. Tzetzes, *Schol. on Lycophron*, 156; Lucian, *Charidemus*, 19); that of Erechtheus, king of Athens, with his daughter Procris; and that of Epopeus, king of Lesbos, with his daughter Nyctimene (compare Hyginus, *Fab*. 204).

[2] The custom of brother and sister marriage seems to have been especially common in royal families. See my note on Pausanias, i. 7. 1 (vol. ii. pp. 84 *sq*.); as to the case of Egypt see below, vol. ii. pp. 213 *sqq*. The true explanation of the custom was first, so far as I know, indicated by J. F. McLennan (*The Patriarchal Theory*, London, 1885, p. 95).

In this connexion it is worth while to remember that at Rome the Flamen Dialis was bound to vacate his priesthood on the death of his wife, the Flaminica.[1] The rule would be intelligible if the Flaminica had originally been the more important functionary of the two, and if the Flamen held office only by virtue of his marriage with her.[2] Elsewhere I have shown reason to suppose that he and his wife represented an old line of priestly kings and queens, who played the parts of Jupiter and Juno, or perhaps rather Dianus and Diana, respectively.[3] If the supposition is correct, the custom which obliged him to resign his priesthood on the death of his wife seems to prove that of the two deities whom they personated, the goddess, whether named Juno or Diana, was indeed the better half. But at Rome the goddess Juno always played an insignificant part; whereas at Nemi her old double, Diana, was all-powerful, casting her mate, Dianus or Virbius, into deep shadow. Thus a rule which points to the superiority of the Flaminica over the Flamen, appears to indicate that the divine originals of the two were Dianus and Diana rather than Jupiter and Juno; and further, that if Jupiter and Juno at Rome stood for the principle of father-kin, or the predominance of the husband over the wife, Dianus and Diana at Nemi stood for the older principle of mother-kin, or the predominance of the wife in matters of inheritance over the husband. If, then, I am right in holding that the kingship at Rome was originally a plebeian institution and descended through women,[4] we must conclude that the people who founded the sanctuary of Diana at Nemi were of the same plebeian stock as the Roman kings, that they traced descent in the female line, and that they worshipped a great Mother Goddess, not a great Father God. That goddess was Diana ; her maternal functions are abundantly proved by the votive offerings found at her ancient shrine among the wooded hills.[5] On the other hand, the

---

[1] Aulus Gellius, x. 15. 22 ; J. Marquardt, *Römische Staatsverwaltung*, iii.² (Leipsic, 1885) p. 328.

[2] Priestesses are said to have preceded priests in some Egyptian cities. See W. M. Flinders Petrie, *The Religion of Ancient Egypt* (London, 1906), p. 74.

[3] *The Magic Art and the Evolution of Kings*, ii. 179, 190 *sqq.*

[4] *The Magic Art and the Evolution of Kings*, ii. 268 *sqq.*

[5] *The Magic Art and the Evolution of Kings*, i. 12 note ¹.

patricians, who afterwards invaded the country, brought with them father-kin in its strictest form, and consistently enough paid their devotions rather to Father Jove than to Mother Juno.

A parallel to what I conjecture to have been the original relation of the Flaminica to her husband the Flamen may to a certain extent be found among the Khasis of Assam, who preserve to this day the ancient system of mother-kin in matters of inheritance and religion. For among these people the propitiation of deceased ancestors is deemed essential to the welfare of the community, and of all their ancestors they revere most the primaeval ancestress of the clan. Accordingly in every sacrifice a priest must be assisted by a priestess; indeed, we are told that he merely acts as her deputy, and that she " is without doubt a survival of the time when, under the matriarchate, the priestess was the agent for the performance of all religious ceremonies." It does not appear that the priest need be the husband of the priestess; but in the Khyrim State, where each division has its own goddess to whom sacrifices are offered, the priestess is the mother, sister, niece, or other maternal relation of the priest. It is her duty to prepare all the sacrificial articles, and without her assistance the sacrifice cannot take place.[1] Here, then, as among the ancient Romans on my hypothesis, we have the superiority of the priestess over the priest based on a corresponding superiority of the goddess or divine ancestress over the god or divine ancestor; and here, as at Rome, a priest would clearly have to vacate office if he had no woman of the proper relationship to assist him in the performance of his sacred duties.

Further, I have conjectured that as representatives of Jupiter and Juno respectively the Flamen and Flaminica at Rome may have annually celebrated a Sacred Marriage for the purpose of ensuring the fertility of the powers of nature.[2] This conjecture also may be supported by an analogous custom which is still observed in India. We have seen how among the Oraons, a primitive hill-tribe of Bengal, the

---

[1] Major P. R. T. Gurdon, *The Khasis* (London, 1907), pp. 109-112, 120 *sq.*

[2] *The Magic Art and the Evolution of Kings*, ii. 191 *sqq.*

marriage of the Sun and the Earth is annually celebrated
by a priest and priestess who personate respectively the god
of the Sun and the goddess of the Earth.[1]   The ceremony
of the Sacred Marriage has been described more fully by a
Jesuit missionary, who was intimately acquainted with the
people and their native religion.   The rite is celebrated in
the month of May, when the *sal* tree is in bloom, and the
festival takes its native name (*khaddi*) from the flower of the
tree.   It is the greatest festival of the year.   " The object
of this feast is to celebrate the mystical marriage of the
Sun-god (*Bhagawan*) with the Goddess-earth (*Dharti-mai*),
to induce them to be fruitful and give good crops."   At the
same time all the minor deities or demons of the village are
propitiated, in order that they may not hinder the beneficent
activity of the Sun God and the Earth Goddess.   On the
eve of the appointed day no man may plough his fields, and
the priest, accompanied by some of the villagers, repairs to
the sacred grove, where he beats a drum and invites all the
invisible guests to the great feast that will await them on
the morrow.   Next morning very early, before cock-crow,
an acolyte steals out as quietly as possible to the sacred
spring to fetch water in a new earthen pot.   This holy water
is full of all kinds of blessings for the crops.   The priest has
prepared a place for it in the middle of his house surrounded
by cotton threads of diverse colours.   So sacred is the water
that it would be defiled and lose all its virtue, were any profane eye to fall on it before it entered the priest's house.
During the morning the acolyte and the priest's deputy go
round from house to house collecting victims for the sacrifice.
In the afternoon the people all gather at the sacred grove,
and the priest proceeds to consummate the sacrifice.   The
first victims to be immolated are a white cock for the Sun
God and a black hen for the Earth Goddess ; and as the
feast is the marriage of these great deities the marriage
service is performed over the two fowls before they are
hurried into eternity.   Amongst other things both birds are
marked with vermilion just as a bride and bridegroom are
marked at a human marriage ; and the earth is also smeared
with vermilion, as if it were a real bride, on the spot where

[1] *The Magic Art and the Evolution of Kings*, ii. 148.

the sacrifice is offered. Sacrifices of fowls or goats to the minor deities or demons follow. The bodies of the victims are collected by the village boys, who cook them on the spot; all the heads go to the sacrificers. The gods take what they can get and are more or less thankful. Meantime the acolyte has collected flowers of the *sal* tree and set them round the place of sacrifice, and he has also fetched the holy water from the priest's house. A procession is now formed and the priest is carried in triumph to his own abode. There his wife has been watching for him, and on his arrival the two go through the marriage ceremony, applying vermilion to each other in the usual way "to symbolise the mystical marriage of the Sun-god with the Earth-goddess." Meantime all the women of the village are standing on the thresholds of their houses each with a winnowing-fan in her hand. In the fan are two cups, one empty to receive the holy water, and the other full of rice-beer for the consumption of the holy man. As he arrives at each house, he distributes flowers and holy water to the happy women, and enriches them with a shower of blessings, saying, "May your rooms and granary be filled with rice, that the priest's name may be great." The holy water which he leaves at each house is sprinkled on the seeds that have been kept to sow next year's crop. Having thus imparted his benediction to the household the priest swigs the beer; and as he repeats his benediction and his potation at every house he is naturally dead-drunk by the time he gets to the end of the village. "By that time every one has taken copious libations of rice-beer, and all the devils of the village seem to be let loose, and there follows a scene of debauchery baffling description —all these to induce the Sun and the Earth to be fruitful."[1]

Thus the people of Cyprus and Western Asia in antiquity were by no means singular in their belief that the profligacy of the human sexes served to quicken the fruits of the earth.[2]

Cinyras is said to have been famed for his exquisite

Marriage of the Sun-god and Earth-goddess acted by a priest and his wife.

---

[1] The late Rev. P. Dehon, S.J., "Religion and Customs of the Uraons," *Memoirs of the Asiatic Society of Bengal*, vol. i. No. 9 (Calcutta, 1906), pp. 144-146.

[2] For more evidence see *The Magic Art and the Evolution of Kings*, ii. 97 *sqq.*

beauty[1] and to have been wooed by Aphrodite herself.[2] Cinyras
Thus it would appear, as scholars have already observed,[3] beloved by
that Cinyras was in a sense a duplicate of his handsome son Aphrodite.
Adonis, to whom the inflammable goddess also lost her
heart.   Further, these stories of the love of Aphrodite for Pygmalion
two members of the royal house of Paphos can hardly be and
dissociated from the corresponding legend told of Pygmalion, Aphrodite.
the Phoenician king of Cyprus, who is said to have fallen in
love with an image of Aphrodite and taken it to his bed.[4]
When we consider that Pygmalion was the father-in-law The
of Cinyras, that the son of Cinyras was Adonis, and that all Phoenician
three, in successive generations, are said to have been con- kings of
cerned in a love-intrigue with Aphrodite, we can hardly help their sons
concluding that the early Phoenician kings of Paphos, or have been
their sons, regularly claimed to be not merely the priests hereditary
of the goddess[5] but also her lovers, in other words, that in of the
their official capacity they personated Adonis. At all events goddess.
Adonis is said to have reigned in Cyprus,[6] and it appears
to be certain that the title of Adonis was regularly borne
by the sons of all the Phoenician kings of the island.[7]   It is
true that the title strictly signified no more than " lord " ;
yet the legends which connect these Cyprian princes with
the goddess of love make it probable that they claimed the

---

[1] Lucian, *Rhetorum praeceptor*, 11 ;
Hyginus, *Fab.* 270.

[2] Clement of Alexandria, *Protrept.*
ii. 33, p. 29, ed. Potter.

[3] W. H. Engel, *Kypros*, ii. 585,
612 ; A. Maury, *Histoire des Religions
de la Grèce Antique* (Paris, 1857–
1859), iii. 197, note[3].

[4] Arnobius, *Adversus Nationes*, vi.
22 ; Clement of Alexandria, *Protrept.*
iv. 57, p. 51, ed. Potter ; Ovid,
Metam. x. 243-297. The authority
for the story is the Greek history of
Cyprus by Philostephanus, cited both
by Arnobius and Clement. In Ovid's
poetical version of the legend Pygmalion is a sculptor, and the image
with which he falls in love is that of a
lovely woman, which at his prayer
Venus endows with life. That King
Pygmalion was a Phoenician is mentioned by Porphyry (*De abstinentia*,
iv. 15) on the authority of Asclepiades,

a Cyprian.

[5] See above, p. 42.

[6] Probus, on Virgil, *Ecl.* x. 18.
I owe this reference to my friend
Mr. A. B. Cook.

[7] In his treatise on the political
institutions of Cyprus, Aristotle reported that the sons and brothers of
the kings were called "lords" (ἄνακτες),
and their sisters and wives " ladies "
(ἄνασσαι).   See Harpocration and
Suidas, *s.v.* Ἄνακτες. Compare Isocrates, ix. 72 ; Clearchus of Soli,
quoted by Athenaeus, vi. 68, p. 256 A.
Now in the bilingual inscription of
Idalium, which furnished the clue to
the Cypriote syllabary, the Greek
version gives the title Fάναξ as the
equivalent of the Phoenician *Adon*
(אדן).   See *Corpus Inscriptionum
Semiticarum*, i. No. 89 ; G. A. Cooke,
*Text-book of North-Semitic Inscrip-
tions*, p. 74, note[1].

divine nature as well as the human dignity of Adonis. The story of Pygmalion points to a ceremony of a sacred marriage in which the king wedded the image of Aphrodite, or rather of Astarte. If that was so, the tale was in a sense true, not of a single man only, but of a whole series of men, and it would be all the more likely to be told of Pygmalion, if that was a common name of Semitic kings in general, and of Cyprian kings in particular. Pygmalion, at all events, is known as the name of the famous king of Tyre from whom his sister Dido fled ;[1] and a king of Citium and Idalium in Cyprus, who reigned in the time of Alexander the Great, was also called Pygmalion, or rather Pumiyathon, the Phoenician name which the Greeks corrupted into Pygmalion.[2] Further, it deserves to be noted that the names Pygmalion and Astarte occur together in a Punic inscription on a gold medallion which was found in a grave at Carthage ; the characters of the inscription are of the earliest type.[3] As the custom of religious prostitution at Paphos is said to have been founded by King Cinyras and

Sacred marriage of the kings of Paphos. observed by his daughters,[4] we may surmise that the kings of Paphos played the part of the divine bridegroom in a less innocent rite than the form of marriage with a statue; in fact, that at certain festivals each of them had to mate with one or more of the sacred harlots of the temple, who played Astarte to his Adonis. If that was so, there is more truth than has commonly been supposed in the reproach cast by the Christian fathers that the Aphrodite worshipped

---

[1] Josephus, *Contra Apionem*, i. 18, ed. B. Niese ; Appian, *Punica*, 1 ; Virgil, *Aen.* i. 346 *sq.* ; Ovid, *Fasti*, iii. 574 ; Justin, xviii. 4 ; Eustathius on Dionysius Periegetes, 195 (*Geographi Graeci Minores*, ed. C. Müller Paris, 1882, ii. 250 *sq.*).

[2] Pumi-yathon, son of Milk-yathon, is known from Phoenician inscriptions found at Idalium. See G. A. Cooke, *Text-book of North-Semitic Inscriptions*, Nos. 12 and 13, pp. 55 *sq.*, 57 *sq.* Coins inscribed with the name of King Pumi-yathon are also in existence. See G. F. Hill, *Catalogue of the Greek Coins of Cyprus* (London, 1904), pp. xl. *sq.*, 21 *sq.*, pl. iv. 20-24. He was deposed by Ptolemy

(Diodorus Siculus, xix. 79. 4). Most probably he is the Pymaton of Citium who purchased the kingdom from a dissolute monarch named Pasicyprus some time before the conquests of Alexander (Athenaeus, iv. 63, p. 167). In this passage of Athenaeus the name Pymaton, which is found in the MSS. and agrees closely with the Phoenician Pumi-yathon, ought not to be changed into Pygmalion, as the latest editor (G. Kaibel) has done.

[3] G. A. Cooke, *op. cit.* p. 55, note [1]. Mr. Cooke remarks that the form of the name (פגמלין instead of פמיחן) must be due to Greek influence.

[4] See above, p. 41.

by Cinyras was a common whore.[1]   The fruit of their union would rank as sons and daughters of the deity, and would in time become the parents of gods and goddesses, like their fathers and mothers before them.   In this manner Paphos, and perhaps all sanctuaries of the great Asiatic goddess where sacred prostitution was practised, might be well stocked with human deities, the offspring of the divine king by his wives, concubines, and temple harlots.   Any one of these might probably succeed his father on the throne[2] or be sacrificed in his stead whenever stress of war or other grave junctures called, as they sometimes did,[3] for the death of a royal victim.   Such a tax, levied occasionally on the king's numerous progeny for the good of the country, would neither extinguish the divine stock nor break the father's heart, who divided his paternal affection among so many. At all events, if, as there seems reason to believe, Semitic kings were often regarded at the same time as hereditary deities, it is easy to understand the frequency of Semitic personal names which imply that the bearers of them were the sons or daughters, the brothers or sisters, the fathers or mothers of a god, and we need not resort to the shifts employed by some scholars to evade the plain sense of the words.[4]   This interpretation is confirmed by a parallel

Sons and daughters, fathers and mothers of a god.

---

[1] Clement of Alexandria, *Protrept.* ii. 13, p. 12; Arnobius, *Adversus Nationes*, v. 9; Firmicus Maternus, *De errore profanarum religionum*, 10.

[2] That the king was not necessarily succeeded by his eldest son is proved by the case of Solomon, who on his accession executed his elder brother Adoni-jah (1 Kings ii. 22-24).   Similarly, when Abimelech became king of Shechem, he put his seventy brothers in ruthless oriental fashion to death. See Judges viii. 29-31, ix. 5 *sq.*, 18. So on his accession Jehoram, King of Judah, put all his brothers to the sword (2 Chronicles xxi. 4).   King Rehoboam had eighty-eight children (2 Chronicles xi. 21) and King Abi-jah had thirty-eight (2 Chronicles xiii. 21). These examples illustrate the possible size of the family of a polygamous king.

[3] *The Dying God*, pp. 160 *sqq.*

[4] The names which imply that a man was the father of a god have proved particularly puzzling to some eminent Semitic scholars.   See W. Robertson Smith, *Religion of the Semites*,[2] p. 45, note[2]; Th. Nöldeke, *s.v.* "Names," *Encyclopaedia Biblica*, iii. 3287 *sqq.*; W. W. Graf Baudissin, *Adonis und Esmun*, pp. 39 *sq.*, 43 *sqq.*   Such names are Abi-baal ("father of Baal"), Abi-el ("father of El"), Abi-jah ("father of Jehovah"), and Abi-melech ("father of a king" or "father of Moloch").   On the hypothesis put forward in the text the father of a god and the son of a god stood precisely on the same footing, and the same person would often be both one and the other.   Where the common practice prevailed of naming a father after his son (*Taboo and the Perils of the Soul*, pp. 331 *sqq.*), a divine king in later life might often be called "father of such-and-such a god."

Egyptian usage; for in Egypt, where the kings were worshipped as divine,[1] the queen was called "the wife of the
god" or "the mother of the god,"[2] and the title "father
of the god" was borne not only by the king's real father
but also by his father-in-law.[3] Similarly, perhaps, among
the Semites any man who sent his daughter to swell the
royal harem may have been allowed to call himself "the
father of the god."

Cinyras, like King David, a harper. If we may judge by his name, the Semitic king who
bore the name of Cinyras was, like King David, a harper;
for the name of Cinyras is clearly connected with the Greek
cinyra, "a lyre," which in its turn comes from the Semitic
kinnor, "a lyre," the very word applied to the instrument
on which David played before Saul.[4] We shall probably
not err in assuming that at Paphos as at Jerusalem the
music of the lyre or harp was not a mere pastime designed
to while away an idle hour, but formed part of the service
of religion, the moving influence of its melodies being perhaps set down, like the effect of wine, to the direct inspiration of a deity. Certainly at Jerusalem the regular clergy
of the temple prophesied to the music of harps, of psalteries,
and of cymbals;[5] and it appears that the irregular clergy
also, as we may call the prophets, depended on some such
stimulus for inducing the ecstatic state which they took for
immediate converse with the divinity.[6] Thus we read of a
band of prophets coming down from a high place with a
psaltery, a timbrel, a pipe, and a harp before them, and
prophesying as they went.[7] Again, when the united forces
of Judah and Ephraim were traversing the wilderness of
Moab in pursuit of the enemy, they could find no water for

The use of music as a means of prophetic inspiration among the Hebrews.

---

[1] *The Magic Art and the Evolution of Kings*, i. 418 *sq.*

[2] A. Erman, *Aegypten und aegyptisches Leben im Altertum* (Tübingen, N.D.), p. 113.

[3] L. Borchardt, "Der ägyptische Titel 'Vater des Gottes' als Bezeichnung für 'Vater oder Schwiegervater des Königs,'" *Berichte über die Verhandlungen der Königlich Sächsischen Gesellschaft der Wissenschaften zu Leipzig, Philolog.-histor. Klasse*, lvii. (1905) pp. 254-270.

[4] F. C. Movers, *Die Phoenizier*, i. 243; Stoll, *s.v.* "Kinyras," in W. H. Roscher's *Lexikon der griech. und röm. Mythologie*, ii. 1191; I Samuel xvi. 23.

[5] I Chronicles xxv. 1-3; compare 2 Samuel vi. 5.

[6] W. Robertson Smith, *The Prophets of Israel*[2] (London, 1902), pp. 391 *sq.*; E. Renan, *Histoire du peuple d'Israel* (Paris, 1893), ii. 280.

[7] I Samuel x. 5.

three days, and were like to die of thirst, they and the beasts
of burden.   In this emergency the prophet Elisha, who was
with the army, called for a minstrel and bade him play.
Under the influence of the music he ordered the soldiers
to dig trenches in the sandy bed of the waterless waddy
through which lay the line of march.   They did so, and
next morning the trenches were full of the water that had
drained down into them underground from the desolate,
forbidding mountains on either hand.   The prophet's success
in striking water in the wilderness resembles the reported
success of modern dowsers, though his mode of procedure
was different.   Incidentally he rendered another service
to his countrymen.   For the skulking Moabites from their
lairs among the rocks saw the red sun of the desert reflected
in the water, and taking it for the blood, or perhaps rather
for an omen of the blood, of their enemies, they plucked up
heart to attack the camp and were defeated with great
slaughter.[1]

Again, just as the cloud of melancholy which from time *The*
to time darkened the moody mind of Saul was viewed as *influence*
an evil spirit from the Lord vexing him, so on the other *of music*
hand the solemn strains of the harp, which soothed and com- *on religion.*
posed his troubled thoughts,[2] may well have seemed to the
hag-ridden king the very voice of God or of his good angel
whispering peace.   Even in our own day a great religious
writer, himself deeply sensitive to the witchery of music, has
said that musical notes, with all their power to fire the blood
and melt the heart, cannot be mere empty sounds and nothing
more ; no, they have escaped from some higher sphere, they
are outpourings of eternal harmony, the voice of angels, the
Magnificat of saints.[3]   It is thus that the rude imaginings
of primitive man are transfigured and his feeble lispings
echoed with a rolling reverberation in the musical prose of
Newman.   Indeed the influence of music on the develop-

---

[1] 2 Kings iii. 4-24. And for the
explanation of the supposed miracle,
see W. Robertson Smith, *The Old
Testament in the Jewish Church*[2]
(London and Edinburgh, 1892), pp.
146 *sq.* I have to thank Professor
Kennett for the suggestion that the
Moabites took the ruddy light on the
water for an omen of blood rather
than for actual gore.

[2] 1 Samuel xvi. 14-23.

[3] J. H. Newman, *Sermons preached
before the University of Oxford*, No.
xv. pp. 346 *sq.* (third edition).

ment of religion is a subject which would repay a sympathetic
study. For we cannot doubt that this, the most intimate and
affecting of all the arts, has done much to create as well as to
express the religious emotions, thus modifying more or less
deeply the fabric of belief to which at first sight it seems
only to minister. The musician has done his part as well
as the prophet and the thinker in the making of religion.
Every faith has its appropriate music, and the difference
between the creeds might almost be expressed in musical
notation. The interval, for example, which divides the wild
revels of Cybele from the stately ritual of the Catholic
Church is measured by the gulf which severs the dissonant
clash of cymbals and tambourines from the grave harmonies
of Palestrina and Handel. A different spirit breathes in the
difference of the music.[1]

The function of string music in Greek and Semitic ritual. The legend which made Apollo the friend of Cinyras[2] may
be based on a belief in their common devotion to the lyre.
But what function, we may ask, did string music perform in
the Greek and the Semitic ritual? Did it serve to rouse the
human mouthpiece of the god to prophetic ecstasy? or did it
merely ban goblins and demons from the holy places and
the holy service, drawing as it were around the worshippers
a magic circle within which no evil thing might intrude?
In short, did it aim at summoning good or banishing evil
spirits? was its object inspiration or exorcism? The
examples drawn from the lives or legends of Elisha and
David prove that with the Hebrews the music of the lyre
might be used for either purpose ; for while Elisha employed
it to tune himself to the prophetic pitch, David resorted to it
for the sake of exorcising the foul fiend from Saul. With
the Greeks, on the other hand, in historical times, it does not
appear that string music served as a means of inducing the
condition of trance or ecstasy in the human mouthpieces of
Apollo and the other oracular gods ; on the contrary, its sober-
ing and composing influence, as contrasted with the exciting
influence of flute music, is the aspect which chiefly impressed

---

[1] It would be interesting to pursue
a similar line of inquiry in regard to
the other arts. What was the influence
of Phidias on Greek religion? How

much does Catholicism owe to Fra
Angelico?

[2] Pindar, *Pyth.* ii. 15 *sq.*

the Greek mind.[1] The religious or, at all events, the superstitious man might naturally ascribe the mental composure
wrought by grave, sweet music to a riddance of evil spirits,
in short to exorcism ; and in harmony with this view, Pindar,
speaking of the lyre, says that all things hateful to Zeus in
earth and sea tremble at the sound of music.[2] Yet the
association of the lyre with the legendary prophet Orpheus
as well as with the oracular god Apollo seems to hint that
in early days its strains may have been employed by the
Greeks, as they certainly were by the Hebrews, to bring on
that state of mental exaltation in which the thick-coming
fancies of the visionary are regarded as divine communica-
tions.[3] Which of these two functions of music, the positive
or the negative, the inspiring or the protective, predominated
in the religion of Adonis we cannot say ; perhaps the
two were not clearly distinguished in the minds of his
worshippers.

A constant feature in the myth of Adonis was his Traditions
premature and violent death. If, then, the kings of Paphos as to the
death of
regularly personated Adonis, we must ask whether they Cinyras.
imitated their divine prototype in death as in life. Tradition
varied as to the end of Cinyras. Some thought that he
slew himself on discovering his incest with his daughter ;[4]
others alleged that, like Marsyas, he was defeated by Apollo
in a musical contest and put to death by the victor.[5] Yet he
cannot strictly be said to have perished in the flower of his
youth if he lived, as Anacreon averred, to the ripe age of one
hundred and sixty.[6] If we must choose between the two
stories, it is perhaps more likely that he died a violent death
than that he survived to an age which surpassed that of

---

[1] On the lyre and the flute in Greek
religion and Greek thought, see L. R.
Farnell, *The Cults of the Greek States*
(Oxford, 1896–1909), iv. 243 *sqq.*

[2] Pindar, *Pyth.* i. 13 *sqq.*

[3] This seems to be the view also of
Dr. Farnell, who rightly connects the
musical with the prophetic side of
Apollo's character (*op. cit.* iv. 245).

[4] Hyginus, *Fab.* 242. So in the
version of the story which made Adonis
the son of Theias, the father is said to
have killed himself when he learned

what he had done (Antoninus Liberalis,
Transform. 34).

[5] Scholiast and Eustathius on
Homer, *Iliad*, xi. 20. Compare F. C.
Movers, *Die Phoenizier*, i. 243 *sq.* ;
W. H. Engel, *Kypros*, ii. 109–116 ;
Stoll, *s.v.* "Kinyras," in W. H.
Roscher's *Lexikon der griech. und röm.
Mythologie*, ii. 1191.

[6] Anacreon, cited by Pliny, *Nat.
Hist.* vii. 154. Nonnus also refers to
the long life of Cinyras (*Dionys.* xxxii.
212 *sq.*).

Thomas Parr by eight years,[1] though it fell far short of the antediluvian standard. The life of eminent men in remote ages is exceedingly elastic and may be lengthened or shortened, in the interests of history, at the taste and fancy of the historian.

[1] *Encyclopaedia Britannica,*[9] xiv. 858.

CHAPTER IV

SACRED MEN AND WOMEN

§ 1. *An Alternative Theory*

IN the preceding chapter we saw that a system of sacred prostitution was regularly carried on all over Western Asia, and that both in Phoenicia and in Cyprus the practice was specially associated with the worship of Adonis. As the explanation which I have adopted of the custom has been rejected in favour of another by writers whose opinions are entitled to be treated with respect, I shall devote the present chapter to a further consideration of the subject, and shall attempt to gather, from a closer scrutiny and a wider survey of the field, such evidence as may set the custom and with it the worship of Adonis in a clearer light. At the outset it will be well to examine the alternative theory which has been put forward to explain the facts.

It has been proposed to derive the religious prostitution of Western Asia from a purely secular and precautionary practice of destroying a bride's virginity before handing her over to her husband in order that "the bridegroom's intercourse should be safe from a peril that is much dreaded by men in a certain stage of culture."[1] Among

[1] L. R. Farnell, "Sociological hypotheses concerning the position of women in ancient religion," *Archiv für Religionswissenschaft*, vii. (1904) p. 88; M. P. Nilsson, *Griechische Feste* (Leipsic, 1906), pp. 366 *sq.*; Fr. Cumont, *Les religions orientales dans le paganisme Romain* [2] (Paris, 1909), pp. 361 *sq.* A different and, in my judgment, a truer view of these customs was formerly taken by Prof. Nilsson. See his *Studia de Dionysiis Atticis* (Lund, 1900), pp. 119-121. For a large collection of facts bearing on this subject and a judicious discussion of them, see W. Hertz, "Die Sage vom Giftmädchen," *Gesammelte Abhandlungen* (Stuttgart and Berlin, 1905), pp. 195-219. My attention was drawn to this last work by Prof. G. L. Hamilton of the University of Michigan after my

the objections which may be taken to this view are the following :—

(1) The theory fails to account for the deeply religious character of the customs as practised in antiquity all over Western Asia. That religious character appears from the observance of the custom at the sanctuaries of a great goddess, the dedication of the wages of prostitution to her, the belief of the women that they earned her favour by prostituting themselves,[1] and the command of a male deity to serve him in this manner.[2]

(2) The theory fails to account for the prostitution of married women at Heliopolis[3] and apparently also at Babylon and Byblus ; for in describing the practice at the two latter places our authorities, Herodotus and Lucian, speak only of women, not of virgins.[4] In Israel also we know from Hosea that young married women prostituted themselves at the sanctuaries on the hilltops under the shadow of the sacred oaks, poplars, and terebinths.[5] The prophet makes no mention of virgins participating in these orgies. They may have done so, but his language does not imply it : he speaks only of "your daughters" and "your daughters-in-law." The prostitution of married women is wholly inexplicable on the hypothesis here criticized. Yet it can hardly be separated from the prostitution of virgins, which in some places at least was carried on side by side with it.

(3) The theory fails to account for the repeated and professional prostitution of women in Lydia, Pontus, Armenia, and apparently all over Palestine.[6] Yet this habitual prostitution can in its turn hardly be separated

---

manuscript had been sent to the printer. With Hertz's treatment of the subject I am in general agreement, and I have derived from his learned treatise several references to authorities which I had overlooked.

[1] Above, p. 37.

[2] Above, p. 38. Prof. Nilsson is mistaken in affirming (*op. cit.* p. 367) that the Lydian practice was purely secular : the inscription which I have cited proves the contrary. Both he

and Dr. Farnell fully recognize the religious aspect of most of these customs in antiquity, and Prof. Nilsson attempts, as it seems to me, unsuccessfully, to indicate how a practice supposed to be purely secular in origin should have come to contract a religious character.

[3] Above, p. 37.

[4] Above, pp. 36 *sq.*, 38.

[5] Hosea iv. 13 *sq.*

[6] Above, pp. 37 *sqq.*

from the first prostitution in a woman's life. Or are we to suppose that the first act of unchastity is to be explained in one way and all the subsequent acts in quite another? that the first act was purely secular and all the subsequent acts purely religious?

(4) The theory fails to account for the *Kedeshim* ("sacred men") side by side with the *Kedeshoth* ("sacred women") at the sanctuaries;[1] for whatever the religious functions of these "sacred men" may have been, it is highly probable that they were analogous to those of the "sacred women" and are to be explained in the same way.

nor for the "sacred men" beside the "sacred women,"

(5) On the hypothesis which I am considering we should expect to find the man who deflowers the maid remunerated for rendering a dangerous service; and so in fact we commonly find him remunerated in places where the supposed custom is really practised.[2] But in Western Asia it was just the contrary. It was the woman who was paid, not the man; indeed, so well was she paid that in Lydia and Cyprus the girls earned dowries for themselves in this fashion.[3] This clearly shows that it was the woman, and not the man, who was believed to render the service. Or are we to suppose that the man had to pay for rendering a dangerous service?[4]

and is irreconcilable with the payment of the women.

These considerations seem to prove conclusively that whatever the remote origin of these Western Asiatic customs may have been, they cannot have been observed in his-

---

[1] See above, pp. 17 *sq.*

[2] L. di Varthema, *Travels* (Hakluyt Society, 1863), pp. 141, 202-204 (Malabar); J. A. de Mandlesloe, in J. Harris's *Voyages and Travels*, i. (London, 1744), p. 767 (Malabar); Richard, "History of Tonquin," in J. Pinkerton's *Voyages and Travels*, ix. 760 *sq.* (Aracan); A. de Morga, *The Philippine Islands, Moluccas, Siam, Cambodia, Japan, and China* (Hakluyt Society, 1868), pp. 304 *sq.* (the Philippines); J. Mallat, *Les Philippines* (Paris, 1846), i. 61 (the Philippines); L. Moncelon, in *Bulletins de la Société d'Anthropologie de Paris*, 3me Série, ix. (1886) p. 368 (New Caledonia); H. Crawford Angas, in *Verhandlungen der Berliner Gesellschaft für Anthropologie, Ethnologie*

und Urgeschichte, 1898, p. 481 (Azimba, Central Africa); Sir H. H. Johnston, *British Central Africa* (London, 1897), p. 410 (the Wa-Yao of Central Africa). See further, W. Hertz, "Die Sage vom Giftmädchen," *Gesammelte Abhandlungen*, pp. 198-204.

[3] Herodotus, i. 93; Justin, xviii. 5. 4. Part of the wages thus earned was probably paid into the local temple. See above, pp. 37, 38. However, according to Strabo (xi. 14. 16, p. 532) the Armenian girls of rich families often gave their lovers more than they received from them.

[4] This fatal objection to the theory under discussion has been clearly stated by W. Hertz, *op. cit.* p. 217. I am glad to find myself in agreement with so judicious and learned an inquirer.

torical times from any such motive as is assumed by the
hypothesis under discussion.   At the period when we have
to do with them the customs were to all appearance purely
religious in character, and a religious motive must accordingly
be found for them.   Such a motive is supplied by the
theory I have adopted, which, so far as I can judge,
adequately explains all the known facts.

The
practice of
destroying
virginity
has some-
times had
a religious
character.

At the same time, in justice to the writers whose views
I have criticized, I wish to point out that the practice from
which they propose to derive the sacred prostitution of
Western Asia has not always been purely secular in character.
For, in the first place, the agent employed is sometimes reported to be a priest ; [1] and, in the second place, the sacrifice
of virginity has in some places, for example at Rome and in
parts of India, been made directly to the image of a male
deity. [2]   The meaning of these practices is very obscure, and
in the present state of our ignorance on the subject it is un-
safe to build conclusions on them.   It is possible that what
seems to be a purely secular precaution may be only a
degenerate form of a religious rite ; and on the other hand
it is possible that the religious rite may go back to a purely
physical preparation for marriage, such as is still observed
among the aborigines of Australia. [3]   But even if such an

---

[1] L. di Varthema, *Travels* (Hakluyt
Society, 1863), p. 141 ; J. A. de
Mandlesloe, in J. Harris's *Voyages and
Travels*, i. (London, 1744) p. 767 ;
A. Hamilton, "New Account of the
East Indies," in J. Pinkerton's *Voyages
and Travels*, viii. 374 ; Ch. Lassen,
Indische Alterthumskunde, iv. (Leipsic,
1861), p. 408 ; A. de Herrera, *The
General History of the Vast Conti-
nent and Islands of America*, translated by Captain J. Stevens (London,
1725–1726), iii. 310, 340 ; Fr.
Coreal, *Voyages aux Indes Occidentales*
(Amsterdam, 1722), i. 10 *sq.*, 139
sq. ; C. F. Ph. v. Martius, *Beiträge
zur Ethnographie und Sprachenkunde
Amerika's*, i. (Leipsic, 1867) pp. 113
sq. The first three of these authorities
refer to Malabar ; the fourth refers
to Cambodia ; the last three refer to
the Indians of Central and South
America.   See further W. Hertz,

" Die Sage vom Giftmädchen," *Gesammelte Abhandlungen*, pp. 204-207. For
a criticism of the Malabar evidence see
K. Schmidt, *Jus primae noctis* (Freiburg
im Breisgau, 1881), pp. 312-320.

[2] Lactantius, *Divin. Institut.* i. 20 ;
Arnobius, *Adversus Nationes*, iv. 7 ;
Augustine, *De civitate Dei*, vi. 9, vii.
24 ; D. Barbosa, *Description of the
Coasts of East Africa and Malabar*
(Hakluyt Society, 1866), p. 96 ; Son-
nerat, *Voyage aux Indes Orientales et
à la Chine* (Paris, 1782), i. 68 ; F.
Liebrecht, *Zur Volkskunde* (Heilbronn,
1879), pp. 396 *sq.*, 511 ; W. Hertz,
" Die Sage vom Giftmädchen," *Gesam-
melte Abhandlungen*, pp. 270-272.
According to Arnobius, it was matrons,
not maidens, who resorted to the image.
This suggests that the custom was a
charm to procure offspring.

[3] R. Schomburgk, in *Verhandlungen
der Berliner Gesellschaft für Anthro-*

historical origin could be established, it would not explain the motives from which the customs described in this volume were practised by the people of Western Asia in historical times. The true parallel to these customs is the sacred prostitution which is carried on to this day by dedicated women in India and Africa. An examination of these modern practices may throw light on the ancient customs.

§ 2. Sacred Women in India

In India the dancing-girls dedicated to the service of the Tamil temples take the name of *deva-dasis*, " servants or slaves of the gods," but in common parlance they are spoken of simply as harlots. Every Tamil temple of note in Southern India has its troop of these sacred women. Their official duties are to dance twice a day, morning and evening, in the temple, to fan the idol with Tibetan ox-tails, to dance and sing before it when it is borne in procession, and to carry the holy light called *Kûmbarti*. Inscriptions show that in A.D. 1004 the great temple of the Chola king Rajaraja at Tanjore had attached to it four hundred " women of the temple," who lived at free quarters in the streets round about it and were allowed land free of taxes out of its endowment. From infancy they are trained to dance and sing. In order to obtain a safe delivery expectant mothers will often vow to dedicate their child, if she should prove to be a girl, to the service of God. Among the weavers of Tiru-kalli-kundram, a little town in the Madras Presidency, the eldest daughter of every family is devoted to the temple. Girls thus made over to the deity are formally married, sometimes to the idol, sometimes to a sword, before they enter on their duties ; from which it appears that they are often, if not regularly, regarded as the wives of the god.[1]

Sacred women in the Tamil temples of Southern India.

Such women are sometimes married to the god and possessed by him.

pologie, Ethnologie und Urgeschichte, 1879, pp. 235 *sq.* ; Miklucho-Maclay, *ibid.* 1880, p. 89 ; W. E. Roth, *Studies among the North-West-Central Queensland Aborigines* (Brisbane and London, 1897), pp. 174 *sq.*, 180 ; B. Spencer and F. J. Gillen, *Native Tribes of Central Australia* (London, 1899), pp. 92-95 ; *id., Northern Tribes*

of Central Australia (London, 1904), pp. 133-136. In Australia the observance of the custom is regularly followed by the exercise of what seem to be old communal rights of the men over the women.

[1] J. A. Dubois, *Mœurs, Institutions et Cérémonies des Peuples de l'Inde* (Paris, 1825), ii. 353 *sqq.* ;

Among the Kaikolans, a large caste of Tamil weavers who are spread all over Southern India, at least one girl in every family should be dedicated to the temple service. The ritual, as it is observed at the initiation of one of these girls in Coimbatore, includes "a form of nuptial ceremony. The relations are invited for an auspicious day, and the maternal uncle, or his representative, ties a gold band on the girl's forehead, and, carrying her, places her on a plank before the assembled guests. A Brahman priest recites the *mantrams*, and prepares the sacred fire (*hōmam*). The uncle is presented with new cloths by the girl's mother. For the actual nuptials a rich Brahman, if possible, and, if not, a Brahman of more lowly status is invited. A Brahman is called in, as he is next in importance to, and the representative of the idol. It is said that, when the man who is to receive her first favours, joins the girl, a sword must be placed, at least for a few minutes, by her side." When one of these dancing-girls dies, her body is covered with a new cloth which has been taken for the purpose from the idol, and flowers are supplied from the temple to which she belonged. No worship is performed in the temple until the last rites have been performed over her body, because the idol, being deemed her husband, is held to be in that state of ceremonial pollution common to human mourners which debars him from the offices of religion.[1] In Mahratta such a female devotee is called Murli. Common folk believe that from time to time the shadow of the god falls on her and

---

J. Shortt, "The Bayadère or dancing-girls of Southern India," *Memoirs of the Anthropological Society of London*, iii. (1867-69) pp. 182-194; Edward Balfour, *Cyclopaedia of India*[3] (London, 1885), i. 922 *sqq.*; W. Francis, in *Census of India, 1901*, vol. xv., *Madras*, Part I. (Madras, 1902) pp. 151 *sq.*; E. Thurston, *Ethnographic Notes in Southern India* (Madras, 1906), pp. 36 *sq.*, 40 *sq.* The office of these sacred women has in recent years been abolished, on the ground of immorality, by the native Government of Mysore. See *Homeward Mail*, 6th June 1909 (extract kindly sent me by General Begbie).

[1] Edgar Thurston, *Castes and Tribes of Southern India* (Madras, 1909), iii. 37-39. Compare *id.*, *Ethnographic Notes in Southern India* (Madras, 1906), pp. 29 *sq.* In Southern India the maternal uncle often takes a prominent part in the marriage ceremony to the exclusion of the girl's father. See, for example, E. Thurston, *Castes and Tribes of Southern India*, ii. 497, iv. 147. The custom is derived from the old system of mother-kin, under which a man's heirs are not his own children but his sister's children. As to this system see below, Chapter XII., "Mother-kin and Mother Goddesses."

ossesses her person.   At such times the possessed woman
ocks herself to and fro, and the people occasionally consult
er as a soothsayer, laying money at her féet and accepting
s an oracle the words of wisdom or folly that drop from
er lips.[1]   Nor is the profession of a temple prostitute
dopted only by girls.   In Tulava, a district of Southern
ndia, any woman of the four highest castes who wearies
f her husband or, as a widow and therefore incapable of
narriage, grows tired of celibacy, may go to a temple and
at of the rice offered to the idol.   Thereupon, if she is a
3rahman, she has the right to live either in the temple or
utside of its precincts, as she pleases.   If she decides to
ive in it, she gets a daily allowance of rice, and must sweep
he temple, fan the idol, and confine her amours to the
3rahmans.   The male children of these women form a
pecial class called Moylar, but are fond of assuming the
itle of Stanikas.   As many of them as can find employment
ang about the temple, sweeping the areas, sprinkling them
vith cow-dung, carrying torches before the gods, and doing
ther odd jobs.   Some of them, debarred from these holy
ffices, are reduced to the painful necessity of earning their
read by honest work.   The daughters are either brought
p to live like their mothers or are given in marriage to the
itanikas.   Brahman women who do not choose to live in
he temples, and all the women of the three lower castes,
ohabit with any man of pure descent, but they have to pay
 fixed sum annually to the temple.[2]

   In Travancore a dancing-girl attached to a temple is *In Travan-*
:nown as a *Dâsî*, or *Dêvadâsî*, or *Dêvaratiâl*, "a servant of *core the dancing-*
;od."   The following account of her dedication and way of *girls are*
ife deserves to be quoted because, while it ignores the baser *regularly married to*
ide of her vocation, it brings clearly out the idea of her *the god.*
narriage to the deity.   "Marriage in the case of a *Dêvaratiâl*
n its original import is a renunciation of ordinary family life
nd a consecration to the service of God.   With a lady-nurse
t a Hospital, or a sister at a Convent, a *Dêvadâsî* at a Hindu
hrine, such as she probably was in the early ages of Hindu

[1] E. Balfour, *op. cit.* ii. 1012.   Mysore, Canara, and Malabar," in J.
[2] Francis Buchanan, "A Journey   Pinkerton's *Voyages and Travels*, viii.
om Madras through the countries of   (London, 1811) p. 749.

spirituality, would have claimed favourable comparison. In the ceremonial of the dedication-marriage of the *Dâst* elements are not wanting which indicate a past quite the reverse of disreputable.   The girl to be married is generally from six to eight years in age.   The bridegroom is the presiding deity of the local temple.   The ceremony is done at his house.   The expenses of the celebration are supposed to be partly paid from his funds.   To instance the practice at the Suchîndram temple, a *Yôga* or meeting of the chief functionaries of the temple arranges the preliminaries.   The girl to be wedded bathes and goes to the temple with two pieces of cloth, a *tâli*, betel, areca-nut, etc.   These are placed by the priest at the feet of the image.   The girl sits with the face towards the deity.   The priest kindles the sacred fire and goes through all the rituals of the *Tirukkalyânam* festival.   He then initiates the bride into the *Panchâkshara mantra*, if in a Saiva temple, and the *Ashtâkshara*, if in a Vaishnava temple.   On behalf of the divine bridegroom, he presents one of the two cloths she has brought as offering and ties the *Tâli* around her neck.   The practice, how old it is not possible to say, is then to take her to her house where the usual marriage festivities are celebrated for four days.   As in Brahminical marriages, the *Nalunku* ceremony, *i.e.* the rolling of a cocoanut by the bride to the bridegroom and *vice versa* a number of times to the accompaniment of music, is gone through, the temple priest playing the bridegroom's part.   Thenceforth she becomes the wife of the deity in the sense that she formally and solemnly dedicates the rest of her life to his service with the same constancy and devotion that a faithful wife united in holy matrimony shows to her wedded lord.   The life of a *Dêvadâsî* bedecked with all the accomplishments that the muses could give was one of spotless purity.   Even now she is maintained by the temple.   She undertakes fasts in connection with the temple festivals, such as the seven days' fast for the *Apamârgam* ceremony.   During the period of this fast, strict continence is enjoined ; she is required to take only one meal, and that within the temple—in fact to live and behave at least for a term, in the manner ordained for her throughout life.   Some of the details of her daily work seem interesting ; she attends

the *Dîpâradhana*, the waving of lighted lamps in front of the
deity at sunset every day ; sings hymns in his praise, dances
before his presence, goes round with him in his processions
with lights in hand.   After the procession, she sings a song
or two from Jayadêva's *Gîtagôvinda* and with a few lullaby
hymns, her work for the night is over.   When she grows
physically unfit for these duties, she is formally invalided by
a special ceremony, *i.e. Tôtuvaikkuka*, or the laying down of
the ear-pendants.   It is gone through at the Maha Raja's
palace, whereafter she becomes a *Tâikkizhavi* (old mother),
entitled only to a subsistence-allowance.   When she dies,
the temple contributes to the funeral expenses.   On her
death-bed, the priest attends and after a few ceremonies
immediately after death, gets her bathed with saffron-
powder." [1]

§ 3. *Sacred Men and Women in West Africa*

Still more instructive for our present purpose are the
West African customs.   Among the Ewe-speaking peoples
of the Slave Coast " recruits for the priesthood are obtained
in two ways, viz. by the affiliation of young persons, and by
the direct consecration of adults.   Young people of either
sex dedicated or affiliated to a god are termed *kosio*, from
kono, 'unfruitful,' because a child dedicated to a god passes
into his service and is practically lost to his parents, and *si*,
'to run away.'   As the females become the 'wives' of the
god to whom they are dedicated, the termination *si* in *vŏdu-si*
[another name for these dedicated women], has been translated 'wife' by some Europeans ; but it is never used in
the general acceptation of that term, being entirely restricted
to persons consecrated to the gods.   The chief business of
the female *kosi* is prostitution, and in every town there is at
least one institution in which the best-looking girls, between
ten and twelve years of age, are received.   Here they remain
for three years, learning the chants and dances peculiar to
the worship of the gods, and prostituting themselves to the

*Among
the Ewe
peoples
of West
Africa the
sacred pro-
stitutes are
regarded
as the
wives of
the god.*

---

[1] N. Subramhanya Aiyar, in *Census
of India, 1901*, vol. xxvi., *Travancore*,
Part i. (Trivandrum, 1903), pp. 276
sq.   I have to thank my friend Mr.
W. Crooke for referring me to this and
other passages on the sacred dancing-
girls of India.

priests and the inmates of the male seminaries; and at the termination of their novitiate they become public prostitutes. This condition, however, is not regarded as one for reproach; they are considered to be married to the god, and their excesses are supposed to be caused and directed by him. Properly speaking, their libertinage should be confined to the male worshippers at the temple of the god, but practically it is indiscriminate. Children who are born from such unions belong to the god."[1] These women are not allowed to marry since they are deemed the wives of a god.[2]

The human wives of the python-god.

Again, in this part of Africa "the female *Kosio* of Dañh-gbi, or *Dañh-sio*, that is, the wives, priestesses, and temple prostitutes of Dañh-gbi, the python-god, have their own organization. Generally they live together in a group of houses or huts inclosed by a fence, and in these inclosures the novices undergo their three years of initiation. Most new members are obtained by the affiliation of young girls; but any woman whatever, married or single, slave or free, by publicly simulating possession, and uttering the conventional cries recognized as indicative of possession by the god, can at once join the body, and be admitted to the habitations of the order. The person of a woman who has joined in this manner is inviolable, and during the period of her novitiate she is forbidden, if single, to enter the house of her parents, and, if married, that of her husband. This inviolability, while it gives women opportunities of gratifying an illicit passion, at the same time serves occasionally to save the persecuted slave, or neglected wife, from the ill-treatment of the lord and master; for she has only to go through the conventional form of possession and an asylum is assured."[3] The python-god marries these women secretly in his temple, and they father their offspring on him; but it is the priests who consummate the union.[4]

For our purpose it is important to note that a close

---

[1] A. B. Ellis, *The Ewe-speaking Peoples of the Slave Coast of West Africa* (London, 1890), pp. 140 *sq.*

[2] A. B. Ellis, *op. cit.* p. 142.

[3] A. B. Ellis, *op. cit.* pp. 148 *sq.* Compare Des Marchais, *Voyage en Guinée et à Cayenne* (Amsterdam, 1731), ii. 144-151; P. Bouche, *La Côte des Esclaves* (Paris, 1885), p. 128. The Abbé Bouche calls these women *danwés*.

[4] A. B. Ellis, *op. cit.* p. 60; Des Marchais, *op. cit.* ii. 149 *sq.*

connexion is apparently supposed to exist between the
fertility of the soil and the marriage of these women to
the serpent.   For the time when new brides are sought for
the reptile-god is the season when the millet is beginning to
sprout.   Then the old priestesses, armed with clubs, run
frantically through the streets shrieking like mad women
and carrying off to be brides of the serpent any little girls
between the ages of eight and twelve whom they may find
outside of the houses.   Pious people at such times will
sometimes leave their daughters at their doors on purpose
that they may have the honour of being dedicated to the
god.[1]   The marriage of wives to the serpent-god is probably
deemed necessary to enable him to discharge the important
function of making the crops to grow and the cattle to
multiply ; for we read that these people " invoke the snake
in excessively wet, dry, or barren seasons ; on all occasions
relating to their government and the preservation of their
cattle ; or rather, in one word, in all necessities and difficulties,
in which they do not apply to their new batch of gods." [2]
Once in a bad season the Dutch factor Bosman found the
King of Whydah in a great rage.   His Majesty explained
the reason of his discomposure by saying " that that year he
had sent much larger offerings to the snake-house than
usual, in order to obtain a good crop ; and that one of his
vice-roys (whom he shewed me) had desired him afresh, in
the name of the priests, who threatened a barren year, to
send yet more.   To which he answered that he did not intend
to make any further offerings this year ; and if the snake
would not bestow a plentiful harvest on them, he might let it
alone ; for (said he) I cannot be more damaged thereby, the
greatest part of my corn being already rotten in the field." [3]

The Akikuyu of British East Africa "have a custom
which reminds one of the West African python-god and his
wives.   At intervals of, I believe, several years the medicine-
men order huts to be built for the purpose of worshipping a
river snake.   The snake-god requires wives, and women or

Supposed
connexion
between
the fertility
of the soil
and the
marriage
of women
to the
serpent.

Human
wives of
a snake-
god among
the
Akikuyu.

---

[1] Des Marchais, *Voyage en Guinée
et à Cayenne* (Amsterdam, 1731), ii.
146 *sq.*

[2] W. Bosman, "Description of the
Coast of Guinea," in J. Pinkerton's
Voyages and Travels, xvi. (London,
1814) p. 494.

[3] W. Bosman, *l.c.*   The name of
Whydah is spelt by Bosman as Fida,
and by Des Marchais as Juda.

more especially girls go to the huts.   Here the union is
consummated by the medicine-men.   If the number of
females who go to the huts voluntarily is not sufficient,
girls are seized and dragged there.   I believe the offspring
of such a union is said to be fathered by God (Ngai): at
any rate there are children in Kikuyu who are regarded as
the children of God." [1]

Among the negroes of the Slave Coast there are, as we
have seen, male *kosio* as well as female *kosio* ; that is, there
are dedicated men as well as dedicated women, priests as
well as priestesses, and the ideas and customs in regard to
them seem to be similar.   Like the women, the men undergo
a three years' novitiate, at the end of which each candidate
has to prove that the god accepts him and finds him worthy
of inspiration.   Escorted by a party of priests he goes to a
shrine and seats himself on a stool that belongs to the deity.
The priests then anoint his head with a mystic decoction and
invoke the god in a long and wild chorus.   During the
singing the youth, if he is acceptable to the deity, trembles
violently, simulates convulsions, foams at the mouth, and
dances in a frenzied style, sometimes for more than an hour.
This is the proof that the god has taken possession of him.
After that he has to remain in a temple without speaking
for seven days and nights.   At the end of that time, he is
brought out, a priest opens his mouth to show that he may
now use his tongue, a new name is given him, and he is
fully ordained. [2]   Henceforth he is regarded as the priest
and medium of the deity whom he serves, and the words
which he utters in that morbid state of mental excitement
which passes for divine inspiration, are accepted by the
hearers as the very words of the god spoken by the mouth
of the man. [3]   Any crime which a priest committed in a state
of frenzy used to remain unpunished, no doubt because the
act was thought to be the act of the god.   But this benefit
of clergy was so much abused that under King Gezo the law
had to be altered ; and although, while he is still possessed

[1] MS. notes, kindly sent to me by
the author, Mr. A. C. Hollis, 21st
May, 1908.

[2] A. B. Ellis, *The Ewe - speaking
Peoples of the Slave Coast*, pp. 142-144 ;

Le R. P. Baudin, "Féticheurs ou
ministres religieux des Nègres de la
Guinée," *Les Missions Catholiques*,
No. 787 (4 juillet 1884), p. 322.

[3] A. B. Ellis, *op. cit.* pp. 150 *sq.*

by the god, the inspired criminal is safe, he is now liable to punishment as soon as the divine spirit leaves him. Nevertheless on the whole among these people "the person of a priest or priestess is sacred. Not only must a layman not lay hands on or insult one; he must be careful not even to knock one by accident, or jostle against one in the street. The Abbé Bouche relates[1] that once when he was paying a visit to the chief of Agweh, one of the wives of the chief was brought into the house by four priestesses, her face bloody, and her body covered with stripes. She had been savagely flogged for having accidentally trodden upon the foot of one of them; and the chief not only dared not give vent to his anger, but had to give them a bottle of rum as a peace-offering."[2]

Among the Tshi-speaking peoples of the Gold Coast, who border on the Ewe-speaking peoples of the Slave Coast to the west, the customs and beliefs in regard to the dedicated men and dedicated women, the priests and priestesses, are very similar. These persons are believed to be from time to time possessed or inspired by the deity whom they serve; and in that state they are consulted as oracles. They work themselves up to the necessary pitch of excitement by dancing to the music of drums; each god has his special hymn, sung to a special beat of the drum, and accompanied by a special dance. It is while thus dancing to the drums that the priest or priestess lets fall the oracular words in a croaking or guttural voice which the hearers take to be the voice of the god. Hence dancing has an important place in the education of priests and priestesses; they are trained in it for months before they may perform in public. These mouthpieces of the deity are consulted in almost every concern of life and are handsomely paid for their services.[3] Priests marry like any other members of the community, and purchase wives; but priestesses are never married, nor can any 'head money' be paid for a priestess. The reason appears to be that a priestess belongs to the god she serves, and therefore cannot become the property of a man, as would

Similarly among the Tshi peoples of the Gold Coast there are sacred men and women, who are supposed to be inspired by the deity.

---

[1] *La Côte des Esclaves*, pp. 127 7.

[2] A. B. Ellis, *op. cit.* p. 147.

[3] A. B. Ellis, *The Tshi-speaking Peoples of the Gold Coast of West Africa* (London, 1887), pp. 120-138.

be the case if she married one.   This prohibition extends to
marriage only, and a priestess is not debarred from sexual
commerce.   The children of a priest or priestess are not
ordinarily educated for the priestly profession, one generation
being usually passed over, and the grandchildren selected.
Priestesses are ordinarily most licentious, and custom allows
them to gratify their passions with any man who may chance
to take their fancy " [1]   The ranks of the hereditary priesthood are constantly recruited by persons who devote themselves or who are devoted by their relations or masters to
the profession.   Men, women, and even children can thus
become members of the priesthood.   If a mother has lost
several of her children by death, she will not uncommonly
vow to devote the next born to the service of the gods ; for
in this way she hopes to save the child's life.   So when the
child is born it is set apart for the priesthood, and on arriving
at maturity generally fulfils the vow made by the mother
and becomes a priest or priestess.   At the ceremony of
ordination the votary has to prove his or her vocation for
the sacred life in the usual way by falling into or simulating
convulsions, dancing frantically to the beat of drums, and
speaking in a hoarse unnatural voice words which are deemed
to be the utterance of the deity temporarily lodged in the
body of the man or woman.[2]

§ 4. *Sacred Women in Western Asia*

In like
manner the
sacred
prostitutes
of Western
Asia may
have been
viewed as
possessed
by the
deity and
married to
the god.

Thus in Africa, and sometimes if not regularly in India,
the sacred prostitutes attached to temples are regarded as
the wives of the god, and their excesses are excused on the
ground that the women are not themselves, but that they act
under the influence of divine inspiration.   This is in substance
the explanation which I have given of the custom of sacred
prostitution as it was practised in antiquity by the peoples

[1] A. B. Ellis, *op. cit.* p. 121.

[2] A. B. Ellis, *op. cit.* pp. 120 *sq.*,
129-138.   The slaves, male and female,
dedicated to a god from childhood are
often mentioned by the German missionary Mr. J. Spieth in his elaborate
work on the Ewe people (*Die Ewe-*

Stämme : Material zur Kunde des Ewe-
Volkes in Deutsch-Togo, Berlin, 1906,
pp. 228, 229, 309, 450, 474, 792,
797, etc.).   But his information does
not illustrate the principal points to
which I have called attention in the
text.

of Western Asia.   In their licentious intercourse at the
temples the women, whether maidens or matrons or professional harlots, imitated the licentious conduct of a great
goddess of fertility for the purpose of ensuring the fruitfulness of fields and trees, of man and beast ; and in discharging
this sacred and important function the women were probably
supposed, like their West African sisters, to be actually
possessed by the goddess.   The hypothesis at least explains
all the facts in a simple and natural manner ; and in assuming that women could be married to gods it assumes a
principle which we know to have been recognized in Babylon,
Assyria, and Egypt.[1]   At Babylon a woman regularly slept
in the great bed of Bel or Marduk, which stood in his temple
on the summit of a lofty pyramid ; and it was believed that
the god chose her from all the women of Babylon and slept
with her in the bed.   However, unlike the Indian and West
African wives of gods, this spouse of the Babylonian deity
is reported by Herodotus to have been chaste.[2]   Yet we may
doubt whether she was so ; for these wives or perhaps para-
mours of Bel are probably to be identified with the wives or
votaries of Marduk mentioned in the code of Hammurabi,
and we know from the code that female votaries of the gods
might be mothers and married to men.[3]   At Babylon the
sun-god Shamash as well as Marduk had human wives
formerly dedicated to his service, and they like the votaries
of Marduk might have children.[4]   It is significant that a
name for these Babylonian votaries was *kadishtu*, which is
the same word as *kedesha*, " consecrated woman," the regular
Hebrew word for a temple harlot.[5]   It is true that the law

[1] *The Magic Art and the Evolution
of Kings*, ii. 129-135.
[2] Herodotus, i. 181 *sq*. It is not
clear whether the same or a different
woman slept every night in the temple.
[3] H. Winckler, *Die Gesetze Hammurabi*[2] (Leipsic, 1903), p. 31, § 182 ;
C. H. W. Johns, *Babylonian and
Assyrian Laws, Contracts, and Letters*
(Edinburgh, 1904), pp. 54, 55, 59, 60,
61 (§§ 137, 144, 145, 146, 178, 182,
187, 192, 193, of the Code of Hammurabi).   As to these female votaries
see especially C. H. W. Johns, " Notes
on the Code of Hammurabi," *Ameri-*

*can Journal of Semitic Languages and
Literatures*, xix. (January 1903) pp.
98-107.   Compare S. A. Cook, *The
Laws of Moses and the Code of Hammurabi* (London, 1903), pp. 147-150.
[4] C. H. W. Johns, " Notes on the
Code of Hammurabi," *l.c.*, where we
read (p. 104) of a female votary of
Shamash who had a daughter.
[5] *Code of Hammurabi*, § 181 ;
C. H. W. Johns, " Notes on the Code
of Hammurabi," *op. cit.* pp. 100 *sq.*;
S. A. Cook, *op. cit.* p. 148.   Dr.
Johns translates the name by " temple
maid" (*Babylonian and Assyrian Laws,*

severely punished any disrespect shown to these sacred women;[1] but the example of West Africa warns us that a formal respect shown to such persons, even when it is enforced by severe penalties, need be no proof at all of their virtuous character.[2] In Egypt a woman used to sleep in the temple of Ammon at Thebes, and the god was believed to visit her.[3] Egyptian texts often mention her as " the divine consort," and in old days she seems to have usually been the Queen of Egypt herself.[4] But in the time of Strabo, at the beginning of our era, these consorts or concubines of Ammon, as they were called, were beautiful young girls of noble birth, who held office only till puberty. During their term of office they prostituted themselves freely to any man who took their fancy. After puberty they were given in marriage, and a ceremony of mourning was performed for them as if they were dead.[5] When they died in good earnest, their bodies were laid in special graves.[6]

§ 5. Sacred Men in Western Asia

Similarly the sacred men (*kedeshim*) of Western Asia may have been regarded as possessed by the deity and as acting and speaking in his name. As in West Africa the dedicated women have their counterpart in the dedicated men, so it was in Western Asia; for there the sacred men (*kedeshim*) clearly corresponded to the sacred women (*kedeshoth*), in other words, the sacred male slaves[7] of the temples were the complement of the sacred female slaves. And as the characteristic feature of the dedicated men in West Africa is their supposed possession or inspiration by the deity, so we may conjecture was it with the sacred male slaves (the *kedeshim*) of Western Asia; they, too, may have been regarded as temporary or permanent embodiments of the deity, possessed from time to time by

---

Contracts, and Letters, p. 61). He is scrupulously polite to these ladies, but I gather from him that a far less charitable view of their religious vocation is taken by Father Scheil, the first editor and translator of the code.

[1] Any man proved to have pointed the finger of scorn at a votary was liable to be branded on the forehead (*Code of Hammurabi*, § 127).

[2] See above, pp. 66, 69.

[3] Herodotus, i. 182.

[4] A. Wiedemann, *Herodots Zweites Buch* (Leipsic, 1890), pp. 268 sq. See further *The Magic Art and the Evolution of Kings*, ii. 130 sqq.

[5] Strabo, xvii. 1. 46, p. 816. The title " concubines of Zeus (Ammon) " is mentioned by Diodorus Siculus (i. 47).

[6] Diodorus Siculus, i. 47.

[7] The ἱερόδουλοι, as the Greeks called them.

his divine spirit, acting in his name, and speaking with his voice.[1] At all events we know that this was so at the sanctuary of the Moon among the Albanians of the Caucasus. The sanctuary owned church lands of great extent peopled by sacred slaves, and it was ruled by a high-priest, who ranked next after the king. Many of these slaves were inspired by the deity and prophesied ; and when one of them had been for some time in this state of divine frenzy, wandering alone in the forest, the high-priest had him caught, bound with a sacred chain, and maintained in luxury for a year. Then the poor wretch was led out, anointed with unguents, and sacrificed with other victims to the Moon. The mode of sacrifice was this. A man took a sacred spear, and thrust it through the victim's side to the heart. As he staggered and fell, the rest observed him closely and drew omens from the manner of his fall. Then the body was dragged or carried away to a certain place, where all his fellows stood upon it by way of purification.[2] In this custom the prophet, or rather the maniac, was plainly supposed to be moon-struck in the most literal sense, that is, possessed or inspired by the deity of the Moon, who was perhaps thought by the Albanians, as by the Phrygians,[3] to be a male god, since his chosen minister and mouthpiece was a man, not a woman.[4] It can hardly therefore be deemed improbable that at other sanctuaries of Western Asia, where sacred men were kept, these ministers of religion should have discharged a similar prophetic function, even though they did not share the tragic

---

[1] I have to thank the Rev. Professor R. H. Kennett for this important suggestion as to the true nature of the *ḳedeshim*. The passages of the Bible in which mention is made of these men are Deuteronomy xxiii. 17 (in Hebrew 18) ; 1 Kings xiv. 24, xv. 12, xxii. 46 (in Hebrew 47) ; 2 Kings xxiii. 7 ; Job xxxvi. 14 (where *ḳedeshim* is translated "the unclean" in the English version). The usual rendering of *ḳedeshim* in the English Bible is not justified by any of these passages ; but it may perhaps derive support from a reference which Eusebius makes to the profligate rites observed at Aphaca (*Vita Constantini*, iii. 55 ; Migne's *Patrologia Graeca*, xx.

1120) ; Γύνιδες γοῦν τινες ἄνδρες οὐκ ἄνδρες, τὸ σέμνον τῆς φύσεως ἀπαρνησάμενοι, θηλείᾳ νόσῳ τὴν δαίμονα ἱλεοῦντο. But probably Eusebius is here speaking of the men who castrated themselves in honour of the goddess, and thereafter wore female attire. See Lucian, *De dea Syria*, 51 ; and below, pp. 269 *sq.*

[2] Strabo, xi. 4. 7, p. 503.

[3] Drexler, in W. H. Roscher's *Lexikon der griech. und röm. Mythologie*, *s.v.* "Men," ii. 2687 *sqq.*

[4] It is true that Strabo (*l.c.*) speaks of the Albanian deity as a goddess, but this may be only an accommodation to the usage of the Greek language, in which the moon is feminine.

fate of the moon-struck Albanian prophet.   Nor was the influence of these Asiatic prophets confined to Asia.   In Sicily the spark which kindled the devastating Servile War was struck by a Syrian slave, who simulated the prophetic ecstasy in order to rouse his fellow-slaves to arms in the name of the Syrian goddess.   To inflame still more his inflammatory words this ancient Mahdi ingeniously inter-larded them with real fire and smoke, which by a common conjurer's trick he breathed from his lips.[1]

Resem-
blance of
the Hebrew
prophets
to the
sacred men
of Western
Africa. In like manner the Hebrew prophets were believed to be temporarily possessed and inspired by a divine spirit who spoke through them, just as a divine spirit is supposed by West African negroes to speak through the mouth of the dedicated men his priests.   Indeed the points of resem-blance between the prophets of Israel and West Africa are close and curious.   Like their black brothers, the Hebrew prophets employed music in order to bring on the prophetic trance;[2] like them, they received the divine spirit through the application of a magic oil to their heads;[3] like them, they were apparently distinguished from common people by certain marks on the face;[4] and like

---

[1] Florus, *Epitoma*, ii. 7 ; Diodorus Siculus, Frag. xxxiv. 2 (vol. v. pp. 87 *sq.*, ed. L. Dindorf, in the Teubner series).

[2] Above, pp. 52 *sq.*

[3] 1 Kings xix. 16 ; Isaiah lx. 1.

[4] 1 Kings xx. 41.   So in Africa "priests and priestesses are readily distinguishable from the rest of the community.   They wear their hair long and unkempt, while other people, except the women in the towns on the sea-board, have it cut close to the head. . . . Frequently both appear with white circles painted round their eyes, or with various white devices, marks, or lines painted on the face, neck, shoulders, or arms" (A. B. Ellis, *The Tshi-speaking Peoples of the Gold Coast*, p. 123).   "Besides the ordinary tribal tattoo-marks borne by all natives, the priesthood in Dahomi bear a variety of such marks, some very elaborate, and an expert can tell by the marks on a priest to what god he is vowed, and what rank he holds in the order.

These hierarchical marks consist of lines, scrolls, diamonds, and other patterns, with sometimes a figure, such as that of the crocodile or chameleon. The shoulders are frequently seen covered with an infinite number of small marks like dots, set close together. All these marks are considered sacred, and the laity are forbidden to touch them" (A. B. Ellis, *The Ewe-speaking Peoples of the Slave Coast*, p. 146). The reason why the prophet's shoulders are especially marked is perhaps given by the statement of a Zulu that "the sensitive part with a doctor [medicine-man] is his shoulders.   Everything he feels is in the situation of his shoulders. That is the place where black men feel the Amatongo" (ancestral spirits). See H. Callaway, *The Religious System of the Amazulu*, part ii. p. 159.   These African analogies suggest that the "wounds between the arms" (literally, "between the hands") which the prophet Zechariah mentions (xiii. 6) as the badge of a Hebrew prophet were

hem they were consulted not merely in great national
emergencies but in the ordinary affairs of everyday life, in
which they were expected to give information and advice
for a small fee.   For example, Samuel was consulted about
lost asses,[1] just as a Zulu diviner is consulted about lost
cows;[2] and we have seen Elisha acting as a dowser when
water ran short.[3]   Indeed, we learn that the old name for a
prophet was a seer,[4] a word which may be understood to
imply that his special function was divination rather than
prophecy in the sense of prediction.   Be that as it may,
prophecy of the Hebrew type has not been limited to Israel ;
it is indeed a phenomenon of almost world-wide occurrence ;
in many lands and in many ages the wild, whirling words of
frenzied men and women have been accepted as the utterances
of an indwelling deity.[5]   What does distinguish Hebrew prophecy from all others is that the genius of a few members of
the profession wrested this vulgar but powerful instrument
from baser uses, and by wielding it in the interest of a high
morality rendered a service of incalculable value to humanity.
That is indeed the glory of Israel, but it is not the side of
prophecy with which we are here concerned.

More to our purpose is to note that prophecy of the
ordinary sort appears to have been in vogue at Byblus,
the sacred city of Adonis, centuries before the life-time of
the earliest Hebrew prophet whose writings have come
down to us.   When the Egyptian traveller, Wen-Ammon,
was lingering in the port of Byblus, under the King's orders
to quit the place, the spirit of God came on one of the royal

Inspired
prophets
at Byblus.

---

marks tattooed on his shoulders in
token of his holy office.   The suggestion is confirmed by the prophet's own
statement (*l.c.*) that he had received
the wounds in the house of his lovers
(בֵּית מְאַהֲבָי) ; for the same word lovers
is repeatedly applied by the prophet
Hosea to the Baalim (Hosea, ii. 5, 7,
10, 12, 13, verses 7, 9, 12, 14, 15 in
Hebrew).

[1] I Samuel ix. 1-20.
[2] H. Callaway, *The Religious System
of the Amazulu*, part iii. pp. 300 *sqq.*
[3] See above, pp. 52 *sq.*
[4] I Samuel ix. 9.   In the Wiimbaio

tribe of South - Eastern Australia a
medicine - man used to be called
" *mekigar*, from *meki*, ' eye ' or ' to
see,' otherwise ' one who sees,' that is,
sees the causes of maladies in people,
and who could extract them from the
sufferer, usually in the form of quartz
crystals " (A. W. Howitt, *The Native
Tribes of South-East Australia*, London, 1904, p. 380).

[5] That the prophet's office in Canaan
was developed out of the widespread
respect for insanity is duly recognized
by Ed. Meyer, *Geschichte des Altertums*,[2] i. 2. p. 383.

pages or henchmen, and in a prophetic frenzy he announced
that the King should receive the Egyptian stranger as a
messenger sent from the god Ammon.[1]   The god who thus
took possession of the page and spoke through him was
probably Adonis, the god of the city.   With regard to the
office of these royal pages we have no information ; but as
ministers of a sacred king and liable to be inspired by the
deity, they would naturally be themselves sacred ; in fact
they may have belonged to the class of sacred slaves or
ḳedeshim.   If that was so it would confirm the conclusion to
which the foregoing investigation points, namely, that originally no sharp line of distinction existed between the prophets
and the *ḳedeshim* ; both were " men of God," as the prophets
were constantly called ; [2] in other words, they were inspired
mediums, men in whom the god manifested himself from
time to time by word and deed, in short temporary incarnations of the deity.   But while the prophets roved freely about
the country, the *ḳedeshim* appear to have been regularly
attached to a sanctuary ; and among the duties which they
performed at the shrines there were clearly some which
revolted the conscience of men imbued with a purer
morality.   What these duties were, we may surmise partly
from the behaviour of the sons of Eli to the women who
came to the tabernacle,[3] partly from the beliefs and practices

[1] W. Max Müller, in *Mitteilungen
der Vorderasiatischen Gesellschaft*,
1900, No. 1, p. 17 ; A. Erman,
"Eine Reise nach Phönizien im
11 Jahrhundert v. Chr." *Zeitschrift
für Ägyptische Sprache und Altertums-
kunde*, xxxviii. (1900) pp. 6 *sq.* ;
G. Maspero, *Les contes populaires de
l'Égypte Ancienne*,[3] p. 192 ; A. Wiedemann, *Altägyptische Sagen und Mär-
chen* (Leipsic, 1906), pp. 99 *sq.* ;
H. Gressmann, *Altorientalische Texte
und Bilder zum Alten Testamente*
(Tübingen, 1909), p. 226. Scholars
differ as to whether Wen-Ammon's
narrative is to be regarded as history
or romance ; but even if it were proved
to be a fiction, we might safely assume
that the incident of the prophetic
frenzy at Byblus was based upon
familiar facts. Prof. Wiedemann thinks
that the god who inspired the page

was the Egyptian Ammon, not the
Phoenician Adonis, but this view
seems to me less probable.

[2] 1 Samuel ix. 6-8, 10 ; 1 Kings
xiii. 1, 4-8, 11 etc.

[3] 1 Samuel ii. 22.   Totally different
from their Asiatic namesakes were the
"sacred men" and "sacred women"
who were charged with the superin-
tendence of the mysteries at Andania
in Messenia. They were chosen by
lot and held office for a year. The
sacred women might be either married
or single ; the married women had to
swear that they had been true to their
husbands. See G. Dittenberger, *Sylloge Inscriptionum Graecarum*[2] (Leipsic, 1898-1901), vol. ii. pp. 461 *sqq.*,
No. 653 ; Ch. Michel, *Recueil d'Inscriptions Grecques* (Brussels, 1900),
pp. 596 *sqq.*, No. 694 ; *Leges Graecorum Sacrae*, ed. J. de Prott, L.

as to "holy men" which survive to this day among the Syrian peasantry.

Of these "holy men" we are told that "so far as they are not impostors, they are men whom we would call insane, known among the Syrians as *mejnûn*, possessed by a *jinn* or spirit. They often go in filthy garments, or without clothing. Since they are regarded as intoxicated by deity, the most dignified men, and of the highest standing among the Moslems, submit to utter indecent language at their bidding without rebuke, and ignorant Moslem women do not shrink from their approach, because in their superstitious belief they attribute to them, as men possessed by God, a divine authority which they dare not resist. Such an attitude of compliance may be exceptional, but there are more than rumours of its existence. These 'holy men' differ from the ordinary derwishes whom travellers so often see in Cairo, and from the ordinary madmen who are kept in fetters, so that they may not do injury to themselves and others. But their appearance, and the expressions regarding them, afford some illustrations of the popular estimate of ancient seers, or prophets, in the time of Hosea: 'The prophet is a fool, the man that hath the spirit is mad';[1] and in the time of Jeremiah,[2] the man who made himself a prophet was considered as good as a madman."[3] To complete the parallel these vagabonds "are also believed to be possessed of prophetic power, so that they are able to foretell the future, and warn the people among whom they live of impending danger."[4]

"Holy men" in modern Syria.

Ziehen, Pars Altera, Fasciculus i. (Leipsic, 1906), No. 58, pp. 166 *sqq.*

[1] Hosea ix. 7.

[2] Jeremiah xxix. 26.

[3] S. I. Curtiss, *Primitive Semitic Religion To-day* (Chicago, New York, Toronto, 1902), pp. 150 *sq.*

[4] S. I. Curtiss, *op. cit.* p. 152. As to these "holy men," see further C. R. Conder, *Tent-work in Palestine* (London, 1878), ii. 231 *sq.* : "The most peculiar class of men in the country is that of the Derwîshes, or sacred personages, who wander from

village to village, performing tricks, living on alms, and enjoying certain social and domestic privileges, which very often lead to scandalous scenes. Some of these men are mad, some are fanatics, but the majority are, I imagine, rogues. They are reverenced not only by the peasantry, but also sometimes by the governing class. I have seen the Kady of Nazareth ostentatiously preparing food for a miserable and filthy beggar, who sat in the justice-hall, and was consulted as if he had been inspired. A Derwîsh of peculiar eminence is often dressed in

The licence
accorded
to such
" holy
men " may
be ex-
plained by
the desire
of women
for off-
spring.

We may conjecture that with women a powerful motive for submitting to the embraces of the " holy men " is a hope of obtaining offspring by them. For in Syria it is still believed that even dead saints can beget children on barren women, who accordingly resort to their shrines in order to obtain the wish of their hearts. For example, at the Baths of Solomon in Northern Palestine, blasts of hot air escape from the ground ; and one of them, named Abu Rabah, is a famous resort of childless wives who wish to satisfy their maternal longings. They let the hot air stream up over their bodies and really believe that children born to them after such a visit are begotten by the saint of the shrine.[1] But the saint who enjoys the highest reputation in this respect is St. George. He reveals himself at his shrines which are scattered all over the country ; at each of them there is a tomb or the likeness of a tomb. The most celebrated of these sanctuaries is at Kalat el Hosn in Northern Syria. Barren women of all sects, including Moslems, resort to it. " There are many natives who shrug their shoulders when this shrine is mentioned in connection with women. But it is doubtless true that many do not know what seems to be its true character, and who think that the most puissant saint, as they believe, in the world can give them sons." " But the true character of the place is beginning to be recognized, so that many Moslems have forbidden their wives to visit it." [2]

§ 6. *Sons of God*

Belief that
men and
women
may be the
offspring
of a god.

Customs like the foregoing may serve to explain the belief, which is not confined to Syria, that men and women may be in fact and not merely in metaphor the sons and

---

good clothes, with a spotless turban, and is preceded by a banner-bearer, and followed by a band, with drum, cymbal, and tambourine. . . . It is natural to reflect whether the social position of the Prophets among the Jews may not have resembled that of the Derwîshes."

[1] S. I. Curtiss, *op. cit.* pp. 116 *sq.*
[2] S. I. Curtiss, *op. cit.* pp. 118, 119.

In India also some Mohammedan saints are noted as givers of children. Thus at Fatepur-Sikri, near Agra, is the grave of Salim Chishti, and child-less women tie rags to the delicate tracery of the tomb, " thus bringing them into direct communion with the spirit of the holy man " (W. Crooke, *Natives of Northern India*, London, 1907, p. 203).

daughters of a god; for these modern saints, whether Christian or Moslem, who father the children of Syrian mothers, are nothing but the old gods under a thin disguise. If in antiquity as at the present day Semitic women often repaired to shrines in order to have the reproach of barrenness removed from them—and the prayer of Hannah is a familiar example of the practice,[1] we could easily understand not only the tradition of the sons of God who begat children on the daughters of men,[2] but also the exceedingly common occurrence of the divine titles in Hebrew names of human beings.[3] Multitudes of men and women, in fact, whose mothers had resorted to holy places in order to procure offspring, would be regarded as the actual children of the god and would be named accordingly. Hence Hannah called her infant Samuel, which means "name of God" or "his name is God";[4] and probably she sincerely believed that the child was actually begotten in her womb by the deity.[5] The dedication of such children to the service of God at the sanctuary was merely giving back the divine son to the divine father. Similarly in West Africa, when a woman has got a child at the shrine of Agbasia, the god who alone bestows offspring on women, she dedicates him or her as a sacred slave to the deity.[6]

Thus in the Syrian beliefs and customs of to-day we probably have the clue to the religious prostitution practised in the very same regions in antiquity. Then as now women looked to the local god, the Baal or Adonis of old, the Abu Rabah or St. George of to-day, to satisfy the natural craving of a woman's heart; and then as now, apparently, the part

The saints in modern Syria are the equivalents of the ancient Baal or Adonis.

---

[1] 1 Samuel i.

[2] Genesis vi. 1-3. In this passage "the sons of God (or rather of the gods)" probably means, in accordance with a common Hebrew idiom, no more than "the gods," just as the phrase "sons of the prophets" means the prophets themselves. For more examples of this idiom, see Brown, Driver, and Briggs, *Hebrew and English Lexicon*, p. 121.

[3] For example, all Hebrew names ending in *-el* or *-iah* are compounds of El or Yahweh, two names of the divinity. See G. B. Gray, *Studies in Hebrew Proper Names* (London, 1896), pp. 149 *sqq.*

[4] Brown, Driver, and Briggs, *Hebrew and English Lexicon*, p. 1028. But compare *Encyclopaedia Biblica*, iii. 3285, iv. 4452.

[5] A trace of a similar belief perhaps survives in the narratives of Genesis xxxi. and Judges xiii., where barren women are represented as conceiving children after the visit of God, or of an angel of God, in the likeness of a man.

[6] J. Spieth, *Die Ewe - Stämme* (Berlin, 1906), pp. 446, 448-450.

of the local god was played by sacred men, who in personating him may often have sincerely believed that they were
acting under divine inspiration, and that the functions which
they discharged were necessary for the fertility of the land
as well as for the propagation of the human species. The
purifying influence of Christianity and Mohammedanism has
restricted such customs within narrow limits; even under
Turkish rule they are now only carried on in holes and corners.
Yet if the practice has dwindled, the principle which it
embodies appears to be fundamentally the same; it is a
desire for the continuance of the species, and a belief that
an object so natural and legitimate can be accomplished by
divine power manifesting itself in the bodies of men and
women.

Belief in the physical fatherhood of God not confined to Syria.

The belief in the physical fatherhood of God has not
been confined to Syria in ancient and modern times. Elsewhere many men have been counted the sons of God in
the most literal sense of the word, being supposed to have
been begotten by his holy spirit in the wombs of mortal
women. Here I shall merely illustrate the creed by a few
examples drawn from classical antiquity.[1] Thus in order to

Sons of the serpent-god.

obtain offspring women used to resort to the great sanctuary
of Aesculapius, situated in a beautiful upland valley, to
which a path, winding through a long wooded gorge, leads
from the bay of Epidaurus. Here the women slept in the
holy place and were visited in dreams by a serpent; and
the children to whom they afterwards gave birth were
believed to have been begotten by the reptile.[2] That the
serpent was supposed to be the god himself seems certain;
for Aesculapius repeatedly appeared in the form of a serpent,[3]
and live serpents were kept and fed in his sanctuaries for
the healing of the sick, being no doubt regarded as his
incarnations.[4] Hence the children born to women who had

[1] For more instances see H. Usener,
Das Weihnachtsfest[2] (Bonn, 1911), i. 71
sqq.

[2] G. Dittenberger, *Sylloge Inscriptionum Graecarum*,[2] vol. ii. pp. 662,
663, No. 803, lines 117 *sqq.*, 129
sqq.

[3] Pausanias, ii. 10. 3 (with my
note), iii. 23. 7; Livy, xi. Epitome;

Pliny, *Nat. Hist.* xxix. 72; Valerius
Maximus, i. 8. 2; Ovid, *Metam.* xv.
626-744; Aurelius Victor, *De viris
illustr.* 22; Plutarch, *Quaest. Rom.*
94.

[4] Aristophanes, *Plutus*, 733; Pausanias, ii. 11. 8; Herodas, *Mimiambi*,
iv. 90 *sq.*; G. Dittenberger, *Sylloge
Inscriptionum Graecarum*,[2] vol. ii. p.

thus visited a sanctuary of Aesculapius were probably fathered on the serpent-god. Many celebrated men in classical antiquity were thus promoted to the heavenly hierarchy by similar legends of a miraculous birth. The famous Aratus of Sicyon was certainly believed by his countrymen to be a son of Aesculapius; his mother is said to have got him in intercourse with a serpent.[1] Probably she slept either in the shrine of Aesculapius at Sicyon, where a figurine of her was shown seated on a serpent,[2] or perhaps in the more secluded sanctuary of the god at Titane, not many miles off, where the sacred serpents crawled among ancient cypresses on the hill-top which overlooks the narrow green valley of the Asopus with the white turbid river rushing in its depths.[3] There, under the shadow of the cypresses, with the murmur of the Asopus in her ears, the mother of Aratus may have conceived, or fancied she conceived, the future deliverer of his country. Again, the mother of Augustus is said to have got him by intercourse with a serpent in a temple of Apollo; hence the emperor was reputed to be the son of that god.[4] Similar tales were told of the Messenian hero Aristomenes, Alexander the Great, and the elder Scipio : all of them were reported to have been begotten by snakes.[5] In the time of Herod a serpent, according to Aelian, in like manner made love to a Judean maid.[6] Can the story be a distorted rumour of the parentage of Christ ?

In India even stone serpents are credited with a power of bestowing offspring on women. Thus the Komatis of Mysore " worship *Nága* or the serpent god. This worship is generally confined to women and is carried on on a large

Women fertilized by stone serpents in India.

655, No. 802, lines 116 *sqq.*; Ch. Michel, *Recueil d'Inscriptions Grecques*, p. 826, No. 1069.

[1] Pausanias, ii. 10. 3, iv. 14. 7 *sq.*

[2] Pausanias, ii. 10. 4.

[3] Pausanias, ii. 11. 5-8.

[4] Suetonius, *Divus Augustus*, 94 ; Dio Cassius, xlv. 1. 2. Tame serpents were kept in a sacred grove of Apollo in Epirus. A virgin priestess fed them, and omens of plenty and

health or the opposites were drawn from the way in which the reptiles took their food from her. See Aelian, *Nat. Hist.* xi. 2.

[5] Pausanias, iv. 14. 7 ; Livy, xxvi. 19 ; Aulus Gellius, vi. 1 ; Plutarch, *Alexander*, 2. All these cases have been already cited in this connexion by L. Deubner, *De incubatione* (Leipsic, 1900), p. 33 note.

[6] Aelian, *De natura animalium*, vi. 17.

scale once a year on the fifth day of the bright fortnight of Srávana (July and August). The representations of serpents are cut in stone slabs and are set up round an *Asvattha* tree on a platform, on which is also generally planted a margosa tree. These snakes in stones are set up in performance of vows and are said to be specially efficacious in curing bad sores and other skin diseases and in giving children. The women go to such places for worship with milk, fruits, and flowers on the prescribed day which is observed as a feast day." They wash the stones, smear them with turmeric, and offer them curds and fruits. Sometimes they search out the dens of serpents and pour milk into the holes for the live reptiles.[1]

§ 7. *Reincarnation of the Dead*

Belief that
the dead
come to
life in the
form of
serpents.

The reason why snakes were so often supposed to be the fathers of human beings is probably to be found in the common belief that the dead come to life and revisit their old homes in the shape of serpents.

This notion is widely spread in Africa, especially among tribes of the Bantu stock. It is held, for example, by the Zulus, the Thonga, and other Caffre tribes of South Africa;[2] by the Ngoni of British Central Africa;[3] by the Wabondei,[4] the Masai,[5] the Suk,[6] the Nandi,[7] and the Akikuyu of German and British East Africa;[8] and by the Dinkas of

---

[1] H. V. Nanjundayya, *The Ethnographical Survey of Mysore*, vi. *Komati Caste* (Bangalore, 1906), p. 29.

[2] T. Arbousset et F. Daumas, *Voyage d'Exploration au Nord-Est de la Colonie du Cap de Bonne-Espérance* (Paris, 1842), p. 277; H. Callaway, *Religious System of the Amazulu*, part ii. pp. 140-144, 196-200, 208-212; J. Shooter, *The Kafirs of Natal* (London, 1857), p. 162; E. Casalis, *The Basutos* (London, 1861), p. 246; "Words about Spirits," (*South African*) *Folk-lore Journal*, ii. (1880) pp. 101-103; A. Kranz, *Natur- und Kulturleben der Zulus* (Wiesbaden, 1880), p. 112; F. Speckmann, *Die Hermannsburger Mission in Afrika* (Hermannsburg, 1876), pp. 165-167; Dudley Kidd, *The Essential Kafir* (London, 1904),

pp. 85-87; Henri A. Junod, *The Life of a South African Tribe* (Neuchatel, 1912–1913), ii. 358 *sq.*

[3] W. A. Elmslie, *Among the Wild Ngoni* (London, 1899), pp. 71 *sq.*

[4] O. Baumann, *Usambara und seine Nachbargebiete* (Berlin, 1891), pp. 141 *sq.*

[5] S. L. Hinde and H. Hinde, *The Last of the Masai* (London, 1901), pp. 101 *sq.*; A. C. Hollis, *The Masai* (Oxford, 1905), pp. 307 *sq.*; Sir H. Johnston, *The Uganda Protectorate* (London, 1904), ii. 832.

[6] M. W. H. Beech, *The Suk* (Oxford, 1911), p. 20.

[7] A. C. Hollis, *The Nandi* (Oxford, 1909), p. 90.

[8] H. R. Tate, "The Native Law of the Southern Gikuyu of British East

the Upper Nile.[1]   It prevails also among the Betsileo and other tribes of Madagascar.[2]   Among the Iban or Sea Dyaks of Borneo a man's guardian spirit (*Tua*) "has its external manifestation in a snake, a leopard or some other denizen of the forest.   It is supposed to be the spirit of some ancestor renowned for bravery or some other virtue who at death has taken an animal form.   It is a custom among the Iban when a person of note in the tribe dies, not to bury the body but to place it on a neighbouring hill or in some solitary spot above ground.   A quantity of food is taken to the place every day, and if after a few days the body disappears, the deceased is said to have become a *Tua* or guardian spirit.   People who have been suffering from some chronic complaint often go to such a tomb, taking with them an offering to the soul of the deceased to obtain his help.   To such it is revealed in a dream what animal form the honoured dead has taken.   The most frequent form is that of a snake.   Thus when a snake is found in a Dyak house it is seldom killed or driven away ; food is offered to it, for it is a guardian spirit who has come to inquire after the welfare of its clients and bring them good luck.   Anything that may be found in the mouth of such a snake is taken and kept as a charm."[3]   Similarly in

Africa," *Journal of the African Society*, No. xxxv. April 1910, p. 243.

[1] E. de Pruyssenaere, *Reisen und Forschungen im Gebiete des Weissen und Blauen Nil* (Gotha, 1877), p. 27 (*Petermann's Mittheilungen, Ergänzungsheft*, No. 50). Compare G. Schweinfurth, *The Heart of Africa*[3] (London, 1878), i. 55. Among the Bahima of Ankole dead chiefs turn into serpents, but dead kings into lions. See J. Roscoe, "The Bahima, a Cow Tribe of Enkole in the Uganda Protectorate," *Journal of the Anthropological Institute*, xxxvii. (1907), pp. 101 *sq.*; Major J. A. Meldon, "Notes on the Bahima of Ankole," *Journal of the African Society*, No. xxii. (January 1907), p. 151. Major Leonard holds that the pythons worshipped in Southern Nigeria are regarded as reincarnations of the dead ; but this seems very doubtful. See A. G. Leonard, *The*

Lower Niger and its Tribes (London, 1906), pp. 327 *sqq.*   Pythons are worshipped by the Ewe-speaking peoples of the Slave Coast, but apparently not from a belief that the souls of the dead are lodged in them. See A. B. Ellis, *The Ewe-speaking Peoples of the Slave Coast of West Africa*, pp. 54 *sqq.*

[2] G. A. Shaw, "The Betsileo," *The Antananarivo Annual and Madagascar Magazine, Reprint of the First Four Numbers* (Antananarivo, 1885), p. 411 ; H. W. Little, *Madagascar, its History and People* (London, 1884), pp. 86 *sq.* ; A. van Gennep, *Tabou et Totémisme à Madagascar* (Paris, 1904), pp. 272 *sqq.*

[3] "Religious Rites and Customs of the Iban or Dyaks of Sarawak," by Leo Nyuak, translated from the Dyak by the Very Rev. Edm. Dunn, *Anthropos*, i. (1906) p. 182. As to

Kiriwina, an island of the Trobriands Group, to the east of New Guinea, "the natives regarded the snake as one of their ancestral chiefs, or rather as the abode of his spirit, and when one was seen in a house it was believed that the chief was paying a visit to his old home. The natives considered this as an ill omen and so always tried to persuade the animal to depart as soon as possible. The honours of a chief were paid to the snake : the natives passed it in a crouching posture, and as they did so, saluted it as a chief of high rank. Native property was presented to it as an appeasing gift, accompanied by prayers that it would not do them any harm, but would go away quickly. They dared not kill the snake, for its death would bring disease and death upon those who did so." [1]

Serpents which are viewed as ancestors come to life are treated with respect and often fed with milk.

Where serpents are thus viewed as ancestors come to life, the people naturally treat them with great respect and often feed them with milk, perhaps because milk is the food of human babes and the reptiles are treated as human beings in embryo, who can be born again from women. Thus " the Zulu-Caffres imagine that their ancestors generally visit them under the form of serpents. As soon, therefore, as one of these reptiles appears near their dwellings, they hasten to salute it by the name of *father*, place bowls of milk in its way, and turn it back gently, and with the greatest respect." [2]   Among the Masai of East Africa, "when a medicine-man or a rich person dies and is buried, his soul turns into a snake as soon as his body rots ; and the snake goes to his children's kraal to look after them. The Masai in consequence do not kill their sacred snakes, and if a woman sees one in her hut, she pours some milk on the ground for it to lick, after which it will go away." [3]   Among

---

the Sea Dyak reverence for snakes and their belief that spirits (*antus*) are incarnate in the reptiles, see further J. Perham, "Sea Dyak Religion," *Journal of the Straits Branch of the Royal Asiatic Society*, No. 10 (December, 1882), pp. 222-224 ; H. Ling Roth, *The Natives of Sarawak and British North Borneo* (London, 1896), i. 187 *sq.* But from this latter account it does not appear that the spirits (*antus*) which possess the snakes

are supposed to be those of human ancestors.

[1] George Brown, D.D., *Melanesians and Polynesians* (London, 1910), pp. 238 *sq.*

[2] Rev. E. Casalis, *The Basutos* (London, 1861), p. 246.   Compare A. Kranz, *Natur- und Kulturleben der Zulus* (Wiesbaden, 1880), p. 112.

[3] A. C. Hollis, *The Masai* (Oxford, 1905), p. 307.

the Nandi of British East Africa, "if a snake goes on to the woman's bed, it may not be killed, as it is believed that it personifies the spirit of a deceased ancestor or relation, and that it has been sent to intimate to the woman that her next child will be born safely.   Milk is put on the ground for it to drink, and the man or his wife says : '. . . If thou wantest the call, come, thou art being called.'   It is then allowed to leave the house.   If a snake enters the houses of old people they give it milk, and say : 'If thou wantest the call, go to the huts of the children,' and they drive it away."[1] This association of the serpent, regarded as an incarnation of the dead, both with the marriage bed and with the huts of young people, points to a belief that the deceased person who is incarnate in the snake may be born again as a human child into the world.   Again, among the Suk of British East Africa "it seems to be generally believed that a man's spirit passes into a snake at death.   If a snake enters a house, the spirit of the dead man is believed to be very hungry.   Milk is poured on to its tracks, and a little meat and tobacco placed on the ground for it to eat.   It is believed that if no food is given to the snake one or all of the members of the household will die.   It, however, may none the less be killed if encountered outside the house, and if at the time of its death it is inhabited by the spirit of a dead man, 'that spirit dies also.'"[2]   The Akikuyu of British East Africa, who similarly believe that snakes are *ngoma* or spirits of the departed, "do not kill a snake but pour out honey and milk for it to drink, which they say it licks up and then goes its way   If a man causes the death of a snake he must without delay summon the senior Elders in the village and slaughter a sheep, which they eat and cut a *rukwaru* from the skin of its right shoulder for the offender to wear on his right wrist ; if this ceremony is neglected he, his wife and his children will die."[3]   Among

[1] A. C. Hollis, *The Nandi* (Oxford, 1909), p. 90.

[2] Mervyn W. H. Beech, *The Suk, their Language and Folklore* (Oxford, 1911), p. 20.

[3] H. R. Tate (District Commissioner, East Africa Protectorate), "The Native Law of the Southern Gikuyu of British East Africa," *Journal of the African Society*, No. xxxv., April 1910, p. 243.   See further C. W. Hobley, "Further Researches into Kikuyu and Kamba Religious Beliefs and Customs," *Journal of the Royal Anthropological Institute*, xli. (1911) p. 408.   According to Mr. Hobley it is only one parti-

the Baganda the python god Selwanga had his temple on the shore of the lake Victoria Nyanza, where he dwelt in the form of a live python. The temple was a hut of the ordinary conical shape with a round hole in the wall, through which the sinuous deity crawled out and in at his pleasure. A woman lived in the temple, and it was her duty to feed the python daily with fresh milk from a wooden bowl, which she held out to the divine reptile while he drained it. The serpent was thought to be the giver of children; hence young couples living in the neighbourhood always came to the shrine to ensure the blessing of the god on their union, and childless women repaired from long distances to be relieved by him from the curse of barrenness.[1] It is not said that this python god embodied the soul of a dead ancestor, but it may have been so; his power of bestowing offspring on women suggests it.

The Greeks and Romans seem to have shared the belief that the souls of the dead can be reincarnated in serpents.

The Romans and Greeks appear to have also believed that the souls of the dead were incarnate in the bodies of serpents. Among the Romans the regular symbol of the *genius* or guardian spirit of every man was a serpent,[2] and in Roman houses serpents were lodged and fed in such numbers that if their swarms had not been sometimes reduced by conflagrations there would have been no living for them.[3] In Greek legend Cadmus and his wife Harmonia

---

cular sort of snake, called *nyamuyathi*, which is thought to be the abode of a spirit and is treated with ceremonious respect by the Akikuyu. Compare P. Cayzac, "La Religion des Kikuyu," *Anthropos*, v. (1910) p. 312; and for more evidence of milk offered to serpents as embodiments of the dead see E. de Pruyssenaere and H. W. Little, cited above, p. 83, notes 1 and 2.

[1] Rev. J. Roscoe, *The Baganda* (London, 1911), pp. 320 *sq.* My friend Mr. Roscoe tells me that serpents are revered and fed with milk by the Banyoro to the north of Uganda; but he cannot say whether the creatures are supposed to be incarnations of the dead. Some of the Gallas also regard serpents as sacred and offer milk to them, but it is not said that they believe the reptiles to embody the

souls of the departed. See Rev. J. L. Krapf, *Travels, Researches and Missionary Labours in Eastern Africa* (London, 1860), pp. 77 *sq.* The negroes of Whydah in Guinea likewise feed with milk the serpents which they worship. See Thomas Astley's *New General Collection of Voyages and Travels*, iii. (London, 1746) p. 29.

[2] L. Preller, *Römische Mythologie*[3] (Berlin, 1881–1883), ii. 196 *sq.*; G. Wissowa, *Religion und Kultus der Römer*[2] (Munich, 1912), pp. 176 *sq.* The worship of the *genius* was very popular in the Roman Empire. See J. Toutain, *Les Cultes Païens dans l'Empire Romain*, Première Partie, i. (Paris, 1907) pp. 439 *sqq.*

[3] Pliny, *Nat. Hist.* xxix. 72. Compare Seneca, *De Ira*, iv. 31. 6.

were turned at death into snakes.[1]   When the Spartan king
Cleomenes was slain and crucified in Egypt, a great serpent
coiled round his head on the cross and kept off the vultures
from his face.   The people regarded the prodigy as a proof
that Cleomenes was a son of the gods.[2]   Again, when
Plotinus lay dying, a snake crawled from under his bed
and disappeared into a hole in the wall, and at the same
moment the philosopher expired.[3]   Apparently superstition
saw in these serpents the souls of the dead men.   In Greek
religion the serpent was indeed the regular symbol or
attribute of the worshipful dead,[4] and we can hardly doubt
that the early Greeks, like the Zulus and other African
tribes at the present day, really believed the soul of the
departed to be lodged in the reptile.   The sacred serpent
which lived in the Erechtheum at Athens, and was fed with
honey - cakes once a month, may have been supposed to
house the soul of the dead king Erechtheus, who had reigned
in his lifetime on the same spot.[5]   Perhaps the libations
of milk which the Greeks poured upon graves[6] were intended to be drunk by serpents as the embodiments of the
deceased ; on two tombstones found at Tegea a man and a
woman are respectively represented holding out to a serpent
a cup which may be supposed to contain milk.[7]   We have
seen that various African tribes feed serpents with milk
because they imagine the reptiles to be incarnations of their
dead kinsfolk ;[8] and the Dinkas, who practise the custom,
also pour milk on the graves of their friends for some time
after the burial.[9]   It is possible that a common type in
Greek art, which exhibits a woman feeding a serpent out of

---

[1] Apollodorus, *Bibliotheca*, iii. 5. 4 ;
Hyginus, *Fab.* 6 ; Ovid, *Metam.* iv.
563-603.

[2] Plutarch, *Cleomenes*, 39.

[3] Porphyry, *De vita Plotini*, p. 103,
Didot edition (appended to the lives of
Diogenes Laertius).

[4] Plutarch, *Cleomenes*, 39; Scholiast
on Aristophanes, *Plutus*, 733.

[5] Herodotus, viii. 41 ; Plutarch,
Themistocles, 10 ; Aristophanes, *Ly-
sistra*, 758 *sq.*, with the Scholium ;

Philostratus, *Imag.* ii. 17. 6.   See
further my note on Pausanias, i. 18. 2
(vol. ii. pp. 168 *sqq.*).

[6] Sophocles, *Electra*, 893 *sqq.* ;
Euripides, *Orestes*, 112 *sqq.*

[7] *Mittheilungen des Deutsch. Archäo-
log. Institutes in Athen*, iv. (1879)
pl. viii.   Compare *ib.* pp. 135 *sq.*,
162 *sq.*

[8] Above, pp. 84 *sq.*

[9] E. de Pruyssenaere, *l.c.* (above,
p. 83, note [1]).

a saucer, may have been borrowed from a practice of thus ministering to the souls of the departed.[1]

The serpents fed at the Thesmophoria may have been deemed incarnations of the dead.

Further, at the sowing festival of the Thesmophoria, held by Greek women in October, it was customary to throw cakes and pigs to serpents, which lived in caverns or vaults sacred to the corn-goddess Demeter.[2] We may guess that the serpents thus propitiated were deemed to be incarnations of dead men and women, who might easily be incommoded in their earthy beds by the operations of husbandry. What indeed could be more disturbing than to have the roof of the narrow house shaken and rent over their heads by clumsy oxen dragging a plough up and down on the top of it? No wonder that at such times it was thought desirable to appease them with offerings. Sometimes, however, it is not the dead but the Earth Goddess herself who is disturbed by the husbandman. An Indian prophet at Priest Rapids, on the Middle Columbia River, dissuaded his many followers from tilling the ground because "it is a sin to wound or cut, tear up or scratch our common mother by agricultural pursuits."[3] · "You ask me," said this Indian sage, "to plough the ground. Shall I take a knife and tear my mother's bosom? You ask me to dig for stone. Shall I dig under her skin for her bones? You ask me to cut grass and hay and sell it and be rich like white men. But

Reluctance to disturb the Earth Goddess or the spirits of the earth by the operations of digging and ploughing.

[1] See C. O. Müller, *Denkmäler der alten Kunst*[2] (Göttingen, 1854), pl. lxi. with the corresponding text in vol. i. (where the eccentric system of paging adopted renders references to it practically useless). In these groups the female figure is commonly, and perhaps correctly, interpreted as the Goddess of Health (Hygieia). It is to be remembered that Hygieia was deemed a daughter of the serpent-god Aesculapius (Pausanias, i. 23. 4), and was constantly associated with him in ritual and art. See, for example, Pausanias, i. 40. 6, ii. 4. 5, ii. 11. 6, ii. 23. 4, ii. 27. 6, iii. 22. 13, v. 20. 3, v. 26. 2, vii. 23. 7, viii. 28. 1, viii. 31. 1, viii. 32. 4, viii. 47. 1. The snake-entwined goddess whose image was found in a prehistoric shrine at Gournia in Crete may have been a predecessor of the serpent-feeding Hygieia. See R. M. Burrows, *The Discoveries in Crete* (London, 1907), pp. 137 *sq.* The snakes, which were the regular symbol of the Furies, may have been originally nothing but the emblems or rather embodiments of the dead; and the Furies themselves may, like Aesculapius, have been developed out of the reptiles, sloughing off their serpent skins through the anthropomorphic tendency of Greek thought.

[2] Scholia on Lucian, *Dial. Meretr.* ii. (*Scholia in Lucianum*, ed. H. Rabe, Leipsic, 1906, pp. 275 *sq.*). As to the Thesmophoria, see my article, "Thesmophoria," *Encyclopaedia Britannica*,[9] xxiii. 295 *sqq.*; *Spirits of the Corn and of the Wild*, ii. 17 *sqq.*

[3] A. S. Gatschet, *The Klamath Indians of South-Western Oregon* (Washington, 1890), p. xcii.

how dare I cut off my mother's hair?"[1]   The Baigas, a primitive Dravidian tribe of the Central Provinces in India, used to practise a fitful and migratory agriculture, burning down patches of jungle and sowing seed in the soil fertilized by the ashes after the breaking of the rains.   "One explanation of their refusal to till the ground is that they consider it a sin to lacerate the breast of their mother earth with a ploughshare."[2]   In China the disturbance caused to the earth-spirits by the operations of digging and ploughing was so very serious that Chinese philosophy appears to have contemplated a plan for allowing the perturbed spirits a close time by forbidding the farmer to put his spade or his plough into the ground except on certain days, when the earth-spirits were either not at home or kindly consented to put up with some temporary inconvenience for the good of man.   This we may infer from a passage in a Chinese author who wrote in the first century of our era.   "If it is true," he says, "that the spirits who inhabit the soil object to it being disturbed and dug up, then it is proper for us to select special good days for digging ditches and ploughing our fields.   (But this is never done); it therefore follows that the spirits of the soil, even though really annoyed when it is disturbed, pass over such an offence if man commits it without evil intent.   As he commits it merely to ensure his rest and comfort, the act cannot possibly excite any anger against him in the perfect heart of those spirits ; and this being the case, they will not visit him with misfortune even if he do not choose auspicious days for it.   But if we believe that the earth-spirits cannot excuse man on account of the object he pursues, and detest him for annoying them by disturbing the ground, what advantage then can he derive from selecting proper days for doing so?"[3]   What advantage indeed?   In that case the only logical conclusion is, with the Indian prophet, to forbid agriculture altogether, as an impious encroachment on the spiritual world.   Few peoples, however, who have once contracted the habit of agri-

---

[1] Washington Matthews, "Myths of Gestation and Parturition," *American Anthropologist*, New Series, iv. (New York, 1902) p. 738.

[2] *Central Provinces, Ethnographic Survey*, iii. *Draft Articles on Forest Tribes* (Allahabad, 1907), p. 23.

[3] J. J. M. de Groot, *The Religious System of China*, v. (Leyden, 1907) pp. 536 *sq.*

culture are willing to renounce it out of a regard for the
higher powers ; the utmost concession which they are willing to make to religion in the matter is to prohibit agricultural operations at certain times and seasons, when the
exercise of them would be more than usually painful to the
earth-spirits.   Thus in Bengal the chief festival in honour
of Mother Earth is held at the end of the hot season, when
she is supposed to suffer from the impurity common to
women, and during that time all ploughing, sowing, and
other work cease.[1]   On a certain day of the year, when
offerings are made to the Earth, the Ewe farmer of West
Africa will not hoe the ground, and the Ewe weaver will not
drive a sharp stake into it, " because the hoe and the stake
would wound the Earth and cause her pain." [2]   When
Ratumaimbulu, the god who made fruit-trees to blossom
and bear fruit, came once a year to Fiji, the people had to
live very quietly for a month lest they should disturb him
at his important work.   During this time they might not
plant nor build nor sail about nor go to war ; indeed most
kinds of work were forbidden.   The priests announced the
time of the god's arrival and departure.[3]   These periods of
rest and quiet would seem to be the Indian and Fijian Lent.

Thus behind the Greek notion that women may conceive
by a serpent-god [4] seems to lie the belief that they can conceive by the dead in the form of serpents.   If such a belief
was ever held, it would be natural that barren women should
resort to graves in order to have their wombs quickened, and
this may explain why they visited the shrine of the serpent-
god Aesculapius for that purpose ; the shrine was perhaps
at first a grave.   It is significant that in Syria the shrines
of St. George, to which childless women go to get offspring,
always include a tomb or the likeness of one ; [5] and further,

[1] W. Crooke, *Natives of Northern India* (London, 1907), p. 232.
[2] J. Spieth, *Die Ewe - Stämme* (Berlin, 1906), p. 796.
[3] J. E. Erskine, *Journal of a Cruise among the Islands of the Western Pacific* (London, 1853), pp. 245 *sq.*
[4] Persons initiated into the mysteries of Sabazius had a serpent drawn through the bosom of their robes, and the reptile

was identified with the god (ὁ διὰ κόλπου θεός, Clement of Alexandria, *Protrept.* ii. 16, p. 14, ed. Potter).   This may be a trace of the belief that women can be impregnated by serpents, though it does not appear that the ceremony was performed only on women.
[5] See above, p. 78.   Among the South Slavs women go to graves to get children.   See below, p. 96.

that in the opinion of Syrian peasants at the present day
women may, without intercourse with a living man, bear
children to a dead husband, a dead saint, or a jinnee.[1]   In
the East Indies also it is still commonly believed that spirits
can consort with women and beget children on them.   The
Olo Ngadjoe of Borneo imagine that albinoes are the offspring of the spirit of the moon by mortal women, the pallid
hue of the human children naturally reflecting the pallor of
their heavenly father.[2]

Such beliefs are closely akin to the idea, entertained by
many peoples, that the souls of the dead may pass directly into
the wombs of women and be born again as infants.   Thus
the Hurons used to bury little children beside the paths in
the hope that their souls might enter the passing squaws
and be born again;[3] and similarly some negroes of West
Africa throw the bodies of infants into the bush in order
that their souls may choose a new mother from the women
who pass by.[4]   Among the tribes of the Lower Congo "a
baby is always buried near the house of its mother, never
in the bush.   They think that, if the child is not buried
near its mother's house, she will be unlucky and never have
any more children."   The notion probably is that the dead
child, buried near its mother's house, will enter into her
womb and be born again, for these people believe in the
reincarnation of the dead.   They think that "the only new
thing about a child is its body.   The spirit is old and
formerly belonged to some deceased person, or it may have
the spirit of some living person."   For example, if a child
is like its mother, father, or uncle, they imagine that it must

*Reincar-
nation of
the dead in
America
and Africa.*

---

[1] S. I. Curtiss, *Primitive Semitic
Religion To-day*, pp. 115 *sqq.*

[2] A. C. Kruijt, *Het Animisme in den
Indischen Archipel* (The Hague, 1906),
p. 398.

[3] *Relations des Jésuites*, 1636, p.
130 (Canadian reprint, Quebec, 1858).
A similar custom was practised for a
similar reason by the Musquakie
Indians.   See Miss Mary Alicia Owen,
*Folk-lore of the Musquakie Indians of
North America* (London, 1904), pp.
22 *sq.*, 86.   Some of the instances
here given have been already cited by

Mr. J. E. King, who suggests, with
much probability, that the special
modes of burial adopted for infants in
various parts of the world may often
have been intended to ensure their rebirth.   See J. E. King, "Infant
Burial," *Classical Review*, xvii. (1903)
pp. 83 *sq.*   For a large collection of
evidence as to the belief in the reincarnation of the dead, see E. S. Hartland, *Primitive Paternity* (London,
1909–1910), i. 156 *sqq.*

[4] Mary H. Kingsley, *Travels in
West Africa* (London, 1897), p. 478.

have the spirit of the relative whom it resembles, and that
therefore the person whose soul has thus been abstracted by
the infant will soon die.[1]   Among the Bangalas, a tribe of
cannibals in Equatorial Africa, to the north of the Congo, a
woman was one day seen digging a hole in the public road.
Her husband entreated a Belgian officer to let her alone,
promising to mend the road afterwards, and explaining that
his wife wished to become a mother.   The good-natured
officer complied with his request and watched the woman.
She continued to dig till she had uncovered a little skeleton,
the remains of her first-born, which she tenderly embraced,
humbly entreating the dead child to enter into her and give
her again a mother's joy.   The officer rightly did not smile.[2]
The Bagishu, a Bantu tribe of Mount Elgon, in the Uganda
Protectorate, practise the custom of throwing out their dead
" except in the case of the youngest child or the old grand-
father or grandmother, for whom, like the child, a prolonged
life on earth is desired. . . . When it is desired to perpetuate on the earth the life of some old man or woman, or
that of some young baby, the corpse is buried inside the
house or just under the eaves, until another child is born to
the nearest relation of the corpse.   This child, male or
female, takes the name of the corpse, and the Bagishu
firmly believe that the spirit of the dead has passed into
this new child and lives again on earth.   The remains are
then dug up and thrown out into the open."[3]

Measures
taken to
prevent the
rebirth of
undesir-
able spirits.

Again, just as measures are adopted to facilitate the rebirth
of good ghosts, so on the other hand precautions are taken
to prevent the rebirth of bad ones.   Thus, with regard to the
Baganda of Central Africa we read that, "while the present
generation know the cause of pregnancy, the people in the
earlier times were uncertain as to its real cause, and thought
that it was possible to conceive without any intercourse with
the male sex.   Hence their precautions in passing places where

[1] Rev. John H. Weeks, "Notes on
some Customs of the Lower Congo
People," Folk-lore, xix. (1908) p.
422.

[2] Th. Masui, Guide de la Section de
l'État Indépendant du Congo à l'Ex-
position de Bruxelles - Tervueren en
1897 (Brussels, 1897), pp. 113 sq.

[3] J. B. Purvis, Through Uganda to
Mount Elgon (London, 1909), pp.
302 sq.   As to the Bagishu or Bageshu
and their practice of throwing out the
dead, see Rev. J. Roscoe, "Notes on
the Bageshu," Journal of the Royal
Anthropological Institute, xxxix. (1909)
pp. 181 sqq.

either a suicide had been burnt, or a child born feet first had been buried. Women were careful to throw grass or sticks on such a spot, for by so doing they thought that they could prevent the ghost of the dead from entering into them, and being reborn."[1] The fear of being got with child by such ghosts was not confined to married women, it was shared by all women alike, whether young or old, whether married or single ; and all of them sought to avert the danger in the same way.[2] And Baganda women imagined that without the help of the other sex they could be impregnated not only by these unpleasant ghosts but also by the flower of the banana. If while a woman was busy in her garden under the shadow of the banana trees, a great purple bloom chanced to fall from one of the trees on her back or shoulders, it was quite enough, in the opinion of the Baganda, to get her with child ; and were a wife accused of adultery because she gave birth to a child who could not possibly have been begotten by her husband, she had only to father the infant on a banana flower to be honourably acquitted of the charge. The reason why this remarkable property was ascribed to the bloom of the banana would seem to be that ghosts of ancestors were thought to haunt banana groves, and that the afterbirths of children, which the Baganda regarded as twins of the children, were commonly buried at the root of the trees.[3] What more natural than that a ghost should lurk in each flower, and dropping adroitly in the likeness of a blossom on a woman's back effect a lodgment in her womb?

Again, when a child dies in Northern India it is usually buried under the threshold of the house, " in the belief that as

Belief of the Baganda that a woman can be impregnated by the flower of the banana.

---

[1] Rev. J. Roscoe, *The Baganda* (London, 1911), pp. 46 *sq.* Women adopted a like precaution at the grave of twins to prevent the ghosts of the twins from entering into them and being born again (*id.*, pp. 124 *sq.*). The Baganda always strangled children that were born feet first and buried their bodies at cross-roads. The heaps of sticks or grass thrown on these graves by passing women and girls rose in time into mounds large enough to deflect the path and to attract the notice of travellers. See J. Roscoe, *op. cit.* pp. 126 *sq.*, 289.

[2] Rev. J. Roscoe, *op. cit.* pp. 126 *sq.* In the Senegal and Niger region of Western Africa it is said to be commonly believed by women that they can conceive without any carnal knowledge of a man. See Maurice Delafosse, *Haut - Sénégal - Niger, Le Pays, les Peuples, les Langues, l'Histoire, les Civilisations* (Paris, 1912), iii. 171.

[3] Rev. J. Roscoe, *The Baganda*, pp. 47 *sq.* ; *Totemism and Exogamy*, ii. 506 *sq.* As to the custom of depositing the afterbirths of children at the foot of banana (plantain) trees, see J. Roscoe, *op. cit.* pp. 52, 54 *sq.*

Reincar-
nation of
the dead
in India.
Means
taken to
facilitate
the rebirth
of dead
children.

the parents tread daily over its grave, its soul will be reborn
in the family.   Here, as Mr. Rose suggests, we reach an
explanation of the rule that children of Hindus are buried,
not cremated.   Their souls do not pass into the ether with the
smoke of the pyre, but remain on earth to be reincarnated
in the household." [1]   In the Punjaub this belief in the reincarnation of dead infants gives rise to some quaint or
pathetic customs.   Thus, " in the Hissar District, Bishnois
bury dead infants at the threshold, in the belief that it would
facilitate the return of the soul to the mother.   The practice
is also in vogue in the Kangra District, where the body is
buried in front of the back door.   In some places it is
believed that, if the child dies in infancy and the mother
drops her milk for two or three days on the ground, the soul
of the child comes back to be born again.   For this purpose
milk diluted with water is placed in a small earthen pot
and offered to the dead child's spirit for three consecutive
evenings.   There is also a belief in the Ambala and Gujrat
Districts that if jackals and dogs dig out the dead body of
the child and bring it towards the town or village, it means
that the child will return to its mother, but if they take it
to some other side, the soul will reincarnate in some other
family.   For this purpose, the second day after the infant's
death, the mother goes out early in the morning to see
whether the dogs have brought the body towards the village.
When the child is being taken away for burial the mother
cuts off and preserves a piece of its garment with a view to
persuade the soul to return to her.   Barren women or those
who have lost children in infancy tear a piece off the clothing
of a dead child and stitch it to their wearing apparel,
believing that the soul of the child will return to them
instead of its own mother.   On this account, people take
great care not to lose the clothes of dead children, and
some bury them in the house." [2]   In Bilaspore " a still-born
child, or one who has passed away before the *Chhatti* (the
sixth day, the day of purification) is not taken out of the

[1] W. Crooke, *Natives of Northern
India* (London, 1907), p. 202.   As to
the Hindoo custom of burying infants
but burning older persons, see *The
Belief in Immortality and the Worship*
of the Dead, i. 162 *sq.*
[2] *Census of India, 1911*, vol. xiv.
Punjab, Part i., Report, by Pandit
Harikishan Kaul (Lahore, 1912), p.
299.

house for burial, but is placed in an earthen vessel and is buried in the doorway or in the yard of the house. Some say that this is done in order that the mother may bear another child."[1] Here in Bilaspore the people have devised a very simple way of identifying a dead person when he or she is born again as an infant. When anybody dies, they mark the body with soot or oil, and the next baby born in the family with a similar mark is hailed as the departed come to life again.[2] Among the Kois of the Godavari district, in Southern India, the dead are usually burnt, but the bodies of children and of young men and women are buried. If a child dies within a month of its birth, it is generally buried close to the house " so that the rain, dripping from the eaves, may fall upon the grave, and thereby cause the parents to be blessed with another child."[3] Apparently it is supposed that the soul of the dead child, refreshed and revived by the rain, will pass again into the mother's womb. Indian criminal records contain many cases in which " the ceremonial killing of a male child has been performed as a cure for barrenness, the theory being that the soul of the murdered boy becomes reincarnated in the woman, who performs the rite with a desire to secure offspring. Usually she effects union with the spirit of the child by bathing over its body or in the water in which the corpse has been washed. Cases have recently occurred in which the woman actually bathed in the blood of the child."[4]

On the fifth day after a death the Gonds perform the ceremony of bringing back the soul. They go to the bank of a river, call aloud the name of the deceased, and entering the water catch a fish or an insect. This creature they then take home and place among the sainted dead of the family, supposing that in this manner the spirit of the departed has been brought back to the house. Sometimes the fish or

Bringing back the soul of the dead in a fish or insect.

---

[1] E. M. Gordon, *Indian Folk Tales* (London, 1908), p. 49. Other explanations of the custom are reported by the writer, but the original motive was probably a desire to secure the reincarnation of the dead child in the mother.

[2] E. M. Gordon, *op. cit.* pp. 50 *sq.*

[3] E. Thurston, *Ethnographic Notes in Southern India* (Madras, 1906), p. 155; *id., Castes and Tribes of Southern India* (Madras, 1909), iv. 52.

[4] W. Crooke, *Natives of Northern India*, p. 202; *Census of India, 1901*, vol. xvii. *Punjab*, Part i., Report, by H. A. Rose (Simla, 1902), pp. 213 *sq.*

Stories of the Virgin Birth.

insect is eaten in the belief that it will be thus reborn as a child.[1] This last custom explains the widely diffused story of virgins who have conceived by eating of a plant or an animal or merely by taking it to their bosom.[2] In all such cases we may surmise that the plant or animal was thought to contain the soul of a dead person, which thus passed into the virgin's womb and was born again as an infant. Among the South Slavs childless women often resort to a grave in which a pregnant woman is buried. There they bite some grass from the grave, invoke the deceased by name, and beg her to give them the fruit of her womb. After that they take a little of the mould from the grave and carry it about with them thenceforth under their girdle.[3] Apparently they imagine that the soul of the unborn infant is in the grass or the mould and will pass from it into their body.

Reincarnation of the dead among the South Slavs.

Belief of the Kai that women may be impregnated without sexual intercourse.

Among the Kai of German New Guinea, "impossible as it may be thought, it is yet a fact that women here and there deny in all seriousness the connexion between sexual intercourse and pregnancy. Of course most people are clear as to the process. The ignorance of some individuals is perhaps based on the consideration that not uncommonly married women remain childless for years or for life. Finally, the animistic faith contributes its share to support the

---

[1] *Census of India, 1901*, vol. xiii. *Central Provinces*, Part i., Report, by R. V. Russell (Nagpur, 1902), p. 93.

[2] For stories of such virgin births see Comte H. de Charency, *Le folklore dans les deux Mondes* (Paris, 1894), pp. 121-256; E. S. Hartland, *The Legend of Perseus*, vol. i. (London, 1894) pp. 71 *sqq.*; and my note on Pausanias vii. 17. 11 (vol. iv. pp. 138-140). To the instances there cited by me add : A. Thevet, *Cosmographie Universelle* (Paris, 1575), ii. 918 [wrongly numbered 952]; K. von den Steinen, *Unter den Naturvölkern Zentral-Brasiliens* (Berlin, 1884), pp. 370, 373; H. A. Coudreau, *La France Equinoxiale*, ii. (Paris, 1887) pp. 184 *sq.*; *Relations des Jésuites*, 1637, pp. 123 *sq.* (Canadian reprint, Quebec, 1858); Franz Boas, *Indianische Sagen von der Nord-Pacifischen Küste Amerikas* (Berlin, 1895), pp. 311 *sq.*; A.

G. Morice, *Au pays de l'Ours Noir* (Paris and Lyons, 1897, p. 153; A. Raffray, "Voyage à la côte nord de la Nouvelle Guinée," *Bulletin de la Société de Géographie* (Paris), VIe Série, xv. (1878) pp. 392 *sq.*; J. L. van der Toorn, "Het animisme bij den Minangkabauer der Padangsche Bovenlanden," *Bijdragen tot de Taal- Land- en Volkenkunde van Nederlandsch-Indië*, xxxix. (1890) p. 78; E. Aymonier, "Les Tchames et leurs religions," *Revue de l'Histoire des Religions*, xxiv. (1901) pp. 215 *sq.*; Major P. R. T. Gurdon, *The Khasis* (London, 1907), p. 195. In some stories the conception is brought about not by eating food but by drinking water. But the principle is the same.

[3] F. S. Krauss, *Sitte und Brauch der Süd-Slaven* (Vienna, 1885), p. 531.

ignorance."[1]   In some islands of Southern Melanesia the
natives appear similarly to believe that sexual intercourse is
not necessary to impregnation, and that a woman can conceive through the simple passage into her womb of a spirit-
animal or a spirit-fruit without the help of a man.   In the
island of Mota, one of the Banks' group, " the course of events
is usually as follows : a woman sitting down in her garden
or in the bush or on the shore finds an animal or fruit in her
loincloth.   She takes it up and carries it to the village,
where she asks the meaning of the appearance.   The people
say that she will give birth to a child who will have the
characters of this animal or even, it appeared, would be
himself or herself the animal.   The woman then takes the
creature back to the place where she had found it and places
it in its proper home ; if it is a land animal on the land ; if
a water animal in the pool or stream from which it had
probably come.   She builds up a wall round it and goes to
feed and visit it every day.   After a time the animal will
disappear, and it is believed that that is because the animal
has at the time of its disappearance entered into the woman.
It seemed quite clear that there was no belief in physical
impregnation on the part of the animal, nor of the entry of
a material object in the form of the animal into her womb,
but so far as I could gather, an animal found in this way
was regarded as more or less supernatural, a spirit animal
and not one material, from the beginning.   It has happened
in the memory of an old man now living in Mota that a
woman who has found an animal in her loincloth has carried
it carefully in her closed hands to the village, but that when
she opened her hands to show it to the people, the animal
has gone, and in this case it was believed that the entry had
taken place while the woman was on her way from the bush
to the village. . . .   When the child is born it is regarded as
being in some sense the animal or fruit which had been found
and tended by the mother.   The child may not eat the
animal during the whole of its life, and if it does so, will
suffer serious illness, if not death.   If it is a fruit which has
been found, the child may not eat this fruit or touch the tree

*Belief in
the island
of Mota
that a
woman can
conceive
through
the
entrance
into her of
a spirit
animal or
fruit.*

[1] Ch. Keysser, "Aus dem Leben   *Neu - Guinea*, iii. (Berlin, 1911) p.
der Kaileute," in R. Neuhauss's *Deutsch*   26.

on which it grows, the latter restriction remaining in those
cases in which the fruit is inedible. . . . I inquired into the
idea at the bottom of the prohibition of the animal as food,
and it appeared to be that the person would be eating
himself. It seemed that the act would be regarded as a kind
of cannibalism. It was evident that there is a belief in the
most intimate relation between the person and all individuals
of the species with which he is identified.

" A further aspect of the belief in the animal nature of
a child is that it partakes of the physical and mental characters of the animal with which it is identified. Thus, if the
animal found has been a sea-snake, and this is a frequent
occurrence, the child would be weak, indolent and slow ; if
an eel, there will be a similar disposition ; if ｜a hermit crab,
the child will be hot-tempered ; if a flying fox, it will also
be hot-tempered and the body will be dark ; if a brush
turkey, the disposition will be good ; if a lizard, the child
will be soft and gentle ; if a rat, thoughtless, hasty and
intemperate. If the object found has been a fruit, here also
the child will partake of its nature. In the case of a wild
Malay apple (*malmalagaviga*) the child will have a big
belly, and a person with this condition will be asked, ' Do
you come from the *malmalagaviga*? ' Again, if the fruit is
one called *womarakaraqat*, the child will have a good
disposition.

Similar
belief in
the island
of Motlav. " In the island of Motlav not far from Mota they have
the same belief that if a mother has found an animal in her
dress, the child will be identified with that animal and will
not be allowed to eat it. Here again the child is believed
to have the characters of the animal, and two instances given
were that a child identified with a yellow crab will have a
good disposition and be of a light colour, while if a hermit
crab has been found, the child will be angry and disagreeable.
In this island a woman who desires her child to have certain
characters will frequent a place where she will be likely to
encounter the animal which causes the appearance of these
characters. Thus, if she wants to have a light coloured child,
she will go to a place where there are light coloured crabs." [1]

[1] W. H. R. Rivers, " Totemism in   *the Royal Anthropological Institute,*
Polynesia and Melanesia," *Journal of*   xxxix. (1909) pp. 173-175. Compare

Throughout a large part of Australia, particularly in the Australian beliefs as to the birth of children. Centre, the North, and the West, the aborigines hold that the commerce of the human sexes is not necessary to the production of children; indeed many of them go further and deny that sexual intercourse is the real cause of the propagation of the species. Among the Arunta, Kaitish, Luritcha, Ilpirra and other tribes, who roam the barren steppes of Central Australia, it appears to be a universal article of belief that every person is the reincarnation of a deceased ancestor, and that the souls of the dead pass directly Reincarnation of the dead in Central Australia. into the wombs of women, who give them birth without the need of commerce with the other sex. They think that the spirits of the departed gather and dwell at particular spots, marked by a natural feature such as a rock or a tree, and that from these lurking-places they dart out and enter the bodies of passing women or girls. When a woman feels her womb quickened, she knows that a spirit has made its way into her from the nearest abode of the dead. This is their regular explanation of conception and childbirth. " The natives, one and all in these tribes, believe that the child is the direct result of the entrance into the mother of an ancestral spirit individual. They have no idea of pro-creation as being associated with sexual intercourse, and firmly believe that children can be born without this taking place." [1]   The spots where the souls thus congregate wait-

---

Totemism and Exogamy, ii. 89 *sqq.* As to this Melanesian belief that animals can enter into women and be born from them as human children with animal characteristics, Dr. Rivers observes (p. 174): "It was clear that this belief was not accompanied by any ignorance of the physical *rôle* of the human father, and that the father played the same part in conception as in cases of birth unaccompanied by an animal appearance. We found it im-possible to get definitely the belief as to the nature of the influence exerted by the animal on the woman, but it must be remembered that any belief of this kind can hardly have escaped the many years of European influence and Christian teaching which the people of this group have received. It is doubtful

whether even a prolonged investigation of this point could now elicit the ori-ginal belief of the people about the nature of the influence." To me it seems that the belief described by Dr. Rivers in the text is incompatible with the recognition of human fatherhood as a necessary condition for the birth of children, and that though the people may now recognize that necessity, perhaps as a result of intercourse with Europeans, they certainly cannot have recognized it at the time when the belief in question originated.

[1] Baldwin Spencer and F. J. Gillen, *Northern Tribes of Central Australia* (London, 1904), p. 330, compare *id. ibid.* pp. xi, 145, 147-151, 155 *sq.*, 161 *sq.*, 169 *sq.*, 173 *sq.*, 174-176, 606; *id., Native Tribes of Central*

ing to be born again are usually the places where the remote ancestors of the dream-time are said to have passed into the ground ; that is, they are the places where the fore-fathers of the tribe are supposed to have died or to have been buried.   For example, in the Warramunga tribe the ancestor of the Black-snake clan is said to have left many spirits of Black-snake children in the rocks and trees which border a certain creek.   Hence no woman at the present day dares to strike one of these trees with an axe, being quite convinced that the blow would release one of the spirit-children, who would at once enter her body.   They imagine that the spirit is no larger than a grain of sand, and that it enters the woman through her navel and grows into a child in her womb.[1]   Again, at several places in the wide terri-tory of the Arunta tribe there are certain stones which are in like manner thought to be the abode of souls awaiting re-birth.   Hence the stones are called " child-stones."   In one of them there is a hole through which the spirit-children look out for passing women, and it is firmly believed that a visit to the stone would result in conception.   If a young woman is obliged to pass near the stone and does not wish to have a child, she will carefully disguise her youth, pulling a wry face and hobbling along on a stick.   She will bend herself double like a very old woman, and imitating the cracked voice of age she will say, " Don't come to me, I am an old woman."   Nay, it is thought that women may conceive by the stone without visiting it.   If a man and his wife both wish for a child, the husband will tie his hair-girdle round the stone, rub it, and mutter a direction to the spirits to give heed to his wife.   And it is believed that by performing a similar ceremony a malicious man can cause women and even children at a distance to be pregnant.[2]

Reincarna-tion of the dead in Northern Australia.

Such beliefs are not confined to the tribes of Central Australia but prevail among all the tribes from Lake Eyre northwards to the sea and the Gulf of Carpentaria.[3]   Thus

---

Australia (London, 1899), pp. 52, 123-125, 126, 132 *sq.*, 265, 335-338.

[1] B. Spencer and F. J. Gillen, *Northern Tribes of Central Australia*, pp. 162, 330 *sq.*

[2] B. Spencer and F. J. Gillen,

Native Tribes of Central Australia, pp. 337 *sq.*

[3] W. Baldwin Spencer, *An Intro-duction to the Study of Certain Native Tribes of the Northern Territory* (Mel-bourne, 1912), p. 6: "The two

the Mungarai say that in the far past time their old ancestors walked about the country, making all the natural features of the landscape and leaving spirit-children behind them where they stopped.   These children emanated from the bodies of the ancestors, and they still wait at various spots looking out for women into whom they may go and be born.   For example, near McMinn's bar on the Roper River there is a large gum tree full of spirit-children, who all belong to one particular totem and are always agog to enter into women of that totem.   Again, at Crescent Lagoon an ancestor, who belonged to the thunder totem, deposited numbers of spirit-children ; and if a woman of the Gnaritjbellan subclass so much as dips her foot in the water, one of the spirit-children passes up her leg and into her body and in due time is born as a child, who has thunder for its totem.   Or if the woman stoops and drinks water, one of the sprites will enter her through the mouth.   Again, there are lagoons along the Roper River where red lilies grow ; and the water is full of spirit-children which were deposited there by a kangaroo man. So when women of the Gnaritjbellan subclass wade into the water to gather lilies, little sprites swarm up their legs and are born as kangaroo children.   Again, in the territory of the Nullakun tribe there is a certain spring where a man once deposited spirit-children of the rainbow totem ; and to this day when a woman of the right totem comes to drink at the spring, the spirit of a rainbow child will dart into her and be born.   Once more, in the territory of the Yungman tribe the trees and stones near Elsey Creek are full of spirit-children who belong to the sugar-bag (honeycomb) totem ; and these sugar-bag children are constantly entering into the right women and being born into the world.[1]

---

fundamental beliefs of reincarnation and of children not being of necessity the result of sexual intercourse, are firmly held by the tribes in their normal wild state.   There is no doubt whatever of this, and we now know that these two beliefs extend through all the tribes northwards to Katherine Creek and eastwards to the Gulf of Carpentaria."   In a letter (dated Melbourne, July 27th, 1913) Professor Baldwin

Spencer writes to me that the natives on the Alligator River in the Northern Territory "have detailed traditions— as also have all the tribes—of how great ancestors wandered over the country leaving numbers of spirit children behind them who have been reincarnated time after time.   They know who everyone is a reincarnation of, as the names are perpetuated."

[1] W. Baldwin Spencer, *An Intro-*

Theories
as to the
birth of
children
among the
tribes of
Queens-
land.

The natives of the Tully River in Queensland do not
recognize sexual intercourse as a cause of conception in
women, though curiously enough they do recognize it as the
cause of conception in all animals, and pride themselves on
their superiority to the brutes in that they are not indebted
for the continuance of their species to such low and vulgar
means. The true causes of conception in a woman, according
to them, are four in number. First, she may have received
a particular species of black bream from a man whom the
European in his ignorance would call the father; this she
may have roasted and sat over the fire inhaling the savoury
smell of the roast fish. That is quite sufficient to get her
with child. Or, secondly, she may have gone out on
purpose to catch a certain kind of bull-frog, and if she
succeeds in capturing it, that again is a full and satisfactory
explanation of her pregnancy. Thirdly, some man may
have told her to conceive a child, and the mere command
produces the desired effect. Or, fourth and lastly, she may
have simply dreamed that the child was put into her, and
the dream necessarily works its own fulfilment. Whatever
white men may think about the matter, these are the real
causes why babies are born among the blacks on the Tully
River.[1] About Cape Bedford in Queensland the natives
believe that babies are sent by certain long-haired spirits,
with two sets of eyes in the front and back of their heads,
who live in the dense scrub and underwood. The children
are made in the far west where the sun goes down, and they
are made not in the form of infants but full grown; but on
their passage from the sunset land to the wombs they are
changed into the shape of spur-winged plovers, if they are
girls, or of pretty snakes, if they are boys. So when the cry
of a plover is heard by night, the blacks prick up their ears
and say, " Hallo! there is a baby somewhere about." And
if a woman is out in the bush searching for food and sees
one of the pretty snakes, which are really baby boys on the
look out for mothers, she will call out to her mates, and

---

duction to the *Study of Certain Native
Tribes of the Northern Territory* (Melbourne, 1912), pp. 41-45.

[1] Walter E. Roth, *North Queensland*

Ethnography, Bulletin No. 5, *Superstition, Magic, and Medicine* (Brisbane,
1903), pp. 22, § 81.

they will come running and turn over stones, and leaves, and logs in the search for the snake; and if they cannot find it they know that it has gone into the woman and that she will soon give birth to a baby boy.[1]   On the Penne-father River in Queensland the being who puts babies into women is called Anje-a.   He takes a lump of mud out of one of the mangrove swamps, moulds it into the shape of an infant, and insinuates it into a woman's womb.   You can never see him, for he lives in the depths of the woods, among the rocks, and along the mangrove swamps; but sometimes you can hear him laughing there to himself, and when you hear him you may know that he has got a baby ready for somebody.[2]   Among the tribes of the Cairns district in North Queensland "the acceptance of food from a man by a woman was not merely regarded as a marriage ceremony, but as the actual cause of conception."[3]

Similarly among the Australian tribes of the Northern Territory, about Port Darwin and the Daly River, especially among the Larrekiya and Wogait, "conception is not regarded as a direct result of cohabitation."   The old men of the Wogait say that there is an evil spirit who takes babies from a big fire and puts them in the wombs of women, who must give birth to them.   In the ordinary course of events, when a man is out hunting and kills game or collects other food, he gives it to his wife and she eats it, believing that the game or other food will cause her to conceive and bring forth a child.   When the child is born, it may on no account partake of the food

Theories as to the birth of children in Northern and Western Australia. Belief that conception in women is caused by the food they eat.

---

[1] Walter E. Roth, *op. cit.* p. 23, § 82.

[2] Walter E. Roth, *op. cit.* p. 23, § 83.   Mr. Roth adds, very justly: "When it is remembered that as a rule in all these Northern tribes, a little girl may be given to and will live with her spouse as wife long before she reaches the stage of puberty—the relationship of which to fecundity is not recognised—the idea of conception not being necessarily due to sexual connection becomes partly intelligible."

[3] The Bishop of North Queensland (Dr. Frodsham) in a letter to me, dated Bishop's Lodge, Townsville, Queensland, July 9th, 1909.   The Bishop's authority for the statement is the Rev. C. W. Morrison, M.A., acting head of the Yarrubah Mission. In the same letter Dr. Frodsham, speaking from personal observation, refers to "the belief, practically universal among the northern tribes, that copulation is not the cause of conception."   See J. G. Frazer, "Beliefs and Customs of the Australian Aborigines," *Folk-lore,* xx. (1909) pp. 350-352; *Man,* ix. (1909) pp. 145-147; *Totemism and Exogamy,* i. 577 *sq.*

which caused conception in the mother until it has got its
first teeth.[1]   A similar belief that conception is caused by
the food which a woman eats is held by some tribes of
Western Australia.   On this subject Mr. A. R. Brown reports
as follows: " In the Ingarda tribe at the mouth of the
Gascoyne River, I found a belief that a child is the product
of some food of which the mother has partaken just before
her first sickness in pregnancy.   My principal informant on
this subject told me that his father had speared a small
animal called *bandaru*, probably a bandicoot, but now extinct
in this neighbourhood.   His mother ate the animal, with the
result that she gave birth to my informant.   He showed me
the mark in his side where, as he said, he had been speared
by his father before being eaten by his mother.   A little
girl was pointed out to me as being the result of her mother
eating a domestic cat, and her brother was said to have been
produced from a bustard. . . . The bustard was one of the
totems of the father of these two children and, therefore, of
the children themselves.   This, however, seems to have been
purely accidental.   In most cases the animal to which conception is due is not one of the father's totems.   The species
that is thus connected with an individual by birth is not
in any way sacred to him.   He may kill or eat it; he
may marry a woman whose conceptional animal is of the
same species, and he is not by the accident of his birth
entitled to take part in the totemic ceremonies connected
with it.

" I found traces of this same belief in a number of tribes
north of the Ingarda, but everywhere the belief seemed to be
sporadic ; that is to say, some persons believed in it and
others did not.   Some individuals could tell the animal or
plant from which they or others were descended, while others
did not know or in some cases denied that conception was
so caused.   There were to be met with, however, some
beliefs of the same character.   A woman of the Buduna
tribe said that native women nowadays bear half-caste
children because they eat bread made of white flour.   Many

---

[1] Herbert Basedow, *Anthropological Notes on the Western Coastal Tribes of the Northern Territory of South Aus-* *tralia*, pp. 4 *sq.* (separate reprint from the *Transactions of the Royal Society of South Australia*, vol. xxxi. 1907).

of the men believed that conception is due to sexual intercourse, but as these natives have been for many years in
contact with the whites this cannot be regarded as satisfactory evidence of the nature of their original beliefs.

"In some tribes further to the north I found a more
interesting and better organised system of beliefs.   In the
Kariera, Namal, and Injibandi tribes the conception of a
child is believed to be due to the agency of a particular man,
who is not the father.   This man is the *wororu* of the child
when it is born.   There were three different accounts of how
the *wororu* produces conception, each of them given to me
on several different occasions.   According to the first, the
man gives some food, either animal or vegetable, to the
woman, and she eats this and becomes pregnant.   According
to the second, the man when he is out hunting kills an
animal, preferably a kangaroo or an emu, and as it is dying
he tells its spirit or ghost to go to a particular woman.   The
spirit of the dead animal goes into the woman and is born
as a child.   The third account is very similar to the last.
A hunter, when he has killed a kangaroo or an emu, takes a
portion of the fat of the dead animal which he places on
one side.   This fat turns into what we may speak of as a
spirit-baby, and follows the man to his camp.   When the
man is asleep at night the spirit-baby comes to him and
he directs it to enter a certain woman who thus becomes
pregnant.   When the child is born the man acknowledges
that he sent it, and becomes its *wororu*.   In practically
every case that I examined, some forty in all, the *wororu* of
a man or woman was a person standing to him or her in the
relation of father's brother own or tribal.   In one case a man
had a *wororu* who was his father's sister.   The duties of a
man to his *wororu* are very vaguely defined.   I was told
that a man 'looks after' his *wororu*, that is, performs small
services for him, and, perhaps, gives him food.   The conceptional animal or plant is not the totem of either the child or the
wororu.   The child has no particular magical connection with
the animal from which he is derived.   In a very large number
of cases that animal is either the kangaroo or the emu." [1]

Marginal note: Conception supposed to be caused by a man who is not the father.

[1] A. R. Brown, "Beliefs concerning
Childbirth in some Australian Tribes,"
Man, xii. (1912) pp. 180 *sq.*   Com-
pare *id.*, "Three Tribes of Western

Some rude
races still
ignorant as
to the
cause of
procrea-
tion.

Thus it appears that a childlike ignorance as to the physical process of procreation still prevails to some extent among certain rude races of mankind, who are accordingly driven to account for it in various fanciful ways such as might content the curiosity of children. We may safely assume that formerly a like ignorance was far more widely spread than it is now; indeed in the long ages which elapsed before any portion of mankind emerged from savagery, it is probable that the true cause of childbirth was universally unknown, and that people made shift to explain the mystery by some such theories as are still current among the savage or barbarous races of Central Africa, Melanesia, and Australia. A little reflection on the conditions of savage life may satisfy us that the ignorance is by no means so surprising as it may seem at first sight to a civilized observer, or, to put it otherwise, that the true cause of the birth of children is not nearly so obvious as we are apt to think. Among low savages, such as all men were originally, it is customary for boys and girls to cohabit freely with each other under the age of puberty, so that they are familiar with a commerce of the sexes which is not and cannot be attended with the birth of children. It is, therefore, not very wonderful that they should confidently deny the connexion of sexual intercourse with the production of offspring. Again, the long interval of time which divides the act of conception from the first manifest symptoms of pregnancy might easily disguise from the heedless savage the vital relation between the two. These considerations may remove or lessen the hesitation which civilized man naturally feels at admitting that a considerable part or even the whole of his species should ever have doubted or denied what seems to him one of the most obvious and elementary truths of nature.[1]

In the light of the foregoing evidence, stories of the

Australia," *Journal of the Royal Anthropological Institute*, xliii. (1913) p. 168.

[1] Those who desire to pursue this subject further may consult with advantage Mr. E. S. Hartland's learned treatise *Primitive Paternity* (London, 1909–1910), which contains an ample collection of facts and a careful discussion of them. Elsewhere I have argued that the primitive ignorance of paternity furnishes the key to the origin of totemism. See *Totemism and Exogamy*, i. 155 *sqq.*, iv. 40 *sqq.*

miraculous birth of gods and heroes from virgin mothers Legends of virgin mothers.
lose much of the glamour that encircled them in days of old,
and we view them simply as relics of superstition surviving
like fossils to tell us of a bygone age of childlike ignorance
and credulity.

§ 8. Sacred Stocks and Stones among the Semites

Traces of beliefs and customs like the foregoing may Procreative virtue apparently ascribed to the sacred stocks and stones at Semitic sanctuaries.
perhaps be detected among the ancient Semites. When the
prophet Jeremiah speaks of the Israelites who said to a
stock or to a tree (for in Hebrew the words are the same),
"Thou art my father," and to a stone, "Thou hast brought
me forth,"[1] it is probable that he was not using vague
rhetorical language, but denouncing real beliefs current
among his contemporaries. Now we know that at all the
old Canaanite sanctuaries, including the sanctuaries of
Jehovah down to the reformations of Hezekiah and Josiah,
the two regular objects of worship were a sacred stock and
a sacred stone,[2] and that these sanctuaries were the seats of
profligate rites performed by sacred men (kedeshim) and
sacred women (kedeshoth). Is it not natural to suppose
that the stock and stone which the superstitious Israelites
regarded as their father and mother were the sacred stock
(asherah) and the sacred stone (massebah) of the sanctuary,
and that the children born of the loose intercourse of the
sexes at these places were believed to be the offspring or
emanations of these uncouth but worshipful idols in which,
as in the sacred trees and stones of Central Australia, the
souls of the dead may have been supposed to await rebirth?
On this view the sacred men and women who actually begot

---

[1] Jeremiah ii. 27. The ancient
Greeks seem also to have had a notion
that men were sprung from trees or
rocks. See Homer, Od. xix. 163;
F. G. Welcker, Griechische Götterlehre
(Göttingen, 1857–1862), i. 777 sqq.;
A. B. Cook, "Oak and Rock,"
Classical Review, xv. (1901) pp. 322
sqq.

[2] The ashera and the masseba. See
1 Kings xiv. 23; 2 Kings xviii. 4,
xxiii. 14; Micah v. 13 sq. (in Hebrew,

12 sq.); Deuteronomy xvi. 21 sq.;
W. Robertson Smith, Religion of the
Semites,[2] pp. 187 sqq., 203 sqq.; G. F.
Moore, in Encyclopaedia Biblica, svv.,
"Asherah" and "Massebah." In the
early religion of Crete also the two
principal objects of worship seem to
have been a sacred tree and a sacred
pillar. See A. J. Evans, "Mycenaean
Tree and Pillar Cult," Journal of
Hellenic Studies, xxi. (1901) pp. 99
sqq.

or bore the children were deemed the human embodiments of the two divinities, the men perhaps personating the sacred stock, which appears to have been a tree stripped of its branches, and the women personating the sacred stone, which seems to have been in the shape of a cone, an obelisk, or a pillar.[1]

These conclusions confirmed by the excavation of a sanctuary at the Canaanitish city of Gezer.

These conclusions are confirmed by the result of recent researches at Gezer, an ancient Canaanitish city, which occupied a high, isolated point on the southern border of Ephraim, between Jerusalem and the sea. Here the English excavations have laid bare the remains of a sanctuary with the sacred stone pillars or obelisks (*masseboth*) still standing in a row, while between two of them is set a large socketed stone, beautifully squared, which perhaps contained the sacred stock or pole (*asherah*). In the soil which had accumulated over the floor of the temple were found vast numbers of male emblems rudely carved out of soft limestone ; and tablets of terra-cotta, representing in low relief the mother-goddess, were discovered throughout the strata. These objects were no doubt votive-offerings presented by the worshippers to the male and female deities who were represented by the sacred stock and the sacred stones ; and their occurrence in large quantities raises a strong presumption that the divinities of the sanctuary were a god and goddess

The infants buried in the sanctuary may have been expected to be born again.

regarded as above all sources of fertility. The supposition is further strengthened by a very remarkable discovery. Under the floor of the temple were found the bones of many new-born children, none more than a week old, buried in large jars. None of these little bodies showed any trace of mutilation or violence ; and in the light of the customs practised in many other lands[2] we seem to be justified in

---

[1] As to conical images of Semitic goddesses, see above, pp. 34 *sqq.* The sacred pole (*asherah*) appears also to have been by some people regarded as the embodiment of a goddess (Astarte), not of a god. See above, p. 18, note [2]. Among the Khasis of Assam the sacred upright stones, which resemble the Semitic *masseboth*, are regarded as males, and the flat table-stones as female. See P. R. T. Gurdon, *The Khasis* (London, 1907), pp. 112 *sq.*,

150 *sqq.* So in Nikunau, one of the Gilbert Islands in the South Pacific, the natives had sandstone slabs or pillars which represented gods and goddesses. "If the stone slab represented a goddess it was not placed erect, but laid down on the ground. Being a lady they thought it would be cruel to make her stand so long." See G. Turner, LL.D., *Samoa* (London, 1884), p. 296.

[2] See above, pp. 91 *sqq.*

conjecturing that the infants were still-born or died soon after birth, and that they were buried by their parents in the sanctuary in the hope that, quickened by the divine power, they might enter again into the mother's womb and again be born into the world.[1]   If the souls of these buried babes were supposed to pass into the sacred stocks and stones and to dart from them into the bodies of would-be mothers who resorted to the sanctuary, the analogy with Central Australia would be complete.   That the analogy is real and not fanciful is strongly suggested by the modern practice of Syrian women who still repair to the shrines of saints to procure offspring, and who still look on " holy men " as human embodiments of divinity.   In this, as in many other dark places of superstition, the present is the best guide to the interpretation of the past ; for while the higher forms of religious faith pass away like clouds, the lower stand firm and indestructible like rocks.   The " sacred men " of one age are the dervishes of the next, the Adonis of yesterday is the St. George of to-day.

---

[1] As to the excavations at Gezer, see R. A. Stewart Macalister, *Reports on the Excavation of Gezer* (London, N.D.), pp. 76-89 (reprinted from the *Quarterly Statement of the Palestine Exploration Fund*) ; *id.*, *Bible Side-lights from the Mound of Gezer* (London, 1906), pp. 57-67, 73-75.   Professor Macalister now inclines to regard the socketed stone as a laver rather than as the base of the sacred pole.   He supposes that the buried infants were first-born children sacrificed in accordance with the ancient law of the dedication of the first-born.   The explanation which I have adopted in the text agrees better with the uninjured state of the bodies, and it is further confirmed by the result of the Austrian excavations at Tell Ta'annek (Taanach) in Palestine, which seem to prove that there children up to the age of two years were not buried in the family graves but interred separately in jars.   Some of these sepulchral jars were deposited under or beside the houses, but many were grouped round a rock-hewn altar in a different part of the hill.   There is nothing to indicate that any of the children were sacrificed : the size of some of the skeletons precludes the idea that they were slain at birth. Probably they all died natural deaths, and the custom of burying them in or near the house or beside an altar was intended to ensure their rebirth in the family.   See Dr. E. Sellin, "Tell Ta'annek," *Denkschriften der Kaiser. Akademie der Wissenschaften, Philosophisch-historische Klasse*, l. (Vienna, 1904), No. iv. pp. 32-37, 96 *sq.*   Compare W. W. Graf Baudissin, *Adonis und Esmun*, p. 59 n.[3].   I have to thank Professor R. A. Stewart Macalister for kindly directing my attention to the excavations at Tell Ta'annek (Taanach).   It deserves to be mentioned that in an enclosure close to the standing stones at Gezer, there was found a bronze model of a cobra (R. A. Stewart Macalister, *Bible Side-lights*, p. 76).   Perhaps the reptile was the deity of the shrine, or an embodiment of an ancestral spirit.

CHAPTER V

THE BURNING OF MELCARTH

Semitic custom of sacrificing a member of the royal family.

IF a custom of putting a king or his son to death in the character of a god has left small traces of itself in Cyprus, an island where the fierce zeal of Semitic religion was early tempered by Greek humanity, the vestiges of that gloomy rite are clearer in Phoenicia itself and in the Phoenician colonies, which lay more remote from the highways of Grecian commerce. We know that the Semites were in the habit of sacrificing some of their children, generally the first-born, either as a tribute regularly due to the deity or to appease his anger in seasons of public danger and calamity.[1] If commoners did so, is it likely that kings, with all their heavy responsibilities, could exempt themselves from this dreadful sacrifice for the fatherland? In point of fact, history informs us that kings steeled themselves to do as others did.[2] It deserves to be noticed that if Mesha, king of Moab, who sacrificed his eldest son by fire, claimed to be a son of his god,[3] he would no doubt transmit his divinity to his offspring; and further, that the same sacrifice is said to have been performed in the same way by the divine founder of Byblus, the great seat of the worship of Adonis.[4] This suggests that the human representatives of Adonis formerly perished in the flames. At all events, a custom of periodically burning the chief god of the city in effigy appears to have prevailed

The burning of Melcarth at Tyre.

[1] *The Dying God*, pp. 166 *sqq.* See Note I., "Moloch the King;" at the end of this volume.

[2] Philo of Byblus, quoted by Eusebius, *Praepar. Evang.* i. 10. 29 *sq.*; 2 Kings iii. 27.

[3] See above, p. 15.

[4] Philo of Byblus, in *Fragmenta Historicorum Graecorum*, ed. C. Müller, iii. pp. 569, 570, 571. See above, p. 13.

at Tyre and in the Tyrian colonies down to a late time, and the effigy may well have been a later substitute for a man. For Melcarth, the great god of Tyre, was identified by the Greeks with Hercules,[1] who is said to have burned himself to death on a great pyre, ascending up to heaven in a cloud and a peal of thunder.[2] The common Greek legend, immortalized by Sophocles, laid the scene of the fiery tragedy on the top of Mount Oeta, but another version transferred it significantly to Tyre itself.[3] Combined with the other evidence which I shall adduce, this latter tradition raises a strong presumption that an effigy of Hercules, or rather of Melcarth, was regularly burned at a great festival in Tyre. That festival may have been the one known as "the awakening of Hercules," which was held in the month of Peritius, answering nearly to January.[4] The name of the festival suggests that the dramatic representation of the death of the god on the pyre was followed by a semblance of his resurrection. The mode in which the resurrection was supposed to be effected is perhaps indicated by the statement of a Greek writer that the Phoenicians used to sacrifice quails to Hercules, because Hercules on his journey to Libya had been slain by Typhon and brought to life again by Iolaus, who held a quail under his nose : the dead god snuffed at the bird and revived.[5] According to another account Iolaus burnt a quail alive, and the dead hero, who

[1] See above, p. 16.

[2] Sophocles, *Trachiniae*, 1191 *sqq.*; Apollodorus, *Bibliotheca*, ii. 7. 7 ; Diodorus Siculus, iv. 38 ; Hyginus, *Fab.* 36.

[3] [S. Clementis Romani,] *Recognitiones*, x. 24, p. 233, ed. E. G. Gersdorf (Migne's *Patrologia Graeca*, i. 1434).

[4] Josephus, *Antiquit. Jud.* viii. 5. 3, *Contra Apionem*, i. 18. Whether the quadriennial festival of Hercules at Tyre (2 Maccabees iv. 18-20) was a different celebration, or only "the awakening of Melcarth," celebrated with unusual pomp once in four years, we do not know.

[5] Eudoxus of Cnidus, quoted by Athenaeus, ix. 47, p. 392 D, E. That the death and resurrection of Melcarth were celebrated in an annual festival at

Tyre has been recognised by scholars. See Raoul-Rochette, "Sur l'Hercule Assyrien et Phénicien," *Mémoires de l'Académie des Inscriptions et Belles-Lettres*, xvii. Deuxième Partie (Paris, 1848), pp. 25 *sqq.* ; H. Hubert et M. Mauss, "Essai sur le sacrifice," *L'Année Sociologique*, ii. (1899) pp. 122, 124 ; M. J. Lagrange, *Études sur les Religions Sémitiques*,[2] pp. 308-311. Iolaus is identified by some modern scholars with Eshmun, a Phoenician and Carthaginian deity about whom little is known. See F. C. Movers, *Die Phoenizier*, i. (Bonn, 1841) pp. 536 *sqq.* ; F. Baethgen, *Beiträge zur semitischen Religionsgeschichte* (Berlin, 1888), pp. 44 *sqq.* ; C. P. Tiele, *Geschichte der Religion im Altertum* (Gotha, 1896-1903), i. 268 ; W. W. Graf Baudissin, *Adonis und Esmun*, pp. 282 *sqq.*

loved quails, came to life again through the savoury smell of the roasted bird.[1]   This latter tradition seems to point to a custom of burning the quails alive in the Phoenician sacrifices to Melcarth.[2]   A festival of the god's resurrection might appropriately be held in spring, when the quails migrate northwards across the Mediterranean in great bands, and immense numbers of them are netted for the market.[3]   In the month of March the birds return to Palestine by myriads in a single night, and remain to breed in all the open plains, marshes, and cornfields.[4]   Certainly a close connexion seems to have subsisted between quails and Melcarth; for legend ran that Asteria, the mother of the Tyrian Hercules, that is, of Melcarth, was transformed into a quail.[5]   It was probably to this annual festival of the death and resurrection of Melcarth that the Carthaginians were wont to send ambassadors every year to Tyre, their mother-city.[6]

Worship of Melcarth at Gades, and trace of a custom of burning him there in effigy.

In Gades, the modern Cadiz, an early colony of Tyre on the Atlantic coast of Spain,[7] there was an ancient, famous, and wealthy sanctuary of Hercules, the Tyrian Melcarth. Indeed the god was said to be buried on the spot.   No image stood in his temple, but a perpetual fire burned on the altar, and incense was offered by white-robed priests, with bare feet and shorn heads, who were bound to chastity. Neither women nor pigs might pollute the holy place by their presence.   In later times many distinguished Romans went on pilgrimage to this remote shrine on the Atlantic shore when they were about to embark on some perilous

---

[1] Zenobius, *Centur.* v. 56 (*Paroemiographi Graeci*, ed. E. L. Leutsch et F. G. Schneidewin, Göttingen, 1839–1851, vol. i. p. 143).

[2] Quails were perhaps burnt in honour of the Cilician Hercules or Sandan at Tarsus.   See below, p. 126, note [2].

[3] Alfred Newton, *Dictionary of Birds* (London, 1893–96), p. 755.

[4] H. B. Tristram, *The Fauna and Flora of Palestine* (London, 1884), p. 124.   For more evidence as to the migration of quails see Aug. Dillmann's commentary on Exodus xvi. 13, pp. 169 *sqq.* (Leipsic, 1880).

[5] The Tyrian Hercules was said to be a son of Zeus and Asteria (Eudoxus of Cnidus, quoted by Athenaeus, ix. 47, p. 392 D; Cicero, *De natura deorum,* iii. 16. 42).   As to the transformation of Asteria into a quail see Apollodorus, *Bibliotheca,* i. 4. 1; J. Tzetzes, *Schol. on Lycophron,* 401; Hyginus, *Fab.* 53; Servius on Virgil, *Aen.* iii. 73.   The name Asteria may be a Greek form of Astarte.   See W. W. Graf Baudissin, *Adonis und Esmun,* p. 307.

[6] Quintus Curtius, iv. 2. 10; Arrian, *Anabasis,* ii. 24. 5.

[7] Strabo, iii. 5. 5, pp. 169 *sq.*; Mela, iii. 46; Scymnus Chius, *Orbis Descriptio,* 159-161 (*Geographi Graeci Minores,* ed. C. Müller, i. 200 *sq.*).

enterprise, and they returned to it to pay their vows when their petitions had been granted.[1] One of the last things Hannibal himself did before he marched on Italy was to repair to Gades and offer up to Melcarth prayers which were never to be answered. Soon after he dreamed an ominous dream.[2] Now it would appear that at Gades, as at Tyre, though no image of Melcarth stood in the temple, an effigy of him was made up and burned at a yearly festival. For a certain Cleon of Magnesia related how, visiting Gades, he was obliged to sail away from the island with the rest of the multitude in obedience to the command of Hercules, that is, of Melcarth, and how on their return they found a monstrous man of the sea stranded on the beach and burning; for the god, they were told, had struck him with a thunderbolt.[3] We may conjecture that at the annual festival of Melcarth strangers were obliged to quit the city, and that in their absence the mystery of burning the god was consummated. What Cleon and the rest saw on their return to Gades would, on this hypothesis, be the smouldering remains of a gigantic effigy of Melcarth in the likeness of a man riding on a sea-horse, just as he is represented on coins of Tyre.[4] In like manner the Greeks portrayed the sea-god Melicertes, whose name is only a slightly altered form of Melcarth, riding on a dolphin or stretched on the beast's back.[5]

At Carthage, the greatest of the Tyrian colonies, a

[1] Silius Italicus, iii. 14-32; Mela, iii. 46; Strabo, iii. 5. 3, 5, 7, pp. 169, 170, 172; Diodorus Siculus, v. 20. 2; Philostratus, *Vita Apollonii*, v. 4 *sq.*; Appian, *Hispanica*, 65. Compare Arrian, *Anabasis*, ii. 16. 4. That the bones of Hercules were buried at Gades is mentioned by Mela (*l.c.*). Compare Arnobius, *Adversus Nationes*, i. 36. In Italy women were not allowed to participate in sacrifices offered to Hercules (Aulus Gellius, xi. 6. 2; Macrobius, *Saturn.* i. 12. 28; Sextus Aurelius Victor, *De origine gentis Romanae*, vi. 6; Plutarch, *Quaestiones Romanae*, 60). Whether the priests of Melcarth at Gades were celibate, or had only to observe continence at certain seasons, does not appear. At Tyre the priest of Melcarth might be married (Justin, xviii.

4. 5). The worship of Melcarth under the name of Hercules continued to flourish in the south of Spain down to the time of the Roman Empire. See J. Toutain, *Les Cultes païens dans l'Empire Romain*, Première Partie, i. (Paris, 1907) pp. 400 *sqq.*

[2] Livy, xxi. 21. 9, 22. 5-9; Cicero, *De Divinatione*, i. 24. 49; Silius Italicus, iii. 1 *sqq.*, 158 *sqq.*

[3] Pausanias, x. 4. 5.

[4] B. V. Head, *Historia Numorum* (Oxford, 1887), p. 674; G. A. Cooke, *Text-Book of North-Semitic Inscriptions*, p. 351.

[5] F. Imhoof-Blumer and P. Gardner, *Numismatic Commentary on Pausanias*, pp. 10-12, with pl. A; Stoll, *s.v.* "Melikertes," in W. H. Roscher's *Lexikon der griech. und röm. Mythologie*, ii. 2634.

Evidence of a custom of burning a god or goddess at Carthage.

reminiscence of the custom of burning a deity in effigy seems to linger in the story that Dido or Elissa, the foundress and queen of the city, stabbed herself to death upon a pyre, or leaped from her palace into the blazing pile, to escape the fond importunities of one lover or in despair at the cruel desertion of another.[1] We are told that Dido was worshipped as a goddess at Carthage so long as the country maintained its independence.[2] Her temple stood in the centre of the city shaded by a grove of solemn yews and firs.[3] The two apparently contradictory views of her character as a queen and a goddess may be reconciled if we suppose that she was both the one and the other ; that in fact the queen of Carthage in early days, like the queen of Egypt down to historical times, was regarded as divine, and had, like human deities elsewhere, to die a violent death either at the end of a fixed period or whenever her bodily and mental powers began to fail. In later ages the stern old custom might be softened down into a pretence by substituting an effigy for the queen or by allowing her to

The fire-walk at Tyre.

pass through the fire unscathed. A similar modification of the ancient rule appears to have been allowed at Tyre itself, the mother-city of Carthage. We have seen reason to think that the kings of Tyre, from whom Dido was descended, claimed to personate the god Melcarth, and that the deity was burned either in effigy or in the person of a man at an annual festival.[4] Now in the same chapter in which Ezekiel charges the king of Tyre with claiming to be a god, the prophet describes him as walking " up and down amidst the stones of fire." [5] The description becomes at once intelligible

---

[1] Justin, xviii. 6. 1-7 ; Virgil, *Aen.* iv. 473 *sqq.*, v. i. *sqq.* ; Ovid, *Fasti*, iii. 545 *sqq.* ; Timaeus, in *Fragmenta Historicorum Graecorum*, ed. C. Müller, i. 197. Compare W. Robertson Smith, *Religion of the Semites*,[2] pp. 373 *sqq.* The name of Dido has been plausibly derived by Gesenius, Movers, E. Meyer, and A. H. Sayce from the Semitic *dôd*, " beloved." See F. C. Movers, *Die Phoenizier*, i. 616 ; Meltzer, *s.v.* " Dido," in W. H. Roscher's *Lexikon der griech. und röm. Mythologie*, i. 1017 *sq.* ; A. H. Sayce, *Lectures on the Religion of the Ancient Baby-*

lonians (London and Edinburgh, 1887), pp. 56 *sqq.* If they are right, the divine character of Dido becomes more probable than ever, since "the Beloved " (*Dodah*) seems to have been a title of a Semitic goddess, perhaps Astarte. See above, p. 20, note[2]. According to Varro it was not Dido but her sister Anna who slew herself on a pyre for love of Aeneas (Servius on Virgil, *Aen.* iv. 682).

[2] Justin, xviii. 6. 8.

[3] Silius Italicus, i. 81 *sqq.*

[4] See above, pp. 16, 110 *sqq.*

[5] Ezekiel xxviii. 14, compare 16.

if we suppose that in later times the king of Tyre compounded for being burnt in the fire by walking up and down
on hot stones, thereby saving his life at the expense perhaps
of a few blisters on his feet.   It is possible that when all
went well with the commonwealth, children whom strict law
doomed to the furnace of Moloch may also have been
mercifully allowed to escape on condition of running the
fiery gauntlet.   At all events, a religious rite of this sort has
been and is still practised in many parts of the world : the
performers solemnly pace through a furnace of heated stones
or glowing wood-ashes in the presence of a multitude of
spectators.   Examples of the custom have been adduced
in another part of this work.[1]   Here I will cite only
one.   At Castabala, in Southern Cappadocia, there was   The fire
worshipped an Asiatic goddess whom the Greeks called   walk at
the Perasian Artemis.   Her priestesses used to walk bare-   Castabala.
foot over a fire of charcoal without sustaining any injury.
That this rite was a substitute for burning human beings
alive or dead is suggested by the tradition which placed the
adventure of Orestes and the Tauric Artemis at Castabala ;[2]
for the men or women sacrificed to the Tauric Artemis
were first put to the sword and then burned in a pit of
sacred fire.[3]   Among the Carthaginians another trace of   The Car-
such a practice may perhaps be detected in the story that   thaginian
at the desperate battle of Himera, fought from dawn of day   Hamilcar
till late in the evening, the Carthaginian king Hamilcar   sacrifices
remained in the camp and kept sacrificing holocausts of   the fire.
victims on a huge pyre ; but when he saw his army giving

[1] *Balder the Beautiful*, ii. 1 *sqq.*
But, as I have there pointed out, there
are grounds for thinking that the custom
of walking over fire is not a substitute
for human sacrifice, but merely a stringent form of purification.   On fire as a
purificatory agent see below, pp. 179
sqq., 188 *sq.*

[2] Strabo, xii. 2. 7, p. 537.   In
Greece itself accused persons used to
prove their innocence by walking
through fire (Sophocles, *Antigone*, 264
sq., with Jebb's note).   Possibly the
fire-walk of the priestesses at Castabala was designed to test their chastity.   For this purpose the priests and
priestesses of the Tshi-speaking people

of the Gold Coast submit to an ordeal,
standing one by one in a narrow circle
of fire.   This "is supposed to show
whether they have remained pure, and
refrained from sexual intercourse, during
the period of retirement, and so are
worthy of inspiration by the gods.   If
they are pure they will receive no injury
and suffer no pain from the fire" (A. B.
Ellis, *The Tshi-speaking Peoples of the
Gold Coast*, London, 1887, p. 138).
These cases favour the purificatory
explanation of the fire-walk.

[3] Euripides, *Iphigenia in Tauris*,
621-626.   Compare Diodorus Siculus,
xx. 14. 6.

way before the Greeks, he flung himself into the flames and was burned to death. Afterwards his countrymen sacrificed to him and erected a great monument in his honour at Carthage, while lesser monuments were reared to his memory in all the Punic colonies.[1]   In public emergencies which called for extraordinary measures a king of Carthage may well have felt bound in honour to sacrifice himself in the old way for the good of his country.   That the Carthaginians regarded the death of Hamilcar as an act of heroism and not as a mere suicide of despair, is proved by the posthumous honours they paid him.

The death of Hercules a Greek version of the burning of Melcarth.

The foregoing evidence, taken altogether, raises a strong presumption, though it cannot be said to amount to a proof, that a practice of burning a deity, and especially Melcarth, in effigy or in the person of a human representative, was observed at an annual festival in Tyre and its colonies.   We can thus understand how Hercules, in so far as he represented the Tyrian god, was believed to have perished by a voluntary death on a pyre.   For on many a beach and headland of the Aegean, where the Phoenicians had their trading factories, the Greeks may have watched the bale-fires of Melcarth blazing in the darkness of night, and have learned with wonder that the strange foreign folk were burning their god.   In this way the legend of the voyages of Hercules and his death in the flames may be supposed to have originated.   Yet with the legend the Greeks borrowed the custom of burning the god; for at the festivals of Hercules a pyre used to be kindled in memory of the hero's fiery death on Mount Oeta.[2]   We may surmise, though we are not expressly told, that an effigy of Hercules was regularly burned on the pyre.

[1] Herodotus, vii. 167. This was the Carthaginian version of the story. According to another account, Hamilcar was killed by the Greek cavalry (Diodorus Siculus, xi. 22. 1).   His worship at Carthage is mentioned by Athenagoras (*Supplicatio pro Christianis*, p. 64, ed. J. C. T. Otto, Jena, 1857.) I have called Hamilcar a king in accordance with the usage of Greek writers (Herodotus, vii. 165 *sq.* ; Aristotle, *Politics*, ii. 11; Polybius, vi. 51; Diodorus Siculus, xiv. 54. 5).   But the *suffetes*, or supreme magistrates, of Carthage were two in number; whether they were elected for a year or for life seems to be doubtful. Cornelius Nepos, who calls them kings, says that they were elected annually (*Hannibal*, vii. 4), and Livy (xxx. 7. 5) compares them to the consuls; but Cicero (*De re publica*, ii. 23. 42 *sq.*) seems to imply that they held office for life.   See G. A. Cooke, *Text-book of North-Semitic Inscriptions*, pp. 115 *sq.*

[2] Lucian, *Amores*, 1 and 54.

CHAPTER VI

THE BURNING OF SANDAN

§ 1. *The Baal of Tarsus*

IN Cyprus the Tyrian Melcarth was worshippped side by side with Adonis at Amathus,[1] and Phoenician inscriptions prove that he was revered also at Idalium and Larnax Lapethus. At the last of these places he seems to have been regarded by the Greeks as a marine deity and identified with Poseidon.[2] A remarkable statue found at Amathus may represent Melcarth in the character of the lion-slayer, a character which the Greeks bestowed on Hercules. The statue in question is of colossal size, and exhibits a thick-set, muscular, hirsute deity of almost bestial aspect, with goggle eyes, huge ears, and a pair of stumpy horns on the top of his head. His beard is square and curly: his hair falls in three pigtails on his shoulders: his brawny arms appear to be tattooed. A lion's skin, clasped by a buckle, is knotted round his loins; and he holds the skin of a lioness in front of him, grasping a hind paw with each hand, while the head of the beast, which is missing, hung down between his legs. A fountain must have issued from the jaws of the lioness, for a rectangular hole, where the beast's head should be, communicates by a channel with another hole in the back of the statue. Greek artists working on this or a similar barbarous model produced the refined type of the Grecian Hercules with the lion's scalp thrown like a cowl over

The Tyrian Melcarth in Cyprus.

The lion-slaying god.

---

[1] See above, p. 32.

[2] G. A. Cooke, *Text-book of North-* *Semitic Inscriptions,* Nos. 23 and 29, pp. 73, 83 *sq.,* with the notes on pp. 81, 84.

his head.   Statues of him have been found in Cyprus, which represent intermediate stages in this artistic evolution.[1]   But there is no proof that in Cyprus the Tyrian Melcarth was burned either in effigy or in the person of a human representative.[2]

The Baal of Tarsus, an Oriental god of corn and grapes.   On the other hand, there is clear evidence of the observance of such a custom in Cilicia, the country which lies across the sea from Cyprus, and from which the worship of Adonis, according to tradition, was derived.[3] Whether the Phoenicians ever colonized Cilicia or not is doubtful,[4] but at all events the natives of the country, down to late times, worshipped a male deity who, in spite of a superficial assimilation to a fashionable Greek god, appears to have been an Oriental by birth and character. He had his principal seat at Tarsus, in a plain of luxuriant fertility and almost tropical climate, tempered by breezes from the snowy range of Tarsus on the north and from the sea on the south.[5]   Though Tarsus boasted of a school of Greek philosophy which at the beginning of our era surpassed those of Athens and Alexandria,[6] the city apparently remained in manners and spirit essentially Oriental.   The women went about the streets muffled up to the eyes in Eastern fashion, and Dio Chrysostom reproaches the natives with resembling the most dissolute of the Phoenicians rather than the Greeks

[1] G. Perrot et Ch. Chipiez, *Histoire de l'Art dans l'Antiquité*, iii. 566-578. The colossal statue found at Amathus may be related, directly or indirectly, to the Egyptian god Bes, who is represented as a sturdy misshapen dwarf, wearing round his body the skin of a beast of the panther tribe, with its tail hanging down. See E. A. Wallis Budge, *The Gods of the Egyptians* (London, 1904), ii. 284 *sqq.* ; A. Wiedemann, *Religion of the Ancient Egyptians* (London, 1897), pp. 159 *sqq.* ; A. Furtwängler, *s.v.* " Herakles," in W. H. Roscher's *Lexikon der griech. und röm. Mythologie*, i. 2143 *sq.*

[2] However, human victims were burned at Salamis in Cyprus. See below, p. 145.

[3] See above, p. 41.

[4] For traces of Phoenician influence in Cilicia see F. C. Movers, *Die Phoenizier*, ii. 2, pp. 167-174, 207 *sqq.* Herodotus says (vii. 91) that the Cilicians were named after Cilix, a son of the Phoenician Agenor.

[5] As to the fertility and the climate of the plain of Tarsus, which is now very malarious, see E. J. Davis, *Life in Asiatic Turkey* (London, 1879), chaps. i.-vii.   The gardens for miles round the city are very lovely, but wild and neglected, full of magnificent trees, especially fine oak, ash, orange, and lemon-trees.   The vines run to the top of the highest branches, and almost every garden resounds with the song of the nightingale (E. J. Davis, *op. cit.* p. 35).

[6] Strabo, xiv. 5. 13, pp. 673 *sq.*

whose civilization they aped.[1]   On the coins of the city
they assimilated their native deity to Zeus by representing
him seated on a throne, the upper part of his body bare,
the lower limbs draped in a flowing robe, while in one
hand he holds a sceptre, which is topped sometimes with
an eagle but often with a lotus flower.   Yet his foreign
nature is indicated both by his name and his attributes ;
for in Aramaic inscriptions on the coins he bears the name
of the Baal of Tarsus, and in one hand he grasps an ear of
corn and a bunch of grapes.[2]   These attributes clearly
mark him out as a god of fertility in general, who con-
ferred on his worshippers the two things which they prized
above all other gifts of nature, the corn and the wine.
He was probably therefore a Semitic, or at all events an
Oriental, rather than a Greek deity.   For while the Semite
cast all his gods more or less in the same mould, and
expected them all to render him nearly the same services,
the Greek, with his keener intelligence and more pictorial
imagination, invested his deities with individual characteristics, allotting to each of them his or her separate function
in the divine economy of the world.   Thus he assigned the
production of the corn to Demeter, and that of the grapes
to Dionysus ; he was not so unreasonable as to demand
both from the same hard-worked deity.

§ 2. *The God of Ibreez*

Now the suspicion that the Baal of Tarsus, for all his
posing in the attitude of Zeus, was really an Oriental is
confirmed by a remarkable rock-hewn monument which is
to be seen at Ibreez in Southern Cappadocia.   Though the

The Baal
of Tarsus
has his
counter-
part at
Ibreez in
Cappa-
docia.

[1] Dio Chrysostom, *Or.* xxxiii. vol.
ii. pp. 14 *sq.*, 17, ed. L. Dindorf
(Leipsic, 1857).

[2] F. C. Movers, *Die Phoenizier*, ii.
2, pp. 171 *sq.* ; P. Gardner, *Types of
Greek Coins* (Cambridge, 1883), pl. x.
Nos. 29, 30 ; B. V. Head, *Historia
Numorum* (Oxford, 1887), p. 614 ;
G. F. Hill, *Catalogue of Greek Coins
of Lycaonia, Isauria, and Cilicia*
(London, 1900), pp. 167-176, pl.

xxix.-xxxii. ; G. Macdonald, *Catalogue of Greek Coins in the Hunterian
Collection* (Glasgow, 1899-1905), ii.
547 ; G. Perrot et Ch. Chipiez, *Histoire
de l'Art dans l'Antiquité*, iv. 727.   In
later times, from about 175 B.C. onward, the Baal of Tarsus was completely assimilated to Zeus on the
coins. See B. V. Head, *op. cit.* p.
617 ; G. F. Hill, *op. cit.* pp. 177,
181.

place is distant little more than fifty miles from Tarsus as the crow flies, yet the journey on horseback occupies five days; for the great barrier of the Taurus mountains rises like a wall between. The road runs through the famous pass of the Cilician Gates, and the scenery throughout is of the grandest Alpine character. On all sides the mountains tower skyward, their peaks sheeted in a dazzling pall of snow, their lower slopes veiled in the almost inky blackness of dense pine-forests, torn here and there by impassable ravines, or broken into prodigious precipices of red and grey rock which border the narrow valley for miles. The magnificence of the landscape is enhanced by the exhilarating influence of the brisk mountain air, all the more by contrast with the sultry heat of the plain of Tarsus which the traveller has left behind. When he emerges from the defile on the wide open tableland of Anatolia he feels that in a sense he has passed out of Asia, and that the highroad to Europe lies straight before him. The great mountains on which he now looks back formed for centuries the boundary between the Christian West and the Mohammedan East; on the southern side lay the domain of the Caliphs, on the northern side the Byzantine Empire. The Taurus was the dam that long repelled the tide of Arab invasion; and though year by year the waves broke through the pass of the Cilician Gates and carried havoc and devastation through the tableland, the refluent waters always retired to the lower level of the Cilician plains. A line of beacon lights stretching from the Taurus to Constantinople flashed to the Byzantine capital tidings of the approach of the Moslem invaders.[1]

The village of Ibreez is charmingly situated at the northern foot of the Taurus, some six or seven miles south of the town of Eregli, the ancient Cybistra. From the town to the village the path goes through a richly cultivated district of wheat and vines along green lanes more lovely than those of Devonshire, lined by thick hedges and rows of willow, poplar, hazel, hawthorn, and huge old walnut-trees, where in early summer the nightingales warble on

The pass of the Cilician Gates.

The rock-sculptures at Ibreez represent a god of corn and grapes adored by his worshipper, a priest or king.

---

[1] Sir W. M. Ramsay, *Luke the Physician, and other Studies in the History of Religion* (London, 1908), pp. 112 *sqq.*

every side. Ibreez itself is embowered in the verdure of
orchards, walnuts, and vines. It stands at the mouth of
a deep ravine enclosed by great precipices of red rock.
From the western of these precipices a river clear as crystal,
but of a deep blue tint, bursts in a powerful jet, and being
reinforced by a multitude of springs becomes at once a
raging impassable torrent foaming and leaping with a roar
of waters over the rocks in its bed. A little way from the
source a branch of the main stream flows in a deep narrow
channel along the foot of a reddish weather-stained rock
which rises sheer from the water. On its face, which has
been smoothed to receive them, are the sculptures. They
consist of two colossal figures, representing a god adored by
his worshipper. The deity, some fourteen feet high, is a
bearded male figure, wearing on his head a high pointed
cap adorned with several pairs of horns, and plainly clad in
a short tunic, which does not reach his knees and is drawn
in at the waist by a belt. His legs and arms are bare ; the
wrists are encircled by bangles or bracelets. His feet are
shod in high boots with turned-up toes. In his right hand
he holds a vine-branch laden with clusters of grapes, and in
his raised left hand he grasps a bunch of bearded wheat,
such as is still grown in Cappadocia ; the ears of corn project
above his fingers, while the long stalks hang down to his
feet. In front of him stands the lesser figure, some eight
feet high. He is clearly a priest or king, more probably
perhaps both in one. His rich vestments contrast with the
simple costume of the god. On his head he wears a round
but not pointed cap, encircled by flat bands and ornamented
in front with a rosette or bunch of jewels, such as is still
worn by Eastern princes. He is draped from the neck to
the ankles in a long robe heavily fringed at the bottom, over
which is thrown a shawl or mantle secured at the breast by
a clasp of precious stones. Both robe and shawl are elabor-
ately carved with patterns in imitation of embroidery. A
heavy necklace of rings or beads encircles the neck ; a
bracelet or bangle clasps the one wrist that is visible ; the
feet are shod in boots like those of the god. One or perhaps
both hands are raised in the act of adoration. The large
aquiline nose, like the beak of a hawk, is a conspicuous

feature in the face both of the god and of his worshipper; the hair and beard of both are thick and curly.[1]

The fertility of Ibreez contrasted with the desolation of the surrounding country.
The situation of this remarkable monument resembles that of Aphaca on the Lebanon;[2] for in both places we see a noble river issuing abruptly from the rock to spread fertility through the rich vale below. Nowhere, perhaps, could man more appropriately revere those great powers of nature to whose favour he ascribes the fruitfulness of the earth, and through it the life of animate creation. With its cool bracing air, its mass of verdure, its magnificent stream of pure ice-cold water—so grateful in the burning heat of summer—and its wide stretch of fertile land, the valley may well have been the residence of an ancient prince or high-priest, who desired to testify by this monument his devotion and gratitude to the god. The seat of this royal or priestly potentate may have been at Cybistra,[3] the modern Eregli, now a decayed and miserable place straggling amid orchards and gardens full of luxuriant groves of walnut, poplar, willow, mulberry, and oak. The place is a paradise of birds. Here

---

[1] E. J. Davis, "On a New Hamathite Inscription at Ibreez," *Transactions of the Society of Biblical Archaeology*, iv. (1876) pp. 336-346; *id.*, *Life in Asiatic Turkey* (London, 1879), pp. 245-260; G. Perrot et Ch. Chipiez, *Histoire de l'Art dans l'Antiquité*, iv. 723-729; Ramsay and Hogarth, "Prehellenic Monuments of Cappadocia," *Recueil de Travaux relatifs à la Philologie et à l'Archéologie Égyptiennes et Assyriennes*, xiv. (1903) pp. 77-81, 85 *sq.*, with plates iii. and iv.; L. Messerschmidt, *Corpus Inscriptionum Hettiticarum* (Berlin, 1900), Tafel xxxiv.; Sir W. M. Ramsay, *Luke the Physician* (London, 1908), pp. 171 *sqq.*; John Garstang, *The Land of the Hittites* (London, 1910), pp. 191-195, 378 *sq.* Of this sculptured group Messrs. W. M. Ramsay and D. G. Hogarth say that "it yields to no rock-relief in the world in impressive character" (*American Journal of Archaeology*, vi. (1890) p. 347). Professor Garstang would date the sculptures in the tenth or ninth century B.C. Another inscribed Hittite monument found at Bor, near the site of the ancient Tyana, exhibits a very similar figure of a priest or king in an attitude of adoration. The resemblance extends even to the patterns embroidered on the robe and shawl, which include the well-known *swastika* carved on the lower border of the long robe. The figure is sculptured in high relief on a slab of stone and would seem to have been surrounded by inscriptions, though a portion of them has perished. See J. Garstang, *op. cit.* pp. 185-188, with plate lvi. For the route from Tarsus to Ibreez (Ivriz) see E. J. Davis, *Life in Asiatic Turkey*, pp. 198-244; J. Garstang, *op. cit.* pp. 44 *sqq.*

[2] See above, pp. 28 *sq.*

[3] Strabo, xii. 2. 7, p. 537. When Cicero was proconsul of Cilicia (51-50 B.C.) he encamped with his army for some days at Cybistra, from which two of his letters to Atticus are dated. But hearing that the Parthians, who had invaded Syria, were threatening Cilicia, he hurried by forced marches through the pass of the Cilician Gates to Tarsus. See Cicero, *Ad Atticum*, v. 18, 19, 20; *Ad Familiares*, xv. 2, 4.

the thrush and the nightingale sing full-throated, the hoopoe waves his crested top-knot, the bright-hued woodpeckers flit from bough to bough, and the swifts dart screaming by hundreds through the air. Yet a little way off, beyond the beneficent influence of the springs and streams, all is desolation—in summer an arid waste broken by great marshes and wide patches of salt, in winter a broad sheet of stagnant water, which as it dries up with the growing heat of the sun exhales a poisonous malaria. To the west, as far as the eye can see, stretches the endless expanse of the dreary Lycaonian plain, barren, treeless, and solitary, till it fades into the blue distance, or is bounded afar off by abrupt ranges of jagged volcanic mountains, on which in sunshiny weather the shadows of the clouds rest, purple and soft as velvet.[1] No wonder that the smiling luxuriance of the one landscape, sharply contrasting with the bleak sterility of the other, should have rendered it in the eyes of primitive man a veritable garden of God.

Among the attributes which mark out the deity of Ibreez as a power of fertility the horns on his high cap should not be overlooked. They are probably the horns of a bull; for to primitive cattle-breeders the bull is the most natural emblem of generative force. At Carchemish, the great Hittite capital on the Euphrates, a relief has been discovered which represents a god or a priest clad in a rich robe, and wearing on his head a tall horned cap surmounted by a disc.[2] Sculptures found at the palace of Euyuk in North-Western Cappadocia prove that the Hittites worshipped the bull and sacrificed rams to it.[3] Similarly the Greeks conceived the vine-god Dionysus in the form of a bull.[4]

The horned god.

---

[1] E. J. Davis, in *Transactions of the Society of Biblical Archaeology*, iv. (1876) pp. 336 *sq.*, 346; *id.*, *Life in Asiatic Turkey*, pp. 232 *sq.*, 236 *sq.*, 264 *sq.*, 270-272. Compare W. J. Hamilton, *Researches in Asia Minor, Pontus, and Armenia* (London, 1842), ii. 304-307.

[2] L. Messerschmidt, *The Hittites* (London, 1903), pp. 49 *sq.* On an Assyrian cylinder, now in the British Museum, we see a warlike deity with bow and arrows standing on a lion, and wearing a similar bonnet decorated with horns and surmounted by a star

or sun. See De Vogüé, *Mélanges d'Archéologie Orientale* (Paris, 1868), p. 46, who interprets the deity as the great Asiatic goddess. As to the horned god of Ibreez "it is a plausible theory that the horns may, in this case, be analogous to the Assyrian emblem of divinity. The sculpture is late and its style rather suggests Semitic influence" (Professor J. Garstang, in some MS. notes with which he has kindly furnished me).

[3] See below, p. 132.

[4] *Spirits of the Corn and of the Wild*, i. 16 *sq.*, ii. 3 *sqq.*

§ 3. *Sandan of Tarsus*

The god
of Ibreez
a Hittite
deity.

That the god of Ibreez, with the grapes and corn in his hands, is identical with the Baal of Tarsus, who bears the same emblems, may be taken as certain.[1] But what was his name? and who were his worshippers? The Greeks apparently called him Hercules; at least in Byzantine times the neighbouring town of Cybistra adopted the name of Heraclea, which seems to show that Hercules was deemed the principal deity of the place.[2] Yet the style and costume of the figures at Ibreez prove unquestionably that the god was an Oriental. If any confirmation of this view were needed, it is furnished by the inscriptions carved on the rock beside the sculptures, for these inscriptions are composed in the peculiar system of hieroglyphics now known as Hittite. It follows, therefore, that the deity worshipped at Tarsus and Ibreez was a god of the Hittites, that ancient and little-known people who occupied the centre of Asia Minor, invented a system of writing, and extended their influence, if not their dominion, at one time from the Euphrates to the Aegean. From the lofty and arid table-lands of the interior, a prolongation of the great plateau of Central Asia, with a climate ranging from the most burning heat in summer to the most piercing cold in winter,[3] these hardy highlanders seem to have swept down through the mountain-passes and established themselves at a very early date in the rich southern lowlands of Syria and Cilicia.[4]

---

[1] The identification is accepted by E. Meyer (*Geschichte des Altertums*,[2] i. 2. p. 641), G. Perrot et Ch. Chipiez (*Histoire de l'Art dans l'Antiquité*, iv. 727), and P. Jensen (*Hittiter und Armenier*, Strasburg, 1898, p. 145).

[2] Ramsay and Hogarth, "Pre-Hellenic Monuments of Cappadocia," *Recueil de Travaux relatifs à la Philologie et à l'Archéologie Égyptiennes et Assyriennes*, xiv. (1893) p. 79.

[3] G. Maspero, *Histoire Ancienne des Peuples de l'Orient Classique*, ii. 360-362; G. Perrot et Ch. Chipiez, *Histoire de l'Art dans l'Antiquité*, iv. 572 *sqq.*, 586 *sq.*

[4] That the cradle of the Hittites was in the interior of Asia Minor, particularly in Cappadocia, and that they spread from there south, east, and west, is the view of A. H. Sayce, W. M. Ramsay, D. G. Hogarth, W. Max Müller, F. Hommel, L. B. Paton, and L. Messerschmidt. See *Palestine Exploration Fund Quarterly Statement for 1884*, p. 49; A. H. Sayce, *The Hittites*[3] (London, 1903), pp. 80 *sqq.*: W. Max Müller, *Asien und Europa* (Leipsic, 1893), pp. 319 *sqq.*; Ramsay and Hogarth, "Pre-Hellenic Monuments of Cappadocia," *Recueil de Travaux relatifs à la Philologie et à l'Archéologie Égyptiennes et Assyriennes*, xv. (1893) p. 94; F. Hommel, *Grund-*

Their language and race are still under discussion, but a great preponderance of opinion appears to declare that neither the one nor the other was Semitic.[1]

In the inscription attached to the colossal figure of the god at Ibreez two scholars have professed to read the name of Sandan or Sanda.[2] Be that as it may, there are independent grounds for thinking that Sandan, Sandon, or Sandes may have been the name of the Cappadocian and Cilician god of fertility. For the god of Ibreez in Cappadocia appears, as we saw, to have been identified by the Greeks with Hercules, and we are told that a Cappadocian and Cilician name of Hercules was Sandan or Sandes.[3]

The burning of Sandan or Hercules at Tarsus.

---

riss der Geographie und Geschichte des alten Orients (Munich, 1904), pp. 42, 48, 54; L. B. Paton, The Early History of Syria and Palestine (London, 1902), pp. 103 sqq.; L. Messerschmidt, The Hittites (London, 1903), pp. 12, 13, 19, 20; D. G. Hogarth, "Recent Hittite Research," Journal of the Royal Anthropological Institute, xxxix. (1909) pp. 408 sqq. Compare Ed. Meyer, Geschichte des Altertums,[2] i. 2. (Stuttgart and Berlin, 1909) pp. 617 sqq. ; J. Garstang, The Land of the Hittites, pp. 315 sqq. The native Hittite writing is a system of hieroglyphics which has not yet been read, but in their intercourse with foreign nations the Hittites used the Babylonian cuneiform script. Clay tablets bearing inscriptions both in the Babylonian and in the Hittite language have been found by Dr. H. Winckler at Boghaz-Keui, the great Hittite capital in Cappadocia ; so that the sounds of the Hittite words, though not their meanings, are now known. According to Professor Ed. Meyer, it seems certain that the Hittite language was neither Semitic nor Indo-European. As to the inscribed tablets of Boghaz-Keui, see H. Winckler, "Vorläufige Nachrichten über die Ausgrabungen in Boghaz-köi im Sommer 1907, I. Die Tontafelfunde," Mitteilungen der Deutschen Orient-Gesellschaft zu Berlin, No. 35, December 1907, pp. 1-59 ; "Hittite Archives from Boghaz-Keui," translated from the German transcripts of Dr. Winckler by Meta E. Williams,

Annals of Archaeology and Anthropology, iv. (Liverpool, 1912), pp. 90-98.

[1] G. Maspero, Histoire Ancienne des Peuples de l'Orient Classique, ii. 351, note [3], with his references ; L. B. Paton, op. cit. p. 109 ; L. Messerschmidt, The Hittites, p. 10 ; F. Hommel, op. cit. p. 42 ; W. Max Müller, Asien und Europa, p. 332. See the preceding note.

[2] A. H. Sayce, "The Hittite Inscriptions," Recueil de Travaux relatifs à la Philologie et à l'Archéologie Égyptiennes et Assyriennes, xiv. (1893) pp. 48 sq. ; P. Jensen, Hittiter und Armenier (Strasburg, 1898), pp. 42 sq.

[3] Georgius Syncellus, Chronographia, vol. i. p. 290, ed. G. Dindorf (Bonn, 1829) : Ἡρακλέα τινές φασιν ἐν Φοινίκῃ γνωρίζεσθαι Σάνδαν ἐπιλεγόμενον, ὡς καὶ μεχρὶ νῦν ὑπὸ Καππαδὸκων καὶ Κιλίκων. In this passage Σάνδαν is a correction of F. C. Movers's (Die Phoenizier, i. 460) for the MS. reading Δισανδάν, the ΔΙ having apparently arisen by dittography from the preceding ΑΙ ; and Κιλίκων is a correction of E. Meyer's ("Über einige semitische Götter," Zeitschrift der Deutschen Morgenländischen Gesellschaft, xxxi. 737) for the MS. reading Ἰλίων. Compare Jerome (quoted by Movers and Meyer, ll.cc.) : "Hercules cognomento Desanaus in Syria Phoenice clarus habetur. Inde ad nostram usque memoriam a Cappadocibus et Eliensibus (al. Deliis) Desanaus

Now this Sandan or Hercules is said to have founded
Tarsus, and the people of the city commemorated him at
an annual or, at all events, periodical festival by erecting
a fine pyre in his honour.[1] Apparently at this festival, as
at the festival of Melcarth, the god was burned in effigy
on his own pyre. For coins of Tarsus often exhibit the
pyre as a conical structure resting on a garlanded altar or
basis, with the figure of Sandan himself in the midst of it,
while an eagle with spread wings perches on the top of the
pyre, as if about to bear the soul of the burning god in the
pillar of smoke and fire to heaven.[2] In like manner when a
Roman emperor died leaving a son to succeed him on the

---

adhuc dicitur." If the text of Jerome
is here sound, he would seem to have
had before him a Greek original which
was corrupt like the text of Syncellus
or of Syncellus's authority. The Cilician
Hercules is called Sandes by Nonnus
(*Dionys.* xxxiv. 183 *sq.*). Compare
Raoul-Rochette in *Mémoires de l'Académie des Inscriptions et Belles-Lettres*,
xvii. Deuxième Partie (Paris, 1848),
pp. 159 *sqq.*

[1] Ammianus Marcellinus, xiv. 8. 3;
Dio Chrysostom, *Or.* xxxiii. vol. ii. p. 16,
ed. L. Dindorf (Leipsic, 1857). The pyre
is mentioned only by Dio Chrysostom,
whose words clearly imply that its
erection was a custom observed periodically. On Sandan or Sandon see K.
O. Müller, "Sandon und Sardanapal," *Kunstarchaeologische Werke*, iii.
6 *sqq.*; F. C. Movers, *Die Phoenizier*,
i. 458 *sqq.*: Raoul-Rochette, "Sur
l'Hercule Assyrien et Phénicien,"
*Mémoires de l'Académie des Inscriptions
et Belles-Lettres*, xvii. Deuxième Partie
(Paris, 1848), pp. 178 *sqq.*; E. Meyer,
"Über einige Semitische Götter,"
*Zeitschrift der Deutschen Morgen-
ländischen Gesellschaft*, xxxi. (1877)
pp. 736-740 : *id.*, *Geschichte des Altertums*,[2] i. 2. pp. 641 *sqq.* § 484.

[2] P. Gardner, *Catalogue of Greek
Coins, the Seleucid Kings of Syria*
(London, 1878), pp. 72, 78, 89, 112,
pl. xxi. 6, xxiv. 3, xxviii. 8; G. F.
Hill, *Catalogue of the Greek Coins of
Lycaonia, Isauria, and Cilicia* (Lon-
don, 1900), pp. 180, 181, 183, 190,
221, 224, 225, pl. xxxiii. 2, 3, xxxiv.

10, xxxvii. 9 ; F. Imhoof-Blumer,
"Coin-types of some Kilikian Cities,"
Journal of Hellenic Studies, xviii.
(1898) p. 169, pl. xiii. 1, 2. The
structure represented on the coins is
sometimes called not the pyre but the
monument of Sandan or Sardanapalus.
Certainly the cone resting on the square
base reminds us of the similar structure
on the coins of Byblus as well as of the
conical image of Aphrodite at Paphos
(see above, pp. 14, 34); but the words
of Dio Chrysostom make it probable
that the design on the coins of Tarsus
represents the pyre. At the same
time, the burning of the god may well
have been sculptured on a permanent
monument of stone. The legend
OPTTTΘOΘHPA, literally "quail-hunt,"
which appears on some coins of Tarsus
(G. F. Hill, *op. cit.* pp. lxxxvi. *sq.*),
may refer to a custom of catching
quails and burning them on the pyre.
We have seen (above, pp. 111 *sq.*)
that quails were apparently burnt in
sacrifice at Byblus. This explanation
of the legend on the coins of Tarsus
was suggested by Raoul-Rochette
(*op. cit.* pp. 201-205). However,
Mr. G. F. Hill writes to me that
"the interpretation of Ὀρτυγοθήρα
as anything but a personal name is
rendered very unlikely by the analogy
of all the other inscriptions on coins of
the same class." Doves were burnt on
a pyre in honour of Adonis (below, p.
147). Similarly birds were burnt on a
pyre in honour of Laphrian Artemis at
Patrae (Pausanias, vii. 18. 12).

throne, a waxen effigy was made in the likeness of the
deceased and burned on a huge pyramidal pyre, which was
reared upon a square basis of wood ; and from the summit
of the blazing pile an eagle was released for the purpose of
carrying to heaven the soul of the dead and deified emperor.[1]
The Romans may have borrowed from the East a grandiose
custom which savours of Oriental adulation rather than of
Roman simplicity.[2]

The type of Sandan or Hercules, as he is portrayed on
the coins of Tarsus, is that of an Asiatic deity standing on
a lion.   It is thus that he is represented on the pyre, and
it is thus that he appears as a separate figure without the
pyre.   From these representations we can form a fairly
accurate conception of the form and attributes of the god.
They exhibit him as a bearded man standing on a horned
and often winged lion.   Upon his head he wears a high
pointed cap or mitre, and he is clad sometimes in a long
robe, sometimes in a short tunic.   On at least one coin his
feet are shod in high boots with flaps.   At his side or over
his shoulder are slung a sword, a bow-case, and a quiver,
sometimes only one or two of them.   His right hand is
raised and sometimes holds a flower.   His left hand grasps
a double-headed axe, and sometimes a wreath either in
addition to the axe or instead of it ; but the double-headed
axe is one of Sandan's most constant attributes.[3]

Sandan of Tarsus an Asiatic god with the symbols of the lion and the double axe.

---

[1] Herodian, iv. 2.
[2] See Franz Cumont, "L'Aigle
funéraire des Syriens et l'Apothéose
des Empereurs," *Revue de l'Histoire
des Religions*, lxii. (1910) pp. 119-
163.
[3] F. Imhoof - Blumer, *Monnaies
Grecques* (Amsterdam, 1883), pp. 366
sq., 433, 435, with plates F. 24, 25,
H. 14 (*Verhandelingen der Konink.
Akademie von Wetenschappen*, Afdeeling Letterkunde, xiv.) ; F. Imhoof-
Blumer und O. Keller, *Tier- und
Pflanzenbilder auf Münzen und Gem-
men des klassischen Altertums* (Leipsic,

1889), pp. 70 *sq.*, with pl. xii. 7, 8, 9 ;
F. Imhoof- Blumer, "Coin-types of
some Kilikian Cities," *Journal of Hellenic Studies*, xviii. (1898) pp. 169-
171 ; P. Gardner, *Types of Greek
Coins*, pl. xiii. 20 ; G. F. Hill, *Catalogue of the Greek Coins of Lycaonia,
Isauria, and Cilicia*, pp. 178, 179,
184, 186, 206, 213, with plates xxxii.
13, 14, 15, 16, xxxiv. 2, xxxvi. 9 ;
G. Macdonald, *Catalogue of Greek
Coins in the Hunterian Collection*, ii.
548, with pl. lx. 11.   The booted
Sandan is figured by G. F. Hill, *op.
cit.* pl. xxxvi. 9.

§ 4. *The Gods of Boghaz-Keui*

Boghaz-
Keui the
ancient
capital of
a Hittite
kingdom
in Cappa-
docia.

Now a deity of almost precisely the same type figures prominently in the celebrated group of Hittite sculptures which is carved on the rocks at Boghaz-Keui in North-Western Cappadocia. The village of Boghaz-Keui, that is, "the village of the defile," stands at the mouth of a deep, narrow, and picturesque gorge in a wild upland valley, shut in by rugged mountains of grey limestone. The houses are built on the lower slopes of the hills, and a stream issuing from the gorge flows past them to join the Halys, which is distant about ten hours' journey to the west. Immediately above the modern village a great ancient city, enclosed by massive fortification walls, rose on the rough broken ground of the mountain-side, culminating in two citadels perched on the tops of precipitous crags. The walls are still standing in many places to a height of twelve feet or more. They are about fourteen feet thick and consist of an outer and inner facing built of large blocks with a core of rubble between them. On the outer side they are strengthened at intervals of about a hundred feet by projecting towers or buttresses, which seem designed rather as architectural supports than as military defences. The masonry, composed of large stones laid in roughly parallel courses, resembles in style that of the walls of Mycenae, with which it may be contemporary ; and the celebrated Lion-gate at Mycenae has its counterpart in the southern gate of Boghaz-Keui, which is flanked by a pair of colossal stone lions executed in the best style of Hittite art. The eastern gate is adorned on its inner side with the figure of a Hittite warrior or Amazon carved in high relief. A dense undergrowth of stunted oak coppice now covers much of the site. The ruins of a large palace or temple, built of enormous blocks of stone, occupy a terrace in a commanding situation within the circuit of the walls. This vast city, some four or five miles in circumference, appears to have been the ancient Pteria, which Croesus, king of Lydia, captured in his war with Cyrus. It was probably the capital of a powerful Hittite empire before the Phrygians made their way from

Europe into the interior of Asia Minor and established a rival state to the west of the Halys.[1]

From the village of Boghaz-Keui a steep and rugged path leads up hill to a sanctuary, distant about a mile and a half to the east. Here among the grey limestone cliffs there is a spacious natural chamber or hall of roughly oblong shape, roofed only by the sky, and enclosed on three sides by high rocks. One of the short sides is open, and through it you look out on the broken slopes beyond and the more distant mountains, which make a graceful picture set in a massy frame. The length of the chamber is about a hundred feet; its breadth varies from twenty-five to fifty feet. A nearly level sward forms the floor. On the right-hand side, as you face inward, a narrow opening in the rock leads into another but much smaller chamber, or rather corridor, which would seem to have been the inner sanctuary or Holy of Holies. It is a romantic spot, where the deep shadows of the rocks are relieved by the bright foliage of walnut-trees and by the sight of the sky and clouds overhead. On the rock-walls of both chamber are carved the famous bas-reliefs. In the outer sanctuary these reliefs represent two great processions which defile along the two long sides of the chamber and meet face to face on the short wall at the inner end. The figures on the left-hand wall are for the most part men clad in the characteristic Hittite costume, which consists of a high pointed cap, shoes with turned-up toes, and a tunic drawn in at the waist and

The sanctuary in the rocks.

The rock-sculptures in the outer sanctuary at Boghaz-Keui represent two processions meeting.

---

[1] Herodotus, i. 76; Stephanus Byzantius, *s.v.* Πτέριον. As to the situation of Boghaz-Keui and the ruins of Pteria see W. J. Hamilton, *Researches in Asia Minor, Pontus, and Armenia* (London, 1842), i. 391 *sqq.*; H. Barth, "Reise von Trapezunt durch die nördliche Hälfte Klein-Asiens," *Ergänzungsheft zu Petermann's Geographischen Mittheilungen*, No. 2 (1860), pp. 44-52; H. F. Tozer, *Turkish Armenia and Eastern Asia Minor* (London, 1881), pp. 64, 71 *sqq.*; W. M. Ramsay, "Historical Relations of Phrygia and Cappadocia," *Journal of the Royal Asiatic Society*, N.S., xv. (1883) p. 103; *id.*, *His-torical Geography of Asia Minor* (London, 1890), pp. 28 *sq.*, 33 *sq.*; G. Perrot et Ch. Chipiez, *Histoire de l'Art dans l'Antiquité*, iv. 596 *sqq.*; K. Humann und O. Puchstein, *Reisen in Kleinasien und Nordsyrien* (Berlin, 1890), pp. 71-80, with Atlas, plates xi.-xiv.; E. Chantre, *Mission en Cappadoce* (Paris, 1898), pp. 13 *sqq.*; O. Puchstein, "Die Bauten von Boghaz-Köi," *Mitteilungen der Deutschen Orient-Gesellschaft zu Berlin*, No. 35, December 1907, pp. 62 *sqq.*; J. Garstang, *The Land of the Hittites* (London, 1910), pp. 196 *sqq.*

falling short of the knees.[1]   The figures on the right-hand
wall are women wearing tall, square, flat-topped bonnets
with ribbed sides ; their long dresses fall in perpendicular
folds to their feet, which are shod in shoes like those of the
men.   On the short wall, where the processions meet, the
greater size of the central figures, as well as their postures
and attributes, mark them out as divine.   At the head of
the male procession marches or is carried a bearded deity
clad in the ordinary Hittite costume of tall pointed cap,
short tunic, and turned-up shoes ; but his feet rest on the
bowed heads of two men, in his right hand he holds on his
shoulder a mace or truncheon topped with a knob, while his
extended left hand grasps a symbol, which apparently
consists of a trident surmounted by an oval with a cross-bar.
Behind him follows a similar, though somewhat smaller,
figure of a man, or perhaps rather of a god, carrying a mace
or truncheon over his shoulder in his right hand, while with
his left he holds aloft a long sword with a flat hilt ; his feet
rest not on two men but on two flat-topped pinnacles, which
perhaps represent mountains.   At the head of the female
procession and facing the great god who is borne on the
two men, stands a goddess on a lioness or panther.   Her
costume does not differ from that of the women : her
hair hangs down in a long plait behind : in her extended
right hand she holds out an emblem to touch that of the
god.   The shape and meaning of her emblem are obscure.
It consists of a stem with two pairs of protuberances,
perhaps leaves or branches, one above the other, the whole
being surmounted, like the emblem of the god, by an oval
with a cross-bar.   Under the outstretched arms of the two
deities appear the front parts of two animals, which have
been usually interpreted as bulls but are rather goats ;
each of them wears on its head the high conical Hittite
cap, and its body is concealed by that of the deity.
Immediately behind the goddess marches a smaller and
apparently youthful male figure, standing like her upon a
lioness or panther.   He is beardless and wears the Hittite

The central figures.

---

[1] This procession of men is broken
(*a*) by two women clad in long plaited
robes like the women on the opposite
wall; (*b*) by two winged monsters;
and (*c*) by the figure of a priest or king
as to which see below, pp. 131 *sq.*

dress of high pointed cap, short tunic, and shoes with
turned-up toes. A crescent-hilted sword is girt at his side ;
in his left hand he holds a double-headed axe, and in his
right a staff topped by an armless doll with the symbol of
the cross-barred oval instead of a head. Behind him follow
two women, or rather perhaps goddesses, resembling the
goddess at the head of the procession, but with different
emblems and standing not on a lioness but on a single two-
headed eagle with outspread wings.

The entrance to the smaller chamber is guarded on
either side by the figure of a winged monster carved on the
rock ; the bodies of both figures are human, but one of them
has the head of a dog, the other the head of a lion. In the
inner sanctuary, to which this monster-guarded passage
leads, the walls are also carved in relief. On one side we
see a procession of twelve men in Hittite costume marching
with curved swords in their right hands. On the opposite
wall is a colossal erect figure of a deity with a human head
and a body curiously composed of four lions, two above and
two below, the latter standing on their heads. The god
wears the high conical Hittite hat : his face is youthful and
beardless like that of the male figure standing on the lioness
in the large chamber ; and the ear turned to the spectator
is pierced with a ring. From the knees downwards the
legs, curiously enough, are replaced by a device which has
been interpreted as the tapering point of a great dagger or
dirk with a midrib. To the right of this deity a square
panel cut in the face of the rock exhibits a group of two
figures in relief. The larger of the two figures closely
resembles the youth on the lioness in the outer sanctuary.
His chin is beardless ; he wears the same high pointed cap,
the same short tunic, the same turned-up shoes, the same
crescent-hilted sword, and he carries a similar armless doll
in his right hand. But his left arm encircles the neck of
the smaller figure, whom he seems to clasp to his side in an
attitude of protection. The smaller figure thus embraced
by the god is clearly a priest or priestly king. His face is
beardless ; he wears a skull-cap and a long mantle reaching
to his feet with a sort of chasuble thrown over it. The
crescent-shaped hilt of a sword projects from under his

The rock-
sculptures
in the
inner
sanctuary
at Boghaz-
Keui.

The lion-
god.

The god
protecting
his priest.

mantle. The wrist of his right arm is clasped by the god's left hand ; in his left hand the priest holds a crook or pastoral staff which ends below in a curl. Both the priest and his protector are facing towards the lion-god. In an upper corner of the panel behind them is a divine emblem composed of a winged disc resting on what look like two Ionic columns, while between them appear three symbols of doubtful significance. The figure of the priest or king in this costume, though not in this attitude, is a familiar one ; for it occurs twice in the outer sanctuary and is repeated twice at the great Hittite palace of Euyuk, distant about four and a half hours' ride to the north-east of Boghaz-Keui. In the outer sanctuary at Boghaz-Keui we see the priest marching in the procession of the men, and holding in one hand his curled staff, or *lituus*, and in the other a symbol like that of the goddess on the lioness : above his head appears the winged disc without the other attributes. Moreover he occupies a conspicuous place by himself on the right-hand wall of the outer sanctuary, quite apart from the two processions, and carved on a larger scale than any of the other figures in them. Here he stands on two heaps, perhaps intended to represent mountains, and he carries in his right hand the emblem of the winged disc supported on two Ionic columns with the other symbols between them, except that the central symbol is replaced by a masculine figure wearing a pointed cap and a long robe decorated with a dog-tooth pattern. On one of the reliefs at the palace of Euyuk we see the priest with his characteristic dress and staff followed by a priestess, each of them with a hand raised as if in adoration : they are approaching the image of a bull which stands on a high pedestal with an altar before it. Behind them a priest leads a flock of rams to the sacrifice. On another relief at Euyuk the priest, similarly attired and followed by a priestess, is approaching a seated goddess and apparently pouring a libation at her feet. Both these scenes doubtless represent acts of worship paid in the one case to a goddess, in the other to a bull.[1]

Other representations of the priest at Boghaz-Keui and Euyuk.

---

[1] W. J. Hamilton, *Researches in Asia Minor, Pontus, and Armenia* (London, 1842), i. 393-395 ; H. F. Tozer, *Turkish Armenia and Eastern Asia Minor*, pp. 59 *sq.*, 66-78 ; W. M. Ramsay, " Historical Relations of

We have still to inquire into the meaning of the rock-carvings at Boghaz-Keui. What are these processions which are meeting? Who are the personages represented? and what are they doing? Some have thought that the scene is historical and commemorates a great event, such as a treaty of peace between two peoples or the marriage of a king's son to a king's daughter.[1] But to this view it has

The two deities at the head of the processions at Boghaz-Keui appear to be the great Asiatic goddess and her consort.

Phrygia and Asia Minor," *Journal of the Royal Asiatic Society*, N.S. xv. (1883) pp. 113-120 ; G. Perrot et Ch. Chipiez, *Histoire de l'Art dans l'Antiquité*, iv. 623-656, 666-672 ; K. Humann und O. Puchstein, *Reisen in Kleinasien und Nordsyrien*, pp. 55-70, with Atlas, plates vii.-x. ; E. Chantre, *Mission en Cappadoce*, pp. 3-5, 16-26 ; L. Messerschmidt, *The Hittites*, pp. 42-50 ; Th. Macridy-Bey, *La Porte des Sphinx à Eyuk*, pp. 13 *sq.* (*Mitteilungen der Vorderasiatischen Gesellschaft*, 1908, No. 3, Berlin) ; Ed. Meyer, *Geschichte des Altertums*,[2] i. 2. pp. 631 *sq.* ; J. Garstang, *The Land of the Hittites* (London, 1910), pp. 196 *sqq.* (Boghaz-Keui) 256 *sqq.* (Eyuk). Compare P. Jensen, *Hittiter und Armenier*, pp. 165 *sqq.* In some notes with which my colleague Professor J. Garstang has kindly furnished me he tells me that the two animals wearing Hittite hats, which appear between the great god and goddess in the outer sanctuary, are not bulls but certainly goats ; and he inclines to think that the two heaps on which the priest stands in the outer sanctuary are fir-cones. Professor Ed. Meyer holds that the costume which the priestly king wears is that of the Sun-goddess, and that the corresponding figure in the procession of males on the left-hand side of the outer sanctuary does not represent the priestly king but the Sun-goddess in person. "The attributes of the King," he says (*op. cit.* p. 632), "are to be explained by the circumstance that he, as the Hittite inscriptions prove, passed for an incarnation of the Sun, who with the Hittites was a female divinity ; the temple of the Sun is therefore his emblem." As to the title of "the

Sun" bestowed on Hittite kings in inscriptions, see H. Winckler, "Vorläufige Nachrichten über die Ausgrabungen in Boghaz-köi im Sommer 1907," *Mitteilungen der Deutschen Orient-Gesellschaft zu Berlin*, No. 35, December 1907, pp. 32, 33, 36, 44, 45, 53. The correct form of the national name appears to be Chatti or Hatti rather than Hittites, which is the Hebrew form (חתי) of the name. Compare M. Jastrow, in *Encyclopaedia Biblica*, ii. coll. 2094 *sqq.*, *s.v.* "Hittites."

An interesting Hittite symbol which occurs both in the sanctuary at Boghaz-Keui and at the palace of Euyuk is the double-headed eagle. In both places it serves as the support of divine or priestly personages. After being adopted as a badge by the Seljuk Sultans in the Middle Ages, it passed into Europe with the Crusaders and became in time the escutcheon of the Austrian and Russian empires. See W. J. Hamilton, *op. cit.* i. 383 ; G. Perrot et Ch. Chipiez, *op. cit.* iv. 681-683, with pl. viii. E ; L. Messerschmidt, *The Hittites*, p. 50.

[1] W. J. Hamilton, *Researches in Asia Minor, Pontus, and Armenia*, i. 394 *sq.* ; H. Barth, in *Monatsberichte der königl. Preuss. Akademie der Wissenschaften*, 1859, pp. 128 *sqq.* ; *id.*, "Reise von Trapezunt," *Ergänzungsheft zu Petermann's Geograph. Mittheilungen*, No. 2 (Gotha, 1860), pp. 45 *sq.* ; H. F. Tozer, *Turkish Armenia and Eastern Asia Minor*, p. 69 ; E. Chantre, *Mission en Cappadoce*, pp. 20 *sqq.* According to Barth, the scene represented is the marriage of Aryenis, daughter of Alyattes, king of Lydia, to Astyages, son of Cyaxares, king of the Medes

been rightly objected that the attributes of the principal figures prove them to be divine or priestly, and that the scene is therefore religious or mythical rather than historical. With regard to the two personages who head the processions and hold out their symbols to each other, the most probable opinion appears to be that they stand for the great Asiatic goddess of fertility and her consort, by whatever names these deities were known ; for under diverse names a similar divine couple appears to have been worshipped with similar rites all over Western Asia.[1]   The bearded god who, grasping a trident in his extended left hand, heads the procession of male figures is probably the Father deity, the great Hittite god of the thundering sky, whose emblems were the thunderbolt and the bull ; for the trident which he carries may reasonably be interpreted as a thunderbolt.   The deity is represented in similar form on two stone monuments of Hittite art which were found at Zenjirli in Northern Syria and at Babylon respectively.   On both we see a bearded male god wearing the usual Hittite costume of tall cap, short tunic, and shoes turned up at the toes : a crescent-hilted sword is girt at his side : his hands are raised : in the right he holds a single-headed axe or hammer, in the left a trident of wavy lines, which is thought to stand for forked lightning or a bundle of thunderbolts.   On the Babylonian slab, which bears a long Hittite inscription, the god's cap is ornamented with a pair of horns.[2]   The horns on the cap are probably

The Hittite god of the thundering sky.

(Herodotus, i. 74).   For a discussion of various interpretations which have been proposed see G. Perrot et Ch. Chipiez, *Histoire de l'Art dans l'Antiquité*, iv. 630 *sqq.*

[1] This is in substance the view of Raoul - Rochette, Lajard, W. M. Ramsay, G. Perrot, C. P. Tiele, Ed. Meyer, and J. Garstang. See Raoul-Rochette, " Sur l'Hercule Assyrien et Phénicien," *Mémoires de l'Académie des Inscriptions et Belles-Lettres*, xvii. Deuxième Partie (Paris, 1848), p. 180 note[1]; W. M. Ramsay, " On the Early Historical Relations between Phrygia and Cappadocia," *Journal of the Royal Asiatic Society*, N.S. xv. (1883) pp. 113-120 ; G. Perrot et Ch.

Chipiez, *Histoire de l'Art dans l'Antiquité*, iv. 630 *sqq.* ; C. P. Tiele, *Geschichte der Religion im Altertum*, i. 255-257 ; Ed. Meyer, *Geschichte des Altertums*,[2] i. 2. pp. 633 *sq.* ; J. Garstang, *The Land of the Hittites*, pp. 235-237 ; *id.*, *The Syrian Goddess* (London, 1913), pp. 5 *sqq.*

[2] K. Humann und O. Puchstein, *Reisen in Kleinasien und Nordsyrien* (Berlin, 1902), Atlas, pl. xlv. 3; *Ausgrabungen zu Sendschirli*, iii. (Berlin, 1902) pl. xli. ; J. Garstang, *The Land of the Hittites*, p. 291, with plate lxxvii. ; R. Koldewey, *Die Hettitische Inschrift gefunden in der Königsburg von Babylon* (Leipsic, 1900), plates 1 and 2 (*Wissenschaftl·*

those of a bull ; for on another Hittite monument, found at Malatia on the Euphrates, there is carved a deity in the usual Hittite costume standing on a bull and grasping a trident or thunderbolt in his left hand, while facing him stands a priest clad in a long robe, holding a crook or curled staff in one hand and pouring a libation with the other.[1] The Hittite thunder-god is also known to us from a treaty of alliance which about the year 1290 B.C. was contracted between Hattusil, King of the Hittites, and Rameses II., King of Egypt. By a singular piece of good fortune we possess copies of this treaty both in the Hittite and in the

---

liche Veröffentlichungen der Deutschen Orient - Gesellschaft, Heft 1) ; L. Messerschmidt, *Corpus Inscriptionum Hettiticarum,* pl. i. 5 and 6 ; *id., The Hittites* (London, 1903), pp. 40-42, with fig. 6 on p. 41 ; M. J. Lagrange, *Études sur les Religions Sémitiques*[2] (Paris, 1905), p. 93. The name of the god is thought to have been Teshub or Teshup ; for a god of that name is known from the Tel-el-Amarna letters to have been the chief deity of the Mitani, a people of Northern Mesopotamia akin in speech and religion to the Hittites, but ruled by an Aryan dynasty. See Ed. Meyer, *Geschichte des Altertums,*[2] i. 2. pp. 578, 591 *sq.,* 636 *sq.* ; R. F. Harper, *Assyrian and Babylonian Literature,* pp. 222, 223 (where the god's name is spelt Tishub). The god is also mentioned repeatedly in the Hittite archives which Dr. H. Winckler found inscribed on clay tablets at Boghaz - Keui. See H. Winckler, " Vorläufige Nachrichten über die Ausgrabungen in Boghaz-köi im Sommer 1907," *Mitteilungen der Deutschen Orient-Gesellschaft zu Berlin,* No. 35, December 1907, pp. 13 *sq.,* 32, 34, 36, 38, 39, 43, 44, 51 *sq.,* 53 ; " Hittite Archives from Boghaz - Keui," translated from the German transcripts of Dr. Winckler, *Annals of Archaeology and Anthropology,* iv. (Liverpool and London, 1912) pp. 90 *sqq.* As to the Mitani, their language and their gods, see H. Winckler, *op. cit.* pp. 30 *sqq.,* 46 *sqq.* In thus interpreting the

Hittite god who heads the procession at Boghaz-Keui I follow my colleague Prof. J. Garstang (*The Land of the Hittites,* p. 237 ; *The Syrian Goddess,* pp. 5 *sqq.*), who has kindly furnished me with some notes on the subject. I formerly interpreted the deity as the Hittite equivalent of Tammuz, Adonis, and Attis. But against that view it may be urged that (1) the god is bearded and therefore of mature age, whereas Tammuz and his fellows were regularly conceived as youthful ; (2) the thunderbolt which he seems to carry would be quite inappropriate to Tammuz, who was not a god of thunder but of vegetation ; and (3) the Hittite Tammuz is appropriately represented in the procession of women immediately behind the Mother Goddess (see below, pp. 137 *sq.*), and it is extremely improbable that he should be represented twice over with different attributes in the same scene. These considerations seem to me conclusive against the interpretation of the bearded god as a Tammuz and decisive in favour of Professor Garstang's view of him.

[1] J. Garstang, " Notes of a Journey through Asia Minor," *Annals of Archaeology and Anthropology,* i. (Liverpool and London, 1908) pp. 3 *sq.,* with plate iv.; *id., The Land of the Hittites,* pp. 138, 359, with plate xliv. In this sculpture the god on the bull holds in his right hand what is described as a triangular bow instead of a mace, an axe, or a hammer.

Egyptian language. The Hittite copy was found some years ago inscribed in cuneiform characters on a clay tablet at Boghaz-Keui ; two copies of the treaty in the Egyptian language are engraved on the walls of temples at Thebes. From the Egyptian copies, which have been read and translated, we gather that the thunder-god was the principal deity of the Hittites, and that the two Hittite seals which were appended to the treaty exhibited the King embraced by the thunder-god and the Queen embraced by the sun-goddess of Arenna.[1] This Hittite divinity of the thundering sky appears to have long survived at Doliche in Commagene, for in later Roman art he reappears under the title of Jupiter Dolichenus, wearing a Phrygian cap, standing on a bull, and wielding a double axe in one hand and a thunderbolt in the other. In this form his worship was transported from his native Syrian home by soldiers and slaves, till it had spread over a large part of the Roman empire, especially on the frontiers, where it flourished in the camps of the legions.[2] The combination of the bull with the thunderbolt as emblems of the deity suggests that the animal may have been chosen to represent the sky-god for the sake not merely of its virility but of its voice ; for in the peal of thunder primitive man may well have heard the bellowing of a celestial bull.

Jupiter Dolichenus.

[1] A. Wiedemann, *Ägyptische Geschichte* (Gotha, 1884), ii. 438-440 ; G. Maspero, *Histoire Ancienne des Peuples de l'Orient Classique*, ii. (Paris, 1897) pp. 401 *sq.* ; W. Max Müller, *Der Bündnisvortrag Ramses' II. und des Chetitirkönigs*, pp. 17-19, 21 *sq.*, 38-44 (*Mitteilungen der Vorderasiatischen Gesellschaft*, 1902, No. 5, Berlin) ; L. Messerschmidt, *The Hittites*, pp. 14-19 ; J. H. Breasted, *Ancient Records of Egypt* (Chicago, 1906-1907), iii. 163-174 ; *id.*, *A History of the Ancient Egyptians* (London, 1908), p. 311 ; Ed. Meyer, *Geschichte des Altertums*,[2] i. 2. pp. 631, 635 *sqq.*; J. Garstang, *The Land of the Hittites*, pp. 347-349. The Hittite copy of the treaty was discovered by Dr. H. Winckler at Boghaz-Keui in 1906. The identification of Arenna or Arinna is uncertain. In a forthcoming article, " The Sun God[dess] of Arenna," to

be published in the Liverpool *Annals of Archaeology and Anthropology*, Professor J. Garstang argues that Arenna is to be identified with the Cappadocian Comana.

[2] Ed. Meyer, "Dolichenus," in W. H. Roscher's *Lexikon der griech. und röm. Mythologie*, i. 1191-1194; A. von Domaszewski, *Die Religion des römischen Heeres* (Treves, 1895), pp. 59 *sq.*, with plate iiii. fig. 1 and 2 ; Franz Cumont, *s.v.* "Dolichenus," in Pauly-Wissowa's *Real-Encyclopädie der classischen Altertumswissenschaft*, v. i. coll. 1276 *sqq.*; J. Toutain, *Les Cultes païens dans l'Empire Romain*, ii. (Paris, 1911) pp. 35-43. For examples of the inscriptions which relate to his worship see H. Dessau, *Inscriptiones Latinae Selectae*, vol. ii. Pars i. (Berlin, 1902) pp. 167-172, Nos. 4296-4324.

The goddess who at the head of the procession of women confronts the great sky-god in the sanctuary at Boghaz-Keui is generally recognized as the divine Mother, the great Asiatic goddess of life and fertility. The tall flat-topped hat with perpendicular grooves which she wears, and the lioness or panther on which she stands, remind us of the turreted crown and lion-drawn car of Cybele, who was worshipped in the neighbouring land of Phrygia across the Halys.[1] So Atargatis, the great Syrian goddess of Hiera-polis-Bambyce, was portrayed sitting on lions and wearing a tower on her head.[2] At Babylon an image of a goddess whom the Greeks called Rhea had the figures of two lions standing on her knees.[3]

The Mother Goddess.

But in the rock-hewn sculptures of Boghaz-Keui, who is the youth with the tall pointed cap and double axe who stands on a lioness or panther immediately behind the great goddess? His figure is all the more remarkable because he is the only male who interrupts the long procession of women. Probably he is at once the divine son and the divine lover of the goddess; for we shall find later on that in Phrygian mythology Attis united in himself both these characters.[4]

The youth on the lioness, bearing the double axe, at Boghaz-Keui may be the divine son and lover of the goddess.

---

[1] As to the lions and mural crown of Cybele see Lucretius, ii. 600 *sqq.* ; Catullus, lxiii. 76 *sqq.* ; Macrobius, *Saturn.* i. 23. 20 ; Rapp, *s.v.* " Kybele," in W. H. Roscher's *Lexikon der griech. und röm. Mythologie*, ii. 1644 *sqq.*

[2] Lucian, *De dea Syria*, 31 ; Macro-bius, *Saturn.* i. 23. 19. Lucian's de-scription of her image is confirmed by coins of Hierapolis, on which the goddess is represented wearing a high head-dress and seated on a lion. See B. V. Head, *Historia Numorum* (Oxford, 1887), p. 654; G. Mac-donald, *Catalogue of Greek Coins in the Hunterian Collection* (Glasgow, 1899–1905), iii. 139 *sq.* ; J. Gar-stang, *The Syrian Goddess*, pp. 21 *sqq.*, 70, with fig. 7. That the name of the Syrian goddess of Hierapolis-Bambyce was Atargatis is mentioned by Strabo (xvi. 1. 27, p. 748). On Egyptian monuments the Semitic god-dess Kadesh is represented standing on a lion. See W. Max Müller, *Asien*

und Europa, pp. 314 *sq.* It is to be remembered that Hierapolis-Bambyce was the direct successor of Carchemish, the great Hittite capital on the Euph-rates, and may have inherited many features of Hittite religion. See A. H. Sayce, *The Hittites*,[3] pp. 94 *sqq.*, 105 *sqq.* ; and as to the Hittite monuments at Carchemish, see J. Garstang, *The Land of the Hittites*, pp. 122 *sqq.*

[3] Diodorus Siculus, ii. 9. 5.

[4] In thus interpreting the youth with the double axe I agree with Sir W. M. Ramsay (" On the Early His-torical Relations between Phrygia and Cappadocia," *Journal of the Royal Asiatic Society*, N.S. xv. (1883) pp. 118, 120), C. P. Tiele (*Geschichte der Religion im Altertum*, i. 246, 255), and Prof. J. Garstang (*The Land of the Hittites*, p. 235; *The Syrian Goddess*, p. 8). That the youthful figure on the lioness or panther repre-sents the lover of the great goddess is the view also of Professors Jensen and

The lioness or panther on which he stands marks his affinity with the goddess, who is supported by a similar animal. It is natural that the lion-goddess should have a lion-son and a lion-lover. For we may take it as probable that the Oriental deities who are represented standing or sitting in human form on the backs of lions and other animals were originally indistinguishable from the beasts, and that the complete separation of the bestial from the human or divine shape was a consequence of that growth of knowledge and of power which led man in time to respect himself more and the brutes less. The hybrid gods of Egypt with their human

Hommel. See P. Jensen, *Hittiter und Armenier*, pp. 173-175, 180; F. Hommel, *Grundriss der Geographie und Geschichte des alten Orients*, p. 51. Prof. Perrot holds that the youth in question is a double of the bearded god who stands at the head of the male procession, their costume being the same, though their attributes differ (G. Perrot et Ch. Chipiez, *Histoire de l'Art dans l'Antiquité*, iv. 651). But, as I have already remarked, it is unlikely that the same god should be represented twice over with different attributes in the same scene. The resemblance between the two figures is better explained on the supposition that they are Father and Son. The same two deities, Father and Son, appear to be carved on a rock at Giaour-Kalesi, a place on the road which in antiquity may have led from Ancyra by Gordium to Pessinus. Here on the face of the rock are cut in relief two gigantic figures in the usual Hittite costume of pointed cap, short tunic, and shoes turned up at the toes. Each wears a crescent-hilted sword at his side, each is marching to the spectator's left with raised right hand; and the resemblance between them is nearly complete except that the figure in front is beardless and the figure behind is bearded. See G. Perrot et Ch. Chipiez, *Histoire de l'Art dans l'Antiquité*, iv. 714 *sqq.*, with fig. 352; J. Garstang, *The Land of the Hittites*, pp. 162-164. A similar, but solitary, figure is carved in a niche of the rock at Kara-Bel, but there the

deity, or the man, carries a triangular bow over his right shoulder. See below, p. 185.

With regard to the lionesses or panthers, a bas-relief found at Carchemish, the capital of a Hittite kingdom on the Euphrates, shows two male figures in Hittite costume, with pointed caps and turned-up shoes, standing on a couching lion. The foremost of the two figures is winged and carries a short curved truncheon in his right hand. According to Prof. Perrot, the two figures represent a god followed by a priest or a king. See G. Perrot et Ch. Chipiez, *Histoire de l'Art dans l'Antiquité*, iv. 549 *sq.*; J. Garstang, *The Land of the Hittites*, pp. 123 *sqq.* Again, on a sculptured slab found at Amrit in Phoenicia we see a god standing on a lion and holding a lion's whelp in his left hand, while in his right hand he brandishes a club or sword. See Perrot et Chipiez, *op. cit.* iii. 412-414. The type of a god or goddess standing or sitting on a lion occurs also in Assyrian art, from which the Phoenicians and Hittites may have borrowed it. See Perrot et Chipiez, *op. cit.* ii. 642-644. Much evidence as to the representation of Asiatic deities with lions has been collected by Raoul-Rochette, in his learned dissertation "Sur l'Hercule Assyrien et Phénicien," *Mémoires de l'Académie des Inscriptions et Belles-Lettres*, xvii. Deuxième Partie (Paris, 1848), pp. 106 *sqq.* Compare De Vogüé, *Mélanges d'Archéologie Orientale*, pp. 44 *sqq.*

bodies and animal heads form an intermediate stage in this evolution of anthropomorphic deities out of beasts.

We may now perhaps hazard a conjecture as to the meaning of that strange colossal figure in the inner shrine at Boghaz-Keui with its human head and its body composed of lions. For it is to be observed that the head of the figure is youthful and beardless, and that it wears a tall pointed cap, thus resembling in both respects the youth with the double-headed axe who stands on a lion in the outer sanctuary. We may suppose that the leonine figure in the inner shrine sets forth the true mystic, that is, the old savage nature of the god who in the outer shrine presented himself to his worshippers in the decent semblance of a man. To the chosen few who were allowed to pass the monster-guarded portal into the Holy of Holies, the awful secret may have been revealed that their god was a lion, or rather a lion-man, a being in whom the bestial and human natures mysteriously co-existed.[1] The reader may remember that on the rock beside this leonine divinity is carved a group which represents a god with his arm twined round the neck of his priest in an attitude of protection, holding one of the priest's hands in his own. Both figures are looking and stepping towards the lion-monster, and the god is holding out his right hand as if pointing to it. The scene may represent the deity revealing the mystery to the priest, or preparing him to act his part in some solemn rite for which all his strength and courage will be needed. He seems to be leading his minister onward, comforting him with an assurance that no harm can come near him while the divine arm is around him and the divine hand clasps his. Whither is he leading him? Perhaps to death. The deep shadows of the rocks which fall on the

The mystery of the lion-god.

---

[1] Similarly in Yam, one of the Torres Straits Islands, two brothers named Sigai and Maiau were worshipped in a shrine under the form of a hammer-headed shark and a crocodile respectively, and were represented by effigies made of turtle - shell in the likeness of these animals. But " the shrines were so sacred that no un-initiated persons might visit them, nor did they know what they contained ; they were aware of Sigai and Maiau, but they did not know that the former was a hammer-headed shark and the latter a crocodile ; this mystery was too sacred to be imparted to uninitiates. When the heroes were addressed it was always by their human names, and not by their animal or totem names." See A. C. Haddon, " The Religion of the Torres Straits Islanders," *Anthropological Essays presented to E. B. Tylor* (Oxford, 1907), p. 185.

two figures in the gloomy chasm may be an emblem of darker shadows soon to fall on the priest. Yet still he grasps his pastoral staff and goes forward, as though he said, " Yea, though I walk through the valley of the shadow of death, I will fear no evil; for thou art with me : thy rod and thy staff they comfort me."

The processions at Boghaz-Keui appear to represent the Sacred Marriage of the god and goddess.

If there is any truth in these guesses—for they are little more—the three principal figures in the processional scene at Boghaz-Keui represent the divine Father, the divine Mother, and the divine Son. But we have still to ask, What are they doing? That they are engaged in the performance of some religious rite seems certain. But what is it? We may conjecture that it is the rite of the Sacred Marriage, and that the scene is copied from a ceremony which was periodically performed in this very place by human representatives of the deities.[1] Indeed, the solemn meeting of the male and female figures at the head of their respective processions obviously suggests a marriage, and has been so interpreted by scholars, who, however, regarded it as the historical wedding of a prince and princess instead of the mystic union of a god and goddess, overlooking or explaining away the symbols of divinity which accompany the principal personages.[2] We may suppose that at Boghaz-Keui, as at many other places in the interior of Asia Minor, the government was in the hands of a family who combined royal with priestly functions and personated the gods whose names they bore. Thus at Pessinus in Phrygia, as we shall see later on, the priests of Cybele bore the name of her consort Attis, and doubtless represented him in the ritual.[3]

[1] " There can be no doubt that there is here represented a Sacred Marriage, the meeting of two deities worshipped in different places, like the Horus of Edfu and the Hathor of Denderah " (C. P. Tiele, *Geschichte der Religion im Altertum*, i. 255). This view seems to differ from, though it approaches, the one suggested in the text. That the scene represents a Sacred Marriage between a great god and goddess is the opinion also of Prof. Ed. Meyer (*Geschichte des Altertums*,[2] i. 2. pp. 633 *sq.*), and Prof. J. Garstang (*The Land of the*

Hittites, pp. 238 *sq.* ; *The Syrian Goddess*, p. 7).

[2] See above, p. 133.

[3] See below, p. 285. Compare the remarks of Sir W. M. Ramsay ("Pre-Hellenic Monuments of Cappadocia," *Recueil de Travaux relatifs à la Philologie et à l'Archéologie Égyptiennes et Assyriennes*, xiii. (1890) p. 78): "Similar priest-dynasts are a widespread feature of the primitive social system of Asia Minor ; their existence is known with certainty or inferred with probability at the two towns Komana ; at Venasa not far north.

If this was so at Boghaz-Keui, we may surmise that the chief
pontiff and his family annually celebrated the marriage of
the divine powers of fertility, the Father God and the Mother
Goddess, for the purpose of ensuring the fruitfulness of the
earth and the multiplication of men and beasts. The
principal parts in the ceremony would naturally be played
by the pontiff himself and his wife, unless indeed they
preferred for good reasons to delegate the onerous duty
to others. That such a delegation took place is perhaps
suggested by the appearance of the pontiff himself in a
subordinate place in the procession, as well as by his separate
representation in another place, as if he were in the act of
surveying the ceremony from a distance.[1] The part of the
divine Son at the rite would fitly devolve upon one of the
high-priest's own offspring, who may well have been numerous. For it is probable that here, as elsewhere in Asia
Minor, the Mother Goddess was personated by a crowd of
sacred harlots,[2] with whom the spiritual ruler may have been
required to consort in his character of incarnate deity. But
if the personation of the Son of God at the rites laid a
heavy burden of suffering on the shoulders of the actor, it is
possible that the representative of the deity may have been
drawn, perhaps by lot, from among the numerous progeny
of the consecrated courtesans ; for these women, as incarnations of the Mother Goddess, were probably supposed to
transmit to their offspring some portion of their own divinity.
Be that as it may, if the three principal personages in the
processional scene at Boghaz-Keui are indeed the Father,
the Mother, and the Son, the remarkable position assigned

Traces of
mother-kin
among the
Hittites.

---

of Tyana, at Olba, at Pessinous, at
Aizanoi, and many other places. Now
there are two characteristics which
can be regarded as probable in regard
to most of these priests, and as proved
in regard to some of them : (1) they
wore the dress and represented the
person of the god, whose priests they
were; (2) they were ἱερώνυμοι, losing
their individual name at their succession
to the office, and assuming a sacred
name, often that of the god himself or
some figure connected with the cultus
of the god. The priest of Cybele at

Pessinous was called Attis, the priests
of Sabazios were Saboi, the worshippers of Bacchos Bacchoi." As to the
priestly rulers of Olba, see below,
pp. 144 *sqq.*

[1] See above, p. 132. However,
Prof. Ed. Meyer may be right in
thinking that the priest-like figure in
the procession is not really that of the
priest but that of the god or goddess
whom he personated. See above, p.
133 note.

[2] See above, pp. 36 *sqq.*

to the third of them in the procession, where he walks behind his Mother alone in the procession of women, appears to indicate that he was supposed to be more closely akin to her than to his Father.   From this again we may con-jecturally infer that mother-kin rather than father-kin was the rule which regulated descent among the Hittites.   The conjecture derives some support from Hittite archives, for the names of the Great Queen and the Queen Mother are mentioned along with that of the King in state documents.[1] The other personages who figure in the procession may represent human beings masquerading in the costumes and with the attributes of deities.   Such, for example, are the two female figures who stand on a double-headed eagle; the two male figures stepping on what seem to be two mountains ; and the two winged beings in the procession of men, one of whom may be the Moon-god, for he wears a crescent on his head.[2]

§ 5. *Sandan and Baal at Tarsus*

Sandan at Tarsus appears to be a son of Baal, as Hercules was a son of Zeus.

Whatever may be thought of these speculations, one thing seems fairly clear and certain.   The figure which I have called the divine Son at Boghaz-Keui is identical with the god San-dan, who appears on the pyre at Tarsus.   In both personages the costume, the attributes, the attitude are the same.   Both represent a man clad in a short tunic with a tall pointed cap on his head, a sword at his side, a double-headed axe in his hand, and a lion or panther under his feet.[3]   Accordingly, if we are right in identifying him as the divine Son at Boghaz-

---

[1] H. Winckler, "Vorläufige Nach-richten über die Ausgrabungen in Boghaz-köi im Sommer 1907," *Mit-teilungen der Deutschen Orient-Gesell-schaft*, No. 35, December, 1907, pp. 27 *sq.*, 29 ; J. Garstang, *The Land of the Hittites*, pp. 352 *sq.*; "Hittite Archives from Boghaz-Keui," trans-lated from the German transcripts of Dr. Winckler by Meta E. Williams, *Annals of Archaeology and Anthro-pology*, iv. (Liverpool and London, 1912) p. 98.   We have seen (above, p. 136) that in the seals of the Hittite treaty with Egypt the Queen appears along with the King. If Dr.

H. Winckler is right in thinking (*op. cit.* p. 29) that one of the Hittite queens was at the same time sister to her husband the King, we should have in this relationship a further proof that mother-kin regulated the descent of the kingship among the Hittites as well as among the ancient Egyptians. See above, p. 44, and below, vol. ii. pp. 213 *sqq.*

[2] Compare Ed. Meyer, *Geschichte des Altertums*,[2] i. 2. pp. 629-633.

[3] The figure exhibits a few minor variations on the coins of Tarsus.   See the works cited above, p. 127.

Keui, we may conjecture that under the name of Sandan he bore the same character at Tarsus. The conjecture squares perfectly with the title of Hercules, which the Greeks bestowed on Sandan ; for Hercules was the son of Zeus, the great father-god. Moreover, we have seen that the Baal of Tarsus, with the grapes and the corn in his hand, was assimilated to Zeus.[1] Thus it would appear that at Tarsus as at Boghaz-Keui there was a pair of deities, a divine Father and a divine Son, whom the Greeks identified with Zeus and Hercules respectively. If the Baal of Tarsus was a god of fertility, as his attributes clearly imply, his identification with Zeus would be natural, since it was Zeus who, in the belief of the Greeks, sent the fertilizing rain from heaven.[2] And the identification of Sandan with Hercules would be equally natural, since the lion and the death on the pyre were features common to both. Our conclusion then is that it was the divine Son, the lion-god, who was burned in effigy or in the person of a human representative at Tarsus, and perhaps at Boghaz-Keui. Semitic parallels suggest that the victim who played the part of the Son of God in the fiery furnace ought in strictness to be the king's son.[3] But no doubt in later times an effigy would be substituted for the man.

§ 6. *Priestly Kings of Olba*

Unfortunately we know next to nothing of the kings and priests of Tarsus. In Greek times we hear of an Epicurean philosopher of the city, Lysias by name, who was elected by his fellow-citizens to the office of Crown-wearer, that is, to the priesthood of Hercules. Once raised to that dignity, he would not lay it down again, but played the part of tyrant, wearing a white robe edged with purple, a costly cloak, white shoes, and a golden wreath of laurel. He truckled to the mob by distributing among them the property of the wealthy, while he put to death such as refused to open their money-bags to him.[4] Though we cannot distinguish in this account

Priests of Sandan-Hercules at Tarsus.

---

[1] Above, p. 119.

[2] *The Magic Art and the Evolution of Kings*, ii. 358 *sqq.*

[3] *The Dying God*, pp. 166 *sqq.*

[4] Athenaeus, v. 54, p. 215 B, C. The high-priest of the Syrian goddess at Hierapolis held office for a year, and wore a purple robe and a golden tiara

between the legal and the illegal exercise of authority, yet
we may safely infer that the priesthood of Hercules, that is
of Sandan, at Tarsus continued down to late times to be
an office of great dignity and power, not unworthy to be

Kings of Cilicia related to Sandan. held in earlier times by the kings themselves.   Scanty as is
our information as to the kings of Cilicia, we hear of two
whose names appear to indicate that they stood in some
special relation to the divine Sandan.   One of them was
Sandu'arri, lord of Kundi and Sizu, which have been identified with Anchiale and Sis in Cilicia.[1]   The other was
Sanda-sarme, who gave his daughter in marriage to Ashurbanipal, king of Assyria.[2]   It would be in accordance with
analogy if the kings of Tarsus formerly held the priesthood
of Sandan and claimed to represent him in their own person.

Priestly kings of Olba who bore the names of Teucer and Ajax. We know that the whole of Western or Mountainous
Cilicia was ruled by kings who combined the regal office
with the priesthood of Zeus, or rather of a native deity
whom, like the Baal of Tarsus, the Greeks assimilated to
their own Zeus.   These priestly potentates had their seat
at Olba, and most of them bore the name either of Teucer
or of Ajax,[3] but we may suspect that these appellations are
merely Greek distortions of native Cilician names.   Teucer
(*Teukros*) may be a corruption of Tark, Trok, Tarku, or
Troko, all of which occur in the names of Cilician priests
and kings.   At all events, it is worthy of notice that one,

(Lucian, *De dea Syria*, 42).   We may
conjecture that the priesthood of
Hercules at Tarsus was in later times
at least an annual office.

[1] E. Meyer, *Geschichte des Alterthums*, i. (Stuttgart, 1884) § 389, p.
475; H. Winckler, in E. Schrader's
*Keilinschriften und das Alte Testa-
ment*,[3] p. 88.   Kuinda was the name
of a Cilician fortress a little way inland
from Anchiale (Strabo, xiv. 5. 10, p.
672).

[2] E. Meyer, *op. cit.* i. § 393, p.
480; C. P. Tiele, *Babylonisch-
assyrische Geschichte*, p. 360.   Sandon and Sandas occur repeatedly as
names of Cilician men.   They are
probably identical with, or modified
forms of, the divine name.   See
Strabo, xiv. 5. 14, p. 674; Plutarch,

Poplicola, 17; *Corpus Inscriptionum
Graecarum*, ed. August Boeckh, etc.
(Berlin, 1828–1877) vol. iii. p. 200,
No. 4401; Ch. Michel, *Recueil d'In-
scriptions Grecques* (Brussels, 1900),
p. 718, No. 878; R. Heberdey und
A. Wilhelm, "Reisen in Kilikien,"
*Denkschriften der Kaiser. Akademie
der Wissenschaften, Philosoph.-histor.
Classe*, xliv. (Vienna, 1896) No. vi.
pp. 46, 131 *sq.*, 140 (Inscriptions 115,
218, 232).

[3] Strabo, xiv. 5. 10, p. 672.   The
name of the high-priest Ajax, son of
Teucer, occurs on coins of Olba, dating from about the beginning of our
era (B. V. Head, *Historia Numorum*,
Oxford, 1887, p. 609); and the name
of Teucer is also known from inscriptions.   See below, pp. 145, 151, 159.

if not two, of these priestly Teucers had a father called
Tarkuaris,[1] and that in a long list of priests who served
Zeus at the Corycian cave, not many miles from Olba, the
names Tarkuaris, Tarkumbios, Tarkimos, Trokoarbasis, and
Trokombigremis, besides many other obviously native names,
occur side by side with Teucer and other purely Greek
appellations.[2] In like manner the Teucrids, who traced
their descent from Zeus and reigned at Salamis in Cyprus,[3]
may well have been a native dynasty, who concocted a
Greek pedigree for themselves in the days when Greek
civilization was fashionable. The legend which attributed
the foundation of the Cyprian Salamis to Teucer, son of
Telamon, appears to be late and unknown to Homer.[4]
Moreover, a cruel form of human sacrifice which was
practised in the city down to historical times savours
rather of Oriental barbarity than of Greek humanity. Led
or driven by the youths, a man ran thrice round the altar ;
then the priest stabbed him in the throat with a spear and
burned his body whole on a heaped-up pyre. The sacrifice
was offered in the month of Aphrodite to Diomede, who
along with Agraulus, daughter of Cecrops, had a temple at
Salamis. A temple of Athena stood within the same

The
Teucrids
of Salamis
in Cyprus.

Burnt
sacrifices
of human
victims at
Salamis
and traces
of a similar
custom
elsewhere.

[1] E. L. Hicks, "Inscriptions from
Western Cilicia," *Journal of Hellenic
Studies*, xii. (1891) pp. 226, 263 ; R.
Heberdey und A. Wilhelm, "Reisen
in Kilikien," *Denkschriften der Kaiser.
Akademie der Wissenschaften*, xliv.
(1896) No. vi. pp. 53, 88.

[2] Ch. Michel, *Recueil d'Inscriptions
Grecques*, pp. 718 *sqq.*, No. 878. Tark-
ondimotos was the name of two kings of
Eastern Cilicia in the first century B.C.
One of them corresponded with Cicero
and fell at the battle of Actium. See
Cicero, *Epist. ad Familiares*, xv. 1. 2 ;
Strabo, xiv. 5. 18, p. 676 ; Dio
Cassius, xli. 63. 1, xlvii. 26. 2, l.
14. 2, li. 2. 2, li. 7. 4, liv. 9. 2 ;
Plutarch, *Antoninus*, 61 ; B. V. Head,
Historia Numorum (Oxford, 1887),
p. 618 ; W. Dittenberger, *Orientis
Graeci Inscriptiones Selectae* (Leipsic,
1903-1905), ii. pp. 494 *sq.*, Nos.
752, 753. Moreover, Tarkudimme or
Tarkuwassimi occurs as the name of a
king of Erme (?) or Urmi (?) in a

bilingual Hittite and cuneiform inscription engraved on a silver seal. See
W. Wright, *The Empire of the
Hittites* [2] (London, 1886), pp. 163
sqq. ; L. Messerschmidt, *Corpus Inscriptionum Hettiticarum*, pp. 42 *sq.*,
pl. xlii. 9 ; *id.*, *The Hittites*, pp. 29
sq. ; P. Jensen, *Hittiter und Armenier*
(Strasburg, 1898), pp. 22, 50 *sq.*
In this inscription Prof. Jensen suggests
Tarbibi- as an alternative reading for
Tarku-. Compare P. Kretschmer,
*Einleitung in die Geschichte der
griechischen Sprache* (Göttingen, 1896),
pp. 362-364.

[3] Isocrates, *Or.* ix. 14 and 18 *sq.* ;
Pausanias, ii. 29. 2 and 4 ; W. E.
Engel, *Kypros*, i. 212 *sqq.* As to the
names Teucer and Teucrian see P.
Kretschmer, *op. cit.* pp. 189-191.
Prof. Kretschmer believes that the
native population of Cyprus belonged
to the non-Aryan stock of Asia Minor.

[4] W. E. Engel, *Kypros*, i. 216.

sacred enclosure. It is said that in olden times the sacrifice was offered to Agraulus, and not to Diomede. According to another account it was instituted by Teucer in honour of Zeus. However that may have been, the barbarous custom lasted down to the reign of Hadrian, when Diphilus, king of Cyprus, abolished or rather mitigated it by substituting the sacrifice of an ox for that of a man.[1] On the hypothesis here suggested we must suppose that these Greek names of divine or heroic figures at the Cyprian Salamis covered more or less similar figures of the Asiatic pantheon. And in the Salaminian burnt-sacrifice of a man we may perhaps detect the original form of the ceremony which in historical times appears to have been performed upon an image of Sandan or Hercules at Tarsus. When an ox was sacrificed instead of a man, the old sacrificial rites would naturally continue to be observed in all other respects exactly as before: the animal would be led thrice round the altar, stabbed with a spear, and burned on a pyre. Now at the Syrian Hierapolis the greatest festival of the year bore the name of the Pyre or the Torch. It was held at the beginning of spring. Great trees were then cut down and planted in the court of the temple: sheep, goats, birds, and other creatures were hung upon them: sacrificial victims were led round: then fire was set to the whole, and everything was consumed in the flames.[2] Perhaps here also the burning of animals was a substitute for the burning of men. When the practice of human sacrifice becomes too revolting to humanity to be tolerated, its abolition is commonly effected by substituting

[1] Porphyry, *De abstinentia*, ii. 54 *sq.* ; Lactantius, *Divin. Inst.* i. 21. As to the date when the custom was abolished, Lactantius says that it was done "recently in the reign of Hadrian." Porphyry says that the practice was put down by Diphilus, king of Cyprus, "in the time of Seleucus the Theologian." As nothing seems to be known as to the date of King Diphilus and Seleucus the Theologian, I have ventured to assume, on the strength of Lactantius's statement, that they were contemporaries of Hadrian. But it is curious to find kings of Cyprus reigning so late.

Beside the power of the Roman governors, their authority can have been little more than nominal, like that of native rajahs in British India. Seleucus the Theologian may be, as J. A. Fabricius supposed (*Bibliotheca Graeca*,[4] Hamburg, 1780–1809, vol. i. p. 86, compare p. 522), the Alexandrian grammarian who composed a voluminous work on the gods (Suidas, *s.v.* Σέλευκος). Suetonius tells an anecdote (*Tiberius*, 56) about a grammarian named Seleucus who flourished, and faded prematurely, at the court of Tiberius.

[2] Lucian, *De dea Syria*, 49.

either animals or images for living men or women. At
Salamis certainly, and perhaps at Hierapolis, the substitutes
were animals : at Tarsus, if I am right, they were images.
In this connexion the statement of a Greek writer as to the
worship of Adonis in Cyprus deserves attention. He says
that as Adonis had been honoured by Aphrodite, the
Cyprians after his death cast live doves on a pyre to him,
and that the birds, flying away from the flames, fell into
another pyre and were consumed.[1] The statement seems to
be a description of an actual custom of burning doves in
sacrifice to Adonis. Such a mode of honouring him would
be very remarkable, since doves were commonly sacred to
his divine mistress Aphrodite or Astarte. For example, at
the Syrian Hierapolis, one of the chief seats of her worship,
these birds were so holy that they might not even be
touched. If a man inadvertently touched a dove, he was
unclean or tabooed for the rest of the day. Hence the
birds, never being molested, were so tame that they lived
with the people in their houses, and commonly picked up
their food fearlessly on the ground.[2] Can the burning of
the sacred bird of Aphrodite in the Cyprian worship of
Adonis have been a substitute for the burning of a sacred
man who personated the lover of the goddess ?

Burnt sacrifice of doves to Adonis.

If, as many scholars think, Tark or Tarku was the name,
or part of the name, of a great Hittite deity, sometimes
identified as the god of the sky and the lightning,[3] we may

The priestly Teucers of Olba

---

[1] Diogenianus, *Praefatio*, in *Paroemiographi Graeci*, ed. E. L. Leutsch
et F. G. Schneidewin (Göttingen,
1839-1851), i. 180. Raoul-Rochette
regarded the custom as part of the
ritual of the divine death and resurrection. He compared it with the burning
of Melcarth at Tyre. See his memoir,
"Sur l'Hercule Assyrien et Phénicien,"
*Mémoires de l'Académie des Inscriptions
et Belles-Lettres*, xvii. Deuxième Partie
(1848), p. 32.

[2] Lucian, *De dea Syria*, 54.

[3] A. H. Sayce, in W. Wright's
Empire of the Hittites,[2] p. 186 ; W.
M. Ramsay, "Pre-Hellenic Monu-
ments of Cappadocia," *Recueil de
Travaux relatifs à la Philologie et
à l'Archéologie Égyptiennes et Assy-*

riennes, xiv. (1903) pp. 81 *sq.* ; C. P.
Tiele, *Geschichte der Religion im Altertum*, i. 251 ; W. Max Müller,
Asien und Europa, p. 333 ; P. Jensen, *Hittiter und Armenier*, pp. 70,
150 *sqq.*, 155 *sqq.* ; F. Hommel,
*Grundriss der Geographie und Ge-
schichte des alten Orients*, pp. 44, 51
sq. ; L. Messerschmidt, *The Hittites*,
p. 40. Sir W. M. Ramsay thinks
(*l.c.*) that Tark was the native name
of the god who had his sanctuary at
Dastarkon in Cappadocia and who was
called by the Greeks the Cataonian
Apollo : his sanctuary was revered all
over Cappadocia (Strabo, xiv. 2. 5,
p. 537). Prof. Hommel holds that
Tarku or Tarchu was the chief Hittite
deity, worshipped all over the south of

perhaps
personated
a native
god Tark.
conjecture that Tark or Tarku was the native name of the
god of Olba, whom the Greeks called Zeus, and that the
priestly kings who bore the name of Teucer represented
the god Tark or Tarku in their own persons. This conjecture is confirmed by the observation that Olba, the
ancient name of the city, is itself merely a Grecized form
of Oura, the name which the place retains to this day.[1]
The situation of the town, moreover, speaks strongly in
favour of the view that it was from the beginning an
aboriginal settlement, though in after days, like so many
other Asiatic cities, it took on a varnish of Greek culture.
For it stood remote from the sea on a lofty and barren
tableland, with a rigorous winter climate, in the highlands
of Cilicia.

Western
or Rugged
Cilicia.
Great indeed is the contrast between the bleak windy
uplands of Western or Rugged Cilicia, as the ancients called
it, and the soft luxuriant lowlands of Eastern Cilicia, where
winter is almost unknown and summer annually drives the
population to seek in the cool air of the mountains a refuge
from the intolerable heat and deadly fevers of the plains.
In Western Cilicia, on the other hand, a lofty tableland,
ending in a high sharp edge on the coast, rises steadily
inland till it passes gradually into the chain of heights
which divide it from the interior. Looked at from the sea
it resembles a great blue wave swelling in one uniform
sweep till its crest breaks into foam in the distant snows
of the Taurus. The surface of the tableland is almost
everywhere rocky and overgrown, in the intervals of the
rocks, with dense, thorny, almost impenetrable scrub. Only
here and there in a hollow or glen the niggardly soil allows
of a patch of cultivation; and here and there fine oaks and

Asia Minor. Prof. W. Max Müller is
of opinion that Targh or Tarkh did not
designate any particular deity, but was
the general Hittite name for "god."
There are grounds for holding that the
proper name of the Hittite thunder-
god was Teshub or Teshup. See
above, p. 135 note.

[1] J. T. Bent, "Explorations in
Cilicia Tracheia," *Proceedings of the
Royal Geographical Society*, N.S. xii.

(1890) p. 458; *id.*, "A Journey in
Cilicia Tracheia," *Journal of Hellenic
Studies*, xii. (1891) p. 222; W. M.
Ramsay, *Historical Geography of Asia
Minor* (London, 1890), pp. 22, 364.
Sir W. M. Ramsay had shown grounds
for thinking that Olba was a Grecized
form of a native name Ourba (pro-
nounced Ourwa) before Mr. J. T.
Bent discovered the site and the
name.

planes, towering over the brushwood, clothe with a richer
foliage the depth of the valleys.   None but wandering
herdsmen with their flocks now maintain a precarious
existence in this rocky wilderness.   Yet the ruined towns
which stud the country prove that a dense population lived
and throve here in antiquity, while numerous remains of
wine-presses and wine-vats bear witness to the successful
cultivation of the grape.   The chief cause of the present
desolation is lack of water ; for wells are few and brackish,
perennial streams hardly exist, and the ancient aqueducts,
which once brought life and fertility to the land, have long
been suffered to fall into disrepair.

But for ages together the ancient inhabitants of these The Cilician pirates.
uplands earned their bread by less reputable means than
the toil of the husbandman and the vinedresser.   They
were buccaneers and slavers, scouring the high seas with
their galleys and retiring with their booty to the inaccessible fastnesses of their mountains.   In the decline of Greek
power all over the East the pirate communities of Cilicia
grew into a formidable state, recruited by gangs of desper-
adoes and broken men who flocked to it from all sides.
The holds of these robbers may still be seen perched on
the brink of the profound ravines which cleave the tableland at frequent intervals.   With their walls of massive
masonry, their towers and battlements, overhanging dizzy
depths, they are admirably adapted to bid defiance to the
pursuit of justice.   In antiquity the dark forests of cedar,
which clothed much of the country and supplied the pirates
with timber for their ships, must have rendered access to
these fastnesses still more difficult.   The great gorge of the
Lamas River, which eats its way like a sheet of forked
lightning into the heart of the mountains, is dotted every
few miles with fortified towns, some of them still magnificent in their ruins, dominating sheer cliffs high above the
stream.   They are now the haunt only of the ibex and the
bear.   Each of these communities had its own crest or
badge, which may still be seen carved on the corners of the
mouldering towers.   No doubt, too, it blazoned the same
crest on the hull, the sails, or the streamers of the galley
which, manned with a crew of ruffians, it sent out to prey

upon the rich merchantmen in the Golden Sea, as the corsairs called the highway of commerce between Crete and Africa.

The deep gorges of Rugged Cilicia.

A staircase cut in the rock connects one of these ruined castles with the river in the glen, a thousand feet below. But the steps are worn and dangerous, indeed impassable. You may go for miles along the edge of these stupendous cliffs before you find a way down. The paths keep on the heights, for in many of its reaches the gully affords no foothold even to the agile nomads who alone roam these solitudes. At evening the winding course of the river may be traced for a long distance by a mist which, as the heat of the day declines, rises like steam from the deep gorge and hangs suspended in a wavy line of fleecy cloud above it. But even more imposing than the ravine of the Lamas is the terrific gorge known as the *Sheitan dere* or Devil's Glen near the Corycian cave. Prodigious walls of rock, glowing in the intense sunlight, black in the shadow, and spanned by a summer sky of the deepest blue, hem in the dry bed of a winter torrent, choked with rocks and tangled with thickets of evergreens, among which the oleanders with their slim stalks, delicate taper leaves, and bunches of crimson blossom stand out conspicuous.[1]

---

[1] J. Theodore Bent, "Explorations in Cilicia Tracheia," *Proceedings of the Royal Geographical Society*, N.S. xii. (1890) pp. 445, 450-453; *id.*, "A Journal in Cilicia Tracheia," *Journal of Hellenic Studies*, xii. (1891) pp. 208, 210-212, 217-219; R. Heberdey und A. Wilhelm, "Reisen in Kilikien," *Denkschriften der kaiser. Akademie der Wissenschaften, Philosoph.-historische Classe*, xliv. (Vienna, 1896) No. vi. pp. 49, 70; D. G. Hogarth and J. A. R. Munro, "Modern and Ancient Roads in Eastern Asia Minor," *Royal Geographical Society, Supplementary Papers*, vol. iii. part 5 (London, 1893), pp. 653 *sq.* As to the Cilician pirates see Strabo, xiv. 5. 2, pp. 668 *sq.*; Plutarch, *Pompeius*, 24; Appian, *Bellum Mithridat.* 92 *sq.*; Dio Cassius, xxxvi. 20-24 [3-6], ed. L. Dindorf; Cicero, *De imperio Cn. Pompeii*, 11 *sq.*; Th. Mommsen, *Roman History* (London, 1868), iii. 68-70, iv. 40-45, 118-120. As to the crests carved on their towns see J. T. Bent, "Cilician Symbols," *Classical Review*, iv. (1890) pp. 321 *sq.* Among these crests are a club (the badge of Olba), a bunch of grapes, the caps of the Dioscuri, the three-legged symbol, and so on. As to the cedars and shipbuilding timber of Cilicia in antiquity see Theophrastus, *Historia Plantarum*, iii. 2. 6, iv. 5. 5. The cedars and firs have now retreated to the higher slopes of the Taurus. Great destruction is wrought in the forests by the roving Yuruks with their flocks; for they light their fires under the trees, tap the firs for turpentine, bark the cedars for their huts and bee-hives, and lay bare whole tracts of country that the grass may grow for their sheep and goats. See J. T. Bent, in *Proceedings of the Royal Geographical Society*, N.S. xii. (1890) pp. 453-458.

The ruins of Olba, among the most extensive and remarkable in Asia Minor, were discovered in 1890 by Mr. J. Theodore Bent. But three years before another English traveller had caught a distant view of its battlements and towers outlined against the sky like a city of enchantment or dreams.[1] Standing at a height of nearly six thousand feet above the sea, the upper town commands a free, though somewhat uniform, prospect for immense distances in all directions. The sea is just visible far away to the south. On these heights the winter is long and severe. Snow lies on the ground for months. No Greek would have chosen such a site for a city, so bleak and chill, so far from blue water; but it served well for a fastness of brigands. Deep gorges, one of them filled for miles with tombs, surround it on all sides, rendering fortification walls superfluous. But a great square tower, four stories high, rises conspicuous on the hill, forming a landmark and earning for this upper town the native name of *Jebel Hissar*, or the Mountain of the Castle. A Greek inscription cut on the tower proves that it was built by Teucer, son of Tarkuaris, one of the priestly potentates of Olba. Among other remains of public buildings the most notable are forty tall Corinthian columns of the great temple of Olbian Zeus. Though coarse in style and corroded by long exposure to frost and snow, these massive pillars, towering above the ruins, produce an imposing effect. That the temple of which they formed part belonged indeed to Olbian Zeus is shown by a Greek inscription found within the sacred area, which records that the pent-houses on the inner side of the boundary wall were built by King Seleucus Nicator and repaired for Olbian Zeus by " the great high-priest Teucer, son of Zenophanes." About two hundred yards from this great temple are standing five elegant granite columns of a small temple dedicated to the goddess Fortune. Further, the remains of two theatres and many other public buildings attest the former splendour of this mountain city. An arched colonnade, of which some Corinthian columns are standing with their architraves, ran through the town ;

The site and ruins of Olba.

The temple of Olbian Zeus.

---

[1] D. G. Hogarth, *A Wandering Scholar in the Levant* (London, 1896), pp. 57 *sq.*

and an ancient paved road, lined with tombs and ruins, leads down hill to a lower and smaller city two or three miles distant. It is this lower town which retains the ancient name of Oura. Here the principal ruins occupy an isolated fir-clad height bounded by two narrow ravines full of rock-cut tombs. Below the town the ravines unite and form a fine gorge, down which the old road passed seaward.[1]

§ 7. *The God of the Corycian Cave*

Limestone caverns of Western Cilicia.

Nothing yet found at Olba throws light on the nature of the god who was worshipped there under the Greek name of Zeus. But at two places near the coast, distant only some fourteen or fifteen miles from Olba, a deity also called Zeus by the Greeks was revered in natural surroundings of a remarkable kind, which must have stood in close relation with the worship, and are therefore fitted to illustrate it. In both places the features of the landscape are of the same general cast, and at one of them the god was definitely identified with the Zeus of Olba. The country here consists of a tableland of calcareous rock rent at intervals by those great chasms which are characteristic of a limestone formation. Similar fissures, with the accompaniment of streams or rivers which pour into them and vanish under ground, are frequent in Greece, and may be observed in our own country near Ingleborough in Yorkshire. Fossil bones of extinct animals are often found embedded in

---

[1] J. Theodore Bent, "Explorations in Cilicia Tracheia," *Proceedings of the Royal Geographical Society*, N.S. xii. (1890) pp. 445 *sq.*, 458-460 ; *id.*, "A Journey in Cilicia Tracheia," *Journal of Hellenic Studies*, xii. (1890) pp. 220-222 ; E. L. Hicks, "Inscriptions from Western Cilicia," *ib.* pp. 262-270 ; R. Heberdey und A. Wilhelm, "Reisen in Kilikien," *Denkschriften der kaiser. Akademie der Wissenschaften, Philos.-histor. Classe,* xliv. (Vienna, 1896) No. vi. pp. 83-91 ; W. M. Ramsay and D. G. Hogarth, in *American Journal of Archaeology,* vi. (1890) p. 345 ; Ch.

Michel, *Recueil d'Inscriptions Grec-ques*, p. 858, No. 1231. In one place (*Journal of Hellenic Studies*, xii. 222) Bent gives the height of Olba as 3800 feet ; but this is a misprint, for elsewhere (*Proceedings of the Royal Geographical Society*, N.S. xii. 446, 458) he gives the height as exactly 5850 or roughly 6000 feet. The misprint has unfortunately been repeated by Messrs. Heberdey and Wilhelm (*op. cit.* p. 84 note [1]). The tall tower of Olba is figured on the coins of the city. See G. F. Hill, *Catalogue of the Greek Coins of Lycaonia, Isauria, and Cilicia* (London, 1900), pl. xxii. 8.

the stalagmite or breccia of limestone caves.   For example, the famous Kent's Hole near Torquay contained bones of the mammoth, rhinoceros, lion, hyaena, and bear ; and red osseous breccias, charged with the bones of quadrupeds which have long disappeared from Europe, are common in almost all the countries bordering on the Mediterranean.[1] Western Cilicia is richer in Miocene deposits than any other part of Anatolia, and the limestone gorges of the coast near Olba are crowded with fossil oysters, corals, and other shells.[2] Here, too, within the space of five miles the limestone plateau is rent by three great chasms, which Greek religion associated with Zeus and Typhon.   One of these fissures is the celebrated Corycian cave.

To visit this spot, invested with the double charm of natural beauty and legendary renown, you start from the dead Cilician city of Corycus on the sea, with its ruined walls, towers, and churches, its rock-hewn houses and cisterns, its shattered mole, its island-fortress, still imposing in decay.   Viewed from the sea, this part of the Cilician coast, with its long succession of white ruins, relieved by the dark wooded hills behind, presents an appearance of populousness and splendour.   But a nearer approach reveals the nakedness and desolation of the once prosperous land.[3] Following the shore westward from Corycus for about an hour you come to a pretty cove enclosed by wooded heights, where a spring of pure cold water bubbles up close to the sea, giving to the spot its name of *Tatlu-su*, or the Sweet Water.   From this bay a steep ascent of about a mile along an ancient paved road leads inland to a plateau.   Here, threading your way through a labyrinth or petrified sea of jagged calcareous rocks, you suddenly find yourself on the brink of a vast chasm which yawns at your feet.   This is the Corycian cave.   In reality it is not a cave but an immense hollow or trough in the plateau, of oval shape and perhaps half a mile in circumference.   The cliffs which

The city of Corycus.

The Corycian cave.

[1] Sir Charles Lyell, *Principles of Geology* [12] (London, 1875), ii. 518 *sqq.*; *Encyclopaedia Britannica*, Ninth Edition, *s.v.* "Caves," v. 265 *sqq.* Compare my notes on Pausanias, i. 35. 7, viii. 29. 1.

[2] J. T. Bent, in *Proceedings of the Royal Geographical Society*, N.S. xii. (1890) p. 447.

[3] Fr. Beaufort, *Karmania* (London, 1817), pp. 240 *sq.*

enclose it vary from one hundred to over two hundred feet in depth. Its uneven bottom slopes throughout its whole length from north to south, and is covered by a thick jungle of trees and shrubs—myrtles, pomegranates, carobs, and many more, kept always fresh and green by rivulets, underground water, and the shadow of the great cliffs. A single narrow path leads down into its depths. The way is long and rough, but the deeper you descend the denser grows the vegetation, and it is under the dappled shade of whispering leaves and with the purling of brooks in your ears that you at last reach the bottom. The saffron which of old grew here among the bushes is no longer to be found, though it still flourishes in the surrounding district. This luxuriant bottom, with its rich verdure, its refreshing moisture, its grateful shade, is called Paradise by the wandering herdsmen. They tether their camels and pasture their goats in it and come hither in the late summer to gather the ripe pomegranates. At the southern and deepest end of this great cliff-encircled hollow you come to the cavern proper. The ruins of a Byzantine church, which replaced a heathen temple, partly block the entrance. Inwards the cave descends with a gentle slope into the bowels of the earth. The old path paved with polygonal masonry still runs through it, but soon disappears under sand. At about two hundred feet from its mouth the cave comes to an end, and a tremendous roar of subterranean water is heard. By crawling on all fours you may reach a small pool arched by a dripping stalactite - hung roof, but the stream which makes the deafening din is invisible. It was otherwise in antiquity. A river of clear water burst from the rock, but only to vanish again into a chasm. Such changes in the course of streams are common in countries subject to earthquakes and to the disruption caused by volcanic agency. The ancients believed that this mysterious cavern was haunted ground. In the rumble and roar of the waters they seemed to hear the clash of cymbals touched by hands divine.[1]

---

[1] Strabo, xiv. 5. 5, pp. 670 *sq.*; Mela, i. 72-75, ed. G. Parthey; J. T. Bent, " Explorations in Cilicia Tracheia," *Proceedings of the Royal* *Geographical Society*, N.S. xii. (1890) pp. 446-448; *id.*, " A Journey in Cilicia Tracheia," *Journal of Hellenic Studies*, xii. (1891) pp. 212-214; R.

If now, quitting the cavern, we return by the same path Priests of Corycian Zeus. to the summit of the cliffs, we shall find on the plateau the ruins of a town and of a temple at the western edge of the great Corycian chasm. The wall of the holy precinct was built within a few feet of the precipices, and the sanctuary must have stood right over the actual cave and its subterranean waters. In later times the temple was converted into a Christian church. By pulling down a portion of the sacred edifice Mr. Bent had the good fortune to discover a Greek inscription containing a long list of names, probably those of the priests who superintended the worship. One name which meets us frequently in the list is Zas, and it is tempting to regard this as merely a dialectical form of Zeus. If that were so, the priests who bore the name might be supposed to personate the god.[1] But many strange and barbarous-looking names, evidently foreign, occur in the list, and Zas may be one of them. However, it is certain that Zeus was worshipped at the Corycian cave ; for about half a mile from it, on the summit of a hill, are the ruins of a larger temple, which an inscription proves to have been dedicated to Corycian Zeus.[2]

But Zeus, or whatever native deity masqueraded under The cave of the giant Typhon. his name, did not reign alone in the deep dell. A more dreadful being haunted a still more awful abyss which opens in the ground only a hundred yards to the east of the great Corycian chasm. It is a circular cauldron, about a quarter

---

Heberdey und A. Wilhelm, " Reisen in Kilikien," *Denkschriften der kaiser. Akademie der Wissenschaften, Philos.-histor. Classe*, xliv. (1896) No. vi. pp. 70-79. Mr. D. G. Hogarth was so good as to furnish me with some notes embodying his recollections of the Corycian cave. All these modern writers confirm the general accuracy of the descriptions of the cave given by Strabo and Mela. Mr. Hogarth indeed speaks of exaggeration in Mela's account, but this is not admitted by Mr. A. Wilhelm. As to the ruins of the city of Corycus the coast, distant about three miles from the cave, see Fr. Beaufort, *Karmania* (London,

1817), pp. 232-238 ; R. Heberdey und A. Wilhelm, *op. cit.* pp. 67-70.

[1] The suggestion is Mr. A. B. Cook's. See his article, " The European Sky-god," *Classical Review*, xvii. (1903) p. 418, note [2].

[2] J. T. Bent, in *Proceedings of the Royal Geographical Society*, N.S. xii. (1890) p. 448 ; *id.*, in *Journal of Hellenic Studies*, xii. (1891) pp. 214-216. For the inscription containing the names of the priests see R. Heberdey und A. Wilhelm, *op. cit.* pp. 71-79 ; Ch. Michel, *Recueil d'Inscriptions Grecques*, pp. 718 *sqq.*, No. 878 ; above, p. 145.

of a mile in circumference, resembling the Corycian chasm
in its general character, but smaller, deeper, and far more
terrific in appearance. Its sides overhang and stalactites
droop from them. There is no way down into it. The
only mode of reaching the bottom, which is covered with
vegetation, would be to be lowered at the end of a long
rope. The nomads call this chasm Purgatory, to distinguish
it from the other which they name Paradise. They say
that there is a subterranean passage between the two, and
that the smoke of a fire kindled in the Corycian cave may
be seen curling out of the other. The one ancient writer
who expressly mentions this second and more grisly cavern
is Mela, who says that it was the lair of the giant Typhon,
and that no animal let down into it could live.[1] Aeschylus
puts into the mouth of Prometheus an account of "the
earth-born Typhon, dweller in Cilician caves, dread monster,
hundred-headed," who in his pride rose up against the gods,
hissing destruction from his dreadful jaws, while from his
Gorgon eyes the lightning flashed. But him a flaming levin
bolt, crashing from heaven, smote to the very heart, and
now he lies, shrivelled and scorched, under the weight of
Etna by the narrow sea. Yet one day he will belch a fiery
hail, a boiling angry flood, rivers of flame, to devastate the
fat Sicilian fields.[2] This poetical description of the monster,
confirmed by a similar passage of Pindar,[3] clearly proves
that Typhon was conceived as a personification of those
active volcanoes which spout fire and smoke to heaven as
if they would assail the celestial gods. The Corycian caverns
are not volcanic, but the ancients apparently regarded them
as such, else they would hardly have made them the den of
Typhon.

Battle of Zeus and Typhon.

According to one legend Typhon was a monster, half
man and half brute, begotten in Cilicia by Tartarus upon
the goddess Earth. The upper part of him was human, but
from the loins downward he was an enormous snake. In
the battle of the gods and giants, which was fought out in
Egypt, Typhon hugged Zeus in his snaky coils, wrested

[1] Mela, i. 76, ed. G. Parthey (Berlin, 1867). The cave of Typhon is described by J. T. Bent, *ll.cc.*

[2] Aeschylus, *Prometheus Vinctus*, 351-372.

[3] Pindar, *Pyth.* i. 30 *sqq.*, who speaks of the giant as "bred in the many-named Cilician cave."

from him his crooked sword, and with the blade cut the sinews of the god's hands and feet. Then taking him on his back he conveyed the mutilated deity across the sea to Cilicia, and deposited him in the Corycian cave. Here, too, he hid the severed sinews, wrapt in a bear's skin. But Hermes and Aegipan contrived to steal the missing thews and restore them to their divine owner. Thus made whole and strong again, Zeus pelted his beaten adversary with thunderbolts, drove him from place to place, and at last overwhelmed him under Mount Etna. And the spots where the hissing bolts fell are still marked by jets of flame.[1]

It is possible that the discovery of fossil bones of large extinct animals may have helped to localize the story of the giant at the Corycian cave. Such bones, as we have seen, are often found in limestone caverns, and the limestone gorges of Cilicia are in fact rich in fossils. The Arcadians laid the scene of the battle of the gods and the giants in the plain of Megalopolis, where many bones of mammoths have come to light, and where, moreover, flames have been seen to burst from the earth and even to burn for years.[2] These natural conditions would easily suggest a fable of giants who had fought the gods and had been slain by thunderbolts ; the smouldering earth or jets of flame would be regarded as the spots where the divine lightnings had struck the ground. Hence the Arcadians sacrificed to thunder and lightning.[3] In Sicily, too, great quantities of bones of mammoths, elephants, hippopotamuses, and other animals long extinct in the island have been found, and have been appealed to with confidence by patriotic Sicilians as conclusive evidence of the gigantic stature of their ancestors or predecessors.[4] These remains of huge unwieldy creatures which once trampled through the jungle or splashed in the rivers of Sicily may have contributed with the fires of Etna to build up the story of giants imprisoned under the volcano and vomiting smoke and flame from its crater. " Tales of

Fossil bones of extinct animals give rise to stories of giants.

[1] Apollodorus, *Bibliotheca*, i. 6. 3.

[2] Pausanias, viii. 29. 1, with my notes. Pausanias mentions (viii. 32. 5) bones of superhuman size which were preserved at Megalopolis, and which popular superstition identified as the bones of the giant Hopladamus.

[3] Pausanias, viii. 29. 1.

[4] A. Holm, *Geschichte Siciliens im Alterthum* (Leipsic, 1870–1874), i. 57, 356.

giants and monsters, which stand in direct connexion with the finding of great fossil bones, are scattered broadcast over the mythology of the world.   Huge bones, found at Punto Santa Elena, in the north of Guayaquil, have served as a foundation for the story of a colony of giants who dwelt there.   The whole area of the Pampas is a great sepulchre of enormous extinct animals ; no wonder that one great plain should be called the 'Field of the giants,' and that such names as 'the hill of the giant,' 'the stream of the animal,' should be guides to the geologist in his search for fossil bones."[1]

Chasm of Olbian Zeus at Kanytel-ideis.   About five miles to the north-east of the Corycian caverns, but divided from them by many deep gorges and impassable rocks, is another and very similar chasm.   It may be reached in about an hour and a quarter from the sea by an ancient paved road, which ascends at first very steeply and then gently through bush-clad and wooded hills. Thus you come to a stretch of level ground covered with the well-preserved ruins of an ancient town.   Remains of fortresses constructed of polygonal masonry, stately churches, and many houses, together with numerous tombs and reliefs, finely chiselled in the calcareous limestone of the neighbour-hood, bear witness to the extent and importance of the place. Yet it is mentioned by no ancient writer.   Inscriptions prove that its name was Kanyteldeis or Kanytelideis, which still survives in the modern form of Kanidiwan.   The great chasm opens in the very heart of the city.   So crowded are the ruins that you do not perceive the abyss till you are within a few yards of it.   It is almost a complete circle, about a quarter of a mile wide, three-quarters of a mile in circumference, and uniformly two hundred feet or more in depth.   The cliffs go sheer down and remind the traveller of the great quarries at Syracuse.   But like the Corycian caves, the larger of which it closely resembles, the huge fissure is natural ; and its bottom, like theirs, is overgrown with trees and vegetation.   Two ways led down into it in antiquity, both cut through the rock.   One of them was a tunnel, which is now obstructed ; the other is still open.

---

[1] (Sir) Edward B. Tylor, *Researches into the Early History of Mankind*[3]   (London, 1878), p. 322, who adduces much more evidence of the same sort.

Remains of columns and hewn stones in the bottom of the chasm seem to show that a temple once stood there. But there is no cave at the foot of the cliffs, and no stream flows in the deep hollow or can be heard to rumble underground. A ruined tower of polygonal masonry, which stands on the southern edge of the chasm, bears a Greek inscription stating that it was dedicated to Olbian Zeus by the priest Teucer, son of Tarkuaris. The letters are beautifully cut in the style of the third century before Christ. We may infer that at the time of the dedication the town belonged to the priestly kings of Olba, and that the great chasm was sacred to Olbian Zeus.[1]

What, then, was the character of the god who was worshipped under the name of Zeus at these two great natural chasms? The depth of the fissures, opening suddenly and as it were without warning in the midst of a plateau, was well fitted to impress and awe the spectator; and the sight of the rank evergreen vegetation at their bottom, fed by rivulets or underground water, must have presented a striking contrast to the grey, barren, rocky wilderness of the surrounding tableland. Such a spot must have seemed to simple folk a paradise, a garden of God, the abode of higher powers who caused the wilderness to blossom, if not with roses, at least with myrtles and pomegranates for man, and with grass and underwood for his flocks. So to the Semite, as we saw, the Baal of the land is he who fertilizes it by subterranean water rather than by rain from the sky, and who therefore dwells in the depths of earth rather than in the height of heaven.[2] In rainless countries the sky-god is deprived of one of the principal functions which he discharges in cool cloudy climates like that of Europe. He has, in fact, little or nothing to do with the water-supply, and has therefore small excuse for levying a water-rate on his worshippers. Not, indeed, that Cilicia is rainless; but in countries border-

The deity of these great chasms was called Zeus by the Greeks, but he was probably a god of fertility embodied in vegetation and water.

---

[1] J. T. Bent, "Explorations in Cilicia Tracheia," *Proceedings of the Royal Geographical Society*, N.S. xii. (1890) pp. 448 *sq.*; *id.*, "A Journey in Cilicia Tracheia," *Journal of Hellenic Studies*, xii. (1891) pp. 208-210; R.

Heberdey und A. Wilhelm, "Reisen in Kilikien," *Denkschriften der kaiserlichen Akademie der Wissenschaften, Philosophisch-historische Classe*, xliv. (Vienna, 1896) No. vi. pp. 51-61.

[2] See above, pp. 26 *sq.*

ing on the Mediterranean the drought is almost unbroken
through the long months of summer.   Vegetation then
withers : the face of nature is scorched and brown : most
of the rivers dry up ; and only their white stony beds,
hot to the foot and dazzling to the eye, remain to tell
where they flowed.   It is at such seasons that a green
hollow, a shady rock, a murmuring stream, are welcomed
by the wanderer in the South with a joy and wonder
which the untravelled Northerner can hardly imagine.
Never do the broad slow rivers of England, with their
winding reaches, their grassy banks, their grey willows
mirrored with the soft English sky in the placid stream,
appear so beautiful as when the traveller views them for
the first time after leaving behind him the aridity, the
heat, the blinding glare of the white southern landscape,
set in seas and skies of caerulean blue.

Analogy
of the
Corycian
and Olbian
caverns to
Ibreez and
the vale
of the
Adonis. We may take it, then, as probable that the god of the
Corycian and Olbian caverns was worshipped as a source
of fertility.   In antiquity, when the river, which now roars
underground, still burst from the rock in the Corycian
cave, the scene must have resembled Ibreez, where the god
of the corn and the vine was adored at the source of the
stream ; and we may compare the vale of Adonis in the
Lebanon, where the divinity who gave his name to the river
was revered at its foaming cascades.   The three landscapes
had in common the elements of luxuriant vegetation and
copious streams leaping full-born from the rock.   We shall
hardly err in supposing that these features shaped the conception of the deities who were supposed to haunt the
favoured spots.   At the Corycian cave the existence of a
second chasm, of a frowning and awful aspect, might well
suggest the presence of an evil being who lurked in it and
sought to undo the beneficent work of the good god.   Thus
we should have a fable of a conflict between the two, a
battle of Zeus and Typhon.

Two gods
at Olba,
perhaps a
father and
a son, cor-
responding
to the On the whole we conclude that the Olbian Zeus,
worshipped at one of these great limestone chasms, and
clearly identical in nature with the Corycian Zeus, was
also identical with the Baal of Tarsus, the god of the corn
and the vine, who in his turn can hardly be separated from

the god of Ibreez. If my conjecture is right the native Baal and
Sandan of
Tarsus. name of the Olbian Zeus was Tark or Trok, and the priestly Teucers of Olba represented him in their own persons. On that hypothesis the Olbian priests who bore the name of Ajax embodied another native deity of unknown name, perhaps the father or the son of Tark. A comparison of the coin-types of Tarsus with the Hittite monuments of Ibreez and Boghaz-Keui led us to the conclusion that the people of Tarsus worshipped at least two distinct gods, a father and a son, the father-god being known to the Semites as Baal and to the Greeks as Zeus, while the son was called Sandan by the natives, but Hercules by the Greeks. We may surmise that at Olba the names of Teucer and Ajax designated two gods who corresponded in type to the two gods of Tarsus ; and if the lesser figure at Ibreez, who appears in an attitude of adoration before the deity of the corn and the vine, could be interpreted as the divine Son in presence of the divine Father, we should have in all three places the same pair of deities, represented probably in the flesh by successive generations of priestly kings. But the evidence is far too slender to justify us in advancing this hypothesis as anything more than a bare conjecture.

§ 8. *Cilician Goddesses*

So far, the Cilician deities discussed have been males ; Goddesses
less
prominent
than gods
in Cilician
religion. we have as yet found no trace of the great Mother Goddess who plays so important a part in the religion of Cappadocia and Phrygia, beyond the great dividing range of the Taurus. Yet we may suspect that she was not unknown in Cilicia, though her worship certainly seems to have been far less prominent there than in the centre of Asia Minor. The difference may perhaps be interpreted as evidence that mother-kin and hence the predominance of Mother Goddesses survived, in the bleak highlands of the interior, long after a genial climate and teeming soil had fostered the growth of a higher civilization, and with it the advance from female to male kinship, in the rich lowlands of Cilicia. Be that as it may, Cilician goddesses with or without a male partner are known to have been revered in various parts of the country.

The goddess 'Atheh, partner of Baal at Tarsus, seems to have been a form of Atargatis.

Thus at Tarsus itself the goddess 'Atheh was worshipped along with Baal ; their effigies are engraved on the same coins of the city. She is represented wearing a veil and seated upon a lion, with her name in Aramaic letters engraved beside her.[1] Hence it would seem that at Tarsus, as at Boghaz-Keui, the Father God mated with a lion-goddess like the Phrygian Cybele or the Syrian Atargatis. Now the name Atargatis is a Greek rendering of the Aramaic 'Athar-'atheh, a compound word which includes the name of the goddess of Tarsus.[2] Thus in name as well as in attributes the female partner of the Baal of Tarsus appears to correspond to Atargatis, the Syrian Mother Goddess whose image, seated on a lion or lions, was worshipped with great pomp and splendour at Hierapolis - Bambyce near the Euphrates.[3]

The lion-goddess and the bull-god.

[1] B. V. Head, *Historia Numorum* (Oxford, 1887), p. 616. [However, Mr. G. F. Hill writes to me : "The attribution to Tarsus of the 'Atheh coins is unfounded. Head himself only gives it as doubtful. I should think they belong further East." In the uncertainty which prevails on this point I have left the text unchanged. *Note to Second Edition.*]

[2] The name 'Athar-'atheh occurs in a Palmyrene inscription. See G. A. Cooke, *Text - book of North - Semitic Inscriptions*, No. 112, pp. 267-270. In analysing Atargatis into 'Athar-'atheh ('Atar-'ata) I follow E. Meyer (*Geschichte des Altertums*,[2] i. 2. pp. 605, 650 *sq.*), F. Baethgen (*Beiträge zur semitischen Religionsgeschichte*, pp. 68-75), Fr. Cumont (*s.v.* " Atargatis," Pauly-Wissowa, *Real-Encyclopädie der classischen Altertumswissenschaft*, ii. 1896), G. A. Cooke (*l.c.*), C. P. Tiele (*Geschichte der Religion im Altertum*, i. 245), F. Hommel (*Grundriss der Geographie und Geschichte des alten Orients*, pp. 43 *sq.*), Father Lagrange (*Études sur les Religions Sémitiques*,[2] p. 130), and L. B. Paton (*s.v.* " Atargatis," J. Hastings's *Encyclopaedia of Religion and Ethics*, ii. 164 *sq.*). In the great temple at Hierapolis - Bambyce a mysterious golden image stood between the images of Atargatis and her male partner. It resembled neither of them, yet combined the attributes of other gods. Some interpreted it as Dionysus, others as Deucalion, and others as Semiramis ; for a golden dove, traditionally associated with Semiramis, was perched on the head of the figure. The Syrians called the image by a name which Lucian translates " sign' (σημήιον). See Lucian, *De dea Syria*, 33. It has been plausibly conjectured by F. Baethgen that the name which Lucian translates " sign " was really 'Atheh (עתה), which could easily be confused with the Syriac word for "sign" (אתא). See F. Baethgen, *op. cit.* p. 73. A coin of Hierapolis, dating from the third century A.D., exhibits the images of the god and goddess seated on bulls and lions respectively, with the mysterious object between them enclosed in a shrine, which is surmounted by a bird, probably a dove. See J. Garstang, *The Syrian Goddess* (London, 1913), pp. 22 *sqq.*, 70 *sq.*, with fig. 7.

The modern writers cited at the beginning of this note have interpreted the Syrian 'Atheh as a male god, the lover of Atargatis, and identical in name and character with the Phrygian Attis. They may be right ; but none of them seems to have noticed that the same name 'Atheh (עתה) is applied to a goddess at Tarsus.

[3] As to the image, see above, p. 137.

May we go a step farther and find a correspondence between the Baal of Tarsus and the husband - god of Atargatis at Hierapolis-Bambyce ?   That husband-god, like the Baal of Tarsus, was identified by the Greeks with Zeus, and Lucian tells us that the resemblance of his image to the images of Zeus was in all respects unmistakable.   But his image, unlike those of Zeus, was seated upon bulls.[1]   In point of fact he was probably Hadad, the chief male god of the Syrians, who appears to have been a god of thunder and fertility ; for at Baalbec in the Lebanon, where the ruined temple of the Sun is the most imposing monument bequeathed to the modern world by Greek art in its decline, his image grasped in his left hand a thunderbolt and ears of corn,[2] and a colossal statue of the deity, found near Zenjirli in Northern Syria, represents him with a bearded human head and horns, the emblem of strength and fertility.[3]   A similar god of thunder and lightning was worshipped from early times by the Babylonians and Assyrians ; he bore the similar name of Adad and his emblems appear to have been a thunderbolt and a bull.   On an Assyrian relief his image is represented as that of a bearded man clad in a short tunic, wearing a cap with two pairs of horns, and grasping an axe in his right hand and a thunderbolt in his left.   His resemblance to the Hittite god of the thundering sky was therefore very close.   An alternative name for this Babylonian and Assyrian deity was Ramman, an appropriate

---

[1] Lucian, *De dea Syria*, 31.

[2] Macrobius, *Saturn.* i. 23. 12 and 17-19.   The Greek name of Baalbec was Heliopolis, "the City of the Sun."

[3] G. A. Cooke, *Text-book of North-Semitic Inscriptions*, pp. 163, 164. The statue bears a long inscription, which in the style of its writing belongs to the archaic type represented by the Moabite Stone.   The contents of the inscription show that it is earlier than the time of Tiglath-Pileser III. (745–727 B.C.).   On Hadad, the Syrian thunder-god, see F. Baethgen, *Beiträge zur semitischen Religionsgeschichte*, pp. 66-68 ; C. P. Tiele, *Geschichte der Religion im Altertum*, i. 248 *sq.* ; M. J. Lagrange, *Études sur les Religions*

Sémitiques,[2] pp. 92 *sq.*   That Hadad was the consort of Atargatis at Hiera-polis-Bambyce is the opinion of P. Jensen (*Hittiter und Armenier*, p. 171), who also indicates his character as a god both of thunder and of fertility (*ib.*, p. 167).   The view of Prof. J. Garstang is similar (*The Syrian Goddess*, pp. 25 *sqq.*).   That the name of the chief male god of Hierapolis-Bambyce was Hadad is rendered almost certain by coins of the city which were struck in the time of Alexander the Great by a priestly king Abd - Hadad, whose name means "Servant of Hadad."   See B. V. Head, *Historia Numorum* (Oxford, 1887), p. 654 ; J. Garstang, *The Syrian Goddess*, p. 27, with fig. 5.

term, derived from a verb *ramâmu* to "scream" or "roar."[1]
Now we have seen that the god of Ibreez, whose attributes
tally with those of the Baal of Tarsus, wears a cap adorned
with bull's horns;[2] that the Father God at Boghaz-Keui,
meeting the Mother Goddess on her lioness, is attended by
an animal which according to the usual interpretation is a
bull;[3] and that the bull itself was worshipped, apparently as
an emblem of fertility, at Euyuk near Boghaz-Keui.[4] Thus
at Tarsus and Boghaz-Keui, as at Hierapolis-Bambyce, the
Father God and the Mother Goddess would seem to have
had as their sacred animals or emblems the bull and the lion

In later
times the
old
goddess
became the
Fortune of
the City.

respectively. In later times, under Greek influence, the
goddess was apparently exchanged for, or converted into,
the Fortune of the City, who appears on coins of Tarsus as
a seated woman with veiled and turreted head, grasping ears
of corn and a poppy in her hand. Her lion is gone, but a
trace of him perhaps remains on a coin which exhibits the
throne of the goddess adorned with a lion's leg.[5] In general
it would seem that the goddess Fortune, who figures commonly as the guardian of cities in the Greek East, especially
in Syria, was nothing but a disguised form of Gad, the
Semitic god of fortune or luck, who, though the exigencies of
grammar required him to be masculine, is supposed to have
been often merely a special aspect of the great goddess
Astarte or Atargatis conceived as the patroness and protector
of towns.[6] In Oriental religion such permutations or com-
binations need not surprise us. To the gods all things are

---

[1] H. Zimmern, in E. Schrader's *Die
Keilinschriften und das Alte Testa-
ment*,[3] pp. 442-449; M. Jastrow, *Die
Religion Babyloniens und Assyriens*
(Giessen, 1905-1912), i. 146-150,
with *Bildermappe*, plate 32, fig. 97.
The Assyrian relief is also figured in W.
H. Roscher's *Lexikon der griech. und
röm. Mythologie*, s.v. "Marduk," ii.
2350. The Babylonian *ramâmu* "to
scream, roar" has its equivalent in
the Hebrew *ra'am* (רעם) "to thunder."
The two names Adad (Hadad) and
Ramman occur together in the form
Hadadrimmon in Zechariah, xii. 11
(with S. R. Driver's note, *Century
Bible*).

[2] See above, pp. 121, 123.

[3] See above, p. 130. However,
the animal seems to be rather a goat.
See above, p. 133 note.

[4] See above, p. 132.

[5] G. F. Hill, *Catalogue of the
Greek Coins of Lycaonia, Isauria,
and Cilicia*, pp. 181, 182, 185, 188,
190, 228.

[6] E. Meyer, *Geschichte des Alterthums*, i. (Stuttgart, 1884) pp. 246 *sq.*;
F. Baethgen, *Beiträge zur semitischen
Religionsgeschichte*, pp. 76 *sqq.* The
idolatrous Hebrews spread tables for
Gad, that is, for Fortune (Isaiah lxv.
11, Revised Version).

possible.   In Cyprus the goddess of love wore a beard,[1] and Alexander the Great sometimes disported himself in the costume of Artemis, while at other times he ransacked the divine wardrobe to figure in the garb of Hercules, of Hermes, and of Ammon.[2]   The change of the goddess 'Atheh of Tarsus into Gad or Fortune would be easy if we suppose that she was known as Gad-'Atheh, " Luck of 'Atheh," which occurs as a Semitic personal name.[3]   In like manner the goddess of Fortune at Olba, who had her small temple beside the great temple of Zeus,[4] may have been originally the consort of the native god Tark or Tarku.

Another town in Cilicia where an Oriental god and goddess appear to have been worshipped together was Mallus. The city was built on a height in the great Cilician plain near the mouth of the river Pyramus.[5]   Its coins exhibit two winged deities, a male and a female, in a kneeling or running attitude.   On some of the coins the male deity is represented, like Janus, with two heads facing opposite ways, and with two pairs of wings, while beneath him is the fore-part of a bull with a human head.   The obverse of the coins which bear the female deity displays a conical stone, sometimes flanked by two bunches of grapes.[6]   This conical stone, like those of other Asiatic cities,[7] was probably the emblem of a Mother Goddess, and the bunches of grapes indicate her fertilizing powers.   The god with the two heads

The Phoenician god El and his wife at Mallus in Cilicia.

---

[1] Macrobius, *Saturn.* iii. 8. 2 ; Servius on Virgil, *Aen.* ii. 632.

[2] Ephippus, cited by Athenaeus, xii. 53, p. 537.

[3] F. Baethgen, *op. cit.* p. 77 ; G. A. Cooke, *Text-book of North-Semitic Inscriptions*, p. 269.

[4] See above, p. 151.

[5] Strabo, xiv. 5. 16, p. 675.

[6] B. V. Head, *Historia Numorum* (Oxford, 1887), pp. 605 *sq.*; G. F. Hill, *Catalogue of the Greek Coins of Lycaonia, Isauria, and Cilicia*, pp. cxvii. *sqq.*, 95-98, plates xv. xvi. xl. 9 ; G. Macdonald, *Catalogue of Greek Coins in the Hunterian Collection*, ii. 536 *sq.*, pl. lix. 11-14.   The male and female figures appear on separate coins.   The attribution to Mallus of the coins with

the female figure and conical stone has been questioned by Messrs. J. P. Six and G. F. Hill.   I follow the view of Messrs. F. Imhoof-Blumer and B. V. Head. [However, Mr. G. F. Hill writes to me that the attribution of these coins to Mallus is no longer maintained by any one.   Imhoof-Blumer himself now conjecturally assigns them to Aphrodisias in Cilicia, and Mr. Hill regards this conjecture as very plausible. See F. Imhoof-Blumer, *Kleinasiatische Münzen* (Vienna, 1901–1902), ii. 435 *sq.*   In the uncertainty which still prevails on the subject I have left the text unchanged.   For my purpose it matters little whether this Cilician goddess was worshipped at Mallus or at Aphrodisias.   *Note to Second Edition.*]

[7] See above, pp. 34 *sq.*

and four wings can hardly be any other than the Phoenician El, whom the Greeks called Cronus ; for El was characterized by four eyes, two in front and two behind, and by three pairs of wings.[1] A discrepancy in the number of wings can scarcely be deemed fatal to the identification. The god may easily have moulted some superfluous feathers on the road from Phoenicia to Mallus. On later coins of Mallus these quaint Oriental deities disappear, and are replaced by corresponding Greek deities, particularly by a head of Cronus on one side and a figure of Demeter, grasping ears of corn, on the other.[2] The change doubtless sprang from a wish to assimilate the ancient native divinities to the new and fashionable divinities of the Greek pantheon. If Cronus and Demeter, the harvest god and goddess, were chosen to supplant El and his female consort, the ground of the choice must certainly have been a supposed resemblance between the two pairs of deities. We may assume, therefore, that the discarded couple, El and his wife, had also been worshipped by the husbandman as sources of fertility, the givers of corn and wine. One of these later coins of Mallus exhibits Dionysus sitting on a vine laden with ripe clusters, while on the obverse is seen a male figure guiding a yoke of oxen as if in the act of ploughing.[3] These types of the vine-god and the ploughman probably represent another attempt to adapt the native religion to changed conditions, to pour the old Asiatic wine into new Greek bottles. The barbarous monster with the multiplicity of heads and wings has been reduced to a perfectly human Dionysus. The sacred but deplorable old conical stone no longer flaunts proudly on the coins ; it has retired to a decent obscurity in favour of a natural and graceful vine. It is thus that a truly progressive theology keeps pace with the march of intellect. But if these things were done by the apostles of culture at Mallus, we cannot suppose that the clergy of Tarsus, the capital, lagged behind their pro-

Marginal note: Assimilation of native Oriental deities to Greek divinities.

---

[1] Philo of Byblus, in *Fragmenta Historicorum Graecorum*, ed. C. Müller, iii. 569. El is figured with three pairs of wings on coins of Byblus. See G. Maspero, *Histoire Ancienne des Peuples de l'Orient Classique*, ii. 174 ; M. J. Lagrange, *Études sur les Religions Sémitiques*,[2] p. 72.

[2] Imhoof-Blumer, *s.v.* "Kronos," in W. H. Roscher's *Lexikon der griech. und röm. Mythologie*, ii. 1572 ; G. F. Hill, *Catalogue of Greek Coins of Lycaonia, Isauria, and Cilicia*, pp. cxxii. 99, pl. xvii. 2.

[3] G. F. Hill, *op. cit.* pp. cxxi. *sq.*, 98, pl. xvii. 1.

vincial brethren in their efforts to place the ancient faith upon a sound modern basis. The fruit of their labours seems to have been the more or less nominal substitution of Zeus, Fortune, and Hercules for Baal, 'Atheh, and Sandan.[1]

We may suspect that in like manner the Sarpedonian Artemis, who had a sanctuary in South-Eastern Cilicia, near the Syrian border, was really a native goddess parading in borrowed plumes. She gave oracular responses by the mouth of inspired men, or more probably of women, who in their moments of divine ecstasy may have been deemed incarnations of her divinity.[2] Another even more transparently Asiatic goddess was Perasia, or Artemis Perasia, who was worshipped at Hieropolis-Castabala in Eastern Cilicia. The extensive ruins of the ancient city, now known as Bodroum, cover the slope of a hill about three-quarters of a mile to the north of the river Pyramus. Above them towers the acropolis, built on the summit of dark grey precipices, and divided from the neighbouring mountain by a deep cutting in the rock. A mediaeval castle, built of hewn blocks of reddish-yellow limestone, has replaced the ancient citadel. The city possessed a large theatre, and was traversed by two handsome colonnades, of which some columns are still standing among the ruins. A thick growth of brushwood and grass now covers most of the site, and the place is wild and solitary. Only the wandering herdsmen encamp near the deserted city in winter and spring. The neighbourhood is treeless ; yet in May magnificent fields of wheat and barley gladden the eye, and in the valleys the

Marginal notes:
Sarpedonian Artemis.

The goddess Perasia at Hieropolis-Castabala.

---

[1] Another native Cilician deity who masqueraded in Greek dress was probably the Olybrian Zeus of Anazarba or Anazarbus, but of his true nature and worship we know nothing. See W. Dittenberger, *Orientis Graeci Inscriptiones Selectae* (Leipsic, 1903–1905), ii. p. 267, No. 577 ; Stephanus Byzantius, *s.v.* Ἄδανα (where the MS. reading Ὀλυμβρος was wrongly changed by Salmasius into Ὄλυμπος).

[2] Strabo, xiv. 5. 19, p. 676. The expression of Strabo leaves it doubtful whether the ministers of the goddess were men or women. There was a headland called Sarpedon near the mouth of the Calycadnus River in Western Cilicia (Strabo, xiii. 4. 6, p. 627, xiv. 5. 4, p. 670), where Sarpedon or Sarpedonian Apollo had a temple and an oracle. The temple was hewn in the rock, and contained an image of the god. See R. Heberdey und A. Wilhelm, " Reisen in Kilikien," *Denkschriften der kaiser. Akademie der Wissenschaften, Philosoph.-histor. Classe*, xliv. (Vienna, 1896) No. vi. pp. 100, 107. Probably this Sarpedonian Apollo was a native deity akin to Sarpedonian Artemis.

clover grows as high as the horses' knees.[1]   The ambiguous
nature of the goddess who presided over this City of the
Sanctuary (*Hieropolis*)[2] was confessed by a puzzled worshipper,
a physician named Lucius Minius Claudianus, who confided
his doubts to the deity herself in some very indifferent Greek
verses.   He wisely left it to the goddess to say whether she
was Artemis, or the Moon, or Hecate, or Aphrodite, or
Demeter.[3]   All that we know about her is that her true name
was Perasia, and that she was in the enjoyment of certain
revenues.[4]   Further, we may reasonably conjecture that at
the Cilician Castabala she was worshipped with rites like
those which were held in honour of her namesake Artemis
Perasia at another city of the same name, Castabala in
Cappadocia.   There, as we saw, the priestesses of the goddess
walked over fire with bare feet unscathed.[5]   Probably the

The fire-
walk in the
worship of
Perasia.

[1] E. J. Davis, *Life in Asiatic Turkey*,
pp. 128-134; J. T. Bent, "Recent Discoveries in Eastern Cilicia," *Journal of
Hellenic Studies*, xi. (1890) pp. 234
sq.; E. L. Hicks, "Inscriptions from
Eastern Cilicia," *ibid.* pp. 243 *sqq.*;
R. Heberdey und A. Wilhelm, *op. cit.*
pp. 25 *sqq.* The site of Hieropolis-
Castabala was first identified by J. T.
Bent by means of inscriptions.   As to
the coins of the city, see Fr. Imhoof-
Blumer, "Zur Münzkunde Kilikiens,"
Zeitschrift für Numismatik, x. (1883)
pp. 267-290; G. F. Hill, *Catalogue of
the Greek Coins of Lycaonia, Isauria,
and Cilicia*, pp. c.-cii. 82-84, pl. xiv.
1-6; G. Macdonald, *Catalogue of Greek
Coins in the Hunterian Collection*, ii.
534 *sq.*
[2] On the difference between Hieropolis and Hierapolis see (Sir) W. M.
Ramsay, *Historical Geography of Asia
Minor*, pp. 84 *sq.* According to him,
the cities designated by such names
grew up gradually round a sanctuary;
where Greek influence prevailed the
city in time eclipsed the sanctuary and
became known as Hierapolis, or the
Sacred City, but where the native
element retained its predominance the
city continued to be known as Hieropolis, or the City of the Sanctuary.
[3] E. L. Hicks, "Inscriptions from
Eastern Cilicia," *Journal of Hellenic

Studies, xi. (1890) pp. 251-253; R.
Heberdey und A. Wilhelm, *op. cit.* p.
26.   These writers differ somewhat in
their reading and restoration of the
verses, which are engraved on a limestone basis among the ruins.   I follow
the version of Messrs. Heberdey and
Wilhelm.
[4] J. T. Bent and E. L. Hicks, *op. cit.*
pp. 235, 246 *sq.*; R. Heberdey und
A. Wilhelm, *op. cit.* p. 27.
[5] Strabo, xii. 2. 7, p. 537.   See
above, p. 115.   The Cilician Castabala,
the situation of which is identified by
inscriptions, is not mentioned by Strabo.
It is very unlikely that, with his intimate knowledge of Asia Minor, he
should have erred so far as to place the
city in Cappadocia, to the north of the
Taurus mountains, instead of in Cilicia,
to the south of them.   It is more probable that there were two cities of the
same name, and that Strabo has omitted
to mention one of them.   Similarly, there
were two cities called Comana, one in
Cappadocia and one in Pontus; at both
places the same goddess was worshipped
with similar rites.   See Strabo, xii. 2.
3, p. 535, xii. 3. 32, p. 557.   The
situation of the various Castabalas
mentioned by ancient writers is discussed by F. Imhoof-Blumer, "Zur
Münzkunde Kilikiens," *Zeitschrift für
Numismatik*, x. (1883) pp. 285-288.

same impressive ceremony was performed before a crowd of worshippers in the Cilician Castabala also. Whatever the exact meaning of the rite may have been, the goddess was in all probability one of those Asiatic Mother Goddesses to whom the Greeks often applied the name of Artemis.[1] The immunity enjoyed by the priestess in the furnace was attributed to her inspiration by the deity. In discussing the nature of inspiration or possession by a deity, the Syrian philosopher Jamblichus notes as one of its symptoms a total insensibility to pain. Many inspired persons, he tells us, " are not burned by fire, the fire not taking hold of them by reason of the divine inspiration ; and many, though they are burned, perceive it not, because at the time they do not live an animal life. They pierce themselves with skewers and feel nothing. They gash their backs with hatchets, they slash their arms with daggers, and know not what they do, because their acts are not those of mere men. For impassable places become passable to those who are filled with the spirit. They rush into fire, they pass through fire, they cross rivers, like the priestess at Castabala. These things prove that under the influence of inspiration men are beside themselves, that their senses, their will, their life are those neither of man nor of beast, but that they lead another and a diviner life instead, whereby they are inspired and wholly possessed."[2] Thus in traversing the fiery furnace the priestesses of Perasia were believed to be beside themselves, to be filled with the goddess, to be in a real sense incarnations of her divinity.[3]

A similar touchstone of inspiration is still applied by some villagers in the Himalayan districts of North-Western

Insensibility to pain regarded as a mark of inspiration.

---

[1] See *The Magic Art and the Evolution of Kings*, i. 37 *sq.*

[2] Jamblichus, *De mysteriis*, iii. 4.

[3] Another Cilician goddess was Athena of Magarsus, to whom Alexander the Great sacrificed before the battle of Issus. See Arrian, *Anabasis*, ii. 5. 9 ; Stephanus Byzantius, *s.v.* Μάγαρσος ; J. Tzetzes, *Schol. on Lycophron*, 444. The name of the city seems to be Oriental, perhaps derived from the Semitic word for " cave " (מְעָרָה). As to the importance of caves in Semitic religion, see W. Robertson Smith, *Religion of the Semites*,[2] pp. 197 *sqq.* The site of Magarsus appears to be at Karatash, a hill rising from the sea at the southern extremity of the Cilician plain, about forty-five miles due south of Adana. The walls of the city, built of great limestone blocks, are standing to a height of several courses, and an inscription which mentions the priests of Magarsian Athena has been found on the spot. See R. Heberdey und A. Wilhelm, " Reisen in Kilikien," *Denkschriften der kaiser. Akademie der Wissenschaften, Philosoph.-histor. Classe*, xliv. (1896) No. vi. pp. 6-10.

India.   Once a year they worship Airi, a local deity, who is
represented by a trident and has his temples on lonely hills
and desolate tracts.   At his festival the people seat themselves in a circle about a bonfire.   A kettle-drum is beaten,
and one by one his worshippers become possessed by the
god and leap with shouts round the flames.   Some brand
themselves with heated iron spoons and sit down in the fire.
Such as escape unhurt are believed to be truly inspired,
while those who burn themselves are despised as mere pre-
tenders to the divine frenzy.   Persons thus possessed by the
spirit are called Airi's horses or his slaves.   During the
revels, which commonly last about ten days, they wear
red scarves round their heads and receive alms from the
faithful.   These men deem themselves so holy that they
will let nobody touch them, and they alone may touch
the sacred trident, the emblem of their god.[1]   In Western
Asia itself modern fanatics still practise the same austerities
which were practised by their brethren in the days of
Jamblichus.   " Asia Minor abounds in dervishes of different
orders, who lap red-hot iron, calling it their ' rose,' chew
coals of living fire, strike their heads against solid walls,
stab themselves in the cheek, the scalp, the temple, with
sharp spikes set in heavy weights, shouting ' Allah, Allah,'
and always consistently avowing that during such frenzy
they are entirely insensible to pain." [2]

§ 9. *The Burning of Cilician Gods*

*The divine
triad, Baal,
Atheh,
and
Sandan, at
Tarsus may
have been
personated
by priests
and
priestesses.*

On the whole, then, we seem to be justified in concluding
that under a thin veneer of Greek humanity the barbarous
native gods of Cilicia continued long to survive, and that
among them the great Asiatic goddess retained a place,
though not the prominent place which she held in the
highlands of the interior down at least to the beginning of
our era.   The principle that the inspired priest or priestess
represents the deity in person appears, if I am right, to

---

[1] E. T. Atkinson, *The Himalayan
Districts of the North-Western Provinces of India*, ii. (Allahabad, 1884)
pp. 826 *sq.*

[2] The Rev. G. E. White (Missionary
at Marsovan, in the ancient Pontus), in
a letter to me dated 19 Southmoor
Road, Oxford, February 11, 1907.

have been recognized at Castabala and at Olba, as well as at the sanctuary of Sarpedonian Artemis.   There can be no intrinsic improbability, therefore, in the view that at Tarsus also the divine triad of Baal, 'Atheh, and Sandan may also have been personated by priests and priestesses, who, on the analogy of Olba and of the great sanctuaries in the interior of Asia Minor, would originally be at the same time kings and queens, princes and princesses. Further, the burning of Sandan in effigy at Tarsus would, on this hypothesis, answer to the walk of the priestess of Perasia through the furnace at Castabala.   Both were perhaps mitigations of a custom of putting the priestly king or queen, or another member of the royal family, to death by fire.

CHAPTER VII

SARDANAPALUS AND HERCULES

§ 1. *The Burning of Sardanapalus*

Tarsus said to have been founded by the Assyrian king Sardanapalus, who burned himself on a pyre.

THE theory that kings or princes were formerly burned to death at Tarsus in the character of gods is singularly confirmed by another and wholly independent line of argument. For, according to one account, the city of Tarsus was founded not by Sandan but by Sardanapalus, the famous Assyrian monarch whose death on a great pyre was one of the most famous incidents in Oriental legend. Near the sea, within a day's march of Tarsus, might be seen in antiquity the ruins of a great ancient city named Anchiale, and outside its walls stood a monument called the monument of Sardanapalus, on which was carved in stone the figure of the monarch. He was represented snapping the fingers of his right hand, and the gesture was explained by an accompanying inscription, engraved in Assyrian characters, to the following effect :—" Sardanapalus, son of Anacyndaraxes, built Anchiale and Tarsus in one day. Eat, drink, and play, for everything else is not worth that," by which was implied that all other human affairs were not worth a snap of the fingers.[1] The gesture may have been misin-

---

[1] Strabo, xiv. 5. 9, pp. 671 *sq.*; Arrian, *Anabasis*, ii. 5; Athenaeus, xii. 39, p. 530 A, B. Compare Stephanus Byzantius, *s.v.* Ἀγχιάλη; Georgius Syncellus, *Chronographia*, vol. i. p. 312, ed. G. Dindorf (Bonn, 1829). The site of Anchiale has not yet been discovered. At Tarsus itself the ruins of a vast quadrangular structure have sometimes been identified with the monument of Sardanapalus. See E. J. Davis, *Life in Asiatic Turkey*, pp. 37-39; G. Perrot et Ch. Chipiez, *Histoire de l'Art dans l'Antiquité*, iv. 536 *sqq.* But Mr. D. G. Hogarth tells me that the ruins in question seem to be the concrete foundations of a Roman temple. The mistake had already been pointed out by Mr. R. Koldewey. See his article, "Das sogenannte Grab des Sardanapal zu Tarsus," *Aus der Anomia* (Berlin, 1890), pp. 178-185.

terpreted and the inscription mistranslated,[1] but there is no reason to doubt the existence of such a monument, though we may conjecture that it was of Hittite rather than Assyrian origin ; for, not to speak of the traces of Hittite art and religion which we have found at Tarsus, a group of Hittite monuments has been discovered at Marash, in the upper valley of the Pyramus.[2] The Assyrians may have ruled over Cilicia for a time, but Hittite influence was probably much deeper and more lasting.[3] The story that Tarsus was founded by Sardanapalus may well be apocryphal,[4] but there must have been some reason for his association with the city. On the present hypothesis that reason is to be found in the traditional manner of his death. To avoid falling into the hands of the rebels, who laid siege to Nineveh, he built a huge pyre in his palace, heaped it up with gold and silver and purple raiment, and then burnt himself, his wife, his concubines, and his eunuchs in the fire.[5] The story is false of the historical Sardanapalus, that is, of the great Assyrian king Ashurbanipal, but it is true of his brother Shamashshumukin. Being appointed king of Babylon by Ashurbanipal, he revolted against his suzerain and benefactor, and was besieged by him in his capital. The siege was long and the resistance desperate, for the Babylonians knew that they had no mercy to expect from the ruthless Assyrians. But they were decimated by famine and pestilence, and when the city could hold out no more, King Shamashshumukin, determined not to fall alive into the hands of his offended brother, shut himself up in his

Deaths of Babylonian and Assyrian kings on the pyre.

---

[1] See G. Perrot et Ch. Chipiez, *Histoire de l'Art dans l'Antiquité*, iv. 542 *sq.* They think that the figure probably represented the king in a common attitude of adoration, his right arm raised and his thumb resting on his forefinger.

[2] L. Messerschmidt, *Corpus Inscriptionum Hettiticarum*, pp. 17-19, plates xxi.-xxv. ; G. Perrot et Ch. Chipiez, *Histoire de l'Art dans l'Antiquité*, iv. 492, 494 *sq.*, 528-530, 547 ; J. Garstang, *The Land of the Hittites*, pp. 107-122.

[3] Prof. W. Max Müller is of opinion that the Hittite civilization and the

Hittite system of writing were developed in Cilicia rather than in Cappadocia (*Asien und Europa*, p. 350).

[4] According to Berosus and Abydenus it was not Sardanapalus (Ashurbanipal) but Sennacherib who built or rebuilt Tarsus after the fashion of Babylon, causing the river Cydnus to flow through the midst of the city. See *Fragmenta Historicorum Graecorum*, ed. C. Müller, ii. 504, iv. 282 ; C. P. Tiele, *Babylonisch - assyrische Geschichte*, pp. 297 *sq.*

[5] Diodorus Siculus, ii. 27 ; Athenaeus, xii. 38, p. 529 ; Justin, i. 3.

palace, and there burned himself to death, along with his wives, his children, his slaves, and his treasures, at the very moment when the conquerors were breaking in the gates.[1] Not many years afterwards the same tragedy was repeated at Nineveh itself by Saracus or Sinsharishkun, the last king of Assyria. Besieged by the rebel Nabopolassar, king of Babylon, and by Cyaxares, king of the Medes, he burned himself in his palace. That was the end of Nineveh and of the Assyrian empire.[2] Thus Greek history preserved the memory of the catastrophe, but transferred it from the real victims to the far more famous Ashurbanipal, whose figure in after ages loomed vast and dim against the setting sun of Assyrian glory.

§ 2. The Burning of Croesus

Story that Cyrus intended to burn Croesus alive.

Another Oriental monarch who prepared at least to die in the flames was Croesus, king of Lydia. Herodotus tells how the Persians under Cyrus captured Sardes, the Lydian capital, and took Croesus alive, and how Cyrus caused a great pyre to be erected, on which he placed the captive monarch in fetters, and with him twice seven Lydian youths. Fire was then applied to the pile, but at the last moment Cyrus relented, a sudden shower extinguished the flames, and Croesus was spared.[3] But it is most improbable that the Persians, with their profound reverence for the sanctity of fire, should have thought of defiling the sacred element with the worst of all pollutions, the contact of dead bodies.[4] Such an act would have seemed to them sacrilege of the deepest dye. For to them fire was the earthly form of the

It is unlikely that the Persians would thus have polluted the sacred element of fire.

[1] G. Maspero, *Histoire Ancienne des Peuples de l'Orient Classique*, iii. 422 *sq.* For the inscriptions referring to him and a full discussion of them, see C. F. Lehmann (-Haupt), *Šamaš-šumukîn, König von Babylonien, 668–648 v. Chr.* (Leipsic, 1892).

[2] Abydenus, in *Fragmenta Historicorum Graecorum*, ed. C. Müller, iv. 282; Georgius Syncellus, *Chronographia*, i. p. 396, ed. G. Dindorf; E. Meyer, *Geschichte des Alterthums*, i. (Stuttgart, 1884) pp. 576 *sq.* ; G. Maspero, *Histoire Ancienne des Peuples de l'Orient Classique*, iii. 482-485. C. P. Tiele

thought that the story of the death of Saracus might be a popular but mistaken duplicate of the death of Shamash-shumukin (*Babylonisch-assyrische Geschichte*, pp. 410 *sq.*). Zimri, king of Israel, also burned himself in his palace to escape falling into the hands of his enemies (1 Kings xvi. 18).

[3] Herodotus, i. 86 *sq.*

[4] Raoul-Rochette, "Sur l'Hercule Assyrien et Phénicien," *Mémoires de l'Académie des Inscriptions et Belles-Lettres*, xvii. Deuxième Partie (Paris, 1848), p. 274.

heavenly light, the eternal, the infinite, the divine ; death, on the other hand, was in their opinion the main source of corruption and uncleanness.   Hence they took the most stringent precautions to guard the purity of fire from the defilement of death.[1]   If a man or a dog died in a house where the holy fire burned, the fire had to be removed from the house and kept away for nine nights in winter or a month in summer before it might be brought back ; and if any man broke the rule by bringing back the fire within the appointed time, he might be punished with two hundred stripes.[2]   As for burning a corpse in the fire, it was the most heinous of all sins, an invention of Ahriman, the devil ; there was no atonement for it, and it was punished with death.[3]   Nor did the law remain a dead letter.   Down to the beginning of our era the death penalty was inflicted on all who threw a corpse or cow-dung on the fire, nay, even on such as blew on the fire with their breath.[4]   It is hard, therefore, to believe that a Persian king should have commanded his subjects to perpetrate a deed which he and they viewed with horror as the most flagitious sacrilege conceivable.

Another and in some respects truer version of the story of Croesus and Cyrus has been preserved by two older witnesses—namely, by the Greek poet Bacchylides, who was born some forty years after the event,[5] and by a Greek artist who painted the scene on a red-figured vase about, or soon after, the time of the poet's birth.   Bacchylides tells us that when the Persians captured Sardes, Croesus, unable to brook the thought of slavery, caused a pyre to be erected in front of his courtyard, mounted it with his wife and daughters, and bade a page apply a light to the wood.   A bright blaze shot up, but Zeus extinguished it with rain from heaven, and

The older and truer tradition was that in the extremity of his fortunes Croesus attempted to burn himself.

---

[1] J. Darmesteter, *The Zend-Avesta*, vol. i. (Oxford, 1880) pp. lxxxvi., lxxxviii-xc. (*Sacred Books of the East*, vol. iv.).

[2] *Zend-Avesta*, *Vendîdâd*, Fargard, v. 7. 39-44 (*Sacred Books of the East*, iv. 60 *sq.*).

[3] *Zend-Avesta*, translated by J. Darmesteter, i. pp. xc. 9, 110 *sq.* (*Sacred Books of the East*, iv.).

[4] Strabo, xv. 3. 14, p. 732.   Even gold, on account of its resemblance to fire, might not be brought near a corpse (*id.* xv. 3. 18, p. 734).

[5] Sardes fell in the autumn of 546 B.C. (E. Meyer, *Geschichte des Alterthums*, i. (Stuttgart, 1884), p. 604). Bacchylides was probably born between 512 and 505 B.C. See R. C. Jebb, *Bacchylides, the Poems and Fragments* (Cambridge, 1905), pp. 1 *sq.*

Apollo of the Golden Sword wafted the pious king and his daughters to the happy land beyond the North Wind.[1]   In like manner the vase-painter clearly represents the burning of Croesus as a voluntary act, not as a punishment inflicted on him by the conqueror.   He lets us see the king enthroned upon the pyre with a wreath of laurel on his head and a sceptre in one hand, while with the other he is pouring a libation.   An attendant is in the act of applying to the pile two objects which have been variously interpreted as torches to kindle the wood or whisks to sprinkle holy water.   The demeanour of the king is solemn and composed: he seems to be performing a religious rite, not suffering an ignominious death.[2]

Thus we may fairly conclude with some eminent modern scholars[3] that in the extremity of his fortunes Croesus prepared to meet death like a king or a god in the flames.   It was thus that Hercules, from whom the old kings of Lydia claimed to be sprung,[4] ascended from earth to heaven: it was thus that Zimri, king of Israel, passed beyond the reach of his enemies: it was thus that Shamashshumukin, king of Babylon, escaped a brother's vengeance: it was thus that the last king of Assyria expired in the ruins of his capital ; and it was thus that, sixty-six years after the capture of Sardes, the Carthaginian king Hamilcar sought to retrieve a lost battle by a hero's death.[5]

Legend that Semiramis burnt herself on a pyre.   Semiramis herself, the legendary queen of Assyria, is said to have burnt herself on a pyre out of grief at the death of a favourite horse.[6]   Since there are strong grounds for regard-

[1] Bacchylides, iii. 24-62.

[2] F. G. Welcker, *Alte Denkmäler* (Göttingen, 1849–1864), iii. pl. xxxiii. ; A. Baumeister, *Denkmäler des klassischen Altertums* (Munich and Leipsic, 1885–1888), ii. 796, fig. 860 ; A. H. Smith, " Illustrations to Bacchylides," *Journal of Hellenic Studies*, xviii. (1898) pp. 267-269 ; G. Maspero, *Histoire Ancienne des Peuples de l'Orient Classique*, iii. 618 *sq.* It is true that Cambyses caused the dead body of the Egyptian king Amasis to be dragged from the tomb, mangled, and burned ; but the deed is expressly branded by the ancient historian as an

outrage on Persian religion (Herodotus, iii. 16).

[3] Raoul-Rochette, " Sur l'Hercule Assyrien et Phénicien," *Mémoires de l'Académie des Inscriptions et Belles-Lettres*, xvii. Deuxième Partie (Paris, 1848), pp. 277 *sq.* ; M. Duncker, *Geschichte des Alterthums*, iv.[5] 330-332 ; E. Meyer, *Geschichte des Alterthums*, i. (Stuttgart, 1884) p. 604 ; G. Maspero, *Histoire Ancienne des Peuples de l'Orient Classique*, iii. 618.

[4] Herodotus, i. 7.

[5] See above, pp. 115 *sq.*, 173 *sq.*

[6] Hyginus, *Fab.* 243 ; Pliny, viii. 155.

ing the queen in her mythical aspect as a form of Ishtar or Astarte,[1] the legend that Semiramis died for love in the flames furnishes a remarkable parallel to the traditionary death of the love-lorn Dido, who herself appears to be simply an Avatar of the same great Asiatic goddess.[2] When we compare these stories of the burning of Semiramis and Dido with each other and with the historical cases of the burning of Oriental monarchs, we may perhaps conclude that there was a time when queens as well as kings were expected under certain circumstances, perhaps on the death of their consort, to perish in the fire. The conclusion can hardly be deemed extravagant when we remember that the practice of burning widows to death survived in India under English rule down to a time within living memory.[3]

At Jerusalem itself a reminiscence of the practice of burning kings, alive or dead, appears to have lingered as late as the time of Isaiah, who says: "For Tophet is prepared of old; yea, for the king it is made ready; he hath made it deep and large: the pile thereof is fire and much wood; the breath of the Lord, like a stream of brimstone, doth kindle it."[4] We know that "great burnings" were

The "great burnings" for Jewish kings.

---

[1] See W. Robertson Smith, "Ctesias and the Semiramis Legend," *English Historical Review*, ii. (1887) pp. 303-317. But the legend of Semiramis appears to have gathered round the person of a real Assyrian queen, by name Shammuramat, who lived towards the end of the ninth century B.C. and is known to us from historical inscriptions. See C. F. Lehmann-Haupt, *Die historische Semiramis und ihre Zeit* (Tübingen, 1910), pp. 1 *sqq.*; *id.*, *s.v.* "Semiramis," in W. H. Roscher's *Lexikon der griech. und röm. Mythologie*, iv. 678 *sqq.*; *The Scapegoat*, pp. 369 *sqq.*

[2] See above, p. 114.

[3] In ancient Greece we seem to have a reminiscence of widow-burning in the legend that when the corpse of Capaneus was being consumed on the pyre, his wife Evadne threw herself into the flames and perished. See Euripides, *Supplices*, 980 *sqq.*; Apollodorus, *Bibliotheca*, iii. 7. 1; Zenobius, *Cent.* i. 30; Ovid, *Tristia*, v. 14. 38.

[4] Isaiah xxx. 33. The Revised Version has "a Topheth" instead of "Tophet." But Hebrew does not possess an indefinite article (the few passages of the Bible in which the Aramaic חד is so used are no exception to the rule), and there is no evidence that Tophet (Topheth) was ever employed in a general sense. The passage of Isaiah has been rightly interpreted by W. Robertson Smith in the sense indicated in the text, though he denies that it contains any reference to the sacrifice of the children. See his *Lectures on the Religion of the Semites*,[2] pp. 372 *sq.* He observes (p. 372, note 3): "Saul's body was burned (1 Sam. xxxi. 12), possibly to save it from the risk of exhumation by the Philistines, but perhaps rather with a religious intention, and almost as an act of worship, since his bones were buried under the sacred tamarisk at Jabesh." In 1 Chronicles x. 12 the tree under which the bones of Saul were buried is not a tamarisk but a terebinth or an oak.

regularly made for dead kings of Judah,[1] and it can hardly be accidental that the place assigned by Isaiah to the king's pyre is the very spot in the Valley of Hinnom where the first-born children were actually burned by their parents in honour of Moloch "the King." The exact site of the Valley of Hinnom is disputed, but all are agreed in identifying it with one of the ravines which encircle or intersect Jerusalem; and according to some eminent authorities it was the one called by Josephus the Tyropoeon.[2] If this last identification is correct, the valley where the children were burned on a pyre lay immediately beneath the royal palace and the temple. Perhaps the young victims died for God and the king.[3]

The great burnings for Jewish Rabbis at Meiron in Galilee.

With the "great burnings" for dead Jewish kings it seems worth while to compare the great burnings still annually made for dead Jewish Rabbis at the lofty village of Meiron in Galilee, the most famous and venerated place of pilgrimage for Jews in modern Palestine. Here the tombs of the Rabbis are hewn out of the rock, and here on the thirtieth of April, the eve of May Day, multitudes of pilgrims, both men and women, assemble and burn their offerings, which consist of shawls, scarfs, handkerchiefs, books, and the like. These are placed in two stone basins on the top of two low pillars, and being drenched with oil and ignited they are consumed to ashes amid the loud applause, shouts, and cries of the spectators. A man has been known to pay as much as

---

[1] 2 Chronicles xvi. 14, xxi. 19; Jeremiah xxxiv. 5. There is no ground for assuming, as the Authorized version does in Jeremiah xxxiv. 5, that only spices were burned on these occasions; indeed the burning of spices is not mentioned at all in any of the three passages. The "sweet odours and divers kinds of spices prepared by the apothecaries' art," which were laid in the dead king's bed (2 Chronicles xvi. 14), were probably used to embalm him, not to be burned at his funeral. For though "great burnings" were regularly made for the dead kings of Judah, there is no evidence (apart from the doubtful case of Saul) that their bodies were cremated. They are regularly said to have been buried, not burnt. The passage of Isaiah seems to show that what was burned at a royal funeral was a great, but empty, pyre. That the burnings for the kings formed part of a heathen custom was rightly perceived by Renan (*Histoire du peuple d'Israel*, iii. 121, note).

[2] Josephus, *Bell. Jud.* v. 4. 1. See *Encyclopaedia Biblica*, s.v. "Jerusalem," vol. ii. 2423 *sq.*

[3] As to the Moloch worship, see Note I. at the end of the volume. I have to thank the Rev. Professor R. H. Kennett for indicating to me the inference which may be drawn from the identification of the Valley of Hinnom with the Tyropoeon.

two thousand piastres for the privilege of being allowed to open the ceremony by burning a costly shawl. On such occasions the solemn unmoved serenity of the Turkish officials, who keep order, presents a striking contrast to the intense excitement of the Jews.[1] This curious ceremony may be explained by the widespread practice of burning property for the use and benefit of the dead. So, to take a single instance, the tyrant Periander collected the finest raiment of all the women in Corinth and burned it in a pit for his dead wife, who had sent him word by necromancy that she was cold and naked in the other world, because the clothes he buried with her had not been burnt.[2] In like manner, perhaps, garments and other valuables may have been consumed on the pyre for the use of the dead kings of Judah. In Siam, the corpse of a king or queen is burned in a huge structure resembling a permanent palace, which with its many-gabled and high-pitched roofs and multitudinous tinselled spires, soaring to a height of over two hundred feet, sometimes occupies an area of about an acre.[3] The blaze of such an enormous catafalque may resemble, even if it far surpasses, the "great burnings" for the Jewish kings.

§ 3. *Purification by Fire*

These events and these traditions seem to prove that under certain circumstances Oriental monarchs deliberately chose to burn themselves to death. What were these circumstances? and what were the consequences of the act? If the intention had merely been to escape from the hands of a conqueror, an easier mode of death would naturally have been chosen. There must have been a special reason for electing to die by fire. The legendary death of Hercules, the historical death of Hamilcar, and the picture of Croesus enthroned in state on the pyre and pouring a libation, all combine to indicate that to be burnt alive was regarded as a solemn sacrifice, nay, more than that, as an apotheosis which

[margin note:] Death by fire regarded by the ancients as a kind of apotheosis.

---

[1] W. M. Thomson, *The Land and the Book, Central Palestine and Phoenicia* (London, 1883), pp. 575-579; Ed. Robinson, *Biblical Researches in Palestine*[3] (London, 1867), ii. 430 *sq.*;

K. Baedeker, *Palestine and Syria*[4] (Leipsic, 1906), p. 255.
[2] Herodotus, v. 92. 7.
[3] C. Bock, *Temples and Elephants* (London, 1884), pp. 73-76.

Fire was supposed to purge away the mortal parts of men, leaving the immortal.

raised the victim to the rank of a god.[1] For it is to be remembered that Hamilcar as well as Hercules was worshipped after death. Fire, moreover, was regarded by the ancients as a purgative so powerful that properly applied it could burn away all that was mortal of a man, leaving only the divine and immortal spirit behind. Hence we read of goddesses who essayed to confer immortality on the infant sons of kings by burning them in the fire by night ; but their beneficent purpose was always frustrated by the ignorant interposition of the mother or father, who peeping into the room saw the child in the flames and raised a cry of horror, thus disconcerting the goddess at her magic rites. This story is told of Isis in the house of the king of Byblus, of Demeter in the house of the king of Eleusis, and of Thetis in the house of her mortal husband Peleus.[2] In a slightly

---

[1] This view was maintained long ago by Raoul-Rochette in regard to the deaths both of Sardanapalus and of Croesus. He supposed that "the Assyrian monarch, reduced to the last extremity, wished, by the mode of death which he chose, to give to his sacrifice the form of an apotheosis and to identify himself with the national god of his country by allowing himself to be consumed, like him, on a pyre. . . . Thus mythology and history would be combined in a legend in which the god and the monarch would finally be confused. There is nothing in this which is not conformable to the ideas and habits of Asiatic civilization." See his memoir, " Sur l'Hercule Assyrien et Phénicien," *Mémoires de l'Académie des Inscriptions et Belles-Lettres*, xvii. Deuxième Partie (Paris, 1848), pp. 247 *sq.*, 271 *sqq.* The notion of regeneration by fire was fully recognized by Raoul-Rochette (*op. cit.* pp. 30 *sq.*). It deserves to be noted that Croesus burned on a huge pyre the great and costly offerings which he dedicated to Apollo at Delphi. He thought, says Herodotus (i. 50), that in this way the god would get possession of the offerings.

[2] As to Isis see Plutarch, *Isis et Osiris*, 16. As to Demeter see Homer, *Hymn to Demeter*, 231-262 ; Apollodorus, *Bibliotheca*, i. 5. 1 ; Ovid,

Fasti, iv. 547-560. As to Thetis see Apollonius Rhodius, *Argon.* iv. 865-879 ; Apollodorus, *Bibl.* iii. 13. 6. Most of these writers express clearly the thought that the fire consumed the mortal element, leaving the immortal. Thus Plutarch says, περικαίειν τὰ θνητὰ τοῦ σώματος. Apollodorus says (i. 5. 1), εἰς πῦρ κατετίθει τὸ βρέφος καὶ περιῄρει τὰς θνητὰς σάρκας αὐτοῦ, and again (iii. 13. 6), εἰς τὸ πῦρ ἐγκρυβοῦσα τῆς νυκτὸς ἔφθειρεν ὃ ἦν αὐτῷ θνητὸν πατρῷον. Apollonius Rhodius says,

ἡ μὲν γὰρ βροτέας αἰεὶ περὶ σάρκας ἔδαιεν
νύκτα διὰ μέσσην φλογμῷ πυρός.

And Ovid has,

" *Inque foco pueri corpus vivente favilla
Obruit, humanum purget ut ignis
onus.*"

On the custom of passing children over a fire as a purification, see my note, " The Youth of Achilles," *Classical Review*, vii. (1893) pp. 293 *sq.* On the purificatory virtue which the Greeks ascribed to fire see also Erwin Rohde, *Psyche*[3] (Tübingen and Leipsic, 1903), ii. 101, note[2]. The Warramunga of Central Australia have a tradition of a great man who "used to burn children in the fire so as to make them grow strong" (B. Spencer and F. J. Gillen, *The Northern Tribes of Central Australia*, London, 1904, p. 429).

different way the witch Medea professed to give back to the old their lost youth by boiling them with a hell-broth in her magic cauldron ;[1] and when Pelops had been butchered and served up at a banquet of the gods by his cruel father Tantalus, the divine beings, touched with pity, plunged his mangled remains in a kettle, from which after decoction he emerged alive and young.[2] " Fire," says Jamblichus, " destroys the material part of sacrifices, it purifies all things that are brought near it, releasing them from the bonds of matter and, in virtue of the purity of its nature, making them meet for communion with the gods. So, too, it releases us from the bondage of corruption, it likens us to the gods, it makes us meet for their friendship, and it converts our material nature into an immaterial."[3] Thus we can understand why kings and commoners who claimed or aspired to divinity should choose death by fire. It opened to them the gates of heaven. The quack Peregrinus, who ended his disreputable career in the flames at Olympia, gave out that after death he would be turned into a spirit who would guard men from the perils of the night ; and, as Lucian remarked, no doubt there were plenty of fools to believe him.[4] According to one account, the Sicilian philosopher Empedocles, who set up for being a god in his lifetime, leaped into the crater of Etna in order to establish his claim to godhead.[5] There is nothing incredible in the tradition. The crack-brained philosopher, with his itch for notoriety, may well have done what Indian fakirs [6] and the brazen-faced mountebank Peregrinus did in antiquity, and what Russian peasants and Chinese Buddhists have done in modern times.[7] There is no extremity to which fanaticism or vanity, or a mixture of the two, will not impel its victims.

---

[1] She is said to have thus restored the youth of her husband Jason, her father-in-law Aeson, the nurses of Dionysus, and all their husbands (Euripides, *Medea*, Argum. ; Scholiast on Aristophanes, *Knights*, 1321; compare Plautus, *Pseudolus*, 879 *sqq.*); and she applied the same process with success to an old ram (Apollodorus, *Bibl.* i. 9. 27; Pausanias, viii. 11. 2; Hyginus, *Fab.* 24).

[2] Pindar, *Olymp*. i. 40 *sqq.*, with the Scholiast ; J. Tzetzes, *Schol. on Lycophron*, 152.

[3] Jamblichus, *De mysteriis*, v. 12.

[4] Lucian, *De morte Peregrini*, 27 *sq.*

[5] Diogenes Laertius, viii. 2. 69 *sq.*

[6] Lucian, *De morte Peregrini*, 25 ; Strabo, xv. 1. 64 and 68, pp. 715, 717 ; Arrian, *Anabasis*, vii. 3.

[7] *The Dying God*, pp. 42 *sqq.*

§ 4. *The Divinity of Lydian Kings*

The
Lydian
kings
seem to
have
claimed
divinity
on the
ground
of their
descent
from
Hercules,
the god of
the double-
axe and of
the lion ;
and this
Lydian
Hercules
or Sandon
appears to
have been
the same
with the
Cilician
Sandan.
But apart from any general notions of the purificatory
virtues of fire, the kings of Lydia seem to have had a
special reason for regarding death in the flames as their
appropriate end.   For the ancient dynasty of the Heraclids
which preceded the house of Croesus on the throne traced
their descent from a god or hero whom the Greeks called
Hercules ;[1] and this Lydian Hercules appears to have been
identical in name and in substance with the Cilician
Hercules, whose effigy was regularly burned on a great
pyre at Tarsus.   The Lydian Hercules bore the name of
Sandon ;[2] the Cilician Hercules bore the name of Sandan,
or perhaps rather of Sandon, since Sandon is known from
inscriptions and other evidence to have been a Cilician
name.[3]   The characteristic emblems of the Cilician Hercules
were the lion and the double-headed axe ; and both these
emblems meet us at Sardes in connexion with the dynasty
of the Heraclids.   For the double-headed axe was carried
as part of the sacred regalia by Lydian kings from the time
of the legendary queen Omphale down to the reign of
Candaules, the last of the Heraclid kings.   It is said to
have been given to Omphale by Hercules himself, and it
was apparently regarded as a palladium of the Heraclid
sovereignty ; for after the dotard Candaules ceased to carry
the axe himself, and had handed it over to the keeping of
a courtier, a rebellion broke out, and the ancient dynasty of
the Heraclids came to an end.   The new king Gyges did
not attempt to carry the old emblem of sovereignty ; he
dedicated it with other spoils to Zeus in Caria.   Hence the
image of the Carian Zeus bore an axe in his hand and
received the epithet of Labrandeus, from *labrys*, the Lydian
word for " axe."[4]   Such is Plutarch's account ; but we may

[1] Herodotus, i. 7.

[2] Joannes Lydus, *De magistratibus*,
iii. 64.

[3] See above, p. 144, note [2].

[4] Plutarch, *Quaestiones Graecae*, 45.
Zeus Labrandeus was worshipped at
the village of Labraunda, situated in a
pass over the mountains, near Mylasa

in Caria.   The temple was ancient.
A road called the Sacred Way led
downhill for ten miles to Mylasa, a
city of white marble temples and colonnades which stood in a fertile plain at
the foot of a precipitous mountain,
where the marble was quarried.   Processions bearing the holy emblems

suspect that Zeus, or rather the native god whom the Greeks identified with Zeus, carried the axe long before the time of Candaules. If, as is commonly supposed, the axe was the symbol of the Asiatic thunder-god,[1] it would be an appropriate emblem in the hand of kings, who are so often expected to make rain, thunder, and lightning for the good of their people. Whether the kings of Lydia were bound to make thunder and rain we do not know; but at all events, like many early monarchs, they seem to have been held responsible for the weather and the crops. In the reign of Meles the country suffered severely from dearth, so the people consulted an oracle, and the deity laid the blame on the kings, one of whom had in former years incurred the guilt of murder. The soothsayers accordingly declared that King Meles, though his own hands were clean, must be banished for three years in order that the taint of bloodshed should be purged away. The king obeyed and retired to Babylon, where he lived three years. In his absence the kingdom was administered by a deputy, a certain Sadyattes, son of Cadys, who traced his descent from Tylon.[2] As to this Tylon we shall hear more presently. Again, we read that the Lydians rejoiced greatly at the assassination of Spermus, another of their kings, "for he was very wicked, and the land suffered from drought in his reign."[3] Apparently, like the ancient Irish and many modern Africans, they laid the drought at the king's door, and thought that he only got what he deserved under the knife of the assassin.

Lydian kings held responsible for the weather and the crops.

---

went to and fro along the Sacred Way from Mylasa to Labraunda. See Strabo, xiv. 2. 23, pp. 658 *sq.* The double-headed axe figures on the ruins and coins of Mylasa (Ch. Fellows, *An Account of Discoveries in Lycia*, London, 1841, p. 75; B. V. Head, *Historia Numorum*, Oxford, 1887, pp. 528 *sq.*). A horseman carrying a double-headed axe is a type which occurs on the coins of many towns in Lydia and Phrygia. At Thyatira this axe-bearing hero was called Tyrimnus, and games were held in his honour. He was identified with Apollo and the sun. See B. V. Head, *Catalogue of the Greek Coins of Lydia* (London, 1901), p. cxxviii. On a coin of Mostene in Lydia the double-headed axe is represented between a bunch of grapes and ears of corn, as if it were an emblem of fertility (B. V. Head, *op. cit.* p. 162, pl. xvii. 11).

[1] L. Preller, *Griechische Mythologie*, i.[4] (Berlin, 1894) pp. 141 *sq.* As to the Hittite thunder-god and his axe see above, pp. 134 *sqq.*

[2] Nicolaus Damascenus, in *Fragmenta Historicorum Graecorum*, ed. C. Müller, iii. 382 *sq.*

[3] *Ibid.* iii. 381.

The
lion-god
of Lydia.   With regard to the lion, the other emblem of the
Cilician Hercules, we are told that the same king Meles,
who was banished because of a dearth, sought to make the
acropolis of Sardes impregnable by carrying round it a lion
which a concubine had borne to him.   Unfortunately at a
single point, where the precipices were such that it seemed
as if no human foot could scale them, he omitted to carry
the beast, and sure enough at that very point the Persians
afterwards clambered up into the citadel.[1]   Now Meles was
one of the old Heraclid dynasty [2] who boasted their descent
from the lion-hero Hercules ; hence the carrying of a lion
round the acropolis was probably a form of consecration intended to place the stronghold under the guardianship of the
lion-god, the hereditary deity of the royal family.   And the
story that the king's concubine gave birth to a lion's whelp
suggests that the Lydian kings not only claimed kinship
with the beast, but posed as lions in their own persons and
passed off their sons as lion-cubs.   Croesus dedicated at
Delphi a lion of pure gold, perhaps as a badge of Lydia,[3]
and Hercules with his lion's skin is a common type on coins
of Sardes.[4]

Identity
of the
Lydian and
Cilician
Hercules.   Thus the death, or the attempted death, of Croesus on
the pyre completes the analogy between the Cilician and
the Lydian Hercules.   At Tarsus and at Sardes we find
the worship of a god whose symbols were the lion and the
double-headed axe, and who was burned on a great pyre,
either in effigy or in the person of a human representative.
The Greeks called him Hercules, but his native name was
Sandan or Sandon.   At Sardes he seems to have been
personated by the kings, who carried the double-axe and
perhaps wore, like their ancestor Hercules, the lion's skin.
We may conjecture that at Tarsus also the royal family
aped the lion-god.   At all events we know that Sandan,
the name of the god, entered into the names of Cilician

---

[1] Herodotus, i. 84.

[2] Eusebius, *Chronic.* i. 69, ed. A.
Schoene (Berlin, 1866-1875).

[3] Herodotus, i. 50.   At Thebes
there was a stone lion which was said
to have been dedicated by Hercules
(Pausanias, ix. 17. 2).

[4] B. V. Head, *Historia Numorum*
(Oxford, 1887), p. 553 ; *id., Catalogue
of the Greek Coins of Lydia* (London,
1901), pp. xcviii, 239, 240, 241, 244,
247, 253, 254, 264, with plates xxiv.
9-11, 13, xxv. 2, 12, xxvii. 8.

kings, and that in later times the priests of Sandan at Tarsus wore the royal purple.[1]

§ 5. *Hittite Gods at Tarsus and Sardes*

Now we have traced the religion of Tarsus back by a double thread to the Hittite religion of Cappadocia. One thread joins the Baal of Tarsus, with his grapes and his corn, to the god of Ibreez. The other thread unites the Sandan of Tarsus, with his lion and his double axe, to the similar figure at Boghaz - Keui. Without being unduly fanciful, therefore, we may surmise that the Sandon-Hercules of Lydia was also a Hittite god, and that the Heraclid dynasty of Lydia were of Hittite blood. Certainly the influence, if not the rule, of the Hittites extended to Lydia ; for at least two rock - carvings accompanied by Hittite inscriptions are still to be seen in the country. Both of them attracted the attention of the ancient Greeks. One of them represents a god or warrior in Hittite costume armed with a spear and bow. It is carved on the face of a grey rock, which stands out conspicuous on a bushy hillside, where an old road runs through a glen from the valley of the Hermus to the valley of the Cayster. The place is now called Kara - Bel. Herodotus thought that the figure represented the Egyptian king and conqueror Sesostris.[2] The other monument is a colossal seated figure of the Mother of the Gods, locally known in antiquity as Mother Plastene. It is hewn out of the solid rock and occupies a large niche in the face of a cliff at the steep northern foot of Mount Sipylus.[3] Thus it would seem that at some time or other the Hittites carried their arms to the shores of the Aegean. There is no improbability, therefore, in the view that a Hittite dynasty may have reigned at Sardes.[4]

The Cilician and Lydian Hercules (Sandan or Sandon) seems to have been a Hittite · deity.

---

[1] See above, p. 143.

[2] Herodotus, ii. 106; G. Perrot et Ch. Chipiez, *Histoire de l'Art dans l'Antiquité*, iv. 742-752 ; L. Messerschmidt, *Corpus Inscriptionum Hettiticarum*, pp. 33-37, with plates xxxvii., xxxviii. ; J. Garstang, *The Land of the Hittites*, pp. 170-173, with plate liv.

[3] Pausanias, iii. 24. 2, v. 13. 7 with my note ; G. Perrot et Ch. Chipiez, *op.*

cit. iv. 752-759 ; L. Messerschmidt, *op. cit.* pp. 37 *sq.*, pl. xxxix. 1 ; J. Garstang, *The Land of the Hittites*, pp. 167-170, with plate liii. Unlike most Hittite sculptures the figure of Mother Plastene is carved almost in the round. The inscriptions which accompany both these Lydian monuments are much defaced.

[4] The suggestion that the Heraclid

§ 6. The Resurrection of Tylon

The burning of Sandan, like that of Melcarth,[1] was probably followed by a ceremony of his resurrection or awakening, to indicate that the divine life was not extinct, but had only assumed a fresher and purer form. Of that resurrection we have, so far as I am aware, no direct evidence. In default of it, however, there is a tale of a local Lydian hero called Tylon or Tylus, who was killed and brought to life again. The story runs thus. Tylon or Tylus was a son of Earth.[2] One day as he was walking on the banks of the Hermus a serpent stung and killed him. His distressed sister Moire had recourse to a giant named Damasen, who attacked and slew the serpent. But the serpent's mate culled a herb, " the flower of Zeus," in the woods, and bringing it in her mouth put it to the lips of the dead serpent, which immediately revived. In her turn Moire took the hint and restored her brother Tylon to life by touching him with the same plant.[3] A similar incident occurs in many folk - tales. Serpents are often credited with a knowledge of life - giving plants.[4] But Tylon seems to have been more than a mere hero of fairy-tales. He was closely associated with Sardes, for he figures on the coins of the city along with his champion Damasen or Masnes, the dead serpent, and the life-giving branch.[5] And

Death and resurrection of the Lydian hero Tylon.

kings of Lydia were Hittites, or under Hittite influence, is not novel. See W. Wright, *Empire of the Hittites*, p. 59; E. Meyer, *Geschichte des Alterthums*, i. (Stuttgart, 1884) p. 307, § 257; Fr. Hommel, *Grundriss der Geographie und Geschichte des alten Orients*, p. 54, note[2]; L. Messer-schmidt, *The Hittites*, p. 22.

[1] See above, pp. 110 *sqq.*

[2] Dionysius Halicarnasensis, *Antiquit. Roman.* i. 27. 1.

[3] Nonnus, *Dionys.* xxv. 451-551; Pliny, *Nat. Hist.* xxv. 14. The story, as we learn from Pliny, was told by Xanthus, an early historian of Lydia.

[4] Thus Glaucus, son of Minos, was restored to life by the seer Polyidus, who learned the trick from a serpent.

See Apollodorus, *Bibliotheca*, iii. 3. 1. For references to other tales of the same sort see my note on Pausanias, ii. 10. 3 (vol. iii. pp. 65 *sq.*). The serpent's acquaintance with the tree of life in the garden of Eden perhaps belongs to the same cycle of stories.

[5] B. V. Head, *Catalogue of the Greek Coins of Lydia*, pp. cxi-cxiii, with pl. xxvii. 12. On the coins the champion's name appears as Masnes or Masanes, but the reading is doubtful. The name Masnes occurred in Xanthus's history of Lydia (*Fragmenta Historicorum Graecorum*, ed. C. Müller, iv. 629). It is probably the same with Manes, the name of a son of Zeus and Earth, who is said to have been the first king of Lydia (Dionysius

he was related in various ways to the royal family of Lydia ; for his daughter married Cotys, one of the earliest kings of the country,[1] and a descendant of his acted as regent during the banishment of King Meles.[2]   It has been suggested that the story of his death and resurrection was acted as a pageant to symbolize the revival of plant life in spring.[3] At all events, a festival called the Feast of the Golden Feast of Flower was celebrated in honour of Persephone at Sardes,[4] the Golden Flower at probably in one of the vernal months, and the revival of Sardes. the hero and of the goddess may well have been represented together.   The Golden Flower of the Festival would then be the "flower of Zeus" of the legend, perhaps the yellow crocus of nature or rather her more gorgeous sister, the Oriental saffron.   For saffron grew in great abundance at the Corycian cave of Zeus ;[5] and it is an elegant conjecture, if it is nothing more, that the very name of the place meant "the Crocus Cave." [6]   However, on the coins of Sardes the magical plant seems to be a branch rather than a blossom, a Golden Bough rather than a Golden Flower.

Halicarnasensis, *Ant. Rom.* i. 27. 1). Manes was the father of King Atys (Herodotus, i. 94). Thus Tylon was connected with the royal family of Lydia through his champion as well as in the ways mentioned in the text.

[1] Dionysius Halicarnasensis, *l.c.*

[2] See above, p. 183.

[3] B. V. Head, *Catalogue of the Greek Coins of Lydia*, p. cxiii.

[4] B. V. Head, *Catalogue of the Greek Coins of Lydia*, pp. cx, cxiii. The festival seems to be mentioned only on coins.

[5] See above, p. 154.

[6] V. Hehn, *Kulturpflanzen und Haustiere*[7] (Berlin, 1902), p. 261. He would derive the name from the Semitic, or at all events the Cilician language.   The Hebrew word for saffron is *karkôm*.   As to the spring flowers of North-Western Asia Minor, W. M. Leake remarks (April 1, 1800)

that "primroses, violets, and crocuses, are the only flowers to be seen" (*Journal of a Tour in Asia Minor*, London, 1824, p. 143).   Near Mylasa in Caria, Fellows saw (March 20, 1840) the broom covered with yellow blossoms and a great variety of anemones, like "a rich Turkey carpet, in which the green grass did not form a prominent colour amidst the crimson, lilac, blue, scarlet, white, and yellow flowers" (Ch. Fellows, *An Account of Discoveries in Lycia*, London, 1841, pp. 65, 66).   In February the yellow stars of *Gagea arvensis* cover the rocky and grassy grounds of Lycia, and the field-marigold often meets the eye.   At the same season in Lycia the shrub *Colutea arborescens* opens its yellow flowers.   See T. A. B. Spratt and E. Forbes, *Travels in Lycia* (London, 1847), ii. 133.   I must leave it to others to identify the Golden Flower of Sardes.

CHAPTER VIII

VOLCANIC RELIGION

§ 1. *The Burning of a God*

The custom of burning a god may have been intended to recruit his divine energies.

THUS it appears that a custom of burning a god in effigy or in the person of a human representative was practised by at least two peoples of Western Asia, the Phoenicians and the Hittites. Whether they both developed the custom independently, or whether one of them adopted it from the other, we cannot say. And their reasons for celebrating a rite which to us seems strange and monstrous are also obscure. In the preceding inquiry some grounds have been adduced for thinking that the practice was based on a conception of the purifying virtue of fire, which, by destroying the corruptible and perishable elements of man, was supposed to fit him for union with the imperishable and the divine. Now to people who created their gods in their own likeness, and imagined them subject to the same law of decadence and death, the idea would naturally occur that fire might do for the gods what it was believed to do for men, that it could purge them of the taint of corruption and decay, could sift the mortal from the immortal in their composition, and so endow them with eternal youth. Hence a custom might arise of subjecting the deities themselves, or the more important of them, to an ordeal of fire for the purpose of refreshing and renovating those creative energies on the maintenance of which so much depended. To the coarse apprehension of the uninstructed and unsympathetic observer the solemn rite might easily wear a very different aspect. According as he was of a pious or of a sceptical turn of mind, he might

188

denounce it as a sacrilege or deride it as an absurdity. "To burn the god whom you worship," he might say, "is the height of impiety and of folly. If you succeed in the attempt, you kill him and deprive yourselves of his valuable services. If you fail, you have mortally offended him, and sooner or later he will visit you with his severe displeasure." To this the worshipper, if he was patient and polite, might listen with a smile of indulgent pity for the ignorance and obtuseness of the critic. "You are much mistaken," he might observe, "in imagining that we expect or attempt to kill the god whom we adore. The idea of such a thing is as repugnant to us as to you. Our intention is precisely the opposite of that which you attribute to us. Far from wishing to destroy the deity, we desire to make him live for ever, to place him beyond the reach of that process of degeneration and final dissolution to which all things here below appear by their nature to be subject. He does not die in the fire. Oh no! Only the corruptible and mortal part of him perishes in the flames : all that is incorruptible and immortal of him will survive the purer and stronger for being freed from the contagion of baser elements. That little heap of ashes which you see there is not our god. It is only the skin which he has sloughed, the husk which he has cast. He himself is far away, in the clouds of heaven, in the depths of earth, in the running waters, in the tree and the flower, in the corn and the vine. We do not see him face to face, but every year he manifests his divine life afresh in the blossoms of spring and the fruits of autumn. We eat of his broken body in bread. We drink of his shed blood in the juice of the grape."

§ 2. *The Volcanic Region of Cappadocia*

Some such train of reasoning may suffice to explain, though naturally not to justify, the custom which we bluntly call the burning of a god. Yet it is worth while to ask whether in the development of the practice these general considerations may not have been reinforced or modified by special circumstances ; for example, by the natural features of the country where the custom grew up. For the history

The custom of burning a god may have stood in some relation to volcanic phenomena.

of religion, like that of all other human institutions, has been profoundly affected by local conditions, and cannot be fully understood apart from them.   Now Asia Minor, the region where the practice in question appears to have been widely diffused, has from time immemorial been subjected to the action of volcanic forces on a great scale.   It is true that, so far as the memory of man goes back, the craters of its volcanoes have been extinct, but the vestiges of their dead or slumbering fires are to be seen in many places, and the country has been shaken and rent at intervals by tremendous earthquakes.   These phenomena cannot fail to have impressed the imagination of the inhabitants, and thereby to have left some mark on their religion.

The great extinct volcano Mount Argaeus in Cappadocia.
Among the extinct volcanoes of Anatolia the greatest is Mount Argaeus, in the centre of Cappadocia, the heart of the old Hittite country.   It is indeed the highest point of Asia Minor, and one of the loftiest mountains known to the ancients ; for in height it falls not very far short of Mount Blanc.   Towering abruptly in a huge pyramid from the plain, it is a conspicuous object for miles on miles.   Its top is white with eternal snow, and in antiquity its lower slopes were clothed with dense forests, from which the inhabitants of the treeless Cappadocian plains drew their supply of timber.   In these woods, and in the low grounds at the foot of the mountain, the languishing fires of the volcano manifested themselves as late as the beginning of our era.   The ground was treacherous.   Under a grassy surface there lurked pits of fire, into which stray cattle and unwary travellers often fell.   Experienced woodmen used great caution when they went to fell trees in the forest. Elsewhere the soil was marshy, and flames were seen to play over it at night.[1]   Superstitious fancies no doubt

[1] Strabo, xii. 2. 7, p. 538.   Mount Argaeus still retains its ancient name in slightly altered forms (*Ardjeh, Erdjich, Erjäus*).   Its height is about 13,000 feet.   In the nineteenth century it was ascended by at least two English travellers, W. J. Hamilton and H. F. Tozer.   See W. J. Hamilton, *Researches in Asia Minor, Pontus, and Armenia*, ii. 269-281 ; H. F. Tozer,

Turkish Armenia and Eastern Asia Minor, pp. 94, 113-131 ; Élisée Reclus, *Nouvelle Géographie Universelle* (Paris, 1879–1894), ix. 476-478. A Hittite inscription is carved at a place called Tope Nefezi, near Asarjik, on the slope of Mount Argaeus.   See J. Garstang, *The Land of the Hittites*, pp. 152 *sq.*

gathered thick around these perilous spots, but what shape they took we cannot say. Nor do we know whether sacrifices were offered on the top of the mountain, though a curious discovery may perhaps be thought to indicate that they were. Sharp and lofty pinnacles of red porphyry, inaccessible to the climber, rise in imposing grandeur from the eternal snow of the summit, and here Mr. Tozer found that the rock had been perforated in various places with human habitations. One such rock-hewn dwelling winds inward for a considerable distance; rude niches are hollowed in its sides, and on its roof and walls may be seen the marks of tools.[1] The ancients certainly did not climb mountains for pleasure or health, and it is difficult to imagine that any motive but superstition should have led them to provide dwellings in such a place. These rock-cut chambers may have been shelters for priests charged with the performance of religious or magical rites on the summit.

§ 3. *Fire-Worship in Cappadocia*

Under the Persian rule Cappadocia became, and long continued to be, a great seat of the Zoroastrian fire-worship. In the time of Strabo, about the beginning of our era, the votaries of that faith and their temples were still numerous in the country. The perpetual fire burned on an altar, surrounded by a heap of ashes, in the middle of the temple; and the priests daily chanted their liturgy before it, holding in their hands a bundle of myrtle rods and wearing on their heads tall felt caps with cheek-pieces which covered their lips, lest they should defile the sacred flame with their breath.[2] It is reasonable to suppose that the natural fires which burned perpetually on the outskirts of Mount Argaeus attracted the devotion of the disciples of Zoroaster, for elsewhere similar fires have been the object of religious

Persian fire-worship in Cappadocia.

Worship of natural fires which burn perpetually.

---

[1] H. F. Tozer, *op. cit.* pp. 125-127.
[2] Strabo, xv. 3. 14 *sq.*, pp. 732 *sq.* A bundle of twigs, called the Barsom (*Beresma* in the Avesta), is still used by the Parsee priests in chanting their liturgy. See M. Haug, *Essays on the Sacred Language, Writings and Religion of the Parsis*[3] (London, 1884), pp. 4, note [1], 283. When a potter in Southern India is making a pot which is to be worshipped as a household deity, he "should close his mouth with a bandage, so that his breath may not defile the pot." See E. Thurston, *Castes and Tribes of Southern India* (Madras, 1909), iv. 151.

reverence down to modern times.   Thus at Jualamukhi, on
the lower slopes of the Himalayas, jets of combustible gas
issue from the earth ; and a great Hindoo temple, the
resort of many pilgrims, is built over them.   The perpetual
flame, which is of a reddish hue and emits an aromatic
perfume, rises from a pit in the fore-court of the sanctuary.
The worshippers deliver their gifts, consisting usually of
flowers, to the attendant fakirs, who first hold them over
the flame and then cast them into the body of the temple.[1]

The
perpetual
fires of
Baku.Again, Hindoo pilgrims make their way with great difficulty
to Baku on the Caspian, in order to worship the everlasting
fires which there issue from the beds of petroleum.   The
sacred spot is about ten miles to the north-east of the
city.   An English traveller, who visited Baku in the middle
of the eighteenth century, has thus described the place and
the worship.   " There are several ancient temples built with
stone, supposed to have been all dedicated to fire ; most of
them are arched vaults, not above ten to fifteen feet high.
Amongst others there is a little temple, in which the
Indians now worship ; near the altar, about three feet high,
is a large hollow cane, from the end of which issues a blue
flame, in colour and gentleness not unlike a lamp that
burns with spirits, but seemingly more pure.   These Indians
affirm that this flame has continued ever since the flood,
and they believe it will last to the end of the world ; that
if it was resisted or suppressed in that place, it would rise
in some other.   Here are generally forty or fifty of these
poor devotees, who come on a pilgrimage from their own
country, and subsist upon wild sallary, and a kind of
Jerusalem artichokes, which are very good food, with other
herbs and roots, found a little to the northward.   Their
business is to make expiation, not for their own sins only,
but for those of others ; and they continue the longer time,
in proportion to the number of persons for whom they have
engaged to pray.   They mark their foreheads with saffron,
and have a great veneration for a red cow." [2]   Thus it

[1] Baron Charles Hügel, *Travels in
Kashmir and the Panjab* (London,
1845), pp. 42-46 ; W. Crooke, *Things
Indian* (London, 1906), p. 219.

[2] Jonas Hanway, *An Historical
Account of the British Trade over the
Caspian Sea : with the Author's Journal
of Travels*, Second Edition (London,
1754), i. 263.   For later descriptions
of the fires and fire-worshippers of

would seem that a purifying virtue is attributed to the sacred flame, since pilgrims come to it from far to expiate sin.

§ 4. *The Burnt Land of Lydia*

Another volcanic region of Asia Minor is the district of Lydia, to which, on account of its remarkable appearance, the Greeks gave the name of the Burnt Land. It lies to the east of Sardes in the upper valley of the Hermus, and covers an area of about fifty miles by forty. As described by Strabo, the country was wholly treeless except for the vines, which produced a wine inferior to none of the most famous vintages of antiquity. The surface of the plains was like ashes ; the hills were composed of black stone, as if they had been scorched by fire. Some people laid the scene of Typhon's battle with the gods in this Black Country, and supposed that it had been burnt by the thunderbolts hurled from heaven at the impious monster. The philosophic Strabo, however, held that the fires which had wrought this havoc were subterranean, not celestial, and he pointed to three craters, at intervals of about four miles, each in a hill of scoriae which he supposed to have been once molten matter ejected by the volcanoes.[1] His observation and his theory have both been confirmed by modern science. The three extinct volcanoes to which he referred are still conspicuous features of the landscape. Each is a black cone of loose cinders, scoriae, and ashes, with steep sides and a deep crater. From each a flood of rugged black lava has flowed forth, bursting out at the foot of the cone, and then rushing down the dale to the bed of the Hermus. The dark streams follow all the sinuosities of the valleys, their sombre hue contrasting with the rich verdure of the surrounding landscape. Their surface, broken into a thousand fantastic forms, resembles a sea lashed into fury by a gale, and then suddenly hardened into

The Burnt Land of Lydia.

Baku, see J. Reinegg, *Beschreibung des Kaukasus* (Gotha, Hildesheim, and St. Petersburg, 1796-1797), i. 151-159 ; A. von Haxthausen, *Transkaukasia* (Leipsic, 1856), ii. 80-85. Compare

W. Crooke, *Things Indian*, p. 219.
   [1] Strabo, xii. 8. 18 *sq.*, p. 579 ; xiii. 4. 11, p. 628. The wine of the district is mentioned by Vitruvius (viii. 3. 12) and Pliny (*Nat. Hist.* xiv. 75).

stone.	Regarded from the geological point of view, these black cones of cinders and these black rivers of lava are of comparatively recent formation.	Exposure to the weather for thousands of years has not yet softened their asperities and decomposed them into vegetable mould ; they are as hard and ungenial as if the volcanic stream had ceased to flow but yesterday.	But in the same district there are upwards of thirty other volcanic cones, whose greater age is proved by their softened forms, their smoother sides, and their mantle of vegetation.	Some of them are planted with vineyards to their summits.[1]	Thus the volcanic soil is still as favourable to the cultivation of the vine as it was in antiquity.	The relation between the two was noted by the ancients.	Strabo compares the vines of the Burnt Land with the vineyards of Catania fertilized by the ashes of Mount Etna ; and he tells us that some ingenious persons explained the fire-born Dionysus as a myth of the grapes fostered by volcanic agency.[2]

## § 5.	*The Earthquake God*

Earth-
quakes
in Asia
Minor.
But the inhabitants of these regions were reminded of the slumbering fires by other and less agreeable tokens than the generous juice of their grapes.	For not the Burnt Land only but the country to the south, including the whole valley of the Maeander, was subject to frequent and violent shocks of earthquake.	The soil was loose, friable, and full of salts, the ground hollow, undermined by fire and water.	In particular the city of Philadelphia was a great centre of disturbance.	The shocks there, we are told, were continuous. The houses rocked, the walls cracked and gaped ; the few inhabitants were kept busy repairing the breaches or buttress-ing and propping the edifices which threatened to tumble

---

[1] W. J. Hamilton, *Researches in Asia Minor, Pontus, and Armenia,* i. 136-140, ii. 131-138.	One of the three recent cones described by Strabo is now called the *Kara Devlit*, or Black Inkstand.	Its top is about 2500 feet above the sea, but only 500 feet above the surrounding plain.	The adjoining town of Koula, built of the black lava on which it stands, has a sombre and dismal look.	Another of the cones, almost equally high, has a crater of about half a mile in circum-ference and three or four hundred feet deep.

[2] Strabo, xiii. 4. 11, p. 628.	Com-pare his account of the Catanian vineyards (vi. 2. 3, p. 269).

about their ears. Most of the citizens, indeed, had the
prudence to dwell dispersed on their farms. It was a marvel,
says Strabo, that such a city should have any inhabitants at
all, and a still greater marvel that it should ever have been
built.[1] However, by a wise dispensation of Providence, the
earthquakes which shook the foundations of their houses only
strengthened those of their faith. The people of Apameia, Worship of
whose town was repeatedly devastated, paid their devotions Poseidon,
with great fervour to Poseidon, the earthquake god.[2] Again, quake god.
the island of Santorin, in the Greek Archipelago, has
been for thousands of years a great theatre of volcanic
activity. On one occasion the waters of the bay boiled and
flamed for four days, and an island composed of red-hot
matter rose gradually, as if hoisted by machinery, above
the waves. It happened that the sovereignty of the seas
was then with the Rhodians, those merchant-princes whose
prudent policy, strict but benevolent oligarchy, and beautiful
island-city, rich with accumulated treasures of native art,
rendered them in a sense the Venetians of the ancient world.
So when the ebullition and heat of the eruption had subsided,
their sea-captains landed in the new island, and founded a
sanctuary of Poseidon the Establisher or Securer,[3] a compli-
mentary epithet often bestowed on him as a hint not to shake
the earth more than he could conveniently help.[4] In many

---

[1] Strabo, xii. 8. 16-18, pp. 578 *sq.*;
xiii. 4. 10 *sq.*, p. 628.

[2] Strabo, xii. 8. 18, p. 579. Compare Tacitus, *Annals*, xii. 58.

[3] Strabo, i. 3. 16, p. 57. Compare
Plutarch, *De Pythiae oraculis*, 11 ;
Pliny, *Nat. Hist.* ii. 202 ; Justin,
xxx. 4. The event seems to have
happened in 197 B.C. Several other
islands are known to have appeared in
the same bay both in ancient and
modern times. So far as antiquity is
concerned, the dates of their appearance
are given by Pliny, but some confusion
on the subject has crept into his mind,
or rather, perhaps, into his text. See
the discussion of the subject in W.
Smith's *Dictionary of Greek and Roman
Geography* (London, 1873), ii. 1158-
1160. As to the eruptions in the
bay of Santorin, the last of which
occurred in 1866 and produced a

new island, see Sir Charles Lyell,
Principles of Geology [12] (London,
1875), i. 51, ii. 65 *sqq.*; C. Neumann
und J. Partsch, *Physikalische Geographie
von Griechenland* (Breslau, 1885),
pp. 272 *sqq.* There is a monograph
on Santorin and its eruptions (F.
Fouqué, *Santorin et ses éruptions*,
Paris, 1879). Strabo has given a brief
but striking account of Rhodes, its
architecture, its art-treasures, and its
constitution (xiv. 2. 5, pp. 652 *sq.*).
As to the Rhodian schools of art see
H. Brunn, *Geschichte der griechischen
Künstler* (Stuttgart, 1857-1859), i.
459 *sqq.*, ii. 233 *sqq.*, 286 *sq.*

[4] Aristophanes, *Acharn.* 682 ; Pau-
sanias, iii. 11. 9, vii. 21. 7 ; Plutarch,
Theseus, 36 ; Aristides, *Isthmic.* vol. i.
p. 29, ed. G. Dindorf (Leipsic, 1829);
Appian, *Bell. Civ.* v. 98 ; Macrobius,
Saturn. i. 17. 22 ; G. Dittenberger,

places people sacrificed to Poseidon the Establisher, in the hope that he would be as good as his name and not bring down their houses on their heads.[1]

Spartan propitiation of Poseidon during an earthquake.

Another instance of a Greek attempt to quiet the perturbed spirit underground is instructive, because similar efforts are still made by savages in similar circumstances. Once when a Spartan army under King Agesipolis had taken the field, it chanced that the ground under their feet was shaken by an earthquake. It was evening, and the king was at mess with the officers of his staff. No sooner did they feel the shock than, with great presence of mind, they rose from their dinner and struck up a popular hymn in honour of Poseidon. The soldiers outside the tent took up the strain, and soon the whole army joined in the sacred melody.[2] It is not said whether the flute-band, which always played the Spartan redcoats into action,[3] accompanied the deep voices of the men with its shrill music. At all events, the intention of this service of praise, addressed to the earth-shaking god, can only have been to prevail on him to stop. I have spoken of the Spartan redcoats because the uniform of Spartan soldiers was red.[4] As they fought in an extended, not a deep, formation, a Spartan line of battle must always have been, what the British used to be, a thin red line. It was in this order, and no doubt with the music

Sylloge Inscriptionum Graecarum[2] (Leipsic, 1898-1901), ii. p. 230, No. 543.

[1] Cornutus, *Theologiae Graecae Compendium*, 22.

[2] Xenophon, *Hellenica*, iv. 7. 4. As to the Spartan headquarters staff (οἱ περὶ δαμοσίαν), see *id.* iv. 5. 8, vi. 4. 14; Xenophon, *Respublica Lacedaem.* xiii. 1, xv. 4. Usually the Spartans desisted from any enterprise they had in hand when an earthquake happened (Thucydides, iii. 59. 1, v. 50. 5, vi. 95. 1).

[3] Thucydides, v. 70. 1. The use of the music, Thucydides tells us, was not to inspire the men, but to enable them to keep step, and so to march in close order. Without music a long line of battle was apt to straggle in advancing to the charge. As missiles were little

used in Greek warfare, there was no need to hurry the advance over the intervening ground ; so it was made deliberately and with the bands playing. The air to which the Spartans charged was called Castor's tune. It was the king in person who gave the word for the flutes to strike up. See Plutarch, *Lycurgus*, 22.

[4] Xenophon, *Respublica Lacedaem.* xi. 3 ; Aristophanes, *Lysistrata*, 1140 ; Aristotle, cited by a scholiast on Aristophanes, *Acharn.* 320 ; Plutarch, *Instituta Laconica*, 24. When a great earthquake had destroyed the city of Sparta and the Messenians were in revolt, the Spartans sent a messenger to Athens asking for help. Aristophanes (*Lysistrata*, 1138 *sqq.*) describes the man as if he had seen him, sitting as a suppliant on the altar with his pale face and his red coat.

playing and the sun flashing on their arms, that they advanced to meet the Persians at Thermopylae. Like Cromwell's Ironsides, these men could fight as well as sing psalms.[1]

If the Spartans imagined that they could stop an earthquake by a soldiers' chorus, their theory and practice resembled those of many other barbarians. Thus the people of Timor, in the East Indies, think that the earth rests on the shoulder of a mighty giant, and that when he is weary of bearing it on one shoulder he shifts it to the other, and so causes the ground to quake. At such times, accordingly, they all shout at the top of their voices to let him know that there are still people on the earth ; for otherwise they fear lest, impatient of his burden, he might tip it into the sea.[2] The Manichaeans held a precisely similar theory of earthquakes, except that according to them the weary giant transferred his burden from one shoulder to the other at the end of every thirty years,[3] a view which, at all events, points to the observation of a cycle in the recurrence of earthquake shocks. But we are not told that these heretics reduced an absurd theory to an absurd practice by raising a shout in

Modes of stopping an earthquake by informing the god or giant that there are still men on the earth.

---

[1] I have assumed that the sun shone on the Spartans at Thermopylae. For the battle was fought in the height of summer, when the Greek sky is generally cloudless, and on that particular morning the weather was very still. The evening before, the Persians had sent round a body of troops by a difficult pass to take the Spartans in the rear ; day was breaking when they neared the summit, and the first intimation of their approach which reached the ears of the Phocian guards posted on the mountain was the loud crackling of leaves under their feet in the oak forest. Moreover, the famous Spartan saying about fighting in the shade of the Persian arrows, which obscured the sun, points to bright, hot weather. It was at high noon, and therefore probably in the full blaze of the mid-day sun, that the last march-out took place. See Herodotus, vii. 215-226 ; and as to the date of the battle (about the time of the Olympic games) see Herodotus, vii. 206, viii. 12 and 26 ; G. Busolt, *Griechische Geschichte*, ii.[2] (Gotha,

1895) p. 673, note[9].

[2] S. Müller, *Reizen en Onderzoekingen in den Indischen Archipel* (Amsterdam, 1857), ii. 264 *sq.* Compare A. Bastian, *Indonesien* (Berlin, 1884–1889), ii. 3. The beliefs and customs of the East Indian peoples in regard to earthquakes have been described by G. A. Wilken, *Het animisme bij de volken van den Indischen Archipel*, Tweede Stuk (Leyden, 1885), pp. 247-254 ; *id., Verspreide Geschriften* (The Hague, 1912), iii. 274-281. Compare *id., Handleiding voor de vergelijkende Volkenkunde van Nederlandsch-Indië* (Leyden, 1893), pp. 604 *sq.* ; and on primitive conceptions of earthquakes in general, E. B. Tylor, *Primitive Culture*[2] (London, 1873), i. 364-366 ; R. Lasch, "Die Ursache und Bedeutung der Erdbeben im Volksglauben und Volksbrauch," *Archiv für Religionswissenschaft*, v. (1902) pp. 236-257, 369-383.

[3] Epiphanius, *Adversus Haereses*, ii. 2. 23 (Migne's *Patrologia Graeca*, xlii. 68).

order to remind the earth-shaker of the inconvenience he was putting them to. However, both the theory and the practice are to be found in full force in various parts of the East Indies. When the Balinese and the Sundanese feel an earthquake they cry out, " Still alive," or " We still live," to acquaint the earth-shaking god or giant with their existence.[1] The natives of Leti, Moa, and Lakor, islands of the Indian Archipelago, imagine that earthquakes are caused by Grandmother Earth in order to ascertain whether her descendants are still to the fore. So they make loud noises for the purpose of satisfying her grandmotherly solicitude.[2] The Tami of German New Guinea ascribe earthquakes to a certain old Panku who sits under a great rock ; when he stirs, the earth quakes. If the shock lasts a long time they beat on the ground with palm-branches, saying, " You down there ! easy a little ! We men are still here." [3] The Shans of Burma are taught by Buddhist monks that under the world there sleeps a great fish with his tail in his mouth, but sometimes he wakes, bites his tail, and quivering with pain causes the ground to quiver and shake likewise. That is the cause of great earthquakes. But the cause of little earthquakes is different. These are produced by little men who live underground and sometimes feeling lonely knock on the roof of the world over their heads ; these knockings we perceive as slight shocks of earthquakes. When Shans feel such a shock, they run out of their houses, kneel down, and answer the little men saying, " We are here ! We are here ! " [4] Earthquakes are common in the Pampa del Sacramento of Eastern Peru. The Conibos, a tribe of Indians on the left bank of the great Ucayali River, attribute these disturbances to the creator, who usually resides in heaven, but comes down from time to time to see whether the work of his hands still exists. The result of his descent is an earthquake. So when one happens, these Indians rush out

---

[1] H. N. van der Tuuk, "Notes on the Kawi Language and Literature," *Journal of the Royal Asiatic Society*, N.S. xiii. (1881) p. 50.

[2] J. G. F. Riedel, *De sluik- en kroesharige rassen tusschen Selebes en Papua* (The Hague, 1886), p. 398 ;

compare *id.* pp. 330, 428.

[3] G. Bamler, "Tami," in R. Neuhauss's *Deutsch Neu - Guinea*, iii. (Berlin, 1911) p. 492.

[4] Mrs. Leslie Milne, *Shans at Home* (London, 1910), p. 54.

of their huts with extravagant gestures shouting, as if in answer to a question, "A moment, a moment, here I am, father, here I am!" Their intention is, no doubt, to assure their heavenly father that they are still alive, and that he may return to his mansion on high with an easy mind. They never remember the creator nor pay him any heed except at an earthquake.[1] In Africa the Atonga tribe of Lake Nyassa used to believe that an earthquake was the voice of God calling to inquire whether his people were all there. So when the rumble was heard underground they all shouted in answer, "*Ye, ye*," and some of them went to the mortars used for pounding corn and beat on them with pestles. They thought that if any one of them did not thus answer to the divine call he would die.[2] In Ourwira the people think that an earthquake is caused by a dead sultan marching past underground; so they stand up to do him honour, and some raise their hands to the salute. Were they to omit these marks of respect to the deceased, they would run the risk of being swallowed up alive.[3] The Baganda of Central Africa used to attribute earthquakes to a certain god named Musisi, who lived underground and set the earth in a tremor when he moved about. At such times persons who had fetishes to hand patted them and begged the god to be still; women who were with child patted their bellies to keep the god from taking either their own life or that of their unborn babes; others raised a shrill cry to induce him to remain quiet.[4]

When the Bataks of Sumatra feel an earthquake they shout "The handle! The handle!" The meaning of the cry is variously explained. Some say that it contains a delicate allusion to the sword which is thrust up to the hilt into the body of the demon or serpent who shakes the earth. Thus explained the words are a jeer or taunt levelled at that mischievous being.[5] Others say that when Batara-guru, the

Conduct of the Bataks during an earthquake.

---

[1] De St. Cricq, "Voyage du Pérou au Brésil par les fleuves Ucayali et Amazone, Indiens Conibos," *Bulletin de la Société de Géographie* (Paris), iv⁰ Série, vi. (1853) p. 292.

[2] Miss Alice Werner, *The Natives of British Central Africa* (London, 1906), p. 56.

[3] Mgr. Lechaptois, *Aux Rives du Tanganika* (Algiers, 1913), p. 217.

[4] Rev. J. Roscoe, *The Baganda* (London, 1911), pp. 313 *sq.*

[5] W. Ködding, "Die batakschen Götter und ihr Verhältniss zum Brahmanismus," *Allgemeine Missions-Zeitschrift*, xii. (1885) p. 405.

creator, was about to fashion the earth he began by building a raft, which he commanded a certain Naga-padoha to support. While he was hard at work his chisel broke, and at the same moment Naga-padoha budged under his burden. Therefore Batara-guru said, "Hold hard a moment! The handle of the chisel is broken off." And that is why the Bataks call out " The handle of the chisel " during an earthquake. They believe that the deluded Naga-padoha will take the words for the voice of the creator, and that he will hold hard accordingly.[1]

Various modes of prevailing upon the earthquake god to stop. When the earth quakes in some parts of Celebes, it is said that all the inhabitants of a village will rush out of their houses and grub up grass by handfuls in order to attract the attention of the earth-spirit, who, feeling his hair thus torn out by the roots, will be painfully conscious that there are still people above ground.[2]   So in Samoa, during shocks of earthquake, the natives sometimes ran and threw themselves on the ground, gnawed the earth, and shouted frantically to the earthquake god Mafuie to desist lest he should shake the earth to pieces.[3]   They consoled themselves with the thought that Mafuie has only one arm, saying, "If he had two, what a shake he would give!"[4] The Bagobos of the Philippine Islands believe that the earth rests on a great post, which a large serpent is trying to remove. When the serpent shakes the post, the earth quakes. At such times the Bagobos beat their dogs to make them howl, for the howling of the animals frightens the serpent, and he stops shaking the post. Hence so long as an earthquake lasts the howls of dogs may be heard to proceed from every house in a Bagobo village.[5]   The Tongans think that the earth is supported on the prostrate

[1] G. A. Wilken, "Het Animisme bij de volken van den Indischen Archipel," *Verspreide Geschriften*, ii. 279; H. N. van der Tuuk, *op. cit.* pp. 49 *sq.*
[2] J. G. F. Riedel, "De Topantunuasu of oorspronkelijke Volkstammen van Central Selebes," *Bijdragen tot de Taal- Land- en Volkenkunde van Nederlandsch-Indië*, xxxv. (1886) p. 95.
[3] John Williams, *Narrative of Missionary Enterprises in the South Sea Islands* (London, 1838), p. 379.
[4] G. Turner, *Samoa* (London, 1884), p. 211; Ch. Wilkes, *Narrative of the United States Exploring Expedition*, New Edition (New York, 1851), ii. 131.
[5] A. Schadenburg, "Die Bewohner von Süd-Mindanao und der Insel Samal," *Zeitschrift für Ethnologie*, xvii. (1885) p. 32.

form of the god Móooi. When he is tired of lying in one
posture, he tries to turn himself about, and that causes an
earthquake. Then the people shout and beat the ground
with sticks to make him lie still.[1] During an earthquake
the Burmese make a great uproar, beating the walls of their
houses and shouting, to frighten away the evil genius who
is shaking the earth.[2] On a like occasion and for a like
purpose some natives of the Gazelle Peninsula in New
Britain beat drums and blow on shells.[3] The Dorasques,
an Indian tribe of Panama, believed that the volcano of
Chiriqui was inhabited by a powerful spirit, who, in his
anger, caused an earthquake. At such times the Indians
shot volleys of arrows in the direction of the volcano to
terrify him and make him desist.[4] Some of the Peruvian
Indians regarded an earthquake as a sign that the gods
were thirsty, so they poured water on the ground.[5] In
Ashantee several persons used to be put to death after an
earthquake ; they were slain as a sacrifice to Sasabonsun,
the earthquake god, in the hope of satiating his cruelty
for a time. Houses which had been thrown down or
damaged by an earthquake were sprinkled with human
blood before they were rebuilt. When part of the wall of
the king's house at Coomassie was knocked down by an
earthquake, fifty young girls were slaughtered, and the mud
to be used in the repairs was kneaded with their blood.[6]

An English resident in Fiji attributed a sudden access
of piety in Kantavu, one of the islands, to a tremendous earthquake which destroyed many of the natives. The Fijians
think that their islands rest on a god, who causes earthquakes
by turning over in his sleep. So they sacrifice to him
things of great value in order that he may turn as gently as
possible.[7] In Nias a violent earthquake has a salutary

*Religious
and moral
effects of
earth-
quakes.*

[1] W. Mariner, *Account of the
Natives of the Tonga Islands*, Second
Edition (London, 1818), ii. 112 *sq.*
[2] Sangermano, *Description of the
Burmese Empire* (Rangoon, 1885), p.
130.
[3] P. A. Kleintitschen, *Die Küsten-
bewohner der Gazellehalbinsel* (Hiltrup
bei Münster, N.D.), p. 336.
[4] A. Pinart, "Les Indiens de l'État
de Panama," *Revue d'Ethnographie*,

vi. (1887) p. 119.
[5] E. J. Payne, *History of the New
World called America*, i. (Oxford,
1892) p. 469.
[6] A. B. Ellis, *The Tshi-speaking
Peoples of the Gold Coast* (London,
1887), pp. 35 *sq.*
[7] J. Jackson, in J. E. Erskine's
*Journal of a Cruise among the Islands
of the Western Pacific* (London, 1853),
p. 473. My friend, the late Mr.

effect on the morals of the natives.   They suppose that it is brought about by a certain Batoo Bedano, who intends to destroy the earth because of the iniquity of mankind.   So they assemble and fashion a great image out of the trunk of a tree.   They make offerings, they confess their sins, they correct the fraudulent weights and measures, they vow to do better in the future, they implore mercy, and if the earth has gaped, they throw a little gold into the fissure. But when the danger is over, all their fine vows and promises are soon forgotten.[1]

The god of the sea and of the earthquake naturally conceived as one.

We may surmise that in those Greek lands which have suffered severely from earthquakes, such as Achaia and the western coasts of Asia Minor, Poseidon was worshipped not less as an earthquake god than as a sea-god.[2]   It is to be remembered that an earthquake is often accompanied by a tremendous wave which comes rolling in like a mountain from the sea, swamping the country far and wide ; indeed on the coasts of Chili and Peru, which have often been devastated by both, the wave is said to be even more dreaded than the earthquake.[3]   The Greeks often experienced this combination of catastrophes, this conspiracy, as it were, of earth and sea against the life and works of man.[4]

Lorimer Fison, wrote to me (December 15, 1906) that the name of the Fijian earthquake god is Maui, not A Dage, as Jackson says.   Mr. Fison adds, " I have seen Fijians stamping and smiting the ground and yelling at the top of their voices in order to rouse him."

[1] J. T. Nieuwenhuisen en H. C. B. von Rosenberg, " Verslag omtrent het eiland Nias," *Verhandelingen van het Bataviaasch Genootschap van Kunsten en Wetenschappen*, xxx. (Batavia, 1863) p. 118 ; Th. C. Rappard, " Het eiland Nias en zijne bewoners," *Bijdragen tot de Taal-, Land- en Volkenkunde van Nederlandsch-Indië*, lxii. (1909) p. 582. In Soerakarta, a district of Java, when an earthquake takes place the people lie flat on their stomachs on the ground, and lick it with their tongues so long as the earthquake lasts.   This they do in order that they may not lose their teeth prematurely.   See J. W. Winter,

" Beknopte Beschrijving van het hof Soerokarta in 1824," *Bijdragen tot de Taal-, Land- en Volkenkunde van Nederlandsch-Indië*, liv. (1902) p. 85. The connexion of ideas in this custom is not clear.

[2] On this question see C. Neumann und J. Partsch, *Physikalische Geographie von Griechenland* (Breslau, 1885), pp. 332-336.   As to the frequency of earthquakes in Achaia and Asia Minor see Seneca, *Epist.* xiv. 3. 9 ; and as to Achaia in particular see C. Neumann und J. Partsch, *op. cit.* pp. 324-326.   On the coast of Achaia there was a chain of sanctuaries of Poseidon (L. Preller, *Griechische Mythologie*, i.[4] 575).

[3] See Sir Ch. Lyell, *Principles of Geology*,[12] ii. 147 *sqq.* ; J. Milne, *Earthquakes* (London, 1886), pp. 165 *sqq.*

[4] See, for example, Thucydides, iii. 89.

It was thus that Helice, on the coast of Achaia, perished with all its inhabitants on a winter night, overwhelmed by the billows; and its destruction was set down to the wrath of Poseidon.[1]   Nothing could be more natural than that to people familiar with the twofold calamity the dreadful god of the earthquake and of the sea should appear to be one and the same.   The historian Diodorus Siculus observes that Peloponnese was deemed to have been in ancient days the abode of Poseidon, that the whole country was in a manner sacred to him, and that every city in it worshipped him above all the gods.   The devotion to Poseidon he explains partly by the earthquakes and floods by which the land has been visited, partly by the remarkable chasms and subterranean rivers which are a conspicuous feature of its limestone mountains.[2]

§ 6. *The Worship of Mephitic Vapours*

But eruptions and earthquakes, though the most tremendous, are not the only phenomena of volcanic regions which have affected the religion of the inhabitants. Poisonous mephitic vapours and hot springs, which abound especially in volcanic regions,[3] have also had their devotees, and both are, or were formerly, to be found in those western districts of Asia Minor with which we are here concerned. To begin with vapours, we may take as an illustration of their deadly effect the Guevo Upas, or Valley of Poison, near Batur in Java.   It is the crater of an extinct volcano, about half a mile in circumference, and from thirty to thirty-

Poisonous mephitic vapours.

[1] Strabo, viii. 7. 1 *sq.*, pp. 384 *sq.*; Diodorus Siculus, xv. 49; Aelian, *Nat. Anim.* xi. 19; Pausanias, vii. 24. 5 *sq.* and 12, vii. 25. 1 and 4.

[2] Diodorus Siculus, xv. 49. 4 *sq.* Among the most famous seats of the worship of Poseidon in Peloponnese were Taenarum in Laconia, Helice in Achaia, Mantinea in Arcadia, and the island of Calauria, off the coast of Troezen. See Pausanias, ii. 33. 2, iii. 25. 4-8, vii. 24. 5 *sq.*, viii. 10. 2-4. Laconia as well as Achaia has suffered much from earthquakes, and it contained many sanctuaries of Poseidon.

We may suppose that the deity was worshipped here chiefly as the earthquake god, since the rugged coasts of Laconia are ill adapted to maritime enterprise, and the Lacedaemonians were never a seafaring folk. See C. Neumann und J. Partsch, *Physikalische Geographie von Griechenland*, pp. 330 *sq.*, 335 *sq.* For Laconian sanctuaries of Poseidon see Pausanias, iii. 11. 9, iii. 12. 5, iii. 14. 2 and 7, iii. 15. 10, iii. 20. 2, iii. 21. 5, iii. 25. 4.

[3] Sir Ch. Lyell, *Principles of Geology*,[12] i. 391 *sqq.*, 590.

five feet deep.   Neither man nor beast can descend to the
bottom and live.   The ground is covered with the carcases
of tigers, deer, birds, and even the bones of men, all killed
by the abundant emanations of carbonic acid gas which
exhale from the soil.   Animals let down into it die in a
few minutes.   The whole range of hills is volcanic.   Two
neighbouring craters constantly emit smoke.[1]   In another
crater of Java, near the volcano Talaga Bodas, the sulphureous exhalations have proved fatal to tigers, birds, and
countless insects ; and the soft parts of these creatures, such
as fibres, muscles, hair, and skin, are well preserved, while
the bones are corroded or destroyed.[2]

Places of
Pluto or
Charon.

The ancients were acquainted with such noxious vapours
in their own country, and they regarded the vents from
which they were discharged as entrances to the infernal
regions.[3]   The Greeks called them places of Pluto (*Plutonia*)
or places of Charon (*Charonia*).[4]   In Italy the vapours were
personified as a goddess, who bore the name of Mefitis and
was worshipped in various parts of the peninsula.[5]   She had

The
valley of
Amsanc-
tus.

a temple in the famous valley of Amsanctus in the land of
the Hirpini, where the exhalations, supposed to be the breath
of Pluto himself, were of so deadly a character that all who
set foot on the spot died.[6]   The place is a glen, partly wooded
with chestnut trees, among limestone hills, distant about four
miles from the town of Frigento.   Here, under a steep
shelving bank of decomposed limestone, there is a pool of
dark ash-coloured water, which continually bubbles up with
an explosion like distant thunder.   A rapid stream of the
same blackish water rushes into the pool from under the

[1] "Extract from a Letter of Mr.
Alexander Loudon," *Journal of the
Royal Geographical Society,* ii. (1832)
pp. 60-62 ; Sir Ch. Lyell, *Principles
of Geology,*[12] i. 590.

[2] Sir Ch. Lyell, *l.c.*

[3] Lucretius, vi. 738 *sqq.*

[4] Strabo, v. 4. 5, p. 244, xii. 8. 17,
p. 579, xiii. 4. 14, p. 629, xiv. 1. 11
and 44, pp. 636, 649 ; Cicero, *De
divinatione,* i. 36. 79 ; Pliny, *Nat.
Hist.* ii. 208.   Compare [Aristotle,]
De mundo, 4, p. 395 B, ed. Bekker.

[5] Servius on Virgil, *Aen.* vii. 84,

who says that some people looked on
Mefitis as a god, the male partner of
Leucothoë, to whom he stood as
Adonis to Venus or as Virbius to
Diana.   As to Mefitis see L. Preller,
Römische Mythologie[3] (Berlin, 1881–
1883), ii. 144 *sq.* ; R. Peter, *s.v.*
"Mefitis" in W. H. Roscher's *Lexikon
der griech. und röm. Mythologie,* ii.
2519 *sqq.*

[6] Virgil, *Aen.* vii. 563-571, with
the commentary of Servius ; Cicero,
De divinatione, i. 36. 79 ; Pliny,
Nat. Hist. ii. 208.

barren rocky hill, but the fall is not more than a few feet. A little higher up are apertures in the ground, through which warm blasts of sulphuretted hydrogen are constantly issuing with more or less noise, according to the size of the holes.   These blasts are no doubt what the ancients deemed the breath of Pluto.   The pool is now called *Mefite* and the holes *Mefitinelle.*   On the other side of the pool is a smaller pond called the *Coccaio*, or Cauldron, because it appears to be perpetually boiling.   Thick masses of mephitic vapour, visible a hundred yards off, float in rapid undulations on its surface.   The exhalations given off by these waters are sometimes fatal, especially when they are borne on a high wind.   But as the carbonic acid gas does not naturally rise more than two or three feet from the ground, it is possible in calm weather to walk round the pools, though to stoop is difficult and to fall would be dangerous.   The ancient temple of Mefitis has been replaced by a shrine of the martyred Santa Felicita.[1]

Similar discharges of poisonous vapours took place at various points in the volcanic district of Caria, and were the object of superstitious veneration in antiquity.   Thus at the village of Thymbria there was a sacred cave which gave out deadly emanations, and the place was deemed a sanctuary of Charon.[2]   A similar cave might be seen at the village of Acharaca near Nysa, in the valley of the Maeander.   Here, below the cave, there was a fine grove with a temple dedicated to Pluto and Persephone.   The place was sacred to Pluto, yet sick people resorted to it for the restoration of their health.   They lived in the neighbouring village, and the priests prescribed for them according to the revelations which they received from the two deities in dreams.   Often the priests would take the patients to the cave and leave them there for days without food.   Sometimes the sufferers themselves were favoured with revelations in dreams, but

Sanctuaries of Charon or Pluto in Caria.

---

[1] Letter of Mr. Hamilton (British Envoy at the Court of Naples), in *Journal of the Royal Geographical Society*, ii. (1832) pp. 62-65; W. Smith's *Dictionary of Greek and Roman Geography*, i. 127; H. Nissen, *Italische Landeskunde* (Berlin, 1883–1902), i. 242, 271, ii. 819 *sq.*   Another place in Italy infested by poisonous exhalations is the grotto called *dei cani* at Naples.   It is described by Addison in his "Remarks on Several Parts of Italy" (*Works*, London, 1811, vol. ii. pp. 89-91).

[2] Strabo, xiv. 1. 11, p. 636.

they always acted under the spiritual direction of the priests. To all but the sick the place was unapproachable and fatal. Once a year a festival was held in the village, and then afflicted folk came in crowds to be rid of their ailments. About the hour of noon on that day a number of athletic young men, their naked bodies greased with oil, used to carry a bull up to the cave and there let it go. But the beast had not taken a few steps into the cavern before it fell to the ground and expired : so deadly was the vapour.[1]

Another Plutonian sanctuary of the same sort existed at Hierapolis, in the upper valley of the Maeander, on the borders of Lydia and Phrygia.[2] Here under a brow of the hill there was a deep cave with a narrow mouth just large enough to admit the body of a man. A square space in front of the cave was railed off, and within the railing there hung so thick a cloudy vapour that it was hardly possible to see the ground. In calm weather people could step up to the railing with safety, but to pass within it was instant death. Bulls driven into the enclosure fell to the earth and were dragged out lifeless ; and sparrows, which spectators by way of experiment allowed to fly into the mist, dropped dead at once. Yet the eunuch priests of the Great Mother Goddess could enter the railed-off area with impunity ; nay more, they used to go up to the very mouth of the cave, stoop, and creep into it for a certain distance, holding their breath ; but there was a look on their faces as if they were being choked. Some people ascribed the immunity of the priests to the divine protection, others to the use of antidotes.[3]

§ 7. *The Worship of Hot Springs*

The mysterious chasm of Hierapolis, with its deadly mist, has not been discovered in modern times ; indeed it

[1] Strabo, xiv. 1. 44, pp. 649 *sq.* A coin of Nysa shows the bull carried to the sacrifice by six naked youths and preceded by a naked flute-player. See B. V. Head, *Catalogue of the Greek Coins of Lydia*, pp. lxxxiii. 181, pl. xx. 10. Strabo was familiar with this neighbourhood, for he tells us (xiv. 1. 48, p. 650) that in his youth he studied at Nysa under the philosopher Aristodemus.

[2] Some of the ancients assigned Hierapolis to Lydia, and others to Phrygia (W. M. Ramsay, *Cities and Bishoprics of Phrygia*, i. (Oxford, 1895) pp. 84 *sq.*

[3] Strabo, xiii. 4. 14, pp. 629 *sq.* ; Dio Cassius, lxviii. 27. 3 ; Pliny, *Nat. Hist.* ii. 208 ; Ammianus Marcellinus, xxiii. 6. 18.

would seem to have vanished even in antiquity.[1]   It may
have been destroyed by an earthquake.   But another marvel
of the Sacred City remains to this day.   The hot springs
with their calcareous deposit, which, like a wizard's wand,
turns all that it touches to stone, excited the wonder of the
ancients, and the course of ages has only enhanced the
fantastic splendour of the great transformation scene.   The
stately ruins of Hierapolis occupy a broad shelf or terrace
on the mountain-side commanding distant views of extraordinary beauty and grandeur, from the dark precipices and
dazzling snows of Mount Cadmus away to the burnt summits
of Phrygia, fading in rosy tints into the blue of the sky.
Hills, broken by wooded ravines, rise behind the city.
In front the terrace falls away in cliffs three hundred feet
high into the desolate treeless valley of the Lycus.   Over
the face of these cliffs the hot streams have poured or
trickled for thousands of years, encrusting them with a
pearly white substance like salt or driven snow.   The
appearance of the whole is as if a mighty river, some two
miles broad, had been suddenly arrested in the act of falling
over a great cliff and transformed into white marble.   It
is a petrified Niagara.   The illusion is strongest in winter
or in cool summer mornings when the mist from the
hot springs hangs in the air, like a veil of spray resting
on the foam of the waterfall.   A closer inspection of the
white cliff, which attracts the traveller's attention at a
distance of twenty miles, only adds to its beauty and
changes one illusion for another.   For now it seems to be
a glacier, its long pendent stalactites looking like icicles,
and the snowy whiteness of its smooth expanse being tinged
here and there with delicate hues of blue, rose and green,
all the colours of the rainbow.   These petrified cascades of
Hierapolis are among the wonders of the world.   Indeed
they have probably been without a rival in their kind ever
since the famous white and pink terraces or staircases of
Rotomahana in New Zealand were destroyed by a volcanic
eruption.

The hot springs which have wrought these miracles at

The hot springs and petrified cascades of Hierapolis.

---

[1] Ammianus Marcellinus (*l.c.*) speaks as if the cave no longer existed in his
time.

The hot
pool of
Hierapolis
with its
deadly
exhala-
tions.

Hierapolis rise in a large deep pool among the vast and imposing ruins of the ancient city. The water is of a greenish-blue tint, but clear and transparent. At the bottom may be seen the white marble columns of a beautiful Corinthian colonnade, which must formerly have encircled the sacred pool. Shimmering through the green-blue water they look like the ruins of a Naiad's palace. Clumps of oleanders and pomegranate-trees overhang the little lake and add to its charm. Yet the enchanted spot has its dangers. Bubbles of carbonic acid gas rise incessantly from the bottom and mount like flickering particles of silver to the surface. Birds and beasts which come to drink of the water are sometimes found dead on the bank, stifled by the noxious vapour ; and the villagers tell of bathers who have been overpowered by it and drowned, or dragged down, as they say, to death by the water-spirit.

The streams of hot water, no longer regulated by the care of a religious population, have for centuries been allowed to overflow their channels and to spread unchecked over the tableland. By the deposit which they leave behind they have raised the surface of the ground many feet, their white ridges concealing the ruins and impeding the footstep, except where the old channels, filled up solidly to the brim, now form hard level footpaths, from which the traveller may survey the strange scene without quitting the saddle. In antiquity the husbandmen used purposely to lead the water in rills round their lands, and thus in a few years their fields and vineyards were enclosed with walls of solid stone. The water was also peculiarly adapted for the dyeing of woollen stuffs. Tinged with dyes extracted from certain roots, it imparted to cloths dipped in it the finest shades of purple and scarlet.[1]

---

[1] Strabo, xiii. 4. 14, pp. 629, 630 ; Vitruvius, viii. 3. 10. For modern descriptions of Hierapolis see R. Chandler, *Travels in Asia Minor*[2] (London, 1776), pp. 228-235 ; Ch. Fellows, *Journal written during an Excursion in Asia Minor* (London, 1839), pp. 283-285 ; W. J. Hamilton, *Researches in Asia Minor, Pontus, and Armenia*, i. 517-521 ; E. Renan, *Saint Paul*, pp. 357 sq. ; E. J. Davis, *Anatolica* (London, 1874), pp. 97-112 ; É. Reclus, *Nouvelle Géographie Universelle*, ix. 510-512 ; W. Cochran, *Pen and Pencil Sketches in Asia Minor* (London, 1887), pp. 387-390 ; W. M. Ramsay, *Cities and Bishoprics of Phrygia*, i. 84 sqq. The temperature of the hot pool varies from 85 to 90 degrees Fahrenheit. The volcanic district of Tuscany which skirts the Apennines abounds in hot calcareous springs which have produced phenomena like those of Hierapolis. Indeed the

We cannot doubt that Hierapolis owed its reputation as Hercules the patron of hot springs. a holy city in great part to its hot springs and mephitic vapours. The curative virtue of mineral and thermal springs was well known to the ancients, and it would be interesting, if it were possible, to trace the causes which have gradually eliminated the superstitious element from the use of such waters, and so converted many old seats of volcanic religion into the medicinal baths of modern times. It was an article of Greek faith that all hot springs were sacred to Hercules.[1] "Who ever heard of cold baths that were sacred to Hercules?" asks Injustice in Aristophanes ; and Justice admits that the brawny hero's patronage of hot baths was the excuse alleged by young men for sprawling all day in the steaming water when they ought to have been sweating in the gymnasium.[2] Hot springs were said to have been first produced for the refreshment of Hercules after his labours ; some ascribed the kindly thought and deed to Athena, others to Hephaestus, and others to the nymphs.[3] The warm water of these sources appears to have been used especially to heal diseases of the skin ; for a Greek proverb, "the itch of Hercules," was applied to persons in need of hot baths for the scab.[4] On the strength of his connexion with medicinal springs Hercules set up as a patron of the healing art. In heaven, if we can trust Lucian, he even refused to give place to Aesculapius himself, and the difference between the two deities led to a very unseemly brawl. "Do you mean to say," demanded Hercules of his father Zeus, in a burst of indignation, "that this apothecary is to sit down to table

---

whole ground is in some places coated over with tufa and travertine, which have been deposited by the water, and, like the ground at Hierapolis, it sounds hollow under the foot. See Sir Ch. Lyell, *Principles of Geology*,[12] i. 397 *sqq.* As to the terraces of Rotoma-hana in New Zealand, which were destroyed by an eruption of Mount Taravera in 1886, see R. Taylor, *Te Ika A Maui, or New Zealand and its Inhabitants*[2] (London, 1870), pp. 464-469.

[1] Athenaeus, xii. 6. p. 512.

[2] Aristophanes, *Clouds*, 1044-1054.

[3] Scholiast on Aristophanes, *Clouds*, 1050 ; Scholiast on Pindar, *Olymp.* xii. 25 ; Suidas and Hesychius, *s.v.* Ἡράκλεια λουτρά ; Apostolius, viii. 66 ; Zenobius, vi. 49 ; Diogenianus, v. 7 ; Plutarch, *Proverbia Alexandrinorum*, 21 ; Diodorus Siculus, iv. 23. 1, v. 3. 4. Another story was that Hercules, like Moses, produced the water by smiting the rock with his club (Antoninus Liberalis, *Transform.* 4).

[4] Apostolius, viii. 68 ; Zenobius, vi. 49 ; Diogenianus, v. 7 ; Plutarch, *Proverbia Alexandrinorum*, 21.

before me?" To this the apothecary replied with much acrimony, recalling certain painful episodes in the private life of the burly hero. Finally the dispute was settled by Zeus, who decided in favour of Aesculapius on the ground that he died before Hercules, and was therefore entitled to rank as senior god.[1]

Hot springs of Hercules at Thermopylae.

Among the hot springs sacred to Hercules the most famous were those which rose in the pass of Thermopylae, and gave to the defile its name of the Hot Gates.[2] The warm baths, called by the natives "the Pots," were enlarged and improved for the use of invalids by the wealthy sophist Herodes Atticus in the second century of our era. An altar of Hercules stood beside them.[3] According to one story, the hot springs were here produced for his refreshment by the goddess Athena.[4] They exist to this day apparently unchanged, although the recession of the sea has converted what used to be a narrow pass into a wide, swampy flat, through which the broad but shallow, turbid stream of the Sperchius creeps sluggishly seaward. On the other side the rugged mountains descend in crags and precipices to the pass, their grey rocky sides tufted with low wood or bushes wherever vegetation can find a foothold, and their summits fringed along the sky-line with pines. They remind a Scotchman of the "crags, knolls, and mounds confusedly hurled" in which Ben Venue comes down to the Silver Strand of Loch Katrine. The principal spring bursts from the rocks just at the foot of the steepest and loftiest part of the range. After forming a small pool it flows in a rapid stream eastward, skirting the foot of the mountains. The water is so hot that it is almost painful to hold the hands in it, at least near the source, and steam rises thickly from its surface along the course of the brook. Indeed the clouds of white steam and the strong sulphurous smell acquaint the traveller with his approach to the famous spot before he comes in sight of the springs. The water is clear, but has the appearance of being of a deep sea-blue or sea-green

---

[1] Lucian, *Dialogi Deorum*, 13.

[2] Strabo, ix. 4. 13, p. 428.

[3] Herodotus, vii. 176 ; Pausanias,

iv. 35. 9 ; Philostratus, *Vit. Sophist.* ii. 1. 9.

[4] Scholiast on Aristophanes, *Clouds*, 1050.

colour. This appearance it takes from the thick, slimy deposits of blue-green sulphur which line the bed of the stream. From its source the blue, steaming, sulphur-reeking brook rushes eastward for a few hundred yards at the foot of the mountain, and is then joined by the water of another spring, which rises much more tranquilly in a sort of natural bath among the rocks. The sides of this bath are not so thickly coated with sulphur as the banks of the stream ; hence its water, about two feet deep, is not so blue. Just beyond it there is a second and larger bath, which, from its square shape and smooth sides, would seem to be in part artificial. These two baths are probably the Pots mentioned by ancient writers. They are still used by bathers, and a few wooden dressing-rooms are provided for the accommodation of visitors. Some of the water is conducted in an artificial channel to turn a mill about half a mile off at the eastern end of the pass. The rest crosses the flat to find its way to the sea. In its passage it has coated the swampy ground with a white crust, which sounds hollow under the tread.[1]

We may conjecture that these remarkable springs furnished the principal reason for associating Hercules with this district, and for laying the scene of his fiery death on the top of the neighbouring Mount Oeta. The district is volcanic, and has often been shaken by earthquakes.[2] Across the strait the island of Euboea has suffered from the same cause and at the same time ; and on its southern shore sulphureous springs, like those of Thermopylae, but much hotter and more powerful, were in like manner dedicated to Hercules.[3] The strong medicinal qualities of the

Hot springs of Hercules at Aedepsus.

---

[1] I have described Thermopylae as I saw it in November 1895. Compare W. M. Leake, *Travels in Northern Greece* (London, 1835), ii. 33 *sqq.* ; E. Dodwell, *Classical and Topographical Tour through Greece* (London, 1819), ii. 66 *sqq.*; K. G. Fiedler, *Reise durch alle Theile des Königreichs Griechenland* (Leipsic, 1840–1841), i. 207 *sqq.* ; L. Ross, *Wanderungen in Griechenland* (Halle, 1851), i. 90 *sqq.* ; C. Bursian, *Geographie von Griechenland* (Leipsic, 1862–1872), i. 92 *sqq.*

[2] Thucydides, iii. 87 and 89 ; Strabo, i. 3. 20, pp. 60 *sq.* ; C. Neumann und J. Partsch, *Physikalische Geographie von Griechenland*, pp. 321-323.

[3] Aristotle, *Meteora*, ii. 8, p. 366 A, ed. Bekker ; Strabo, ix. 4. 2, p. 425. Aristotle expressly recognized the connexion of the springs with earthquakes, which he tells us were very common in this district. As to the earthquakes of Euboea see also Thucydides, iii. 87, 89 ; Strabo, i. 3. 16 and 20, pp. 58, 60 *sq.*

waters, which are especially adapted for the cure of skin diseases and gout, have attracted patients in ancient and modern times. Sulla took the waters here for his gout;[1] and in the days of Plutarch the neighbouring town of Aedepsus, situated in a green valley about two miles from the springs, was one of the most fashionable resorts of Greece. Elegant and commodious buildings, an agreeable country, and abundance of fish and game united with the health-giving properties of the baths to draw crowds of idlers to the place, especially in the prime of the glorious Greek spring, the height of the season at Aedepsus. While some watched the dancers dancing or listened to the strains of the harp, others passed the time in discourse, lounging in the shade of cloisters or pacing the shore of the beautiful strait with its prospect of mountains beyond mountains immortalized in story across the water.[2] Of all this Greek elegance and luxury hardly a vestige remains. Yet the healing springs flow now as freely as of old. In the course of time the white and yellow calcareous deposit which the water leaves behind it, has formed a hillock at the foot of the mountains, and the stream now falls in a steaming cascade from the face of the rock into the sea.[3] Once, after an earthquake, the springs ceased to flow for three days, and at the same time the hot springs of Thermopylae dried up.[4] The incident proves the relation of these Baths of Hercules on both sides of the strait to each other and to volcanic agency. On another occasion a cold spring suddenly burst out beside the hot springs of Aedepsus, and as its water was supposed to be peculiarly beneficial to health, patients hastened from far and near to drink of it. But the generals of King Antigonus, anxious to raise a revenue, imposed a tax on the use of the water; and the spring, as if in disgust at being turned to so base a use, disappeared as suddenly as it had come.[5]

---

[1] Plutarch, *Sulla*, 26.

[2] Plutarch, *Quaest. Conviviales*, iv. 4. 1; *id.*, *De fraterno Amore*, 17.

[3] As to the hot springs of Aedepsus (the modern *Lipso*) see K. G. Fiedler, *Reise durch alle Theile des Königreichs Griechenland*, i. 487 - 492; H. N. Ulrichs, *Reisen und Forschungen in*

Griechenland (Bremen, 1840—Berlin, 1863), ii. 233-235; C. Bursian, *Geographie von Griechenland*, ii. 409; C. Neumann und J. Partsch, *Physikalische Geographie von Griechenland*, pp. 342-344.

[4] Strabo, i. 3. 20, p. 60.

[5] Athenaeus, iii. 4, p. 73 E, D.

The association of Hercules with hot springs was not confined to Greece itself. Greek influence extended it to Sicily,[1] Italy,[2] and even to Dacia.[3] Why the hero should have been chosen as the patron of thermal waters, it is hard to say. Yet it is worth while, perhaps, to remember that such springs combine in a manner the twofold and seemingly discordant principles of water and fire,[4] of fertility and destruction, and that the death of Hercules in the flames seems to connect him with the fiery element. Further, the apparent conflict of the two principles is by no means as absolute as at first sight we might be tempted to suppose ; for heat is as necessary as moisture to the support of animal and vegetable life. Even volcanic fires have their beneficent aspect, since their products lend a more generous flavour to the juice of the grape. The ancients themselves, as we have seen, perceived the connexion between good wine and volcanic soil, and proposed more or less seriously to interpret the vine-god Dionysus as a child of the fire.[5] As a patron of hot springs Hercules combined the genial elements of heat and moisture, and may therefore have stood, in one of his many aspects, for the principle of fertility.

In Syria childless women still resort to hot springs in order to procure offspring from the saint or the jinnee of the waters.[6]

[1] The hot springs of Himera (the modern *Termini*) were said to have been produced for the refreshment of the weary Hercules. See Diodorus Siculus, iv. 23. 1, v. 3. 4 ; Scholiast on Pindar, *Olymp.* xii. 25. The hero is said to have taught the Syracusans to sacrifice a bull annually to Persephone at the Blue Spring (*Cyane*) near Syracuse ; the beasts were drowned in the water of the pool. See Diodorus Siculus, iv. 23. 4, v. 4. 1 *sq.* As to the spring, which is now thickly surrounded by tall papyrus-plants introduced by the Arabs, see K. Baedeker, *Southern Italy*[7] (Leipsic, 1880), pp. 356, 357.

[2] The splendid baths of Allifae in Samnium, of which there are considerable remains, were sacred to Hercules. See G. Wilmanns, *Exempla Inscriptionum Latinarum* (Berlin, 1873), vol. i. p. 227, No. 735 c ; H. Nissen, *Italische Landeskunde*,

ii. 798. It is characteristic of the volcanic nature of the springs that the same inscription which mentions these baths of Hercules records their destruction by an earthquake.

[3] H. Dessau, *Inscriptiones Latinae Selectae*, vol. ii. Pars i. (Berlin, 1902) p. 113, No. 3891.

[4] Speaking of thermal springs Lyell observes that the description of them " might almost with equal propriety have been given under the head of ' igneous causes,' as they are agents of a mixed nature, being at once igneous and aqueous " (*Principles of Geology*,[12] i. 392).

[5] See above, p. 194.

[6] S. I. Curtiss, *Primitive Semitic Religion To-day* (Chicago, New York, and Toronto, 1902), pp. 116 *sq.* ; Mrs. H. H. Spoer, "The Powers of Evil in Jerusalem," *Folk-lore*, xviii. (1907) p. 55. See above, p. 78.

This, for example, they do at the famous hot springs in the land of Moab which flow through a wild gorge into the Dead Sea. In antiquity the springs went by the Greek name of Callirrhoe, the Fair-flowing. It was to them that the dying Herod, weighed down by a complication of disorders which the pious Jews traced to God's vengeance, repaired in the vain hope of arresting or mitigating the fatal progress of disease. The healing waters brought no alleviation of his sufferings, and he retired to Jericho to die.[1] The hot springs burst in various places from the sides of a deep romantic ravine to form a large and rapid stream of lukewarm water, which rushes down the depths of the lynn, dashing and foaming over boulders, under the dense shade of tamarisk-trees and cane-brakes, the rocks on either bank draped with an emerald fringe of maidenhair fern. One of the springs falls from a high rocky shelf over the face of a cliff which is tinted bright yellow by the sulphurous water. The lofty crags which shut in the narrow chasm are bold and imposing in outline and varied in colour, for they range from red sandstone through white and yellow limestone to black basalt. The waters issue from the line where the sandstone and limestone meet. Their temperature is high, and from great clefts in the mountain-sides you may see clouds of steam rising and hear the rumbling of the running waters. The bottom of the glen is clothed and half choked with rank vegetation; for, situated far below the level of the sea, the hot ravine is almost African in climate and flora. Here grow dense thickets of canes with their feathery tufts that shake and nod in every passing breath of wind: here the oleander flourishes with its dark-green glossy foliage and its beautiful pink blossoms: here tall date-palms rear their stately heads wherever the hot springs flow. Gorgeous flowers, too, carpet the ground. Splendid orobanches, some pinkish purple, some bright yellow, grow in large tufts, each flower-stalk more than three feet high, and covered with blossoms from the ground upwards. An exquisite rose-coloured geranium abounds among the stones; and where the soil is a little richer than

[1] Josephus, *Antiquit. Jud.* xvii. 6. 5. The medical properties of the spring are mentioned by Pliny (*Nat. Hist.* v. 72).

usual it is a mass of the night-scented stock, while the crannies of the rocks are gay with scarlet ranunculus and masses of sorrel and cyclamen. Over all this luxuriant vegetation flit great butterflies of brilliant hues. Looking down the far-stretching gorge to its mouth you see in the distance the purple hills of Judah framed between walls of black basaltic columns on the one side and of bright red sandstone on the other.[1]

Every year in the months of April and May the Arabs resort in crowds to the glen to benefit by the waters. They take up their quarters in huts made of the reeds which they cut in the thickets. They bathe in the steaming water, or allow it to splash on their bodies as it gushes in a powerful jet from a crevice in the rocks. But before they indulge in these ablutions, the visitors, both Moslem and Christian, propitiate the spirit or genius of the place by sacrificing a sheep or goat at the spring and allowing its red blood to tinge the water. Then they bathe in what they call the Baths of Solomon. Legend runs that Solomon the Wise made his bathing-place here, and in order to keep the water always warm he commanded the jinn never to let the fire die down. The jinn obey his orders to this day, but sometimes they slacken their efforts, and then the water runs low and cool. When the bathers perceive that, they say, " O Solomon, bring green wood, dry wood," and no sooner have they said so than the water begins to gurgle and steam as before. Sick people tell the saint or sheikh, who lives invisible in the springs, all about their ailments ; they point out to him the precise spot that is the seat of the malady, it may be the back, or the head, or the legs ; and if the heat of the water diminishes, they call out, " Thy bath is cold, O sheikh, thy bath is cold ! " whereupon the obliging sheikh stokes up the fire, and out comes the water boiling. But if in spite of their remonstrances the temperature of the spring

Prayers and sacrifices offered to the hot springs of Callirrhoe.

---

[1] C. L. Irby and J. Mangles, *Travels in Egypt and Nubia, Syria and the Holy Land* (London, 1844), pp. 144 *sq.* ; W. Smith, *Dictionary of Greek and Roman Geography* (London, 1873), i. 482, *s.v.* "Callirrhoë" ; K. Baedeker, *Syria and Palestine*[4] (Leipsic, 1906), p. 148 ; H. B. Tristram, *The Land of Moab* (London, 1873), pp. 233-250, 285 *sqq.* ; Jacob E. Spafford, "Around the Dead Sea by Motor Boat," *The Geographical Journal*, xxxix. (1912) pp. 39 *sq.* The river formed by the springs is now called the Zerka.

continues low, they say that the sheikh has gone on pilgrimage, and they shout to him to hasten his return. Barren Moslem women also visit these hot springs to obtain children, and they do the same at the similar baths near Kerak. At the latter place a childless woman has been known to address the spirit of the waters saying, " O sheikh Solomon, I am not yet an old woman ; give me children." [1] The respect thus paid by Arab men and women to the sheikh Solomon at his hot springs may help us to understand the worship which at similar spots Greek men and women used to render to the hero Hercules. As the ideal of manly strength he may have been deemed the father of many of his worshippers, and Greek wives may have gone on pilgrimage to his steaming waters in order to obtain the wish of their hearts.

§ 8. *The Worship of Volcanoes in other Lands*

Worship of volcanic phenomena in other lands.

How far these considerations may serve to explain the custom of burning Hercules, or gods identified with him, in effigy or in the person of a human being, is a question which deserves to be considered. It might be more easily answered if we were better acquainted with analogous customs in other parts of the world, but our information with regard to the worship of volcanic phenomena in general appears to be very scanty. However, a few facts may be noted.

The great volcano of Kirauea in Hawaii.

The largest active crater in the world is Kirauea in Hawaii. It is a huge cauldron, several miles in circumference and hundreds of feet deep, the bottom of which is filled with boiling lava in a state of terrific ebullition ; from the red surge rise many black cones or insulated craters belching columns of grey smoke or pyramids of brilliant flame from their roaring mouths, while torrents of blazing lava roll down their sides to flow into the molten, tossing sea of fire below. The scene is especially impressive by night,

---

[1] Antonin Jaussen, *Coutumes des Arabes au pays de Moab* (Paris, 1908), pp. 359 *sq.* The Arabs think that the evil spirits let the hot water out of hell, lest its healing properties should assuage the pains of the damned. See H. B. Tristram, *The Land of Moab* (London, 1873), p. 247.

when flames of sulphurous blue or metallic red sweep across the heaving billows of the infernal lake, casting a broad glare on the jagged sides of the insulated craters, which shoot up eddying streams of fire with a continuous roar, varied at frequent intervals by loud detonations, as spherical masses of fusing lava or bright ignited stones are hurled into the air.[1] It is no wonder that so appalling a spectacle should have impressed the imagination of the natives and filled it with ideas of the dreadful beings who inhabit the fiery abyss. They considered the great crater, we are told, as the primaeval abode of their volcanic deities : the black cones that rise like islands from the burning lake appeared to them the houses where the gods often amused themselves by playing at draughts : the roaring of the furnaces and the crackling of the flames were the music of their dance ; and the red flaming surge was the surf wherein they played, sportively swimming on the rolling wave.[2]

For these fearful divinities they had appropriate names ; one was the King of Steam or Vapour, another the Rain of Night, another the Husband of Thunder, another the Child of War with a Spear of Fire, another the Fiery-eyed Canoe-breaker, another the Red-hot Mountain holding or lifting Clouds, and so on. But above them all was the great goddess Pélé. All were dreaded : they never journeyed on errands of mercy but only to receive offerings or to execute vengeance ; and their arrival in any place was announced by the convulsive trembling of the earth, by the lurid light of volcanic eruption, by the flash of lightning, and the clap of thunder. The whole island was bound to pay them tribute or support their temples and devotees ; and whenever the chiefs or people failed to send the proper offerings, or incurred their displeasure by insulting them or their priests or breaking the taboos which should be observed round about the craters, they filled the huge cauldron on the top of Kirauea with molten lava, and spouted the fiery liquid on the surrounding country ; or they would

The divinities of the volcano.

Offerings to the volcano.

---

[1] W. Ellis, *Polynesian Researches*, Second Edition (London, 1832-1836), iv. 235 *sqq.* Mr. Ellis was the first European to visit and describe the tremendous volcano. His visit was paid in the year 1823. Compare *The Encyclopaedia Britannica*,[9] xi. 531.
[2] W. Ellis, *op. cit.* iv. 246 *sq.*

march to some of their other houses, which mortals call craters, in the neighbourhood of the sinners, and rushing forth in a river or column of fire overwhelm the guilty. If fishermen did not bring them enough fish from the sea, they would go down, kill all the fish, fill the shoals with lava, and so destroy the fishing-grounds. Hence, when the volcano was in active eruption or threatened to break out, the people used to cast vast numbers of hogs, alive or dead, into the craters or into the rolling torrent of lava in order to appease the gods and arrest the progress of the fiery stream.[1] To pluck certain sacred berries, which grow on the mountain, to dig sand on its slopes, or to throw stones into the crater were acts particularly offensive to the deities, who would instantly rise in volumes of smoke, crush the offender under a shower of stones, or so involve him in thick darkness and rain that he could never find his way home. However, it was lawful to pluck and eat of the sacred berries, if only a portion of them were first offered to the goddess Pélé. The offerer would take a branch laden with clusters of the beautiful red and yellow berries, and standing on the edge of the abyss and looking towards the place where the smoke rose in densest volumes, he would say, " Pélé, here are your berries : I offer some to you, some I also eat." With that he would throw some of the berries into the crater and eat the rest.[2] A kind of brittle volcanic glass, of a dark-olive colour and semi-transparent, is found on the mountain in the shape of filaments as fine as human hair ; the natives call it the hair of the goddess Pélé.[3] Worshippers used to cast locks of their own hair into the crater of Kirauea as an offering to the dreadful goddess who dwelt in it. She had also a temple at the bottom of a valley, where stood a number of rude stone idols wrapt in white and yellow cloth. Once a year the priests and devotees of Pélé assembled there to perform certain rites and to feast on hogs, dogs, and fruit, which the

[1] W. Ellis, *op. cit.* iv. 248-250.

[2] W. Ellis, *op. cit.* iv. 207, 234-236. The berries resemble currants in shape and size and grow on low bushes. " The branches small and clear, leaves alternate, obtuse with a point, and serrated ; the flower was monopetalous, and, on being examined, determined the plant to belong to the class *decandria* and order *monogynia*. The native name of the plant is *ohelo* " (W. Ellis, *op. cit.* iv. 234).

[3] W. Ellis, *op. cit.* iv. 263.

pious inhabitants of Hamakua brought to the holy place in great abundance. This annual festival was intended to propitiate the volcanic goddess and thereby to secure the country from earthquakes and floods of molten lava.[1] The goddess of the volcano was supposed to inspire people, though to the carnal eye the inspiration resembled intoxication. One of these inspired priestesses solemnly affirmed to an English missionary that she was the goddess Pélé herself and as such immortal. Assuming a haughty air, she said, " I am Pélé ; I shall never die ; and those who follow me, when they die, if part of their bones be taken to Kirauea (the name of the volcano), will live with me in the bright fires there." [2] For " the worshippers of Pélé threw a part of bones of their dead into the volcano, under the impression that the spirits of the deceased would then be admitted to the society of the volcanic deities, and that their influence would preserve the survivors from the ravages of volcanic fire." [3]

Priestess impersonating the goddess of the volcano.

This last belief may help to explain a custom, which some peoples have observed, of throwing human victims into volcanoes. The intention of such a practice need not be simply to appease the dreadful volcanic spirits by ministering to their fiendish lust of cruelty ; it may be a notion that the souls of the men or women who have been burnt to death in the crater will join the host of demons in the fiery furnace, mitigate their fury, and induce them to spare the works and the life of man. But, however we may explain the custom, it has been usual in various parts of the world to throw human beings as well as less precious offerings into the craters of active volcanoes. Thus the Indians of Nicaragua used to sacrifice men, women, and children to the active volcano Massaya, flinging them into the craters : we are told that the victims went willingly to their fate.[4] In the island of Siao, to the north of Celebes, a child was formerly sacrificed every year in order to keep the volcano Goowoong Awoo quiet. The poor wretch was tortured to death at a festival which lasted nine days. In later times the place of the child has

Sacrifices to volcanoes.

Human victims thrown into volcanoes.

[1] W. Ellis, *op. cit.* iv. 350.
[2] W. Ellis, *op. cit.* iv. 309-311.
[3] W. Ellis, *op. cit.* iv. 361,

[4] Fernandez de Oviedo y Valdés, *Historia General y Natural de las Indias* (Madrid, 1851–1855), iv. 74.

been taken by a wooden puppet, which is hacked to pieces in the same way. The Galelareese of Halmahera say that the Sultan of Ternate used annually to require some human victims, who were cast into the crater of the volcano to save the island from its ravages.[1]   In Java the volcano Bromo or Bromok is annually worshipped by people who throw offerings of coco-nuts, plantains, mangoes, rice, chickens, cakes, cloth, money, and so forth into the crater.[2]   To the Tenggereese, an aboriginal heathen tribe inhabiting the mountains of which Bromo is the central crater, the festival of making offerings to the volcano is the greatest of the year.   It is held at full moon in the twelfth month, the day being fixed by the high priest. Each household prepares its offerings the night before.   Very early in the morning the people set out by moonlight for Mount Bromo, men, women, and children all arrayed in their best.   Before they reach the mountain they must cross a wide sandy plain, where the spirits of the dead are supposed to dwell until by means of the Festival of the Dead they obtain admittance to the volcano.   It is a remarkable sight to see thousands of people streaming across the level sands from three different directions.   They have to descend into it from the neighbouring heights, and the horses break into a gallop when, after the steep descent, they reach the level. The gay and varied colours of the dresses, the fantastic costumes of the priests, the offerings borne along, the whole lit up by the warm beams of the rising sun, lend to the spectacle a peculiar charm.   All assemble at the foot of the crater, where a market is held for offerings and refreshments.   The scene is a lively one, for hundreds of people must now pay the vows which they made during the year.   The priests sit in a long row on mats, and when the high priest appears the people pray, saying, " Bromo, we thank thee for all thy gifts and benefits with which thou ever blessest us, and for which we offer thee our thank-offerings to-day.   Bless us, our children, and our children's children."   The prayers over, the high priest gives a signal, and the whole multitude arises and climbs the mountain.   On reaching the edge of the

Annual sacrifices to the volcano Bromo in Java.

---

[1] A. C. Kruijt, *Het Animisme in den Indischen Archipel* (The Hague, 1906), pp. 497 *sq.*

[2] W. B. d'Almeida, *Life in Java* (London, 1864), i. 166-173.

crater, the pontiff again blesses the offerings of food, clothes, and money, which are then thrown into the crater. Yet few of them reach the spirits for whom they are intended ; for a swarm of urchins now scrambles down into the crater, and at more or less risk to life and limb succeeds in appropriating the greater part of the offerings. The spirits, defrauded of their dues, must take the will for the deed.[1] Tradition says that once in a time of dearth a chief vowed to sacrifice one of his children to the volcano, if the mountain would bless the people with plenty of food. His prayer was answered, and he paid his vow by casting his youngest son as a thank-offering into the crater.[2]

On the slope of Mount Smeroe, another active volcano in Java, there are two small idols, which the natives worship and pray to when they ascend the mountain. They lay food before the images to obtain the favour of the god of the volcano.[3] In antiquity people cast into the craters of Etna vessels of gold and silver and all kinds of victims. If the fire swallowed up the offerings, the omen was good ; but if it rejected them, some evil was sure to befall the offerer.[4]

Other sacrifices to volcanoes.

These examples suggest that a custom of burning men or images may possibly be derived from a practice of throwing them into the craters of active volcanoes in order to appease the dreaded spirits or gods who dwell there. But unless we reckon the fires of Mount Argaeus in Cappadocia[5] and of Mount Chimaera in Lycia,[6] there is apparently no record of any mountain in Western Asia which has been in

No evidence that the Asiatic custom of burning kings or gods was connected with volcanic phenomena.

---

[1] J. H. F. Kohlbrugge, "Die Tĕng-gĕresen, ein alter Javanischer Volks-stamm," *Bijdragen tot de Taal- Land- en Volkenkunde van Nederlandsch-Indië,* liii. (1901) pp. 84, 144-147.

[2] J. H. F. Kohlbrugge, *op. cit.* pp. 100 *sq.*

[3] I. A. Stigand, "The Volcano of Smeroe, Java," *The Geographical Journal,* xxviii. (1906) pp. 621, 624.

[4] Pausanias, iii. 23. 9. Some have thought that Pausanias confused the crater of Etna with the *Lago di Naftia,* a pool near Palagonia in the interior of Sicily, of which the water, impregnated with naphtha and sulphur, is thrown into violent ebullition by jets of volcanic gas. See [Aristotle,] *Mirab. Auscult.*

57 ; Macrobius, *Saturn.* v. 19. 26 *sqq.*; Diodorus Siculus, xi. 89 ; Stephanus Byzantius, *s.v.* Παλική ; E. H. Bunbury, *s.v.* "Palicorum lacus," in W. Smith's *Dictionary of Greek and Roman Geography,* ii. 533 *sq.* The author of the ancient Latin poem *Aetna* says (vv. 340 *sq.*) that people offered incense to the celestial deities on the top of Etna.

[5] See above, pp. 190 *sq.*

[6] On Mount Chimaera in Lycia a flame burned perpetually which neither earth nor water could extinguish. See Pliny, *Nat. Hist.* ii. 236, v. 100 ; Servius on Virgil, *Aen.* vi. 288 ; Seneca, *Epist.* x. 3. 3 ; Diodorus, quoted by Photius, *Bibliotheca,* p. 212

eruption within historical times. On the whole, then, we conclude that the Asiatic custom of burning kings or gods was probably in no way connected with volcanic phenomena. Yet it was perhaps worth while to raise the question of the connexion, even though it has received only a negative answer. The whole subject of the influence which physical environment has exercised on the history of religion deserves to be studied with more attention than it has yet received.[1]

B, 10 *sqq.*, ed. Im. Bekker (Berlin, 1824). This perpetual flame was rediscovered by Captain Beaufort near Porto Genovese on the coast of Lycia. It issues from the side of a hill of crumbly serpentine rock, giving out an intense heat, but no smoke. "Trees, brushwood, and weeds grow close round this little crater, a small stream trickles down the hill hard bye, and the ground does not appear to feel the effect of its heat at more than a few feet distance." The fire is not accompanied by earthquakes or noises; it ejects no stones and emits no noxious vapours. There is nothing but a brilliant and perpetual flame, at which the shepherds often cook their food. See Fr. Beaufort, *Karmania* (London, 1817), p. 46; compare T. A. B. Spratt and E. Forbes, *Travels in Lycia* (London, 1847), ii. 181 *sq.*

[1] In the foregoing discussion I have confined myself, so far as concerns Asia, to the volcanic regions of Cappadocia, Lydia, and Caria. But Syria and Palestine, the home of Adonis and Melcarth, "abound in volcanic appearances, and very extensive areas have been shaken, at different periods, with great destruction of cities and loss of lives. Continual mention is made in history of the

ravages committed by earthquakes in Sidon, Tyre, Berytus, Laodicea, and Antioch, and in the island of Cyprus. The country around the Dead Sea exhibits in some spots layers of sulphur and bitumen, forming a superficial deposit, supposed by Mr. Tristram to be of volcanic origin" (Sir Ch. Lyell, *Principles of Geology*,[12] i. 592 *sq.*). As to the earthquakes of Syria and Phoenicia see Strabo, i. 3. 16, p. 58; Lucretius, vi. 585; Josephus, *Antiquit. Jud.* xv. 5. 2; *id., Bell. Jud.* i. 19. 3; W. M. Thomson, *The Land and the Book, Central Palestine and Phoenicia*, pp. 568-574; Ed. Robinson, *Biblical Researches in Palestine*,[3] ii. 422-424; S. R. Driver, on Amos iv. 11 (Cambridge *Bible for Schools and Colleges*). It is said that in the reign of the Emperor Justin the city of Antioch was totally destroyed by a dreadful earthquake, in which three hundred thousand people perished (Procopius, *De Bello Persico*, ii. 14). The destruction of Sodom and Gomorrah (Genesis xix. 24-28) has been plausibly explained as the effect of an earthquake liberating large quantities of petroleum and inflammable gases. See H. B. Tristram, *The Land of Israel*, Fourth Edition (London, 1882), pp. 350-354; S. R. Driver, *The Book of Genesis*[4] (London, 1905), pp. 202 *sq.*

CHAPTER IX

THE RITUAL OF ADONIS

THUS far we have dealt with the myth of Adonis and the legends which associated him with Byblus and Paphos. A discussion of these legends led us to the conclusion that among Semitic peoples in early times, Adonis, the divine lord of the city, was often personated by priestly kings or other members of the royal family, and that these his human representatives were of old put to death, whether periodically or occasionally, in their divine character. Further, we found that certain traditions and monuments of Asia Minor seem to preserve traces of a similar practice. As time went on, the cruel custom was apparently mitigated in various ways; for example, by substituting an effigy or an animal for the man, or by allowing the destined victim to escape with a merely make-believe sacrifice. The evidence of all this is drawn from a variety of scattered and often ambiguous indications: it is fragmentary, it is uncertain, and the conclusions built upon it inevitably partake of the weakness of the foundation. Where the records are so imperfect, as they happen to be in this branch of our subject, the element of hypothesis must enter largely into any attempt to piece together and interpret the disjointed facts. How far the interpretations here proposed are sound, I leave to future inquiries to determine. *Results of the preceding inquiry.*

From dim regions of the past, where we have had to grope our way with small help from the lamp of history, it is a relief to pass to those later periods of classical antiquity on which contemporary Greek writers have shed the light of their clear intelligence. To them we owe *Our knowledge of Adonis derived chiefly from Greek writers.*

almost all that we know for certain about the rites of Adonis. The Semites who practised the worship have said little about it ; at all events little that they said has come down to us. Accordingly, the following account of the ritual is derived mainly from Greek authors who saw what they describe ; and it applies to ages in which the growth of humane feeling had softened some of the harsher features of the worship.

Festivals of the death and resurrection of Adonis. At the festivals of Adonis, which were held in Western Asia and in Greek lands, the death of the god was annually mourned, with a bitter wailing, chiefly by women ; images of him, dressed to resemble corpses, were carried out as to burial and then thrown into the sea or into springs ;[1] and in some places his revival was celebrated on the following day.[2] But at different places the ceremonies varied somewhat in the manner and apparently also in the season of their celebration. At Alexandria images of Aphrodite and Adonis were displayed on two couches ; beside them were set ripe fruits of all kinds, cakes, plants growing in flower-pots, and green bowers twined with anise. The marriage of the lovers was celebrated one day, and on the morrow women attired as mourners, with streaming hair and bared

The festival at Alexandria.

---

[1] Plutarch, *Alcibiades*, 18 ; *id.*, *Nicias*, 13 ; Zenobius, *Centur.* i. 49 ; Theocritus, xv. 132 *sqq.* ; Eustathius on Homer, *Od.* xi. 590.

[2] Besides Lucian (cited below) see Origen, *Selecta in Ezechielem* (Migne's *Patrologia Graeca*, xiii. 800), δοκοῦσι γὰρ κατ' ἐνιαυτὸν τελετάς τινας ποιεῖν πρῶτον μὲν ὅτι θρηνοῦσιν αὐτὸν [scil. Ἄδωνιν] ὡς τεθνηκότα, δεύτερον δὲ ὅτι χαίρουσιν ἐπ' αὐτῷ ὡς ἀπὸ νεκρῶν ἀναστάντι. Jerome, *Commentar. in Ezechielem*, viii. 13, 14 (Migne's *Patrologia Latina*, xxv. 82, 83): "*Quem nos* Adonidem *interpretati sumus, et Hebraeus et Syrus sermo* Thamuz (תמוז) *vocat : unde quia juxta gentilem fabulam, in mense Junis amasius Veneris et pulcherrimus juvenis occisus, et deinceps revixisse narratur, eundem Junium mensem eodem appellant nomine, et anniversariam ei celebrant solemni-* *tatem, in qua plangitur a mulieribus quasi mortuus, et postea reviviscens canitur atque laudatur . . . interfectionem et resurrectionem Adonidis planctu et gaudio prosequens.*" Cyril of Alexandria, *In Isaiam*, lib. ii. tomus iii. (Migne's *Patrologia Graeca*, lxx. 441), ἐπλάττοντο τοίνυν Ἕλληνες ἑορτὴν ἐπὶ τούτῳ τοιαύτην. Προσεποιοῦντο μὲν γὰρ λυπουμένῃ τῇ Ἀφροδίτῃ, διὰ τὸ τεθνάναι τὸν Ἄδωνιν, συνολοφύρεσθαι καὶ θρηνεῖν· ἀνελθούσης δὲ ἐξ ᾅδου, καὶ μὴν καὶ ηὑρῆσθαι λεγούσης τὸν ζητούμενον, συνήδεσθαι καὶ ἀνασκιρτᾶν· καὶ μεχρὶ τῶν καθ' ἡμᾶς καιρῶν ἐν τοῖς κατ' Ἀλεξάνδρειαν ἱεροῖς ἐτελεῖτο τὸ παίγνιον τοῦτο. From this testimony of Cyril we learn that this festival of the death and resurrection of Adonis was celebrated at Alexandria down to his time, that is, down to the fourth or even the fifth century, long after the official establishment of Christianity.

breasts, bore the image of the dead Adonis to the sea-shore and committed it to the waves. Yet they sorrowed not without hope, for they sang that the lost one would come back again.[1] The date at which this Alexandrian ceremony was observed is not expressly stated; but from the mention of the ripe fruits it has been inferred that it took place in late summer.[2] In the great Phoenician sanctuary of Astarte at Byblus the death of Adonis was annually mourned, to the shrill wailing notes of the flute, with weeping, lamentation, and beating of the breast; but next day he was believed to come to life again and ascend up to heaven in the presence of his worshippers. The disconsolate believers, left behind on earth, shaved their heads as the Egyptians did on the death of the divine bull Apis; women who could not bring themselves to sacrifice their beautiful tresses had to give themselves up to strangers on a certain day of the festival, and to dedicate to Astarte the wages of their shame.[3]

The festival at Byblus.

This Phoenician festival appears to have been a vernal one, for its date was determined by the discoloration of the river Adonis, and this has been observed by modern travellers to occur in spring. At that season the red earth washed down from the mountains by the rain tinges the water of the river, and even the sea, for a great way with a blood-red hue, and the crimson stain was believed to be the blood of Adonis, annually wounded to death by the boar on Mount Lebanon.[4] Again, the

Date of the festival at Byblus.

---

[1] Theocritus, xv.

[2] W. Mannhardt, *Antike Wald- und Feldkulte* (Berlin, 1877), p. 277.

[3] Lucian, *De dea Syria*, 6. See above, p. 38. The flutes used by the Phoenicians in the lament for Adonis are mentioned by Athenaeus (iv. 76, p. 174 F), and by Pollux (iv. 76), who say that the same name *gingras* was applied by the Phoenicians both to the flute and to Adonis himself. Compare F. C. Movers, *Die Phoenizier*, i. 243 *sq.* We have seen that flutes were also played in the Babylonian rites of Tammuz (above, p. 9). Lucian's words, ἐς τὸν ἠέρα πέμπουσι, imply that the ascension of the god was supposed to take place in the

presence, if not before the eyes, of the worshipping crowds. The devotion of Byblus to Adonis is noticed also by Strabo (xvi. 2. 18, p. 755).

[4] Lucian, *De dea Syria*, 8. The discoloration of the river and the sea was observed by H. Maundrell on $\frac{17}{27}$ March $\frac{1696}{1697}$. See his *Journey from Aleppo to Jerusalem*, at Easter, *A.D. 1697*, Fourth Edition (Perth, 1800), pp. 59 *sq.* ; *id.*, in Bohn's *Early Travels in Palestine*, edited by Thomas Wright (London, 1848), pp. 411 *sq.* Renan remarked the discoloration at the beginning of February (*Mission de Phénicie*, p. 283). In his well-known lines on the subject

The
anemone
and the
red rose
the flowers
of Adonis.
scarlet anemone is said to have sprung from the blood of
Adonis, or to have been stained by it ;[1] and as the anemone
blooms in Syria about Easter, this may be thought to show
that the festival of Adonis, or at least one of his festivals,
was held in spring. The name of the flower is probably
derived from Naaman (" darling "), which seems to have been
an epithet of Adonis. The Arabs still call the anemone
" wounds of the Naaman."[2] The red rose also was said to
owe its hue to the same sad occasion ; for Aphrodite,
hastening to her wounded lover, trod on a bush of white
roses ; the cruel thorns tore her tender flesh, and her sacred
blood dyed the white roses for ever red.[3] It would be idle,
perhaps, to lay much weight on evidence drawn from the
calendar of flowers, and in particular to press an argument
so fragile as the bloom of the rose. Yet so far as it
counts at all, the tale which links the damask rose with

Festivals of
Adonis at
Athens and
Antioch.
the death of Adonis points to a summer rather than to
a spring celebration of his passion. In Attica, certainly,
the festival fell at the height of summer. For the fleet
which Athens fitted out against Syracuse, and by the destruction of which her power was permanently crippled,
sailed at midsummer, and by an ominous coincidence the
sombre rites of Adonis were being celebrated at the very
time. As the troops marched down to the harbour to
embark, the streets through which they passed were lined
with coffins and corpse-like effigies, and the air was rent
with the noise of women wailing for the dead Adonis. The
circumstance cast a gloom over the sailing of the most
splendid armament that Athens ever sent to sea.[4] Many

Milton has laid the mourning in
summer :—

" *Thammuz came next behind,*
Whose annual wound in Lebanon
allur'd
The Syrian damsels to lament his fate
In amorous ditties all a summer's day."

[1] Ovid, *Metam.* x. 735 ; Servius on
Virgil, *Aen.* v. 72 ; J. Tzetzes, *Schol.*
on Lycophron, 831. Bion, on the other
hand, represents the anemone as sprung
from the tears of Aphrodite (*Idyl.* i. 66).
[2] W. Robertson Smith, "Ctesias
and the Semiramis Legend," *English*

Historical Review, ii. (1887) p. 307,
following Lagarde. Compare W. W.
Graf Baudissin, *Adonis und Esmun,*
pp. 88 *sq.*
[3] J. Tzetzes, *Schol. on Lycophron,*
831 ; *Geoponica,* xi. 17 ; *Mythographi*
Graeci, ed. A. Westermann, p. 359.
Compare Bion, *Idyl.* i. 66 ; Pausanias,
vi. 24. 7 ; Philostratus, *Epist.* i. and
iii.
[4] Plutarch, *Alcibiades,* 18 ; *id.,*
Nicias, 13. The date of the sailing
of the fleet is given by Thucydides
(vi. 30, θέρους μεσοῦντος ἤδη), who, with
his habitual contempt for the supersti-

ages afterwards, when the Emperor Julian made his first entry into Antioch, he found in like manner the gay, the luxurious capital of the East plunged in mimic grief for the annual death of Adonis : and if he had any presentiment of coming evil, the voices of lamentation which struck upon his ear must have seemed to sound his knell.[1]

The resemblance of these ceremonies to the Indian and European ceremonies which I have described elsewhere is obvious.   In particular, apart from the somewhat doubtful date of its celebration, the Alexandrian ceremony is almost identical with the Indian.[2]   In both of them the marriage of two divine beings, whose affinity with vegetation seems indicated by the fresh plants with which they are surrounded, is celebrated in effigy, and the effigies are afterwards mourned over and thrown into the water.[3] From the similarity of these customs to each other and to the spring and midsummer customs of modern Europe we should naturally expect that they all admit of a common explanation.   Hence, if the explanation which I have adopted of the latter is correct, the ceremony of the death and resurrection of Adonis must also have been a dramatic representation of the decay and revival of plant life.   The inference thus based on the resemblance of the customs is confirmed by the following features in the legend and ritual of Adonis.   His affinity with vegetation comes out at once in the common story of his birth.   He was said to have been born from a myrrh-tree, the bark of which bursting, after a ten months' gestation, allowed the lovely infant to come forth.   According to some, a boar rent the bark with his tusk and so opened a passage for the babe.   A faint rationalistic colour was given to the legend by saying that his mother was a woman named Myrrh, who had been

Marginal notes:
Resemblance of these rites to Indian and European ceremonies.

The death and resurrection of Adonis a mythical expression for the annual decay and revival of plant life.

---

tion of his countrymen, disdains to notice the coincidence.   Adonis was also bewailed by the Argive women (Pausanias, ii. 20. 6), but we do not know at what season of the year the lamentation took place.   Inscriptions prove that processions in honour of Adonis were held in the Piraeus, and that a society of his worshippers existed at Loryma in Caria.   See G.

Dittenberger, *Sylloge Inscriptionum Graecarum*,[2] Nos. 726, 741 (vol. ii. pp. 564, 604).

[1] Ammianus Marcellinus, xxii. 9. 15.

[2] *The Dying God*, pp. 261-266.

[3] In the Alexandrian ceremony, however, it appears to have been the image of Adonis only which was thrown into the sea.

turned into a myrrh-tree soon after she had conceived the
child.[1] The use of myrrh as incense at the festival of
Adonis may have given rise to the fable.[2] We have seen
that incense was burnt at the corresponding Babylonian
rites,[3] just as it was burnt by the idolatrous Hebrews in
honour of the Queen of Heaven,[4] who was no other than
Astarte. Again, the story that Adonis spent half, or
according to others a third, of the year in the lower world
and the rest of it in the upper world,[5] is explained most
simply and naturally by supposing that he represented
vegetation, especially the corn, which lies buried in the
earth half the year and reappears above ground the other
half. Certainly of the annual phenomena of nature there
is none which suggests so obviously the idea of death
and resurrection as the disappearance and reappearance of
vegetation in autumn and spring. Adonis has been taken
for the sun ; but there is nothing in the sun's annual
course within the temperate and tropical zones to suggest
that he is dead for half or a third of the year and alive
for the other half or two-thirds. He might, indeed, be
conceived as weakened in winter, but dead he could not
be thought to be ; his daily reappearance contradicts the
supposition.[6] Within the Arctic Circle, where the sun
annually disappears for a continuous period which varies
from twenty-four hours to six months according to the
latitude, his yearly death and resurrection would certainly
be an obvious idea ; but no one except the unfortunate

*Adonis
sometimes
taken for
the sun.*

---

[1] Apollodorus, *Bibliotheca*, iii. 14.4 ;
Scholiast on Theocritus, i. 109 ; Antoninus Liberalis, *Transform.* 34 ; J.
Tzetzes, *Scholia on Lycophron*, 829 ;
Ovid, *Metamorph.* x. 489 *sqq.* ; Servius
on Virgil, *Aen.* v. 72, and on *Bucol.*
x. 18 ; Hyginus, *Fab.* 58, 164 ; Fulgentius, iii. 8. The word Myrrha or
Smyrna is borrowed from the Phoenician
(Liddell and Scott, *Greek Lexicon, s.v.*
σμύρνα). Hence the mother's name,
as well as the son's, was taken directly
from the Semites.

[2] W. Mannhardt, *Antike Wald- und
Feldkulte*, p. 383, note [2].

[3] Above, p. 9.

[4] Jeremiah xliv. 17-19.

[5] Scholiast on Theocritus, iii. 48 ;
Hyginus, *Astronom.* ii. 7 ; Lucian,
Dialog. deor. xi. 1 ; Cornutus, *Theologiae Graecae Compendium*, 28, p. 54,
ed. C. Lang (Leipsic, 1881) ; Apollodorus, *Bibliotheca*, iii. 14. 4.

[6] The arguments which tell against
the solar interpretation of Adonis are
stated more fully by the learned and
candid scholar Graf Baudissin (*Adonis
und Esmun*, pp. 169 *sqq.*), who himself
formerly accepted the solar theory but
afterwards rightly rejected it in favour
of the view "*dass Adonis die Frühlings-
vegetation darstellt, die im Sommer
abstirbt*" (*op. cit.* p. 169).

astronomer Bailly[1] has maintained that the Adonis worship came from the Arctic regions. On the other hand, the annual death and revival of vegetation is a conception which readily presents itself to men in every stage of savagery and civilization ; and the vastness of the scale on which this ever-recurring decay and regeneration takes place, together with man's intimate dependence on it for subsistence, combine to render it the most impressive annual occurrence in nature, at least within the temperate zones. It is no wonder that a phenomenon so important, so striking, and so universal should, by suggesting similar ideas, have given rise to similar rites in many lands. We may, therefore, accept as probable an explanation of the Adonis worship which accords so well with the facts of nature and with the analogy of similar rites in other lands. More-over, the explanation is countenanced by a considerable body of opinion amongst the ancients themselves, who again and again interpreted the dying and reviving god as the reaped and sprouting grain.[2]

---

[1] Bailly, *Lettres sur l'Origine des Sciences* (London and Paris, 1777), pp. 255 *sq.* ; *id.*, *Lettres sur l'Atlantide de Platon* (London and Paris, 1779), pp. 114-125. Carlyle has described how through the sleety drizzle of a dreary November day poor innocent Bailly was dragged to the scaffold amid the howls and curses of the Parisian mob (*French Revolution*, bk. v. ch. 2). My friend the late Professor C. Bendall showed me a book by a Hindoo gentleman in which it is seriously maintained that the primitive home of the Aryans was within the Arctic regions. See Bâl Gangâdhar Tilak, *The Arctic Home in the Vedas* (Poona and Bombay, 1903).

[2] Cornutus, *Theologiae Graecae Compendium*, 28, pp. 54 *sq.*, ed. C. Lang (Leipsic, 1881), τοιοῦτον γάρ τι καὶ παρ' Αἰγυπτίοις ὁ ζητούμενος καὶ ἀνευρισκόμενος ὑπὸ τῆς Ἴσιδος Ὄσιρις ἐμφαίνει καὶ παρὰ Φοίνιξιν ὁ ἀνὰ μέρος παρ' ἓξ μῆνας ὑπὲρ γῆν τε καὶ ὑπὸ γῆν γινόμενος Ἄδωνις, ἀπὸ τοῦ ἀδεῖν τοῖς ἀνθρώποις οὕτως ὠνομασμένου τοῦ Δημητριακοῦ καρποῦ. τοῦτον δὲ πλήξας

κάπρος ἀνελεῖν λέγεται διὰ τὸ τὰς ὗς δοκεῖν ληιβότειρας εἶναι ἢ τὸν τῆς ὕνεως ὀδόντα αἰνιττομένων αὐτῶν, ὑφ' οὗ κατὰ γῆς κρύπτεται τὸ σπέρμα. Scholiast on Theocritus, iii. 48, ὁ Ἄδωνις, ἤγουν ὁ σῖτος ὁ σπειρόμενος, ἓξ μῆνας ἐν τῇ γῇ ποιεῖ ἀπὸ τῆς σπορᾶς καὶ ἓξ μῆνας ἔχει αὐτὸν ἡ Ἀφροδίτη, τουτέστιν ἡ εὐκρασία τοῦ ἀέρος. καὶ ἐκτότε λαμβάνουσιν αὐτὸν οἱ ἄνθρωποι. Origen, *Selecta in Ezechielem* (Migne's *Patrologia Graeca*, xiii. 800), οἱ δὲ περὶ τὴν ἀναγωγὴν τῶν Ἑλληνικῶν μύθων δεινοὶ καὶ μυθικῆς νομιζομένης θεολογίας, φασὶ τὸν Ἄδωνιν σύμβολον εἶναι τῶν τῆς γῆς καρπῶν, θρηνουμένων μὲν ὅτε σπείρονται, ἀνισταμένων δέ, καὶ διὰ τοῦτο χαίρειν ποιούντων τοὺς γεωργοὺς ὅτε φύονται. Jerome, *Commentar. in Ezechielem*, viii. 13, 14 (Migne's *Patrologia Latina*, xxv. 83), "*Eadem gentilitas hujuscemodi fabulas poetarum, quae habent turpitudinem, interpretatur subtiliter, interfectionem et resurrectionem Adonidis planctu et gaudio prosequens : quorum alterum in seminibus, quae moriuntur in terra, alterum in*

Tammuz
or Adonis
as a
corn-spirit
bruised and
ground in
a mill.

The character of Tammuz or Adonis as a corn-spirit comes out plainly in an account of his festival given by an Arabic writer of the tenth century. In describing the rites and sacrifices observed at the different seasons of the year by the heathen Syrians of Harran, he says: "Tammuz (July). In the middle of this month is the festival of el-Bûgât, that is, of the weeping women, and this is the Tâ-uz festival, which is celebrated in honour of the god Tâ-uz. The women bewail him, because his lord slew him so cruelly, ground his bones in a mill, and then scattered them to the wind. The women (during this festival) eat nothing which has been ground in a mill, but limit their diet to steeped wheat, sweet vetches, dates, raisins, and the like." [1] Tâ-uz, who is no other than Tammuz, is here like Burns's John Barleycorn—

segetibus, quibus mortua semina rena-scuntur, ostendi putat." Ammianus Marcellinus, xix. I. 11, "in sollemnibus Adonidis sacris, quod simulacrum aliquod esse frugum adultarnm religiones mysticae docent." Id. xxii. 9. 15, "amato Veneris, ut fabulae fingunt, apri dente ferali deleto, quod in adulto flore sectarum est indicium frugum." Clement of Alexandria, Hom. 6. 11 (quoted by W. Mannhardt, Antique Wald- und Feldkulte, p. 281), λαμβάνουσι δὲ καὶ Ἄδωνιν εἰς ὡραίους καρπούς. Etymologieum Magnum s.v. Ἄδωνις κύριον· δύναται καὶ ὁ καρπὸς εἶναι ἄδωνις· οἷον ἀδώνειος καρπός, ἀρέσκων. Eusebius, Praepar. Evang. iii. 11. 9, Ἄδωνις τῆς τῶν τελείων καρπῶν ἐκτομῆς σύμβολον. Sallustius philosophus, "De diis et mundo," iv. Fragmenta Philosophorum Graecorum, ed. F. G. A. Mullach, iii. 32, οἱ Αἰγύπτιοι . . . αὐτὰ τὰ σώματα θεοὺς νομίσαντες . . . Ἶσιν μὲν τὴν γῆν . . . Ἄδωνιν δὲ καρπούς. Joannes Lydus, De mensibus, iv. 4, τῷ Ἀδώνιδι, τουτέστι τῷ Μαίῳ . . . ἢ ὡς ἄλλοις, δοκεῖ, Ἄδωνις μέν ἐστιν ὁ καρπός, κτλ. The view that Tammuz or Adonis is a personification of the dying and reviving vegetation is now accepted by

many scholars. See P. Jensen, Kosmologie der Babylonier (Strasburg, 1890), p. 480; id., Assyrisch-babylonische Mythen und Epen, pp. 411, 560; H. Zimmern, in E. Schrader's Keilinschriften und das Alte Testament,[3] p. 397; A. Jeremias, s.v. "Nergal," in W. H. Roscher's Lexikon der griech. und röm. Mythologie, iii. 265; R. Wünsch, Das Frühlingsfest der Insel Malta (Leipsic, 1902), p. 21; M. J. Lagrange, Études sur les Religions Sémitiques,[2] pp. 306 sqq.; W. W. Graf Baudissin, "Tammuz," Realencyclopädie für protestantische Theologie und Kirchengeschichte; id., Esmun und Adonis, pp. 81, 141, 169, etc.; and Ed. Meyer, Geschichte des Altertums,[2] i. 2. pp. 394, 427. Prof. Jastrow regards Tammuz as a god both of the sun and of vegetation (Religion of Babylonia and Assyria, pp. 547, 564, 574, 588). But such a combination of disparate qualities seems artificial and unlikely.

[1] D. Chwolsohn, Die Ssabier und der Ssabismus (St. Petersburg, 1856), ii. 27; id., Ueber Tammûz und die Menschenverehrung bei den alten Babylioniern (St. Petersburg, 1860), p. 38. Compare W. W. Graf Baudissin, Adonis und Esmun, pp. 111 sqq.

> " *They wasted o'er a scorching flame*
> *The marrow of his bones;*
> *But a miller us'd him worst of all—*
> *For he crush'd him between two stones.*"

This concentration, so to say, of the nature of Adonis upon the cereal crops is characteristic of the stage of culture reached by his worshippers in historical times. They had left the nomadic life of the wandering hunter and herdsman far behind them ; for ages they had been settled on the land, and had depended for their subsistence mainly on the products of tillage. The berries and roots of the wilderness, the grass of the pastures, which had been matters of vital importance to their ruder forefathers, were now of little moment to them : more and more their thoughts and energies were engrossed by the staple of their life, the corn ; more and more accordingly the propitiation of the deities of fertility in general and of the corn-spirit in particular tended to become the central feature of their religion. The aim they set before themselves in celebrating the rites was thoroughly practical. It was no vague poetical sentiment which prompted them to hail with joy the rebirth of vegetation and to mourn its decline. Hunger, felt or feared, was the mainspring of the worship of Adonis.

It has been suggested by Father Lagrange that the mourning for Adonis was essentially a harvest rite designed to propitiate the corn-god, who was then either perishing under the sickles of the reapers, or being trodden to death under the hoofs of the oxen on the threshing-floor. While the men slew him, the women wept crocodile tears at home to appease his natural indignation by a show of grief for his death.[2] The theory fits in well with the dates of the festivals, which fell in spring or summer ; for spring and summer, not autumn, are the seasons of the barley and wheat harvests in the lands which worshipped Adonis.[3]

The mourning for Adonis interpreted as a harvest rite.

---

[1] The comparison is due to Felix Liebrecht (*Zur Volkskunde*, Heilbronn, 1879, p. 259).

[2] M. J. Lagrange, *Études sur les Religions Sémitiques*[2] (Paris, 1905), pp. 307 *sq.*

[3] Hence Philo of Alexandria dates the corn-reaping in the middle of spring (Μεσοῦντος δὲ ἔαρος ἄμητος ἐνίσταται, *De special. legibus*, i. 183, vol. v. p. 44, ed. L. Cohn). On this subject Professor W. M. Flinders Petrie writes to me : " The Coptic calendar puts on April 2 beginning of wheat harvest in Upper Egypt, May 2 wheat harvest, Lower Egypt.

Further, the hypothesis is confirmed by the practice of the Egyptian reapers, who lamented, calling upon Isis, when they cut the first corn ;[1] and it is recommended by the analogous customs of many hunting tribes, who testify great respect for the animals which they kill and eat.[2]

But probably Adonis was a spirit of fruits, edible roots, and grass before he became a spirit of the cultivated corn.

Thus interpreted the death of Adonis is not the natural decay of vegetation in general under the summer heat or the winter cold ; it is the violent destruction of the corn by man, who cuts it down on the field, stamps it to pieces on the threshing-floor, and grinds it to powder in the mill. That this was indeed the principal aspect in which Adonis presented himself in later times to the agricultural peoples of the Levant, may be admitted ; but whether from the beginning he had been the corn and nothing but the corn,

---

Barley is two or three weeks earlier than wheat in Palestine, but probably less in Egypt. The Palestine harvest is about the time of that in North Egypt." With regard to Palestine we are told that "the harvest begins with the barley in April ; in the valley of the Jordan it begins at the end of March. Between the end of the barley harvest and the beginning of the wheat harvest an interval of two or three weeks elapses. Thus as a rule the business of harvest lasts about seven weeks" (J. Benzinger, *Hebräische Archäologie*, Freiburg i. B. and Leipsic, 1894, p. 209). "The principal grain crops of Palestine are barley, wheat, lentils, maize, and millet. Of the latter there is very little, and it is all gathered in by the end of May. The maize is then only just beginning to shoot. In the hotter parts of the Jordan valley the barley harvest is over by the end of March, and throughout the country the wheat harvest is at its height at the end of May, excepting in the highlands of Galilee, where it is about a fortnight later" (H. B. Tristram, *The Land of Israel*, Fourth Edition, London, 1882, pp. 583 *sq.*). As to Greece, Professor E. A. Gardner tells me that harvest is from April to May in the plains and about a month later in the mountains. He adds that "barley may, then, be assigned to the latter

part of April, wheat to May in the lower ground, but you know the great difference of climate between different parts ; there is the same difference of a month in the vintage." Mrs. Hawes (Miss Boyd), who excavated at Gournia, tells me that in Crete the barley is cut in April and the beginning of May, and that the wheat is cut and threshed from about the twentieth of June, though the dates naturally vary somewhat with the height of the place above the sea. June is also the season when the wheat is threshed in Euboea (R. A. Arnold, *From the Levant*, London, 1868, i. 250). Thus it seems possible that the spring festival of Adonis coincided with the cutting of the first barley in March, and his summer festival with the threshing of the last wheat in June. Father Lagrange (*op. cit.* pp. 305 *sq.*) argues that the rites of Adonis were always celebrated in summer at the solstice of June or soon afterwards. Baudissin also holds that the summer celebration is the only one which is clearly attested, and that if there was a celebration in spring it must have had a different signification than the death of the god. See his *Adonis und Esmun*, pp. 132 *sq.*

[1] Diodorus Siculus, i. 14. 2. See below, vol. ii. pp. 45 *sq.*

[2] *Spirits of the Corn and of the Wild*, ii. 180 *sqq.*, 204 *sqq.*

may be doubted.   At an earlier period he may have been
to the herdsman, above all, the tender herbage which
sprouts after rain, offering rich pasture to the lean and
hungry cattle.   Earlier still he may have embodied the
spirit of the nuts and berries which the autumn woods
yield to the savage hunter and his squaw.   And just as
the husbandman must propitiate the spirit of the corn
which he consumes, so the herdsman must appease the
spirit of the grass and leaves which his cattle munch, and
the hunter must soothe the spirit of the roots which he digs,
and of the fruits which he gathers from the bough.   In
all cases the propitiation of the injured and angry sprite
would naturally comprise elaborate excuses and apologies,
accompanied by loud lamentations at his decease whenever,
through some deplorable accident or necessity, he happened
to be murdered as well as robbed.   Only we must bear in
mind that the savage hunter and herdsman of those early
days had probably not yet attained to the abstract idea of
vegetation in general ; and that accordingly, so far as Adonis
existed for them at all, he must have been the *Adon* or lord
of each individual tree and plant rather than a personification of vegetable life as a whole.   Thus there would be as
many Adonises as there were trees and shrubs, and each
of them might expect to receive satisfaction for any damage
done to his person or property.   And year by year, when
the trees were deciduous, every Adonis would seem to bleed
to death with the red leaves of autumn and to come to life
again with the fresh green of spring.

We have seen reason to think that in early times
Adonis was sometimes personated by a living man who
died a violent death in the character of the god.   Further,
there is evidence which goes to show that among the
agricultural peoples of the Eastern Mediterranean, the corn-
spirit, by whatever name he was known, was often represented, year by year, by human victims slain on the harvest-
field.[1]   If that was so, it seems likely that the propitiation
of the corn-spirit would tend to fuse to some extent with
the worship of the dead.   For the spirits of these victims

*The pro-
pitiation of
the corn-
spirit may
have fused
with the
worship of
the dead.*

---

[1] W. Mannhardt, *Mythologische Forschungen* (Strasburg, 1884), pp. 1 *sqq.* ;
Spirits of the Corn and of the Wild,
i. 216 *sqq.*

might be thought to return to life in the ears which they had fattened with their blood, and to die a second death at the reaping of the corn. Now the ghosts of those who have perished by violence are surly and apt to wreak their vengeance on their slayers whenever an opportunity offers. Hence the attempt to appease the souls of the slaughtered victims would naturally blend, at least in the popular conception, with the attempt to pacify the slain corn-spirit. And as the dead came back in the sprouting corn, so they might be thought to return in the spring flowers, waked from their long sleep by the soft vernal airs. They had been laid to their rest under the sod. What more natural than to imagine that the violets and the hyacinths, the roses and the anemones, sprang from their dust, were empurpled or incarnadined by their blood, and contained some portion of their spirit?

> " *I sometimes think that never blows so red*
> *The Rose as where some buried Caesar bled;*
> *That every Hyacinth the Garden wears*
> *Dropt in her Lap from some once lovely Head.*

> " *And this reviving Herb whose tender Green*
> *Fledges the River-Lip on which we lean—*
> *Ah, lean upon it lightly, for who knows*
> *From what once lovely Lip it springs unseen?* "

In the summer after the battle of Landen, the most sanguinary battle of the seventeenth century in Europe, the earth, saturated with the blood of twenty thousand slain, broke forth into millions of poppies, and the traveller who passed that vast sheet of scarlet might well fancy that the earth had indeed given up her dead.[1] At Athens the great Commemoration of the Dead fell in spring about the middle of March, when the early flowers are in bloom. Then the dead were believed to rise from their graves and go about the streets, vainly endeavouring to enter the temples and the dwellings, which were barred against these perturbed spirits with ropes, buckthorn, and pitch. The name of the festival, according to the most obvious and natural interpretation, means the Festival of Flowers, and the title would

The festival of the dead a festival of flowers.

---

[1] T. B. Macaulay, *History of England*, chapter xx. vol. iv. (London, 1855) p. 410.

fit well with the substance of the ceremonies if at that season the poor ghosts were indeed thought to creep from the narrow house with the opening flowers.[1] There may therefore be a measure of truth in the theory of Renan, who saw in the Adonis worship a dreamy voluptuous cult of death, conceived not as the King of Terrors, but as an insidious enchanter who lures his victims to himself and lulls them into an eternal sleep. The infinite charm of nature in the Lebanon, he thought, lends itself to religious emotions of this sensuous, visionary sort, hovering vaguely between pain and pleasure, between slumber and tears.[2] It would doubtless be a mistake to attribute to Syrian peasants the worship of a conception so purely abstract as that of death in general. Yet it may be true that in their simple minds the thought of the reviving spirit of vegetation was blent with the very concrete notion of the ghosts of the dead, who come to life again in spring days with the early flowers, with the tender green of the corn and the many-tinted blossoms of the trees. Thus their views of the death and resurrection of nature would be coloured by their views of the death and resurrection of man, by their personal sorrows and hopes and fears. In like manner we cannot doubt that Renan's theory of Adonis was itself deeply tinged by passionate memories, memories of the slumber akin to death which sealed his own eyes on the slopes of the Lebanon, memories of the sister who sleeps in the land of Adonis never again to wake with the anemones and the roses.

---

[1] This explanation of the name *Anthesteria*, as applied to a festival of the dead, is due to Mr. R. Wünsch (*Das Frühlingsfest der Insel Malta*, Leipsic, 1902, pp. 43 *sqq.*). I cannot accept the late Dr. A. W. Verrall's ingenious derivation of the word from a verb ἀναθέσσασθαι in the sense of "to conjure up" ("The Name Anthesteria," *Journal of Hellenic Studies*, xx. (1900) pp. 115-117). As to the festival see E. Rohde, *Psyche*[3] (Tübingen and Leipsic, 1903), i. 236 *sqq.*; Miss J. E. Harrison, *Prolegomena to the Study of Greek Religion*[2] (Cambridge, 1908), pp. 32 *sqq.* In Annam people offer food to their dead on the graves when the earth begins to grow green in spring. The ceremony takes place on the third day of the third month, the sun then entering the sign of Taurus. See Paul Giran, *Magie et Religion Annamites* (Paris, 1912), pp. 423 *sq.*

[2] E. Renan, *Mission de Phénicie* (Paris, 1864), p. 216.

Pots of corn, herbs, and flowers, called the gardens of Adonis.	PERHAPS the best proof that Adonis was a deity of vegetation, and especially of the corn, is furnished by the gardens of Adonis, as they were called. These were baskets or pots filled with earth, in which wheat, barley, lettuces, fennel, and various kinds of flowers were sown and tended for eight days, chiefly or exclusively by women. Fostered by the sun's heat, the plants shot up rapidly, but having no root they withered as rapidly away, and at the end of eight days were carried out with the images of the dead Adonis, and flung with them into the sea or into springs.[1]
These gardens of Adonis were charms to promote the growth of vegetation.	These gardens of Adonis are most naturally interpreted as representatives of Adonis or manifestations of his power; they represented him, true to his original nature, in vegetable form, while the images of him, with which they were carried out and cast into the water, portrayed him in his later human shape. All these Adonis ceremonies, if I am right, were originally intended as charms to promote the growth

[1] For the authorities see Raoul Rochette, "Mémoire sur les jardins d'Adonis," *Revue Archéologique*, viii. (1851) pp. 97-123; W. Mannhardt, *Antike Wald- und Feldkulte*, p. 279, note [2], and p. 280, note [2]. To the authorities cited by Mannhardt add Theophrastus, *Hist. Plant.* vi. 7. 3; *id.*, *De Causis Plant.* i. 12. 2; Gregorius Cyprius, i. 7; Macarius, i. 63; Apostolius, i. 34; Diogenianus, i. 14; Plutarch, *De sera num. vind.* 17. Women only are mentioned as planting the gardens of Adonis by Plutarch, *l.c.*; Julian, *Convivium*, p. 329 ed. Span-

heim (p. 423 ed. Hertlein); Eustathius on Homer, *Od.* xi. 590. On the other hand, Apostolius and Diogenianus (*ll.cc.*) say φυτεύοντες ἢ φυτεύουσαι. The earliest extant Greek writer who mentions the gardens of Adonis is Plato (*Phaedrus*, p. 276 B). The procession at the festival of Adonis is mentioned in an Attic inscription of 302 or 301 B.C. (G. Dittenberger, *Sylloge Inscriptionum Graecarum*,[2] vol. ii. p. 564, No. 726). Gardens of Adonis are perhaps alluded to by Isaiah (xvii. 10, with the commentators).

or revival of vegetation; and the principle by which they were supposed to produce this effect was homoeopathic or imitative magic. For ignorant people suppose that by mimicking the effect which they desire to produce they actually help to produce it; thus by sprinkling water they make rain, by lighting a fire they make sunshine, and so on. Similarly, by mimicking the growth of crops they hope to ensure a good harvest. The rapid growth of the wheat and barley in the gardens of Adonis was intended to make the corn shoot up; and the throwing of the gardens and of the images into the water was a charm to secure a due supply of fertilizing rain.[1] The same, I take it, was the object of throwing the effigies of Death and the Carnival into water in the corresponding ceremonies of modern Europe.[2] Certainly the custom of drenching with water a leaf-clad person, who undoubtedly personifies vegetation, is still resorted to in Europe for the express purpose of producing rain.[3] Similarly the custom of throwing water on the last corn cut at harvest, or on the person who brings it home (a custom observed in Germany and France, and till quite lately in England and Scotland), is in some places practised with the avowed intent to procure rain for the next year's crops. Thus in Wallachia and amongst the Roumanians in Transylvania, when a girl is bringing home a crown made of the last ears of corn cut at harvest, all who meet her hasten to throw water on her, and two farm-servants are placed at the door for the purpose; for they believe that if this were not done, the crops next year would perish from drought.[4] So

The throwing of the "gardens" into water was a rain-charm.

Parallel European customs of drenching the corn with water at harvest or sowing.

---

[1] In hot southern countries like Egypt and the Semitic regions of Western Asia, where vegetation depends chiefly or entirely upon irrigation, the purpose of the charm is doubtless to secure a plentiful flow of water in the streams. But as the ultimate object and the charms for securing it are the same in both cases, I have not thought it necessary always to point out the distinction.

[2] *The Dying God*, pp. 232, 233 *sqq.*

[3] *The Magic Art and the Evolution of Kings*, i. 272 *sqq.*

[4] W. Mannhardt, *Der Baumkultus der Germanen und ihrer Nachbar-*

stämme (Berlin, 1875), p. 214; W. Schmidt, *Das Jahr und seine Tage in Meinung und Branch der Romänen Siebenbürgens* (Hermannstadt, 1866), pp. 18 *sq.* The custom of throwing water on the last wagon-load of corn returning from the harvest-field has been practised within living memory in Wigtownshire, and at Orwell in Cambridgeshire. See J. G. Frazer, "Notes on Harvest Customs," *Folk-lore Journal*, vii. (1889) pp. 50, 51. (In the first of these passages the Orwell at which the custom used to be observed is said to be in Kent; this was a mistake of mine, which my informant, the Rev.

amongst the Saxons of Transylvania, the person who wears the wreath made of the last corn cut is drenched with water to the skin ; for the wetter he is, the better will be next year's harvest, and the more grain there will be threshed out. Sometimes the wearer of the wreath is the reaper who cut the last corn.[1] In Northern Euboea, when the corn-sheaves have been piled in a stack, the farmer's wife brings a pitcher of water and offers it to each of the labourers that he may wash his hands. Every man, after he has washed his hands, sprinkles water on the corn and on the threshing-floor, expressing at the same time a wish that the corn may last long. Lastly, the farmer's wife holds the pitcher slantingly and runs at full speed round the stack without spilling a drop, while she utters a wish that the stack may endure as long as the circle she has just described.[2] At the spring ploughing in Prussia, when the ploughmen and sowers returned in the evening from their work in the fields, the farmer's wife and the servants used to splash water over them. The ploughmen and sowers retorted by seizing every one, throwing them into the pond, and ducking them under the water. The farmer's wife might claim exemption on payment of a forfeit, but every one else had to be ducked. By observing this custom they hoped to ensure a due supply of rain for the seed.[3] Also after harvest in Prussia, the person who wore a wreath made of the last corn cut was drenched with water, while a prayer was uttered that " as the corn had sprung up and multiplied through the water, so it might spring up and multiply in the barn and granary."[4] At Schlanow, in Brandenburg, when the sowers

---

E. B. Birks, formerly Fellow of Trinity College, Cambridge, afterwards corrected.) Mr. R. F. Davis writes to me (March 4, 1906) from Campbell College, Belfast : " Between 30 and 40 years ago I was staying, as a very small boy, at a Nottinghamshire farmhouse at harvest-time, and was allowed —as a great privilege—to ride home on the top of the last load. All the harvesters followed the waggon, and on reaching the farmyard we found the maids of the farm gathered near the gate, with bowls and buckets of water, which they proceeded to throw on the

men, who got thoroughly drenched."

[1] G. A. Heinrich, *Agrarische Sitten und Gebräuche unter den Sachsen Siebenbürgens* (Hermanstadt, 1880), p. 24 ; H. von Wlislocki, *Sitten und Brauch der Siebenbürger Sachsen* (Hamburg, 1888), p. 32.

[2] G. Drosinis, *Land und Leute in Nord-Euböa* (Leipsic, 1884), p. 53.

[3] Matthäus Prätorius, *Deliciae Prussicae* (Berlin, 1871), p. 55 ; W. Mannhardt, *Baumkultus*, pp. 214 *sq.*, note.

[4] M. Prätorius, *op. cit.* p. 60 ; W. Mannhardt, *Baumkultus*, p. 215, note.

return home from the first sowing they are drenched with water " in order that the corn may grow." [1]   In Anhalt on the same occasion the farmer is still often sprinkled with water by his family; and his men and horses, and even the plough, receive the same treatment. The object of the custom, as people at Arensdorf explained it, is " to wish fertility to the fields for the whole year." [2] So in Hesse, when the ploughmen return with the plough from the field for the first time, the women and girls lie in wait for them and slyly drench them with water.[3]   Near Naaburg, in Bavaria, the man who first comes back from sowing or ploughing has a vessel of water thrown over him by some one in hiding.[4]   At Hettingen in Baden the farmer who is about to begin the sowing of oats is sprinkled with water, in order that the oats may not shrivel up.[5] Before the Tusayan Indians of North America go out to plant their fields, the women sometimes pour water on them; the reason for doing so is that " as the water is poured on the men, so may water fall on the planted fields." [6]   The Indians of Santiago Tepehuacan steep the seed of the maize in water before they sow it, in order that the god of the waters may bestow on the fields the needed moisture.[7]

The opinion that the gardens of Adonis are essentially charms to promote the growth of vegetation, especially of the crops, and that they belong to the same class of customs as those spring and midsummer folk-customs of modern Europe which I have described elsewhere,[8] does not rest for its evidence merely on the intrinsic probability of the case. Fortunately we are able to show that gardens of Adonis (if we may use the expression in a general sense) are still planted, first, by a primitive race at their sowing season,

Gardens of Adonis among the Oraons and Mundas of Bengal.

[1] H. Prahn, "Glaube und Brauch in der Mark Brandenburg," *Zeitschrift des Vereins für Volkskunde*, i. (1891) p. 186.

[2] O. Hartung, "Zur Volkskunde aus Anhalt," *Zeitschrift des Vereins für Volkskunde*, vii. (1897) p. 150.

[3] W. Kolbe, *Hessische Volks-Sitten und Gebräuche* (Marburg, 1888), p. 51.

[4] *Bavaria, Landes- und Volkskunde des Königreichs Bayern*, ii. (Munich, 1863) p. 297.

[5] E. H. Meyer, *Badisches Volksleben* (Strasburg, 1900), p. 420.

[6] J. Walter Fewkes, "The Tusayan New Fire Ceremony," *Proceedings of the Boston Society of Natural History*, xxvi. (1895) p. 446.

[7] "Lettre du curé de Santiago Tepehuacan à son évêque," *Bulletin de la Société de Géographie* (Paris), Deuxième Série, ii. (1834) pp. 181 *sq.*

[8] *The Magic Art and the Evolution of Kings*, ii. 59 *sqq.*

and, second, by European peasants at midsummer. Amongst the Oraons and Mundas of Bengal, when the time comes for planting out the rice which has been grown in seed-beds, a party of young people of both sexes go to the forest and cut a young Karma-tree, or the branch of one. Bearing it in triumph they return dancing, singing, and beating drums, and plant it in the middle of the village dancing-ground. A sacrifice is offered to the tree; and next morning the youth of both sexes, linked arm-in-arm, dance in a great circle round the Karma-tree, which is decked with strips of coloured cloth and sham bracelets and necklets of plaited straw. As a preparation for the festival, the daughters of the headman of the village cultivate blades of barley in a peculiar way. The seed is sown in moist, sandy soil, mixed with turmeric, and the blades sprout and unfold of a pale-yellow or primrose colour. On the day of the festival the girls take up these blades and carry them in baskets to the dancing-ground, where, prostrating themselves reverentially, they place some of the plants before the Karma-tree. Finally, the Karma-tree is taken away and thrown into a stream or tank.[1] The meaning of planting these barley blades and then presenting them to the Karma-tree is hardly open to question. Trees are supposed to exercise a quickening influence upon the growth of crops, and amongst the very people in question — the Mundas or Mundaris—"the grove deities are held responsible for the crops."[2] Therefore, when at the season for planting out the rice the Mundas bring in a tree and treat it with so much respect, their object can only be to foster thereby the growth of the rice which is about to be planted out; and the custom of causing barley blades to sprout rapidly and then presenting them to the tree must be intended to subserve the same purpose, perhaps by reminding the tree-spirit of his duty towards the crops, and stimulating his activity by this visible example of rapid vegetable growth. The throwing of the Karma-tree into the water is to be interpreted as a rain-

---

[1] E. T. Dalton, *Descriptive Ethnology of Bengal* (Calcutta, 1872), p. 259.
[2] E. T. Dalton, *op. cit.* p. 188.

As to the influence which trees are supposed to exercise on the crops, see *The Magic Art and the Evolution of Kings*, ii. 47 *sqq.*

charm. Whether the barley blades are also thrown into the
water is not said ; but if my interpretation of the custom
is right, probably they are so.   A distinction between this
Bengal custom and the Greek rites of Adonis is that in the
former the tree-spirit appears in his original form as a tree ;
whereas in the Adonis worship he appears in human form,
represented as a dead man, though his vegetable nature is
indicated by the gardens of Adonis, which are, so to say, a
secondary manifestation of his original power as a tree-spirit.

Gardens of Adonis are cultivated also by the Hindoos, Gardens of
Adonis in
Rajputana.
with the intention apparently of ensuring the fertility both
of the earth and of mankind.   Thus at Oodeypoor in
Rajputana a festival is held " in honour of Gouri, or Isani,
the goddess of abundance, the Isis of Egypt, the Ceres of
Greece.   Like the Rajpoot Saturnalia, which it follows, it
belongs to the vernal equinox, when nature in these regions
proximate to the tropic is in the full expanse of her charms,
and the matronly Gouri casts her golden mantle over the
verdant Vassanti, personification of spring.   Then the fruits
exhibit their promise to the eye ; the kohil fills the ear with
melody ; the air is impregnated with aroma, and the crimson
poppy contrasts with the spikes of golden grain to form a
wreath for the beneficent Gouri.   Gouri is one of the names
of Isa or Parvati, wife of the greatest of the gods, Mahadeva
or Iswara, who is conjoined with her in these rites, which
almost exclusively appertain to the women.   The meaning
of *gouri* is ' yellow,' emblematic of the ripened harvest, when
the votaries of the goddess adore her effigies, which are
those of a matron painted the colour of ripe corn."   The
rites begin when the sun enters the sign of the Ram, the
opening of the Hindoo year.   An image of the goddess
Gouri is made of earth, and a smaller one of her husband
Iswara, and the two are placed together.   A small trench
is next dug, barley is sown in it, and the ground watered
and heated artificially till the grain sprouts, when the women
dance round it hand in hand, invoking the blessing of Gouri
on their husbands.   After that the young corn is taken up
and distributed by the women to the men, who wear it in
their turbans.   Every wealthy family, or at least every sub-
division of the city, has its own image.   These and other

rites, known only to the initiated, occupy several days, and are performed within doors.   Then the images of the goddess and her husband are decorated and borne in procession to a beautiful lake, whose deep blue waters mirror the cloudless Indian sky, marble palaces, and orange groves. Here the women, their hair decked with roses and jessamine, carry the image of Gouri down a marble staircase to the water's edge, and dance round it singing hymns and love-songs.   Meantime the goddess is supposed to bathe in the water.   No men take part in the ceremony ; even the image of Iswara, the husband-god, attracts little attention.[1] In these rites the distribution of the barley shoots to the men, and the invocation of a blessing on their husbands by the wives, point clearly to the desire of offspring as one motive for observing the custom.   The same motive probably explains the use of gardens of Adonis at the marriage of Brahmans in the Madras Presidency.   Seeds of five or nine sorts are mixed and sown in earthen pots, which are made specially for the purpose and are filled with earth. Bride and bridegroom water the seeds both morning and evening for four days ; and on the fifth day the seedlings are thrown, like the real gardens of Adonis, into a tank or river.[2]

Gardens of Adonis in North-Western and Central India.

In the Himalayan districts of North-Western India the cultivators sow barley, maize, pulse, or mustard in a basket of earth on the twenty-fourth day of the fourth month (*Asárh*), which falls about the middle of July.   Then on the last day of the month they place amidst the new sprouts small clay images of Mahadeo and Parvati and worship them in remembrance of the marriage of those deities. Next day they cut down the green stalks and wear them in their head-dress.[3]   Similar is the barley feast known as Jâyî or Jawâra in Upper India and as Bhujariya in the Central Provinces.   On the seventh day of the light half of the month Sâwan grains of barley are sown in a pot of manure, and spring up so quickly that by the end of the

[1] Lieut.-Col. James Tod, *Annals and Antiquities of Rajast'han*, i. (London, 1829) pp. 570-572.

[2] G. F. D'Penha, "A Collection of Notes on Marriage Customs in the Madras Presidency," *Indian Anti-*

quary, xxv. (1896) p. 144 ; E. Thurston, *Ethnographic Notes in Southern India* (Madras, 1906), p. 2.

[3] E. T. Atkinson, *The Himalayan Districts of the North-Western Provinces of India*, ii. (Allahabad, 1884) p. 870.

month the vessel is full of long, yellowish-green stalks. On the first day of the next month, Bhâdon, the women and girls take the stalks out, throw the earth and manure into water, and distribute the plants among their male friends, who bind them in their turbans and about their dress.[1] At Sargal in the Central Provinces of India this ceremony is observed about the middle of September. None but women may take part in it, though crowds of men come to look on. Some little time before the festival wheat or other grain has been sown in pots ingeniously constructed of large leaves, which are held together by the thorns of a species of acacia. Having grown up in the dark, the stalks are of a pale colour. On the day appointed these gardens of Adonis, as we may call them, are carried towards a lake which abuts on the native city. The women of every family or circle of friends bring their own pots, and having laid them on the ground they dance round them. Then taking the pots of sprouting corn they descend to the edge of the water, wash the soil away from the pots, and distribute the young plants among their friends.[2] At the temple of the goddess Padma-vati, near Pandharpur in the Bombay Presidency, a Nine Nights' festival is held in the bright half of the month Ashvin (September–October). At this time a bamboo frame is hung in front of the image, and from it depend garlands of flowers and strings of wheaten cakes. Under the frame the floor in front of the pedestal is strewn with a layer of earth in which wheat is sown and allowed to sprout.[3] A similar rite is observed in the same month before the images of two other goddesses, Ambabai and Lakhubai, who also have temples at Pandharpur.[4]

[1] W. Crooke, *Popular Religion and Folk-lore of Northern India* (Westminster, 1896), ii. 293 *sq.* Compare Baboo Ishuree Dass, *Domestic Manners and Customs of the Hindoos of Northern India* (Benares, 1860), pp. 111 *sq.* According to the latter writer, the festival of Salono [not Salonan] takes place in August, and the barley is planted by women and girls in baskets a few days before the festival, to be thrown by them into a river or tank when the grain has sprouted to the height of a few inches.

[2] Mrs. J. C. Murray-Aynsley, "Secular and Religious Dances," *Folklore Journal*, v. (1887) pp. 253 *sq.* The writer thinks that the ceremony "probably fixes the season for sowing some particular crop."

[3] *Gazetteer of the Bombay Presidency*, xx. (Bombay, 1884) p. 454. This passage was pointed out to me by my friend Mr. W. Crooke.

[4] *Gazetteer of the Bombay Presidency*, xx. 443, 460.

Gardens of
Adonis in
Bavaria.   In some parts of Bavaria it is customary to sow flax
in a pot on the last three days of the Carnival; from the
seed which grows best an omen is drawn as to whether the
early, the middle, or the late sowing will produce the best

Gardens of
Adonis on
St. John's
Day in
Sardinia.
crop.[1] In Sardinia the gardens of Adonis are still planted
in connexion with the great Midsummer festival which bears
the name of St. John. At the end of March or on the first
of April a young man of the village presents himself to a girl,
and asks her to be his *comare* (gossip or sweetheart), offering
to be her *compare*. The invitation is considered as an honour
by the girl's family, and is gladly accepted. At the end of
May the girl makes a pot of the bark of the cork-tree, fills
it with earth, and sows a handful of wheat and barley in it.
The pot being placed in the sun and often watered, the corn
sprouts rapidly and has a good head by Midsummer Eve
(St. John's Eve, the twenty-third of June). The pot is then
called *Erme* or *Nenneri*. On St. John's Day the young man
and the girl, dressed in their best, accompanied by a long
retinue and preceded by children gambolling and frolicking,
move in procession to a church outside the village. Here
they break the pot by throwing it against the door of the
church. Then they sit down in a ring on the grass and eat
eggs and herbs to the music of flutes. Wine is mixed in a
cup and passed round, each one drinking as it passes.
Then they join hands and sing " Sweethearts of St. John "
(*Compare e comare di San Giovanni*) over and over again,
the flutes playing the while. When they tire of singing
they stand up and dance gaily in a ring till evening. This
is the general Sardinian custom. As practised at Ozieri it
has some special features. In May the pots are made of
cork - bark and planted with corn, as already described.
Then on the Eve of St. John the window-sills are draped
with rich cloths, on which the pots are placed, adorned with
crimson and blue silk and ribbons of various colours. On
each of the pots they used formerly to place a statuette or
cloth doll dressed as a woman, or a Priapus-like figure made
of paste ; but this custom, rigorously forbidden by the
Church, has fallen into disuse. The village swains go about

---

[1] *Bavaria, Landes- und Volkskunde des Königreichs Bayern* (Munich, 1860-
1867), ii. 298.

in a troop to look at the pots and their decorations and to wait for the girls, who assemble on the public square to celebrate the festival. Here a great bonfire is kindled, round which they dance and make merry. Those who wish to be " Sweethearts of St. John " act as follows. The young man stands on one side of the bonfire and the girl on the other, and they, in a manner, join hands by each grasping one end of a long stick, which they pass three times backwards and forwards across the fire, thus thrusting their hands thrice rapidly into the flames. This seals their relationship to each other. Dancing and music go on till late at night.[1] The correspondence of these Sardinian pots of grain to the gardens of Adonis seems complete, and the images formerly placed in them answer to the images of Adonis which accompanied his gardens.

Customs of the same sort are observed at the same season in Sicily. Pairs of boys and girls become gossips of St. John on St. John's Day by drawing each a hair from his or her head and performing various ceremonies over them. Thus they tie the hairs together and throw them up in the air, or exchange them over a potsherd, which they afterwards break in two, preserving each a fragment with pious care. The tie formed in the latter way is supposed to last for life. In some parts of Sicily the gossips of St. John present each other with plates of sprouting corn, lentils, and canary seed, which have been planted forty days before the festival. The one who receives the plate pulls a stalk of the young plants, binds it with a ribbon, and preserves it among his or her greatest treasures, restoring the platter to the giver. At Catania the gossips exchange pots of basil and great cucumbers ; the girls tend the basil, and the thicker it grows the more it is prized.[2]

Gardens of Adonis on St. John's Day in Sicily.

---

[1] Antonio Bresciani, *Dei costumi dell' isola di Sardegna comparati cogli antichissimi popoli orientali* (Rome and Turin, 1866), pp. 427 *sq.* ; R. Tennant, *Sardinia and its Resources* (Rome and London, 1885), p. 187 ; S. Gabriele, " Usi dei contadini della Sardegna," *Archivio per lo Studio delle Tradizioni Popolari*, vii. (1888) pp. 469 *sq.* Tennant says that the pots are kept in a dark warm place, and that the children leap across the fire.

[2] G. Pitrè, *Usi e Costumi, Credenze e Pregiudizi del Popolo Siciliano* (Palermo, 1889), ii. 271-278. Compare *id., Spettacoli e Feste Popolari Siciliane* (Palermo, 1881), pp. 297 *sq.* In the Abruzzi also young men and young women become gossips by exchanging nosegays on St. John's Day,

In these
Sardinian
and Sicilian
ceremonies
St. John
may have
taken the
place of
Adonis.
In these midsummer customs of Sardinia and Sicily it is possible that, as Mr. R. Wünsch supposes,[1] St. John has replaced Adonis. We have seen that the rites of Tammuz or Adonis were commonly celebrated about midsummer; according to Jerome, their date was June.[2] And besides their date and their similarity in respect of the pots of herbs and corn, there is another point of affinity between the two festivals, the heathen and the Christian. In both of them water plays a prominent part. At his midsummer festival in Babylon the image of Tammuz, whose name is said to mean " true son of the deep water," was bathed with pure water: at his summer festival in Alexandria the image of Adonis, with that of his divine mistress Aphrodite, was committed to the waves; and at the midsummer celebration in Greece the gardens of Adonis were thrown into the sea or into springs. Now a great feature of the midsummer festival associated with the name of St. John is, or used to be, the custom of bathing in the sea, springs, rivers, or the dew on Midsummer Eve or the morning of Midsummer Day. Thus, for example, at Naples there is a church dedicated to St. John the Baptist under the name of St. John of the Sea (S. *Giovan a mare*); and it was an old practice for men and women to bathe in the sea on St. John's Eve, that is, on Midsummer Eve, believing that thus all their sins were washed away.[3] In the Abruzzi water is still supposed to acquire certain marvellous and beneficent properties on St. John's Night. They say that on that night the sun and moon bathe in the water. Hence many people take a bath in the sea or in a river at that season, especially at the moment of sunrise. At Castiglione a Casauria they go before sunrise to the Pescara River or to springs, wash their faces and hands, then gird themselves with twigs of bryony (*vitalba*) and twine the plant round their brows, in order that they may be free from pains. At Pescina boys and girls wash each other's faces in a river or a spring, then exchange kisses, and become gossips. The dew, also, that

Custom of
bathing in
water or
washing in
dew on
the Eve or
Day of St.
John (Mid-
summer
Eve or Mid-
summer
Day).

and the tie thus formed is regarded as sacred. See G. Finamore, *Credenze, Usi e Costumi Abruzzesi* (Palermo, 1890), pp. 165 *sq.*

[1] R. Wünsch, *Das Frühlingsfest*

der Insel Malta, pp. 47-57.

[2] See above, pp. 10, note [1], 224 *sq.*, 226.

[3] J. Grimm, *Deutsche Mythologie*,[4] i. 490.

falls on St. John's Night is supposed in the Abruzzi to benefit whatever it touches, whether it be water, flowers, or the human body. For that reason people put out vessels of water on the window-sills or the terraces, and wash themselves with the water in the morning in order to purify themselves and escape headaches and colds. A still more efficacious mode of accomplishing the same end is to rise at the peep of dawn, to wet the hands in the dewy grass, and then to rub the moisture on the eyelids, the brow, and the temples, because the dew is believed to cure maladies of the head and eyes. It is also a remedy for diseases of the skin. Persons who are thus afflicted should roll on the dewy grass. When patients are prevented by their infirmity or any other cause from quitting the house, their friends will gather the dew in sheets or tablecloths and so apply it to the suffering part.[1] At Marsala in Sicily there is a spring of water in a subterranean grotto called the Grotto of the Sibyl. Beside it stands a church of St. John, which has been supposed to occupy the site of a temple of Apollo. On St. John's Eve, the twenty-third of June, women and girls visit the grotto, and by drinking of the prophetic water learn whether their husbands have been faithful to them in the year that is past, or whether they themselves will wed in the year that is to come. Sick people, too, imagine that by bathing in the water, drinking of it, or ducking thrice in it in the name of the Trinity, they will be made whole.[2] At Chiaramonte in Sicily the following custom is observed on St. John's Eve. The men repair to one fountain and the women to another, and dip their heads thrice in the water, repeating at each ablution certain verses in honour of St. John. They believe that this is a cure or preventive of the scald.[3] When Petrarch visited Cologne, he chanced to

---

[1] G. Finamore, *Credenze, Usi e Costumi Abruzzesi*, pp. 156-160. A passage in Isaiah (xxvi. 19) seems to imply that dew possessed the magical virtue of restoring the dead to life. In this passage of Isaiah the customs which I have cited in the text perhaps favour the ordinary interpretation of טַל אֹורֹת as "dew of herbs" (compare 2 Kings iv. 39) against the interpretation "dew of lights," which some modern commentators (Dillmann, Skinner, Whitehouse), following Jerome, have adopted.

[2] G. Pitrè, *Feste patronali in Sicilia* (Turin and Palermo, 1900), pp. 488, 491-493.

[3] G. Pitrè, *Spettacoli e Feste Popolari Siciliane*, p. 307.

arrive in the town on St. John's Eve. The sun was nearly setting, and his host at once led him to the Rhine. A strange sight there met his eyes, for the banks of the river were covered with pretty women. The crowd was great but good-humoured. From a rising ground on which he stood the poet saw many of the women, girt with fragrant herbs, kneel down on the water's edge, roll their sleeves up above their elbows, and wash their white arms and hands in the river, murmuring softly some words which the Italian did not understand. He was told that the custom was a very old one, much honoured in the observance ; for the common folk, especially the women, believed that to wash in the river on St. John's Eve would avert every misfortune in the coming year.[1] On St. John's Eve the people of Copenhagen used to go on pilgrimage to a neighbouring spring, there to heal and strengthen themselves in the water.[2] In Spain people still bathe in the sea or roll naked in the dew of the meadows on St. John's Eve, believing that this is a sovereign preservative against diseases of the skin.[3] To roll in the dew on the morning of St. John's Day is also esteemed a cure for diseases of the skin in Normandy and Perigord. In Perigord a field of hemp is especially recommended for the purpose, and the patient should rub himself with the plants on which he has rolled.[4] At Ciotat in Provence, while the midsummer bonfire blazed, young people used to plunge into the sea and splash each other vigorously. At Vitrolles they bathed in a pond in order that they might not suffer from fever during the year, and at Saint-Maries they watered the horses to protect them from the itch.[5] A custom of drenching people on this occasion with water formerly prevailed in Toulon, Marseilles, and other towns of the south of France. The water was squirted from syringes, poured on the heads of passers-by from windows, and so

[1] Petrarch, *Epistolae de rebus familiaribus*, i. 4 (vol. i. pp. 44-46 ed. J. Fracassetti, Florence, 1859-1862). The passage is quoted by J. Grimm, *Deutsche Mythologie*,[4] i. 489 *sq.*

[2] J. Grimm, *op. cit.* i. 489.

[3] Letter of Dr. Otero Acevado, of Madrid, *Le Temps*, September 1898.

[4] J. Lecœur, *Esquisses du Bocage Normand* (Condé-sur-Noireau, 1883-1887), ii. 8 ; A. de Nore, *Coutumes, Mythes et Traditions des provinces de France* (Paris and Lyons, 1846), p. 150.

[5] A. de Nore, *op. cit.* p. 20 ; Bérenger-Féraud, *Réminiscences populaires de la Provence* (Paris, 1885), pp. 135-141.

forth.[1]   From Europe the practice of bathing in rivers and springs on St. John's Day appears to have passed with the Spaniards to the New World.[2]

It may perhaps be suggested that this wide-spread custom of bathing in water or dew on Midsummer Eve or Midsummer Day is purely Christian in origin, having been adopted as an appropriate mode of celebrating the day dedicated to the Baptist.   But in point of fact the custom is older than Christianity, for it was denounced and forbidden as a heathen practice by Augustine,[3] and to this day it is practised at midsummer by the Mohammedan peoples of North Africa.[4]   We may conjecture that the Church, unable to put down this relic of paganism, followed its usual policy of accommodation by bestowing on the rite of a Christian name and acquiescing, with a sigh, in its observance.   And casting about for a saint to supplant a heathen patron of bathing, the Christian doctors could hardly have hit upon a more appropriate successor than St. John the Baptist.

The custom of bathing at midsummer is pagan, not Christian, in its origin.

But into whose shoes did the Baptist step?   Was the displaced deity really Adonis, as the foregoing evidence seems to suggest?   In Sardinia and Sicily it may have been so, for in these islands Semitic influence was certainly deep and probably lasting.   The midsummer pastimes of Sardinian and Sicilian children may therefore be a direct continuation of the Carthaginian rites of Tammuz.   Yet the midsummer festival seems too widely spread and too deeply rooted in Central and Northern Europe to allow us to trace it everywhere to an Oriental origin in general and to the cult of Adonis in particular.   It has the air of a native of the soil rather than of an exotic imported from the East.   We shall

Old heathen festival of midsummer in Europe and the East.

[1] A. Breuil, "Du Culte de St. Jean Baptiste," *Mémoires de la Société des Antiquaires de Picardie*, viii. (1845) pp. 237 *sq.* Compare *Balder the Beautiful*, i. 193 *sq.*

[2] Diego Duran, *Historia de las Indias de Nueva España*, edited by J. F. Ramirez (Mexico, 1867-1880), ii. 293.

[3] Augustine, *Opera*, v. (Paris, 1683) col. 903 ; *id.*, Pars Secunda, coll. 461 *sq.* The second of these passages occurs in a sermon of doubtful authen-

ticity. Both have been quoted by J. Grimm, *Deutsche Mythologie*,[4] i. 490.

[4] E. Doutté, *Magie et Religion dans l'Afrique du Nord* (Algiers, 1908), pp. 567 *sq.* ; E. Westermarck, "Midsummer Customs in Morocco," *Folklore*, xvi. (1905) pp. 31 *sq.* ; *id.*, *Ceremonies and Beliefs connected with Agriculture, Certain Dates of the Solar Year, and the Weather* (Helsingfors, 1913), pp. 84-86. See *Balder the Beautiful*, i. 216.

do better, therefore, to suppose that at a remote period similar modes of thought, based on similar needs, led men independently in many distant lands, from the North Sea to the Euphrates, to celebrate the summer solstice with rites which, while they differed in some things, yet agreed closely in others ; that in historical times a wave of Oriental influence, starting perhaps from Babylonia, carried the Tammuz or Adonis form of the festival westward till it met with native forms of a similar festival ; and that under pressure of the Roman civilization these different yet kindred festivals fused with each other and crystallized into a variety of shapes, which subsisted more or less separately side by side, till the Church, unable to suppress them altogether, stripped them so far as it could of their grosser features, and dexterously changing the names allowed them to pass muster as Christian.   And what has just been said of the midsummer festivals probably applies, with the necessary modifications, to the spring festivals also.   They, too, seem to have originated independently in Europe and the East, and after ages of separation to have amalgamated under the sway of the Roman Empire and the Christian Church. In Syria, as we have seen, there appears to have been a vernal celebration of Adonis ; and we shall presently meet with an undoubted instance of an Oriental festival of spring in the rites of Attis.   Meantime we must return for a little to the midsummer festival which goes by the name of St. John.

Mid-
summer
fires and
mid-
summer
couples in
relation to
vegetation   The Sardinian practice of making merry round a great bonfire on St. John's Eve is an instance of a custom which has been practised at the midsummer festival from time immemorial in many parts of Europe.   That custom has been more fully dealt with by me elsewhere.[1]   The instances which I have cited in other parts of this work seem to indicate a connexion of the midsummer bonfire with vegetation.   For example, both in Sweden and Bohemia an essential part of the festival is the raising of a May-pole or Midsummer-tree, which in Bohemia is burned in the bonfire.[2]   Again, in a Russian midsummer ceremony a straw figure of Kupalo,

---

[1] *Balder the Beautiful*, i. 160 *sqq.*
[2] *The Magic Art and the Evolution of Kings*, ii. 65 *sq.*

the representative of vegetation, is placed beside a May-pole or Midsummer-tree and then carried to and fro across a bonfire.[1] Kupalo is here represented in duplicate, in tree-form by the Midsummer-tree, and in human form by the straw effigy, just as Adonis was represented both by an image and a garden of Adonis; and the duplicate representatives of Kupalo, like those of Adonis, are finally cast into water. In the Sardinian and Sicilian customs the Gossips or Sweethearts of St. John probably answer, on the one hand to Adonis and Astarte, on the other to the King and Queen of May. In the Swedish province of Blekinge part of the midsummer festival is the election of a Midsummer Bride, who chooses her bridegroom; a collection is made for the pair, who for the time being are looked upon as man and wife.[2] Such Midsummer pairs may be supposed, like the May pairs, to stand for the powers of vegetation or of fertility in general: they represent in flesh and blood what the images of Siva or Mahadeo and Parvati in the Indian ceremonies, and the images of Adonis and Aphrodite in the Alexandrian ceremony, set forth in effigy.

The reason why ceremonies whose aim is to foster the growth of vegetation should thus be associated with bonfires; why in particular the representative of vegetation should be burned in the likeness of a tree, or passed across the fire in effigy or in the form of a living couple, has been discussed by me elsewhere.[3] Here it is enough to have adduced evidence of such association, and therefore to have obviated the objection which might have been raised to my theory of the Sardinian custom, on the ground that the bonfires have nothing to do with vegetation. One more piece of evidence may here be given to prove the contrary. In some parts of Germany and Austria young men and girls leap over midsummer bonfires for the express purpose of making the hemp or flax grow tall.[4] We may, therefore, assume that in the Sardinian custom the blades of wheat and barley which are

Gardens of Adonis intended to foster the growth of vegetation, and especially of the crops.

---

[1] *The Dying God*, p. 262.

[2] L. Lloyd, *Peasant Life in Sweden* (London, 1870), p. 257.

[3] *Balder the Beautiful*, i. 328 *sqq.*, ii. 21 *sqq.*

[4] W. Mannhardt, *Baumkultus*, p. 464; K. von Leoprechting, *Aus dem Lechrain* (Munich, 1855), p. 183. For more evidence see *Balder the Beautiful*, i. 165, 166, 166 *sq.*, 168, 173, 174.

forced on in pots for the midsummer festival, and which correspond so closely to the gardens of Adonis, form one of those widely-spread midsummer ceremonies, the original object of which was to promote the growth of vegetation, and especially of the crops. But as, by an easy extension of ideas, the spirit of vegetation was believed to exercise a beneficent and fertilizing influence on human as well as animal life, the gardens of Adonis would be supposed, like the May-trees or May-boughs, to bring good luck, and more particularly perhaps offspring,[1] to the family or to the person who planted them ; and even after the idea had been abandoned that they operated actively to confer prosperity, they might still be used to furnish omens of good or evil. It is thus that magic dwindles into divination. Accordingly we find modes of divination practised at midsummer which resemble more or less closely the gardens of Adonis. Thus an anonymous Italian writer of the sixteenth century has recorded that it was customary to sow barley and wheat a few days before the festival of St. John (Midsummer Day) and also before that of St. Vitus ; and it was believed that the person for whom they were sown would be fortunate, and get a good husband or a good wife, if the grain sprouted well ; but if it sprouted ill, he or she would be unlucky.[2] In various parts of Italy and all over Sicily it is still customary to put plants in water or in earth on the Eve of St. John, and from the manner in which they are found to be blooming or fading on St. John's Day omens are drawn, especially as to fortune in love. Amongst the plants used for this purpose are *Ciuri di S. Giuvanni* (St. John's wort ?) and nettles.[3] In Prussia two hundred years ago the farmers used to send out their servants, especially their maids, to gather St. John's

Modes of divination at midsummer like the gardens of Adonis.

---

[1] The use of gardens of Adonis to fertilize the human sexes appears plainly in the corresponding Indian practices. See above, pp. 241, 242, 243.

[2] G. Pitrè, *Spettacoli e Feste Popolari Siciliane*, pp. 296 *sq.*

[3] G. Pitrè, *op. cit.* pp. 302 *sq.* ; Antonio de Nino, *Usi e Costumi Abruzzesi* (Florence, 1879–1883), i. 55 *sq.* ; A. de Gubernatis, *Usi Nuziali in Italia e presso gli altri Popoli Indo-Europei* (Milan, 1878), pp. 39 *sq.* Compare

L. Passarini, "Il Comparatico e la Festa di S. Giovanni nelle Marche e in Roma," *Archivio per lo Studio delle Tradizioni Popolari*, i. (1882) p. 135. At Smyrna a blossom of the *Agnus castus* is used on St. John's Day for a similar purpose, but the mode in which the omens are drawn is somewhat different. See Teofilo, "La notte di San Giovanni in Oriente," *Archivio per lo Studio delle Tradizioni Popolari*, vii. (1888) pp. 128-130.

wort on Midsummer Eve or Midsummer Day (St. John's Day). When they had fetched it, the farmer took as many plants as there were persons and stuck them in the wall or between the beams; and it was thought that he or she whose plant did not bloom would soon fall sick or die. The rest of the plants were tied in a bundle, fastened to the end of a pole, and set up at the gate or wherever the corn would be brought in at the next harvest. The bundle was called *Kupole*: the ceremony was known as Kupole's festival; and at it the farmer prayed for a good crop of hay, and so forth.[1] This Prussian custom is particularly notable, inasmuch as it strongly confirms the opinion that Kupalo (doubtless identical with Kupole) was originally a deity of vegetation.[2] For here Kupalo is represented by a bundle of plants specially associated with midsummer in folk-custom; and her influence over vegetation is plainly signified by placing her vegetable emblem over the place where the harvest is brought in, as well as by the prayers for a good crop which are uttered on the occasion. This furnishes a fresh argument in support of the view that the Death, whose analogy to Kupalo, Yarilo, and the rest I have shown elsewhere, originally personified vegetation, more especially the dying or dead vegetation of winter.[3] Further, my interpretation of the gardens of Adonis is confirmed by finding that in this Prussian custom the very same kind of plants is used to form the gardens of Adonis (as we may call them) and the image of the deity. Nothing could set in a stronger light the truth of the theory that the gardens of Adonis are merely another manifestation of the god himself.

In Sicily gardens of Adonis are still sown in spring as well as in summer, from which we may perhaps infer that Sicily as well as Syria celebrated of old a vernal festival of the dead and risen god. At the approach of Easter, Sicilian women sow wheat, lentils, and canary-seed in plates, which they keep in the dark and water every two days. The plants soon shoot up; the stalks are tied together with red ribbons, and the plates containing them are placed on

Sicilian gardens of Adonis in spring.

---

[1] Matthäus Prätorius, *Deliciae Prus-sicae* (Berlin, 1871), p. 56.

[2] *The Dying God*, pp. 261 *sq.*

[3] *The Dying God*, pp. 233 *sqq.*, 261 *sqq.*

the sepulchres which, with the effigies of the dead Christ, are made up in Catholic and Greek churches on Good Friday,[1] just as the gardens of Adonis were placed on the grave of the dead Adonis.[2] The practice is not confined to Sicily, for it is observed also at Cosenza in Calabria,[3] and perhaps in other places. The whole custom—sepulchres as well as plates of sprouting grain—may be nothing but a continuation, under a different name, of the worship of Adonis.

Resemblance of the Easter ceremonies in the Greek Church to the rites of Adonis. Nor are these Sicilian and Calabrian customs the only Easter ceremonies which resemble the rites of Adonis. "During the whole of Good Friday a waxen effigy of the dead Christ is exposed to view in the middle of the Greek churches and is covered with fervent kisses by the thronging crowd, while the whole church rings with melancholy, monotonous dirges. Late in the evening, when it has grown quite dark, this waxen image is carried by the priests into the street on a bier adorned with lemons, roses, jessamine, and other flowers, and there begins a grand procession of the multitude, who move in serried ranks, with slow and solemn step, through the whole town. Every man carries his taper and breaks out into doleful lamentation. At all the houses which the procession passes there are seated women with censers to fumigate the marching host. Thus the community solemnly buries its Christ as if he had just died. At last the waxen image is again deposited in the church, and the same lugubrious chants echo anew. These lamentations, accompanied by a strict fast, continue till midnight on Saturday. As the clock strikes twelve, the bishop appears and announces the glad tidings that 'Christ is risen,' to which the crowd replies, 'He is risen indeed,' and at once the whole city bursts into an uproar of joy, which finds vent in shrieks and shouts, in the endless discharge of carronades and muskets, and the explosion of fire-works of every sort. In the very same hour people plunge from the extremity of the fast into the enjoyment of the Easter lamb and neat wine."[4]

[1] G. Pitrè, *Spettacoli e Feste Popolari Siciliane*, p. 211.

[2] Κήπους ὡσίουν ἐπιταφίους Ἀδώνιδι, Eustathius on Homer, *Od.* xi. 590.

[3] Vincenzo Dorsa, *La tradizione Greco-Latina negli usi e nelle credenze popolari della Calabria Citeriore* (Cosenza, 1884), p. 50.

[4] C. Wachsmuth, *Das alte Griechenland im neuem* (Bonn, 1864), pp. 26

In like manner the Catholic Church has been accustomed to bring before its followers in a visible form the death and resurrection of the Redeemer. Such sacred dramas are well fitted to impress the lively imagination and to stir the warm feelings of a susceptible southern race, to whom the pomp and pageantry of Catholicism are more congenial than to the colder temperament of the Teutonic peoples. The solemnities observed in Sicily on Good Friday, the official anniversary of the Crucifixion, are thus described by a native Sicilian writer. "A truly moving ceremony is the procession which always takes place in the evening in every commune of Sicily, and further the Deposition from the Cross. The brotherhoods took part in the procession, and the rear was brought up by a great many boys and girls representing saints, both male and female, and carrying the emblems of Christ's Passion. The Deposition from the Cross was managed by the priests. The coffin with the dead Christ in it was flanked by Jews armed with swords, an object of horror and aversion in the midst of the profound pity excited by the sight not only of Christ but of the Mater Dolorosa, who followed behind him. Now and then the ' mysteries ' or symbols of the Crucifixion went in front. Sometimes the procession followed the 'three hours of agony' and the 'Deposition from the Cross.' The 'three hours' commemorated those which Jesus Christ passed upon the Cross. Beginning at the eighteenth and ending at the twenty - first hour of Italian time two priests preached alternately on the Passion. Anciently the sermons were delivered in the open air on the place called the Calvary : at last, when the third hour was about to strike, at the words

---

sq. The writer compares these ceremonies with the Eleusinian rites. But I agree with Mr. R. Wünsch (*Das Frühlingsfest der Insel Malta*, pp. 49 *sq.*) that the resemblance to the Adonis festival is still closer. Compare V. Dorsa, *La tradizione Greco - Latina negli usi e nelle credenze popolari della Calabria Citeriore*, pp. 49 *sq.* Prof. Wachsmuth's description seems to apply to Athens. In the country districts the ritual is apparently similar.

See R. A. Arnold, *From the Levant* (London, 1868), pp. 251 *sq.*, 259 *sq.* So in the Church of the Holy Sepulchre at Jerusalem the death and burial of Christ are acted over a life-like effigy. See Henry Maundrell, *Journey from Aleppo to Jerusalem at Easter*, A.D. *1697*, Fourth Edition (Perth, 1800), pp. 110 *sqq.* ; *id.*, in Th. Wright's *Early Travels in Palestine* (London, 1848), pp. 443-445.

emisit spiritum Christ died, bowing his head amid the sobs and tears of the bystanders. Immediately afterwards in some places, three hours afterwards in others, the sacred body was unnailed and deposited in the coffin. In Castronuovo, at the Ave Maria, two priests clad as Jews, representing Joseph of Arimathea and Nicodemus, with their servants in costume, repaired to the Calvary, preceded by the Company of the Whites. There, with doleful verses and chants appropriate to the occasion, they performed the various operations of the Deposition, after which the procession took its way to the larger church. . . . In Salaparuta the Calvary is erected in the church. At the preaching of the death, the Crucified is made to bow his head by means of machinery, while guns are fired, trumpets sound, and amid the silence of the people, impressed by the death of the Redeemer, the strains of a melancholy funeral march are heard. Christ is removed from the Cross and deposited in the coffin by three priests. After the procession of the dead Christ the burial is performed, that is, two priests lay Christ in a fictitious sepulchre, from which at the mass of Easter Saturday the image of the risen Christ issues and is elevated upon the altar by means of machinery."[1] Scenic representations of the same sort, with variations of detail, are exhibited at Easter in the Abruzzi,[2] and probably in many other parts of the Catholic world.[3]

The Christian festival of Easter perhaps grafted on a festival of Adonis.

When we reflect how often the Church has skilfully contrived to plant the seeds of the new faith on the old stock of paganism, we may surmise that the Easter celebration of the dead and risen Christ was grafted upon a similar celebration of the dead and risen Adonis, which, as we have seen reason to believe, was celebrated in Syria at the same season. The type, created by Greek artists, of the sorrowful goddess with her dying lover in her arms, resembles and may have

[1] G. Pitrè, *Spettacoli e Feste Popolari Siciliane*, pp. 217 *sq.*

[2] G. Finamore, *Credenze, Usi e Costumi Abruzzesi*, pp. 118-120; A. de Nino, *Usi e Costumi Abruzzesi*, i. 64 *sq.*, ii. 210-212. At Roccacaramanico part of the Easter spectacle is the death of Judas, who, personated by a living man, pretends to hang himself

upon a tree or a great branch, which has been brought into the church and planted near the high altar for the purpose (A. de Nino, *op. cit.* ii. 211).

[3] The drama of the death and resurrection of Christ was formerly celebrated at Easter in England. See Abbot Gasquet, *Parish Life in Mediaeval England*, pp. 177 *sqq.*, 182 *sq.*

been the model of the *Pietà* of Christian art, the Virgin with
the dead body of her divine Son in her lap, of which the
most celebrated example is the one by Michael Angelo in
St. Peter's.   That noble group, in which the living sorrow of
the mother contrasts so wonderfully with the languor of
death in the son, is one of the finest compositions in marble.
Ancient Greek art has bequeathed to us few works so
beautiful, and none so pathetic.[1]

In this connexion a well-known statement of Jerome
may not be without significance.   He tells us that Bethlehem, the traditionary birthplace of the Lord, was shaded
by a grove of that still older Syrian Lord, Adonis, and
that where the infant Jesus had wept, the lover of Venus
was bewailed.[2]   Though he does not expressly say so,
Jerome seems to have thought that the grove of Adonis
had been planted by the heathen after the birth of Christ
for the purpose of defiling the sacred spot.   In this
he may have been mistaken.   If Adonis was indeed,
as I have argued, the spirit of the corn, a more suitable
name for his dwelling-place could hardly be found than
Bethlehem, " the House of Bread," [3] and he may well have
been worshipped there at his House of Bread long ages
before the birth of Him who said, " I am the bread of life." [4]
Even on the hypothesis that Adonis followed rather than
preceded Christ at Bethlehem, the choice of his sad figure
to divert the allegiance of Christians from their Lord cannot
but strike us as eminently appropriate when we remember the
similarity of the rites which commemorated the death and
resurrection of the two.   One of the earliest seats of the
worship of the new god was Antioch, and at Antioch,

The worship of Adonis at Bethlehem.

---

[1] The comparison has already been
made by A. Maury, who also compares the Easter ceremonies of the
Catholic Church with the rites of
Adonis (*Histoire des Religions de la
Grèce Antique*, Paris, 1857-1859, vol.
iii. p. 221).

[2] Jerome, *Epist.* lviii. 3 (Migne's
Patrologia Latina, xxii. 581).

[3] Bethlehem is בֵּית־לֶחֶם, literally
" House of Bread."   The name is
appropriate, for " the immediate neighbourhood is very fertile, bearing, besides

wheat and barley, groves of olive and
almond, and vineyards.   The wine of
Bethlehem ('Talhamī') is among the
best of Palestine.   So great fertility
must mean that the site was occupied,
in spite of the want of springs, from the
earliest times " (George Adam Smith,
s.v. " Bethlehem," *Encyclopaedia
Biblica*, i. 560).   It was in the harvest-
fields of Bethlehem that Ruth, at least
in the poet's fancy, listened to the
nightingale " amid the alien corn."

[4] John vi. 35.

as we have seen,[1] the death of the old god was annually celebrated with great solemnity. A circumstance which attended the entrance of Julian into the city at the time of the Adonis festival may perhaps throw some light on the date of its celebration. When the emperor drew near to the city he was received with public prayers as if he had been a god, and he marvelled at the voices of a great multitude who cried that the Star of Salvation had dawned upon them in the East.[2] This may doubtless have been no more than a fulsome compliment paid by an obsequious Oriental crowd to the Roman emperor. But it is also possible that the rising of a bright star regularly gave the signal for the festival, and that as chance would have it the star emerged above the rim of the eastern horizon at the very moment of the emperor's approach. The coincidence, if it happened, could hardly fail to strike the imagination of a superstitious and excited multitude, who might thereupon hail the great man as the deity whose coming was announced by the sign in the heavens. Or the emperor may have mistaken for a greeting to himself the shouts which were addressed to the star. Now Astarte, the divine mistress of Adonis, was identified with the planet Venus, and her changes from a morning to an evening star were carefully noted by the Babylonian astronomers, who drew omens from her alternate appearance and disappearance.[3] Hence we may conjecture that the festival of Adonis was regularly timed to coincide with the appearance of Venus as

---

[1] Above, p. 227.

[2] Ammianus Marcellinus, xxii. 9. 14, "*Urbique propinquans in speciem alicujus numinis votis excipitur publicis, miratus voces multitudinis magnae, salutare sidus inluxisse eois partibus adclamantis.*" We may compare the greeting which a tribe of South American Indians used to give to a worshipful star after its temporary disappearance. "The Abipones think that the Pleiades, composed of seven stars, is an image of their ancestor. As the constellation is invisible for some months in the sky of South America, they believe that their ancestor is ill, and every year they are mortally afraid that he will die. But when the said

stars reappear in the month of May, they imagine that their ancestor is recovered from his sickness and has returned ; so they hail him with joyous shouts and the glad music of pipes and war-horns. They congratulate him on his recovery. 'How we thank you ! At last you have come back? Oh, have you happily recovered?' With such cries they fill the air, attesting at once their gladness and their folly." See M. Dobrizhoffer, *Historia de Abiponibus* (Vienna, 1784), ii. 77.

[3] M. Jastrow, *The Religion of Babylonia and Assyria*, pp. 370 *sqq.*; H. Zimmern, in E. Schrader's *Die Keilinschriften und das Alte Testament*,[3] p. 424.

the Morning or Evening Star. But the star which the people of Antioch saluted at the festival was seen in the East; therefore, if it was indeed Venus, it can only have been the Morning Star. At Aphaca in Syria, where there was a famous temple of Astarte, the signal for the celebration of the rites was apparently given by the flashing of a meteor, which on a certain day fell like a star from the top of Mount Lebanon into the river Adonis. The meteor was thought to be Astarte herself,[1] and its flight through the air might naturally be interpreted as the descent of the amorous goddess to the arms of her lover. At Antioch and elsewhere the appearance of the Morning Star on the day of the festival may in like manner have been hailed as the coming of the goddess of love to wake her dead leman from his earthy bed. If that were so, we may surmise that it was the Morning Star which guided the wise men of the East to Bethlehem,[2] the hallowed spot which heard, in the language of Jerome, the weeping of the infant Christ and the lament for Adonis.

The Star of Bethlehem.

[1] Sozomenus, *Historia Ecclesiastica*, ii. 5 (Migne's *Patrologia Graeca*, lxvii. 948). The connexion of the meteor with the festival of Adonis is not mentioned by Sozomenus, but is confirmed by Zosimus, who says (*Hist.* i. 58) that a light like a torch or a globe of fire was seen on the sanctuary at the seasons when the people assembled to worship the goddess and to cast their offerings of gold, silver, and fine raiment into a lake beside the temple. As to Aphaca and the grave of Adonis see above, pp. 28 *sq.*

[2] Matthew ii. 1-12.

BOOK SECOND

ATTIS

CHAPTER I

THE MYTH AND RITUAL OF ATTIS

ANOTHER of those gods whose supposed death and resurrec- Attis the
tion struck such deep roots into the faith and ritual of Phrygian
counter-
Western Asia is Attis. He was to Phrygia what Adonis part of
was to Syria. Like Adonis, he appears to have been a god Adonis.
of vegetation, and his death and resurrection were annually
mourned and rejoiced over at a festival in spring.[1] The
legends and rites of the two gods were so much alike that
the ancients themselves sometimes identified them.[2] Attis His
was said to have been a fair young shepherd or herdsman relation
to Cybele.
beloved by Cybele, the Mother of the Gods, a great
Asiatic goddess of fertility, who had her chief home in
Phrygia.[3] Some held that Attis was her son.[4] His birth, His
like that of many other heroes, is said to have been miraculous
birth.
miraculous. His mother, Nana, was a virgin, who conceived
by putting a ripe almond or a pomegranate in her bosom.
Indeed in the Phrygian cosmogony an almond figured

---

[1] Diodorus Siculus, iii. 59. 7 ; Sallustius philosophus, "De diis et mundo," iv., *Fragmenta Philosophorum Graecorum*, ed. F. G. A. Mullach, iii. 33 ; Scholiast on Nicander, *Alexipharmaca*, 8 ; Firmicus Maternus, *De errore profanarum religionum*, 3 and 22. The ancient evidence, literary and inscriptional, as to the myth and ritual of Attis has been collected and discussed by Mr. H. Hepding in his monograph, *Attis, seine Mythen und sein Kult* (Giessen, 1903).

[2] Hippolytus, *Refutatio omnium haeresium*, v. 9, p. 168 ed. L. Duncker and F. G. Schneidewin (Göttingen, 1859); Socrates, *Historia Ecclesiastica*,

iii. 23. 51 *sqq.*

[3] Ovid, *Fasti*, iv. 223 *sqq.*; Tertullian, *Apologeticus*, 15 ; *id.*, *Ad Nationes*, i. 10 ; Arnobius, *Adversus Nationes*, iv. 35. As to Cybele, the Great Mother, the Mother of the Gods, conceived as the source of all life, both animal and vegetable, see Rapp, in W. H. Roscher's *Lexikon der griech. und röm. Mythologie, s.v.* "Kybele," ii. 1638 *sqq.*

[4] Scholiast on Lucian, *Jupiter Tragoedus*, 8, p. 60 ed. H. Rabe (Leipsic, 1906), (vol. iv. p. 173 ed. C. Jacobitz) ; Hippolytus, *Refutatio omnium haeresium*, v. 9, pp. 168, 170 ed. Duncker and Schneidewin.

as the father of all things,[1] perhaps because its delicate lilac blossom is one of the first heralds of the spring, appearing on the bare boughs before the leaves have opened.   Such tales of virgin mothers are relics of an age of childish ignorance when men had not yet recognized the intercourse of the sexes as the true cause of offspring.   That ignorance, still shared by the lowest of existing savages, the aboriginal tribes of central Australia,[2] was doubtless at one time universal among mankind.   Even in later times, when people are better acquainted with the laws of nature, they sometimes imagine that these laws may be subject to exceptions, and that miraculous beings may be born in miraculous ways by women who have never known a man.   In Palestine to this day it is believed that a woman may conceive by a jinnee or by the spirit of her dead husband.   There is, or was lately, a man at Nebk who is currently supposed to be the offspring of such a union, and the simple folk have never suspected his mother's virtue.[3]   Two different accounts

The death of Attis.

of the death of Attis were current.   According to the one he was killed by a boar, like Adonis.   According to the other he unmanned himself under a pine - tree, and bled to death on the spot.   The latter is said to have been the local story told by the people of Pessinus, a great seat of the worship of Cybele, and the whole legend of which the story forms a part is stamped with a character of rudeness and savagery that speaks strongly for its antiquity.[4]   Both tales might claim the support of custom,

[1] Pausanias, vii. 17. 11; Hippolytus, *Refutatio omnium haeresium*, v. 9, pp. 166, 168 ed. Duncker and Schneidewin; Arnobius, *Adversus Nationes*, v. 6.

[2] See above, pp. 99 *sqq.*

[3] S. I. Curtiss, *Primitive Semitic Religion To-day*, pp. 115 *sq.* See above, pp. 78, 213 *sqq.*

[4] That Attis was killed by a boar was stated by Hermesianax, an elegiac poet of the fourth century B.C. (Pausanias, vii. 17); compare Scholiast on Nicander, *Alexipharmaca*, 8. The other story is told by Arnobius (*Adversus Nationes*, v. 5 *sqq.*) on the authority of Timotheus, who professed to derive it from recondite antiquarian

works and from the very heart of the mysteries.   It is obviously identical with the account which Pausanias (*l.c.*) mentions as the story current in Pessinus.   According to Servius (on Virgil, *Aen.* ix. 115), Attis was found bleeding to death under a pine-tree, but the wound which robbed him of his virility and his life was not inflicted by himself.   The Timotheus cited by Pausanias may be the Timotheus who was consulted by Ptolemy Soter on religious matters and helped to establish the worship of Serapis.   See Plutarch, *Isis et Osiris*, 28 ; Franz Cumont, *Les Religions Orientales dans le Paganisme Romain*[2] (Paris, 1909), pp. 77, 113, 335.

or rather both were probably invented to explain certain customs observed by the worshippers. The story of the self-mutilation of Attis is clearly an attempt to account for the self-mutilation of his priests, who regularly castrated themselves on entering the service of the goddess. The story of his death by the boar may have been told to explain why his worshippers, especially the people of Pessinus, abstained from eating swine.[1] In like manner the worshippers of Adonis abstained from pork, because a boar had killed their god.[2] After his death Attis is said to have been changed into a pine-tree.[3]

The worship of the Phrygian Mother of the Gods was adopted by the Romans in 204 B.C. towards the close of their long struggle with Hannibal. For their drooping spirits had been opportunely cheered by a prophecy, alleged to be drawn from that convenient farrago of nonsense, the Sibylline Books, that the foreign invader would be driven from Italy if the great Oriental goddess were brought to Rome. Accordingly ambassadors were despatched to her sacred city Pessinus in Phrygia. The small black stone which embodied the mighty divinity was entrusted to them and conveyed to Rome, where it was received with great respect and installed in the temple of Victory on the Palatine Hill. It was the middle of April when the goddess arrived,[4] and she went to work at once. For the harvest that year was such as had not been seen for many a long day,[5] and in the very next year Hannibal and his veterans embarked for Africa. As he looked his last on the coast of Italy, fading behind him in the distance, he could not foresee that Europe, which had repelled the arms, would yet yield to the gods, of the Orient. The vanguard of the conquerors had already encamped in

Worship of Cybele introduced into Rome in 204 B.C.

[1] Pausanias, vii. 17. 10; Julian, *Orat.* v. 177 B, p. 229 ed. F. C. Hertlein (Leipsic, 1875–1876). Similarly at Comana in Pontus, the seat of the worship of the goddess Ma, pork was not eaten, and swine might not even be brought into the city (Strabo, xii. 8. 9, p. 575). As to Comana see above, p. 39.

[2] S. Sophronius, "SS. Cyri et Joannis Miracula," Migne's *Patrologia Graeca*, lxxxvii. Pars Tertia, col. 3624,

πρὸς πλάνην Ἑλληνικὴν ἀποκλίνουσαν [*scil.* τὴν Ἰουλίαν] καὶ ταύτῃ διὰ τὸν Ἀδώνιδος θάνατον τὰ κρέα παραιτεῖσθαι τὰ ὕεια.

[3] Ovid, *Metam.* x. 103 *sqq.*

[4] Livy, xxix. chs. 10, 11, and 14; Ovid, *Fasti*, iv. 259 *sqq.*; Herodian, ii. 11. As to the stone which represented the goddess see Arnobius, *Adversus Nationes*, vii. 49.

[5] Pliny, *Nat. Hist.* xviii. 16.

the heart of Italy before the rearguard of the beaten army fell sullenly back from its shores.

Attis and his eunuch priests the Galli at Rome.

We may conjecture, though we are not told, that the Mother of the Gods brought with her the worship of her youthful lover or son to her new home in the West. Certainly the Romans were familiar with the Galli, the emasculated priests of Attis, before the close of the Republic. These unsexed beings, in their Oriental costume, with little images suspended on their breasts, appear to have been a familiar sight in the streets of Rome, which they traversed in procession, carrying the image of the goddess and chanting their hymns to the music of cymbals and tambourines, flutes and horns, while the people, impressed by the fantastic show and moved by the wild strains, flung alms to them in abundance, and buried the image and its bearers under showers of roses.[1]   A further step was taken by the Emperor Claudius when he incorporated the Phrygian worship of the sacred tree, and with it probably the orgiastic rites of Attis, in the established religion of Rome.[2]   The great

[1] Lucretius, ii. 598 *sqq.*; Catullus, lxiii. ; Varro, *Satir. Menipp.*, ed. F. Bücheler (Berlin, 1882), pp. 176, 178; Ovid, *Fasti*, iv. 181 *sqq.*, 223 *sqq.*, 361 *sqq.*; Dionysius Halicarnasensis, *Antiquit. Rom.* ii. 19, compare Polybius, xxii. 18 ed. L. Dindorf (Leipsic, 1866-1868).

[2] Joannes Lydus, *De mensibus*, iv. 41.   See Robinson Ellis, *Commentary on Catullus* (Oxford, 1876), pp. 206 *sq.*; H. Hepding, *Attis*, pp. 142 *sqq.*; Fr. Cumont, *Les Religions Orientales dans le Paganisme Romain*[2] (Paris, 1909), pp. 83 *sq.*

It is held by Prof. A. von Domaszewski that the Claudius who incorporated the Phrygian worship of the sacred tree in the Roman ritual was not the emperor of the first century but the emperor of the third century, Claudius Gothicus, who came to the throne in 268 A.D.   See A. von Domaszewski, " Magna Mater in Latin Inscriptions," *The Journal of Roman Studies*, i. (1911) p. 56.   The later date, it is said, fits better with the slow development of the worship. But on the other hand this view is open to

certain objections.   (1) Joannes Lydus, our only authority on the point, appears to identify the Claudius in question with the emperor of the first century. (2) The great and widespread popularity of the Phrygian worship in the Roman empire long before 268 A.D. is amply attested by an array of ancient writers and inscriptions, especially by a great series of inscriptions referring to the colleges of Tree-bearers (*Dendrophori*), from which we learn that one of these colleges, devoted to the worship of Cybele and Attis, existed at Rome in the age of the Antonines, about a century before the accession of Claudius Gothicus.   (3) Passages of the Augustan historians (Aelius Lampridius, *Alexander Severus*, 37 ; Trebellius Pollio, *Claudius*, iv. 2) refer to the great spring festival of Cybele and Attis in a way which seems to imply that the festival was officially recognized by the Roman government before Claudius Gothicus succeeded to the purple ; and we may hesitate to follow Prof. von Domaszewski in simply excising these passages as the work of an " impudent forger."   (4) The spring festival of Cybele and Attis is best known to us in the form in which it was celebrated at Rome ; but as we are informed that the Roman ceremonies were also Phrygian,[1] we may assume that they differed hardly, if at all, from their Asiatic original. The order of the festival seems to have been as follows.[2]

On the twenty-second day of March, a pine-tree was cut in the woods and brought into the sanctuary of Cybele, where it was treated as a great divinity. The duty of carrying the sacred tree was entrusted to a guild of Tree-bearers. The trunk was swathed like a corpse with woollen bands and decked with wreaths of violets, for violets were said to have sprung from the blood of Attis, as roses and anemones from the blood of Adonis ; and the effigy of a young man, doubtless Attis himself, was tied to the middle of the stem.[3] On the second day of the festival, the twenty-

The spring festival of Cybele and Attis at Rome.

---

official establishment of the bloody Phrygian superstition suits better the life and character of the superstitious, timid, cruel, pedantic Claudius of the first century than the gallant soldier his namesake in the third century. The one lounged away his contemptible days in the safety of the palace, surrounded by a hedge of lifeguards. The other spent the two years of his brief but glorious reign in camps and battlefields on the frontier, combating the barbarian enemies of the empire ; and it is probable that he had as little leisure as inclination to pander to the superstitions of the Roman populace. For these reasons it seems better with Mr. Hepding and Prof. Cumont to acquiesce in the traditional view that the rites of Attis were officially celebrated at Rome from the first century onward.

An intermediate view is adopted by Prof. G. Wissowa, who, brushing aside the statement of Joannes Lydus altogether, would seemingly assign the public institution of the rites to the middle of the second century A.D. on the ground that the earliest extant evidence of their public celebration refers to that period (*Religion und Kultus der Römer*,[2] Munich, 1912, p. 322). But, considering the extremely imperfect evi-

dence at our disposal for the history of these centuries, it seems rash to infer that an official cult cannot have been older than the earliest notice of it which has chanced to come down to us.

[1] Arrian, *Tactica*, 33 ; Servius on Virgil, *Aen.* xii. 836.

[2] On the festival see J. Marquardt, *Römische Staatsverwaltung*, iii.[2] (Leipsic, 1885) pp. 370 *sqq.* ; the calendar of Philocalus, in *Corpus Inscriptionum Latinarum*, vol. i.[2] Pars prior (Berlin, 1893), p. 260, with Th. Mommsen's commentary (pp. 313 *sq.*) ; W. Mannhardt, *Antike Wald- und Feldkulte*, pp. 291 *sqq.*, ; *id.*, *Baumkultus*, pp. 572 *sqq.* ; G. Wissowa, *Religion und Kultus der Römer*,[2] pp. 318 *sqq.* ; H. Hepding, *Attis*, pp. 147 *sqq.* ; J. Toutain, *Les Cultes Païens dans l'Empire Romain*, ii. (Paris, 1911) pp. 82 *sqq.*

[3] Julian, *Orat.* v. 168 C, p. 218 ed. F. C. Hertlein (Leipsic, 1875–1876) ; Joannes Lydus, *De mensibus*, iv. 41 ; Arnobius, *Adversus Nationes*, v. chs. 7, 16, 39 ; Firmicus Maternus, *De errore profanarum religionum*, 27 ; Sallustius philosophus, " De diis et mundo," iv., *Fragmenta Philosophorum Graecorum*, ed. F. G. A. Mullach, iii. 33. As to the guild of

third of March, the chief ceremony seems to have been a
blowing of trumpets.[1]   The third day, the twenty-fourth of
March, was known as the Day of Blood : the Archigallus or
high-priest drew blood from his arms and presented it as an
offering.[2]   Nor was he alone in making this bloody sacrifice.
Stirred by the wild barbaric music of clashing cymbals,
rumbling drums, droning horns, and screaming flutes, the
inferior clergy whirled about in the dance with waggling
heads and streaming hair, until, rapt into a frenzy of excitement and insensible to pain, they gashed their bodies with
potsherds or slashed them with knives in order to bespatter
the altar and the sacred tree with their flowing blood.[3]   The
ghastly rite probably formed part of the mourning for Attis
and may have been intended to strengthen him for the
resurrection.   The Australian aborigines cut themselves in
like manner over the graves of their friends for the purpose,
perhaps, of enabling them to be born again.[4]   Further, we
may conjecture, though we are not expressly told, that
it was on the same Day of Blood and for the same
purpose that the novices sacrificed their virility.   Wrought
up to the highest pitch of religious excitement they dashed
the severed portions of themselves against the image of the
cruel goddess.   These broken instruments of fertility were
afterwards reverently wrapt up and buried in the earth or in
subterranean chambers sacred to Cybele,[5] where, like the

The Day
of Blood.

Tree-bearers (*Dendrophori*) see Joannes
Lydus, *l.c.* ; H. Dessau, *Inscriptiones
Latinae Selectae*, Nos. 4116 *sq.*, 4171-
4174, 4176 ; H. Hepding, *Attis*, pp.
86, 92, 93, 96, 152 *sqq.*; F. Cumont,
s.v. "Dendrophori," in Pauly-Wissowa's *Real - Encyclopädie der classischen Altertumswissenschaft*, v. 1.
coll. 216-219 ; J. Toutain, *Les Cultes
Païens dans l'Empire Romain*, ii.
82 *sq.*, 92 *sq.*

[1] Julian, *l.c.* and 169 C, p. 219 ed.
F. C. Hertlein.   The ceremony may
have been combined with the old *tubi-
lustrium* or purification of trumpets,
which fell on this day.   See Joannes
Lydus, *De mensibus*, iv. 42 ; Varro,
De lingua Latina, vi. 14 ; Festus, pp.
352, 353 ed. C. O. Müller ; W. Warde
Fowler, *Roman Festivals of the Period*

of the Republic (London, 1899), p.
62.

[2] Trebellius Pollio, *Claudius*, 4 ;
Tertullian, *Apologeticus*, 25.

[3] Lucian, *Deorum dialogi*, xii. 1 ;
Seneca, *Agamemnon*, 686 *sqq.*; Martial,
xi. 84.   3 *sq.* ; Valerius Flaccus,
Argonaut. viii. 239 *sqq.*; Statius, *Theb.*
x. 170 *sqq.*; Apuleius, *Metam.* viii. 27;
Lactantius, *Divinarum Institutionum
Epitome*, 23 (18, vol. i. p. 689 ed.
Brandt and Laubmann) ; H. Hepding,
Attis, pp. 158 *sqq.*   As to the music
of these dancing dervishes see also
Lucretius, ii. 618 *sqq.*

[4] *The Magic Art and the Evolution
of Kings*, i. 90 *sq.*, 101 *sq.*

[5] Minucius Felix, *Octavius*, 22 and
24 ; Lactantius, *Divin. Instit.* i. 21.
16; *id., Epitoma*, 8; Schol. on Lucian,

offering of blood, they may have been deemed instrumental in recalling Attis to life and hastening the general resurrection of nature, which was then bursting into leaf and blossom in the vernal sunshine.   Some confirmation of this conjecture is furnished by the savage story that the mother of Attis conceived by putting in her bosom a pomegranate sprung from the severed genitals of a man-monster named Agdestis, a sort of double of Attis.[1]

If there is any truth in this conjectural explanation of the custom, we can readily understand why other Asiatic goddesses of fertility were served in like manner by eunuch priests.   These feminine deities required to receive from their male ministers, who personated the divine lovers, the means of discharging their beneficent functions: they had themselves to be impregnated by the life-giving energy before they could transmit it to the world.   Goddesses thus ministered to by eunuch priests were the great Artemis of Ephesus [2] and the great Syrian Astarte of Hierapolis,[3] whose sanctuary, frequented by swarms of pilgrims and enriched by the offerings of Assyria and Babylonia, of Arabia and Phoenicia, was perhaps in the days of its glory the most popular in the East.[4]   Now the unsexed priests of this Syrian goddess resembled those of Cybele so closely that some people took them to be the same.[5]   And the mode in which they dedicated themselves to the religious life was similar.   The

Eunuch priests in the service of Asiatic goddesses.

Jupiter Tragoedus, 8 (p. 60 ed. H. Rabe); Servius on Virgil, *Aen.* ix. 115; Prudentius, *Peristephan.* x. 1066 *sqq.*; "Passio Sancti Symphoriani," chs. 2 and 6 (Migne's *Patrologia Graeca,* v. 1463, 1466); Arnobius, *Adversus Nationes,* v. 14; Scholiast on Nicander, *Alexipharmaca,* 8; H. Hepding, *Attis,* pp. 163 *sq.* A story told by Clement of Alexandria (*Protrept.* ii. 15, p. 13 ed. Potter) suggests that weaker brethren may have been allowed to sacrifice the virility of a ram instead of their own.   We know from inscriptions that rams and bulls were regularly sacrificed at the mysteries of Attis and the Great Mother, and that the testicles of the bulls were used for a special purpose, probably as a fertility charm.   May not the testicles

of the rams have been employed for the same purpose? and may not those of both animals have been substitutes for the corresponding organs in men?   As to the sacrifices of rams and bulls see G. Zippel, "Das Taurobolium," *Festschrift zum fünfzigjährigen Doctorjubiläum L. Friedlaender* (Leipsic, 1895), pp. 498 *sqq.*; H. Dessau, *Inscriptiones Latinae Selectae,* Nos. 4118 *sqq.*; J. Toutain, *Les Cultes Paiens dans l'Empire Romain,* ii. 84 *sqq.*

[1] Arnobius, *Adversus Nationes,* v. 5 *sq.*

[2] Strabo, xiv. 1. 23, p. 641.

[3] Lucian, *De dea Syria,* 15, 27, 50-53.

[4] Lucian, *op. cit.* 10.

[5] Lucian, *op. cit.* 15.

greatest festival of the year at Hierapolis fell at the beginning
of spring, when multitudes thronged to the sanctuary from
Syria and the regions round about.   While the flutes played,
the drums beat, and the eunuch priests slashed themselves
with knives, the religious excitement gradually spread like a
wave among the crowd of onlookers, and many a one did
that which he little thought to do when he came as a holiday
spectator to the festival.   For man after man, his veins
throbbing with the music, his eyes fascinated by the sight
of the streaming blood, flung his garments from him, leaped
forth with a shout, and seizing one of the swords which
stood ready for the purpose, castrated himself on the spot.
Then he ran through the city, holding the bloody pieces in
his hand, till he threw them into one of the houses which
he passed in his mad career.   The household thus honoured
had to furnish him with a suit of female attire and female
ornaments, which he wore for the rest of his life.[1]   When
the tumult of emotion had subsided, and the man had come
to himself again, the irrevocable sacrifice must often have
been followed by passionate sorrow and lifelong regret.
This revulsion of natural human feeling after the frenzies of
a fanatical religion is powerfully depicted by Catullus in a
celebrated poem.[2]

[1] Lucian, *De dea Syria*, 49-51.

[2] Catullus, *Carm.* lxiii.   I agree
with Mr. H. Hepding (*Attis*, p. 140)
in thinking that the subject of the
poem is not the mythical Attis, but
one of his ordinary priests, who bore
the name and imitated the sufferings of
his god.   Thus interpreted the poem
gains greatly in force and pathos.   The
real sorrows of our fellow-men touch
us more nearly than the imaginary
pangs of the gods.

As the sacrifice of virility and the
institution of eunuch priests appear to
be rare, I will add a few examples.
At Stratonicea in Caria a eunuch
held a sacred office in connexion
with the worship of Zeus and Hecate
(*Corpus Inscriptionum Graecarum*, No.
2715).   According to Eustathius (on
Homer, *Iliad*, xix. 254, p. 1183) the
Egyptian priests were eunuchs who
had sacrificed their virility as a first-

fruit to the gods.   In Corea "during
a certain night, known as *Chu-il*, in
the twelfth moon, the palace eunuchs,
of whom there are some three hundred,
perform a ceremony supposed to ensure
a bountiful crop in the ensuing year.
They chant in chorus prayers, swinging
burning torches around them the while.
This is said to be symbolical of burning
the dead grass, so as to destroy the
field mice and other vermin."   See
W. Woodville Rockhill, "Notes on
some of the Laws, Customs, and
Superstitions of Korea," *The American
Anthropologist*, iv. (Washington, 1891)
p. 185.   Compare Mrs. Bishop, *Korea
and her Neighbours* (London, 1898),
ii. 56 *sq.*   It appears that among the
Ekoi of Southern Nigeria both men
and women are, or used to be, mutilated by the excision of their genital
organs at an annual festival, which is
celebrated in order to produce plentiful

The parallel of these Syrian devotees confirms the view that in the similar worship of Cybele the sacrifice of virility took place on the Day of Blood at the vernal rites of the goddess, when the violets, supposed to spring from the red drops of her wounded lover, were in bloom among the pines. Indeed the story that Attis unmanned himself under a pine-tree [1] was clearly devised to explain why his priests did the same beside the sacred violet-wreathed tree at his festival.

The sacrifice of virility.

---

harvests and immunity from thunderbolts. The victims apparently die from loss of blood. See P. Amaury Talbot, *In the Shadow of the Bush* (London, 1912), pp. 74 *sqq.* Mr. Talbot writes to me : "A horrible case has just happened at Idua, where, at the new yam planting, a man cut off his own *membrum virile*" (letter dated Eket, Nʳ Calabar, Southern Nigeria, Feb. 7th, 1913). Amongst the Ba-sundi and Ba-bwende of the Congo many youths are castrated "in order to more fittingly offer themselves to the phallic worship, which increasingly prevails as we advance from the coast to the interior. At certain villages between Manyanga and Isangila there are curious eunuch dances to celebrate the new moon, in which a white cock is thrown up into the air alive, with clipped wings, and as it falls towards the ground it is caught and plucked by the eunuchs. I was told that originally this used to be a human sacrifice, and that a young boy or girl was thrown up into the air and torn to pieces by the eunuchs as he or she fell, but that of late years slaves had got scarce or manners milder, and a white cock was now substituted" (H. H. Johnston, "On the Races of the Congo," *Journal of the Anthropological Institute*, xiii. (1884) p. 473 ; compare *id.*, *The River Congo*, London, 1884, p. 409). In India, men who are born eunuchs or in some way deformed are sometimes dedicated to a goddess named Huligamma. They wear female attire and might be mistaken for women. Also men who are or believe themselves impotent will vow to dress as women and serve the goddess in the hope of recovering their virility. See F. Fawcett, "On Basivis," *Journal of the Anthropological Society of Bombay*, ii. 343 *sq.* In Pegu the English traveller, Alexander Hamilton, witnessed a dance in honour of the gods of the earth. "Hermaphrodites, who are numerous in this country, are generally chosen, if there are enough present to make a set for the dance. I saw nine dance like mad folks for above half-an-hour ; and then some of them fell in fits, foaming at the mouth for the space of half-an-hour ; and, when their senses are restored, they pretend to foretell plenty or scarcity of corn for that year, if the year will prove sickly or salutary to the people, and several other things of moment, and all by that half hour's conversation that the furious dancer had with the gods while she was in a trance" (A. Hamilton, "A New Account of the East Indies," in J. Pinkerton's *Voyages and Travels*, viii. 427). So in the worship of Attis the Archigallus or head of the eunuch priests prophesied ; perhaps he in like manner worked himself up to the pitch of inspiration by a frenzied dance. See H. Dessau, *Inscriptiones Latinae Selectae*, vol. ii. Pars i. pp. 142, 143, Nos. 4130, 4136 ; G. Wilmanns, *Exempla Inscriptionum Latinarum* (Berlin, 1873), vol. i. p. 36, Nos. 119a, 120 ; J. Toutain, *Les Cultes Païens dans l'Empire Romain*, ii. 93 *sq.* As to the sacrifice of virility in the Syrian religion compare Th. Nöldeke, "Die Selbstentmannung bei den Syrern," *Archiv für Religionswissenschaft*, x. (1907) pp. 150-152.

[1] Arnobius, *Adversus Nationes*, v. 7 and 16 ; Servius on Virgil, *Aen.* ix. 115.

The mourning for Attis.

At all events, we can hardly doubt that the Day of Blood witnessed the mourning for Attis over an effigy of him which was afterwards buried.[1] The image thus laid in the sepulchre was probably the same which had hung upon the tree.[2] Throughout the period of mourning the worshippers fasted from bread, nominally because Cybele had done so in her grief for the death of Attis,[3] but really perhaps for the same reason which induced the women of Harran to abstain from eating anything ground in a mill while they wept for Tammuz.[4] To partake of bread or flour at such a season might have been deemed a wanton profanation of the bruised and broken body of the god. Or the fast may possibly have been a preparation for a sacramental meal.[5]

The Festival of Joy (*Hilaria*) for the resurrection of Attis on March 25th.

But when night had fallen, the sorrow of the worshippers was turned to joy. For suddenly a light shone in the darkness : the tomb was opened : the god had risen from the dead ; and as the priest touched the lips of the weeping mourners with balm, he softly whispered in their ears the glad tidings of salvation. The resurrection of the god was hailed by his disciples as a promise that they too would issue triumphant from the corruption of the grave.[6] On the

[1] Diodorus Siculus, iii. 59 ; Arrian, *Tactica*, 33 ; Scholiast on Nicander, *Alexipharmaca*, 8 ; Firmicus Maternus, *De errore profanarum religionum*, 3 and 22 ; Arnobius, *Adversus Nationes*, v. 16 ; Servius on Virgil, *Aen.* ix. 115.

[2] See above, p. 267.

[3] Arnobius, *l.c.* ; Sallustius philosophus, "De diis et mundo," iv., *Fragmenta Philosophorum Graecorum*, ed. F. G. A. Mullach, iii. 33.

[4] Above, p. 230.

[5] See below, p. 274.

[6] Firmicus Maternus, *De errore profanarum religionum*, 22, "*Nocte quadam simulacrum in lectica supinum ponitur et per numeros digestis fletibus plangitur : deinde cum se ficta lamentatione satiaverint, lumen infertur : tunc a sacerdote omnium qui flebant fauces unguentur, quibus perunctis hoc lento murmure susurrat :*

θαρρεῖτε μύσται τοῦ θεοῦ σεσωσμένου· ἔσται γὰρ ἡμῖν ἐκ πόνων σωτηρία.

Quid miseros hortaris gaudeant ? quid deceptos homines laetari compellis ? quam illis spem, quam salutem funesta persuasione promittis ? Dei tui mors nota est, vita non paret. . . . Idolum sepelis, idolum plangis, idolum de sepultura proferis, et miser cum haec feceris, gaudes. Tu deum tuum liberas, tu jacentia lapidis membra componis, tu insensibile corrigis saxum." In this passage Firmicus does not expressly mention Attis, but that the reference is to his rites is made probable by a comparison with chapter 3 of the same writer's work. Compare also Damascius, in Photius's *Bibliotheca*, p. 345 A, 5 *sqq.*, ed. I. Bekker (Berlin, 1824), τότε τῇ Ἱεραπόλει ἐγκαθευδήσας ἐδόκουν ὄναρ ὁ Ἄττης γένεσθαι, καί μοι ἐπιτελεῖσθαι παρὰ τῆς μητρὸς τῶν θεῶν τὴν τῶν ἱλαρίων καλουμένων ἑορτήν· ὅπερ ἐδήλου τὴν ἐξ ᾅδου γεγονυῖαν ἡμῶν σωτηρίαν. See further Fr. Cumont, *Les Religions Orientales dans le Paganisme Romain*[2] (Paris, 1909), pp. 89 *sq.*

morrow, the twenty-fifth day of March, which was reckoned the vernal equinox, the divine resurrection was celebrated with a wild outburst of glee. At Rome, and probably elsewhere, the celebration took the form of a carnival. It was the Festival of Joy (*Hilaria*). A universal licence prevailed. Every man might say and do what he pleased. People went about the streets in disguise. No dignity was too high or too sacred for the humblest citizen to assume with impunity. In the reign of Commodus a band of conspirators thought to take advantage of the masquerade by dressing in the uniform of the Imperial Guard, and so, mingling with the crowd of merrymakers, to get within stabbing distance of the emperor. But the plot miscarried.[1] Even the stern Alexander Severus used to relax so far on the joyous day as to admit a pheasant to his frugal board.[2] The next day, the twenty-sixth of March, was given to repose, which must have been much needed after the varied excitements and fatigues of the preceding days.[3] Finally, the Roman festival closed on the twenty-seventh of March with a procession to the brook Almo. The silver image of the goddess, with its face of jagged black stone, sat in a wagon drawn by oxen. Preceded by the nobles walking barefoot, it moved slowly, to the loud music of pipes and tambourines, out by the Porta Capena, and so down to the banks of the Almo, which flows into the Tiber just below the walls of Rome. There the high-priest, robed in purple, washed the wagon, the image, and the other sacred objects in the water of the stream. On returning from their bath, the wain and the oxen were strewn with fresh spring flowers. All was mirth and gaiety. No one thought of the blood that had flowed so lately. Even the eunuch priests forgot their wounds.[4]

The procession to the Almo.

---

[1] Macrobius, *Saturn.* i. 21. 10 ; Flavius Vopiscus, *Aurelianus*, i. 1 ; Julian, *Or.* v. pp. 168 D, 169 D ; Damascius, *l.c.* ; Herodian, i. 10. 5-7 ; Sallustius philosophus, "De diis et mundo," *Fragmenta Philosophorum Graecorum*, ed. F. G. A. Mullach, iii. 33. In like manner Easter Sunday, the Resurrection-day of Christ, was called by some ancient writers the Sunday of Joy (*Dominica Gaudii*). The emperors used to celebrate the happy day by releasing from prison all but the worst offenders. See J. Bingham, *The Antiquities of the Christian Church*, bk. xx. ch. vi. §§ 5 *sq.* (Bingham's *Works* (Oxford, 1855), vii. 317 *sqq.*).

[2] Aelius Lampridius, *Alexander Severus*, 37.

[3] *Corpus Inscriptionum Latinarum*, i.[2] Pars prior (Berlin, 1893), pp. 260, 313 *sq.* ; H. Hepding, *Attis*, pp. 51, 172.

[4] Ovid, *Fasti*, iv. 337-346 ; Silius Italicus, *Punic.* viii. 365 ; Valerius

The mysteries of Attis. Such, then, appears to have been the annual solemnization of the death and resurrection of Attis in spring. But besides these public rites, his worship is known to have comprised certain secret or mystic ceremonies, which probably aimed at bringing the worshipper, and especially the novice, into closer communication with his god. Our information as to the nature of these mysteries and the date of their celebration is unfortunately very scanty, but they seem to have included a sacramental meal and a baptism of

The sacrament blood. In the sacrament the novice became a partaker of the mysteries by eating out of a drum and drinking out of a cymbal, two instruments of music which figured prominently in the thrilling orchestra of Attis.[1] The fast which accompanied the mourning for the dead god[2] may perhaps have been designed to prepare the body of the communicant for the reception of the blessed sacrament by purging it of all that could defile by contact the sacred

The baptism of blood. elements.[3] In the baptism the devotee, crowned with gold and wreathed with fillets, descended into a pit, the mouth of which was covered with a wooden grating. A bull, adorned with garlands of flowers, its forehead glittering with gold leaf, was then driven on to the grating and there stabbed to death with a consecrated spear. Its hot reeking blood poured in torrents through the apertures, and was received with devout eagerness by the worshipper on every part of his person and garments, till he emerged from the pit, drenched, dripping, and scarlet from head to foot, to receive the homage, nay the adoration, of his fellows as one who had been born again to eternal life and had washed

---

Flaccus, *Argonaut.* viii. 239 *sqq.*; Martial, iii. 47. 1 *sq.*; Ammianus Marcellinus, xxiii. 3. 7; Arnobius, *Adversus Nationes*, vii. 32; Prudentius, *Peristephan.* x. 154 *sqq.* For the description of the image of the goddess see Arnobius, *Adversus Nationes*, vii. 49. At Carthage the goddess was carried to her bath in a litter, not in a wagon (Augustine, *De civitate Dei*, ii. 4). The bath formed part of the festival in Phrygia, whence the custom was borrowed by the Romans (Arrian, *Tactica*, 33). At Cyzicus the Placianian Mother, a form of Cybele, was

served by women called "marine" (θαλάσσιαι), whose duty it probably was to wash her image in the sea (Ch. Michel, *Recueil d'Inscriptions Grecques* Brussels, 1900, pp. 403 *sq.*, No. 537). See further J. Marquardt, *Römische Staatsverwaltung*, iii.[2] 373; H. Hepding, *Attis*, pp. 133 *sq.*

[1] Clement of Alexandria, *Protrept.* ii. 15, p. 13 ed. Potter; Firmicus Maternus, *De errore profanarum religionum*, 18.

[2] Above, p. 272.

[3] H. Hepding, *Attis*, p. 185.

away his sins in the blood of the bull.[1] For some time afterwards the fiction of a new birth was kept up by dieting him on milk like a new-born babe.[2] The regenera- tion of the worshipper took place at the same time as the regeneration of his god, namely at the vernal equinox.[3] At Rome the new birth and the remission of sins by the shedding of bull's blood appear to have been carried out above all at the sanctuary of the Phrygian goddess on the Vatican Hill, at or near the spot where the great basilica of St. Peter's now stands ; for many inscriptions relating to the rites were found when the church was being enlarged in 1608 or 1609.[4] From the Vatican as a centre this barbarous system of superstition seems to have spread to other parts

The Vatican a centre of the worship of Attis.

---

[1] Prudentius, *Peristephan.* x. 1006-1050 ; compare Firmicus Maternus, *De errore profanarum religionum*, 28. 8. That the bath of bull's blood (*tauro- bolium*) was believed to regenerate the devotee for eternity is proved by an inscription found at Rome, which re- cords that a certain Sextilius Agesilaus Aedesius, who dedicated an altar to Attis and the Mother of the Gods, was *taurobolio criobolioque in aeternum renatus* (*Corpus Inscriptionum Lati- narum*, vi. No. 510; H. Dessau, *Inscrip- tiones Latinae Selectae*, No. 4152). The phrase *arcanis perfusionibus in aeternum renatus* occurs in a dedica- tion to Mithra (*Corpus Inscriptionum Latinarum*, vi. No. 736), which, how- ever, is suspected of being spurious. As to the inscriptions which refer to the *taurobolium* see G. Zippel, " Das Taurobolium," in *Festschrift zum fünfzigjährigen Doctorjubiläum L. Friedlaender dargebracht von seinen Schülern* (Leipsic, 1895), pp. 498-520; H. Dessau, *Inscriptiones Latinae Selectae*, vol. ii. Pars i. pp. 140-147, Nos. 4118-4159. As to the origin of the *taurobolium* and the meaning of the word, see Fr. Cumont, *Textes et Monuments Figurés relatifs aux Mys- tères de Mithra* (Brussels, 1896-1899), i. 334 *sq.*; *id.*, *Les Religions Orientales dans le Paganisme Romain*,[2] pp. 100 *sqq.*; J. Toutain, *Les Cultes Païens dans l'Empire Romain*, ii. 84 *sqq.*; G. Wissowa, *Religion und Kultus der*

Römer,[2] pp. 322 *sqq.* The *tauro- bolium* seems to have formed no part of the original worship of Cybele and to have been imported into it at a com- paratively late date, perhaps in the second century of our era. Its origin is obscure. In the majority of the older inscriptions the name of the rite appears as *tauropolium*, and it has been held that this is the true form, being derived from the worship of the Asiatic goddess Artemis Tauropolis (Strabo, xii. 2. 7, p. 537). This was formerly the view of Prof. F. Cumont (*s.v.* " Anaitis," in Pauly-Wissowa's *Real- Encyclopädie der classischen Alter- tumswissenschaft*, i. 2. col. 2031); but he now prefers the form *taurobolium*, and would deduce both the name and the rite from an ancient Anatolian hunting custom of lassoing wild bulls.

[2] Sallustius philosophus, " De diis et mundo," iv., *Fragmenta Philoso- phorum Graecorum*, ed. F. G. A. Mullach, iii. 33.

[3] Sallustius philosophus, *l.c.*

[4] *Corpus Inscriptionum Latinarum*, vi. Nos. 497-504 ; H. Dessau, *Inscrip- tiones Latinae Selectae*, Nos. 4145, 4147 - 4151, 4153 ; *Inscriptiones Graecae Siciliae et Italiae*, ed. G. Kaibel (Berlin, 1890), p. 270, No. 1020; G. Zippel, *op. cit.* pp. 509 *sq.*, 519; H. Hepding, *Attis*, pp. 83, 86- 88, 176; Ch. Huelsen, *Topographie der Stadt Rom im Alterthum, von H. Jordan*, i. 3 (Berlin, 1907), pp. 658 *sq.*

of the Roman empire.   Inscriptions found in Gaul and
Germany prove that provincial sanctuaries modelled their
ritual on that of the Vatican.[1]   From the same source we
learn that the testicles as well as the blood of the bull
played an important part in the ceremonies.[2]   Probably they
were regarded as a powerful charm to promote fertility and
hasten the new birth.

[1] *Corpus Inscriptionum Latinarum*, xiii. No. 1751; H. Dessau, *Inscriptiones Latinae Selectae*, No. 4131; G. Wilmanns, *Exempla Inscriptionum Latinarum* (Berlin, 1873), vol. ii. p. 125, No. 2278; G. Wissowa, *Religion und Kultus der Römer*,[2] p. 267; H. Hepding, *Attis*, pp. 169-171, 176.

[2] *Corpus Inscriptionum Latinarum*, xiii. No. 1751; G. Wilmanns, *Exempla Inscriptionum Latinarum*, vol. i. pp. 35-37, Nos. 119, 123, 124; H. Dessau, *Inscriptiones Latinae Selectae*, Nos. 4127, 4129, 4131, 4140; G. Wissowa, *Religion und Kultus der Römer*,[2] pp. 322 *sqq.*; H. Hepding, *Attis*, p. 191.

CHAPTER II

ATTIS AS A GOD OF VEGETATION

THE original character of Attis as a tree-spirit is brought out plainly by the part which the pine-tree plays in his legend, his ritual, and his monuments.[1] The story that he was a human being transformed into a pine-tree is only one of those transparent attempts at rationalizing old beliefs which meet us so frequently in mythology. The bringing in of the pine-tree from the woods, decked with violets and woollen bands, is like bringing in the May-tree or Summer-tree in modern folk-custom ; and the effigy which was attached to the pine-tree was only a duplicate representative of the tree-spirit Attis. After being fastened to the tree, the effigy was kept for a year and then burned.[2] The same thing appears to have been sometimes done with the May-pole ; and in like manner the effigy of the corn-spirit, made at harvest, is often preserved till it is replaced by a new effigy at next year's harvest.[3] The original intention of such customs was no doubt to maintain the spirit of vegetation in life throughout the year. Why the Phrygians should have worshipped the pine above other trees we can only guess. Perhaps the sight of its changeless, though sombre, green cresting the ridges of the high hills above the fading splendour of the autumn woods in the valleys may have seemed to their eyes to mark it out as the seat of a diviner life, of something exempt from the sad vicissitudes of the

[1] As to the monuments see H. Dessau, *Inscriptiones Latinae Selectae*, Nos. 4143, 4152, 4153 ; H. Hepding, *Attis*, pp. 82, 83, 88, 89.

[2] Firmicus Maternus, *De errore profanarum religionum*, 27.

[3] *The Magic Art and the Evolution of Kings*, ii. 47 *sq.*, 71 ; *Spirits of the Corn and of the Wild*, i. 138, 143, 152, 153, 154, 155, 156, 157, 158.

seasons, constant and eternal as the sky which stooped to meet it. For the same reason, perhaps, ivy was sacred to Attis ; at all events, we read that his eunuch priests were tattooed with a pattern of ivy leaves.[1] Another reason for the sanctity of the pine may have been its usefulness. The cones of the stone-pine contain edible nut-like seeds, which have been used as food since antiquity, and are still eaten, for example, by the poorer classes in Rome.[2] Moreover, a wine was brewed from these seeds,[3] and this may partly account for the orgiastic nature of the rites of Cybele, which the ancients compared to those of Dionysus.[4] Further, pine-cones were regarded as symbols or rather instruments of fertility. Hence at the festival of the Thesmophoria they were thrown, along with pigs and other agents or emblems of fecundity, into the sacred vaults of Demeter for the purpose of quickening the ground and the wombs of women.[5]

[1] Etymologicum Magnum, p. 220, line 20, Γάλλος, ὁ φιλοπάτωρ Πτολεμαῖος· διὰ τὸ φύλλα κισσοῦ κατέστιχθαι, ὡς οἱ γάλλοι. 'Αεὶ γὰρ ταῖς Διονυσιακαῖς τελεταῖς κισσῷ ἐστεφανοῦντο. But there seems to be some confusion here between the rites of Dionysus and those of Attis ; ivy was certainly sacred to Dionysus (Pausanias, i. 31. 6 with my note). Compare C. A. Lobeck, *Aglaophamus* (Königsberg, 1829), i. 657, who, in the passage quoted, rightly defends the readings κατέστιχθαι and ἐστεφανοῦντο.

[2] *Encyclopaedia Britannica*,[9] xix. 105. Compare Athenaeus, ii. 49, p. 57. The nuts of the silver-pine (*Pinus edulis*) are a favourite food of the Californian Indians (S. Powers, *Tribes of California* (Washington, 1877), p. 421) ; the Wintun Indians hold a pine-nut dance when the nuts are fit to be gathered (*ib.* p. 237). The Shuswap Indians of British Columbia collect the cones of various sorts of pines and eat the nutlets which they extract from them. See G. M. Dawson, "Notes on the Shuswap People of British Columbia," *Proceedings and Transactions of the Royal Society of Canada*, ix. (Montreal, 1892) Transactions, section ii. p. 22. With regard to the Araucanian Indians of South America we read that "the great staple food,

the base of all their subsistence, save among the coast tribes, was the *piñon*, the fruit of the Araucanian pine (*Araucaria imbricata*). Every year during the autumn months excursions are made by the whole tribe to the pine forests, where they remain until they have collected sufficient for the following year. Each tribe has its own district, inherited by custom from generation to generation and inviolate, by unwritten law, from other tribes, even in time of warfare. This harvest was formerly of such supreme importance, that all inter-tribal quarrels and warfares were suspended by mutual accord during this period." See R. E. Latcham, "Ethnology of the Araucanos," *Journal of the Royal Anthropological Institute*, xxxix. (1909) p. 341. The Gilyaks of the Amoor valley in like manner eat the nutlets of the Siberian stone-pine (L. von Schrenk, *Die Völker des Amur-Landes*, iii. 440). See also the commentators on Herodotus, iv. 109 φθειροτραγέουσι.

[3] Pliny, *Nat. Hist.* xiv. 103.

[4] Strabo, x. 3. 12 *sqq.*, pp. 469 *sqq.* However, tipsy people were excluded from the sanctuary of Attis (Arnobius, *Adversus Nationes*, v. 6).

[5] Scholiast on Lucian, *Dial. Meretr.* ii. 1, p. 276 ed. H. Rabe (Leipsic, 1906).

Like tree-spirits in general, Attis was apparently thought Attis as a
corn-god. to wield power over the fruits of the earth or even to be identical with the corn.   One of his epithets was " very fruitful " : he was addressed as the " reaped green (or yellow) ear of corn " ; and the story of his sufferings, death, and resurrection was interpreted as the ripe grain wounded by the reaper, buried in the granary, and coming to life again when it is sown in the ground.[1]   A statue of him in the Lateran Museum at Rome clearly indicates his relation to the fruits of the earth, and particularly to the corn ; for it represents him with a bunch of ears of corn and fruit in his hand, and a wreath of pine-cones, pomegranates, and other fruits on his head, while from the top of his Phrygian cap ears of corn are sprouting.[2]   On a stone urn, which con- Cybele as a
goddess of
fertility. tained the ashes of an Archigallus or high-priest of Attis, the same idea is expressed in a slightly different way.   The top of the urn is adorned with ears of corn carved in relief, and it is surmounted by the figure of a cock, whose tail consists of ears of corn.[3]   Cybele in like manner was conceived as a goddess of fertility who could make or mar the fruits of the earth ; for the people of Augustodunum (Autun) in Gaul used to cart her image about in a wagon for the good of the fields and vineyards, while they danced and sang before it,[4] and we have seen that in Italy an unusually

[1] Hippolytus, *Refutatio omnium haeresium*, v. 8 and 9, pp. 162, 168 ed. Duncker and Schneidewin ; Firmicus Maternus, *De errore profanarum religionum*, 3 ; Sallustius philosophus, "De diis et mundo," *Fragmenta Philosophorum Graecorum*, ed. F. G. A. Mullach, iii. 33.   Others identified him with the spring flowers.   See Eusebius, *Praeparatio Evangelii*, iii. 11. 8 and 12, iii. 13. 10 ed. F. A. Heinichen (Leipsic, 1842–1843) ; Augustine, *De civitate Dei*, vii. 25.

[2] W. Helbig, *Führer durch die öffentlichen Sammlungen klassischer Altertümer in Rom*[2] (Leipsic, 1899), i. 481, No. 721.

[3] The urn is in the Lateran Museum at Rome (No. 1046).   It is not described by W. Helbig in his *Führer*.[2]   The inscription on the urn (*M. Modius Maxximus archigallus coloniae Ostiens*)

is published by H. Dessau (*Inscriptiones Latinae Selectae*, No. 4162), who does not notice the curious and interesting composition of the cock's tail.   The bird is chosen as an emblem of the priest with a punning reference to the word *gallus*, which in Latin means a cock as well as a priest of Attis.

[4] Gregory of Tours, *De gloria confessorum*, 77 (Migne's *Patrologia Latina*, lxxi. 884).   That the goddess here referred to was Cybele and not a native Gallic deity, as I formerly thought (*Lectures on the Early History of the Kingship*, p. 178), seems proved by the "Passion of St. Symphorian," chs. 2 and 6 (Migne s *Patrologia Graeca*, v. 1463, 1466). Gregory and the author of the "Passion of St. Symphorian" call the goddess simply Berecynthia, the latter writer adding "the Mother of the

The
bathing of
her image
either a
rain-charm
or a
marriage-
rite.

fine harvest was attributed to the recent arrival of the Great
Mother.[1] The bathing of the image of the goddess in a
river may well have been a rain-charm to ensure an
abundant supply of moisture for the crops. Or perhaps,
as Mr. Hepding has suggested, the union of Cybele and
Attis, like that of Aphrodite and Adonis, was dramatically
represented at the festival, and the subsequent bath of the
goddess was a ceremonial purification of the bride, such as
is often observed at human marriages.[2] In like manner
Aphrodite is said to have bathed after her union with
Adonis,[3] and so did Demeter after her intercourse with
Poseidon.[4] Hera washed in the springs of the river Burrha
after her marriage with Zeus ;[5] and every year she recovered
her virginity by bathing in the spring of Canathus.[6] However that may be, the rules of diet observed by the worshippers
of Cybele and Attis at their solemn fasts are clearly dictated
by a belief that the divine life of these deities manifested
itself in the fruits of the earth, and especially in such of
them as are actually hidden by the soil. For while the
devotees were allowed to partake of flesh, though not of
pork or fish, they were forbidden to eat seeds and the roots
of vegetables, but they might eat the stalks and upper parts
of the plants.[7]

Demons," which is plainly a Christian
version of the title " Mother of the
Gods."

[1] Above, p. 265. In the island of
Thera an ox, wheat, barley, wine, and
" other first-fruits of all that the seasons
produce" were offered to the Mother
of the Gods, plainly because she was
deemed the source of fertility. See
G. Dittenberger, *Sylloge Inscriptionum
Graecarum,*[2] vol. ii. p. 426, No. 630.

[2] H. Hepding, *Attis,* pp. 215-217 ;
compare *id.* p. 175 note [7].

[3] Ptolemaeus, *Nov. Hist.* i. p. 183 of
A. Westermann's *Mythographi Graeci*
(Brunswick, 1843).

[4] Pausanias, viii. 25. 5 *sq.*

[5] Aelian, *Nat. Anim.* xii. 30. The
place was in Mesopotamia, and the

goddess was probably Astarte. So
Lucian (*De dea Syria*) calls the Astarte
of Hierapolis "the Assyrian Hera."

[6] Pausanias, ii. 38. 2.

[7] Julian, *Orat.* v. 173 *sqq.* (pp. 225
sqq. ed. F. C. Hertlein) ; H. Hepding,
Attis, pp. 155-157. However, apples,
pomegranates, and dates were also
forbidden. The story that the mother
of Attis conceived him through contact
with a pomegranate (above, pp. 263,
269) might explain the prohibition of
that fruit. But the reasons for taboo-
ing apples and dates are not apparent,
though Julian tried to discover them.
He suggested that dates may have been
forbidden because the date-palm does
not grow in Phrygia, the native land
of Cybele and Attis.

CHAPTER III

ATTIS AS THE FATHER GOD

THE name Attis appears to mean simply "father."[1] This The name Attis seems to mean "father." explanation, suggested by etymology, is confirmed by the observation that another name for Attis was Papas;[2] for Papas has all the appearance of being a common form of that word for "father" which occurs independently in many distinct families of speech all the world over. Similarly the mother of Attis was named Nana,[3] which is itself a form of the world-wide word for "mother." "The immense list of such words collected by Buschmann shows that the types *pa* and *ta*, with the similar forms *ap* and *at*, preponderate in the world as names for 'father,' while *ma* and *na*, *am* and *an*, preponderate as names for 'mother.'"[4]

Thus the mother of Attis is only another form of his Relation of Attis to the Mother Goddess. divine mistress the great Mother Goddess,[5] and we are brought back to the myth that the lovers were mother and son. The story that Nana conceived miraculously without commerce with the other sex shows that the Mother Goddess of Phrygia herself was viewed, like other goddesses of the same primitive type, as a Virgin Mother.[6] That view of

[1] P. Kretschmer, *Einleitung in die Geschichte der griechischen Sprache* (Göttingen, 1896), p. 355.

[2] Diodorus Siculus, iii. 58. 4; Hippolytus, *Refutatio omnium haeresium*, i. 9, p. 168 ed. Duncker and Schneidewin. A Latin dedication to *Atte Papa* has been found at Aquileia (F. Cumont, in Pauly-Wissowa's *Real-encyclopädie der classischen Altertumswissenschaft*, ii. 2180, *s.v.* "Attepata"; H. Hepding, *Attis*, p. 86). Greek dedications to Papas or to Zeus Papas

occur in Phrygia (H. Hepding, *Attis*, pp. 78 *sq.*). Compare A. B. Cook, "Zeus, Jupiter, and the Oak," *Classical Review*, xviii. (1904) p. 79.

[3] Arnobius, *Adversus Nationes*, v. 6 and 13.

[4] (Sir) Edward B. Tylor, *Primitive Culture*[2] (London, 1873), i. 223.

[5] Rapp, *s.v.* "Kybele," in W. H. Roscher's *Lexikon der griech. und röm. Mythologie*, ii. 1648.

[6] She is called a "motherless virgin" by Julian (*Or.* v. 166 B, p.

her character does not rest on a perverse and mischievous theory that virginity is more honourable than matrimony. It is derived, as I have already indicated, from a state of savagery in which the mere fact of paternity was unknown. That explains why in later times, long after the true nature of paternity had been ascertained, the Father God was often a much less important personage in mythology than his divine partner the Mother Goddess. With regard to Attis in his paternal character it deserves to be noticed that the Bithynians used to ascend to the tops of the mountains and there call upon him under the name of Papas. The custom is attested by Arrian,[1] who as a native of Bithynia must have had good opportunities of observing it. We may perhaps infer from it that the Bithynians conceived Attis as a sky-god or heavenly father, like Zeus, with whom indeed Arrian identifies him. If that were so, the story of the loves of Attis and Cybele, the Father God and the Mother Goddess, might be in one of its aspects a particular version of the widespread myth which represents Mother Earth fertilized by Father Sky;[2] and, further, the story of the

Attis as a Sky-god or Heavenly Father.

---

215 ed. F. C. Hertlein), and there was a *Parthenon* or virgin's chamber in her sanctuary at Cyzicus (Ch. Michel, *Recueil d'Inscriptions Grecques*, p. 404, No. 538). Compare Rapp, in W. H. Roscher's *Lexikon der griech. und röm. Mythologie*, ii. 1648; Wagner, *s.v.* "Nana," *ibid.* iii. 4 *sq.* Another great goddess of fertility who was conceived as a Virgin Mother was the Egyptian Neith or Net. She is called "the Great Goddess, the Mother of All the Gods," and was believed to have brought forth Ra, the Sun, without the help of a male partner. See C. P. Tiele, *Geschichte der Religion im Altertum*, i. 111; E. A. Wallis Budge, *The Gods of the Egyptians* (London, 1904), i. 457-462. The latter writer says (p. 462); "In very early times Net was the personification of the eternal female principle of life which was self-sustaining and self-existent, and was secret and unknown, and all-pervading; the more material thinkers, whilst admitting that she brought forth her son Rā without the aid of a

husband, were unable to divorce from their minds the idea that a male germ was necessary for its production, and finding it impossible to derive it from a being external to the goddess, assumed that she herself provided not only the substance which was to form the body of Rā but also the male germ which fecundated it. Thus Net was the type of partheno-genesis."

[1] Quoted by Eustathius on Homer, *Il.* v. 408; *Fragmenta Historicorum Graecorum*, ed. C. Müller, iii. 592, Frag. 30.

[2] (Sir) Edward B. Tylor, *Primitive Culture*,[2] i. 321 *sqq.*, ii. 270 *sqq.* For example, the Ewe people of Togo-land, in West Africa, think that the Earth is the wife of the Sky, and that their marriage takes place in the rainy season, when the rain causes the seeds to sprout and bear fruit. These fruits they regard as the children of Mother Earth, who in their opinion is the mother also of men and of gods. See J. Spieth, *Die Ewe-Stämme* (Berlin, 1906), pp. 464, 548. In the

emasculation of Attis would be parallel to the Greek legend
that Cronus castrated his father, the old sky-god Uranus,[1]
and was himself in turn castrated by his own son, the
younger sky-god Zeus.[2] The tale of the mutilation of
the sky-god by his son has been plausibly explained as a
myth of the violent separation of the earth and sky, which
some races, for example the Polynesians, suppose to have
originally clasped each other in a close embrace.[3] Yet it
seems unlikely that an order of eunuch priests like the Galli
should have been based on a purely cosmogonic myth : why
should they continue for all time to be mutilated because
the sky-god was so in the beginning? The custom of
castration must surely have been designed to meet a constantly recurring need, not merely to reflect a mythical
event which happened at the creation of the world. Such
a need is the maintenance of the fruitfulness of the earth,
annually imperilled by the changes of the seasons. Yet

---

regions of the Senegal and the Niger it is believed that the Sky-god and the Earth-goddess are the parents of the principal spirits who dispense life and death, weal and woe, among mankind. The eldest son of Sky and Earth is represented in very various forms, sometimes as a hermaphrodite, sometimes in semi-animal shape, with the head of a bull, a crocodile, a fish, or a serpent. His name varies in the different tribes, but the outward form of his ceremonies is everywhere similar. His rites, which are to some extent veiled in mystery, are forbidden to women. See Maurice Delafosse, *Haut-Sénégal-Niger* (Paris, 1912), iii. 173-175.

[1] Hesiod, *Theogony*, 159 *sqq.*

[2] Porphyry, *De antro nympharum*, 16 ; Aristides, *Or.* iii. (vol. i. p. 35 ed. G. Dindorf, Leipsic, 1829) ; Scholiast on Apollonius Rhodius, *Argon.* iv. 983.

[3] A. Lang, *Custom and Myth* (London, 1884), pp. 45 *sqq.* ; *id.*, *Myth, Ritual, and Religion* (London, 1887), i. 299 *sqq.* In Egyptian mythology the separation of heaven and earth was ascribed to Shu, the god of light, who insinuated himself

between the bodies of Seb (Keb) the earth-god and of Nut the sky-goddess. On the monuments Shu is represented holding up the star-spangled body of Nut on his hands, while Seb reclines on the ground. See A. Wiedemann, *Religion of the Ancient Egyptians* (London, 1897), pp. 230 *sq.* ; E. A. Wallis Budge, *The Gods of the Egyptians*, ii. 90, 97 *sq.*, 100, 105 ; A. Erman, *Die ägyptische Religion*[2] (Berlin, 1909), pp. 35 *sq.* ; C. P. Tiele, *Geschichte der Religion im Altertum*, i. 33 *sq.* Thus contrary to the usual mythical conception the Egyptians regarded the earth as male and the sky as female. An allusion in the *Book of the Dead* (ch. 69, vol. ii. p. 235, E. A. Wallis Budge's translation, London, 1901) has been interpreted as a hint that Osiris mutilated his father Seb at the separation of earth and heaven, just as Cronus mutilated his father Uranus. See H. Brugsch, *Religion und Mythologie der alten Aegypter* (Leipsic, 1885–1888), p. 581 ; E. A. Wallis Budge, *op. cit.* ii. 99 *sq.* Sometimes the Egyptians conceived the sky as a great cow standing with its legs on the earth. See A. Erman, *Die ägyptische Religion*,[2] pp. 7, 8.

the theory that the mutilation of the priests of Attis and the burial of the severed parts were designed to fertilize the ground may perhaps be reconciled with the cosmogonic myth if we remember the old opinion, held apparently by many peoples, that the creation of the world is year by year repeated in that great transformation which depends ultimately on the annual increase of the sun's heat.[1] However, the evidence for the celestial aspect of Attis is too slight to allow us to speak with any confidence on this subject. A trace of that aspect appears to survive in the star-spangled cap which he is said to have received from Cybele,[2] and which is figured on some monuments supposed to represent him.[3] His identification with the Phrygian moon-god Men Tyrannus[4] points in the same direction, but is probably due rather to the religious speculation of a later age than to genuine popular tradition.[5]

[1] Compare *The Dying God*, pp. 105 *sqq.*

[2] Julian, *Or.* v. pp. 165 B, 170 D (pp. 214, 221, ed. F. C. Hertlein); Sallustius philosophus, "De diis et mundo," iv. *Fragmenta Philosophorum Graecorum*, ed. F. G. A. Mullach, iii. 33.

[3] Drexler, *s.v.* "Men," in W. H. Roscher's *Lexikon der griech. und röm. Mythologie*, ii. 2745; H. Hepding, *Attis*, p. 120, note [8].

[4] H. Dessau, *Inscriptiones Latinae Selectae*, vol. ii. Pars i. pp. 145 *sq.*, Nos. 4146-4149; H. Hepding, *Attis*, pp. 82, 86 *sq.*, 89 *sq.* As to Men Tyrannus, see Drexler, *s.v.* "Men," in W. H. Roscher's *Lexikon der griech. und röm. Myth.* ii. 2687 *sqq.*

[5] On the other hand Sir W. M. Ramsay holds that Attis and Men are deities of similar character and origin, but differentiated from each other by development in different surroundings (*Cities and Bishoprics of Phrygia*, i. 169); but he denies that Men was a moon-god (*op. cit.* i. 104, note [4]).

CHAPTER IV

HUMAN REPRESENTATIVES OF ATTIS

FROM inscriptions it appears that both at Pessinus and Rome the high-priest of Cybele regularly bore the name of Attis.[1] It is therefore a reasonable conjecture that he played the part of his namesake, the legendary Attis, at the annual festival.[2] We have seen that on the Day of Blood he drew blood from his arms, and this may have been an imitation of the self-inflicted death of Attis under the pine-tree. It is not inconsistent with this supposition that Attis was also represented at these ceremonies by an effigy ; for instances can be shown in which the divine being is first represented by a living person and afterwards by an effigy, which is then burned or otherwise destroyed.[3] Perhaps we may go a step farther and conjecture that this mimic killing of the priest, accompanied by a real effusion of his blood, was in Phrygia, as it has been elsewhere, a substitute for a human sacrifice which in earlier times was actually offered. Sir W. M. Ramsay, whose authority on all questions relating to Phrygia no one will dispute, is

The high priest of Attis bore the god's name and seems to have personated him.

The drawing of the high priest's blood may have been a substitute for putting him to

---

[1] In letters of Eumenes and Attalus, preserved in inscriptions at Sivrihissar, the priest at Pessinus is addressed as Attis. See A. von Domaszewski, " Briefe der Attaliden an den Priester von Pessinus," *Archaeologische - epigraphische Mittheilungen aus Oesterreich - Ungarn*, viii. (1884) pp. 96, 98 ; Ch. Michel, *Recueil d'Inscriptions Grecques*, pp. 57 *sq.* No. 45 ; W. Dittenberger, *Orientis Graeci Inscriptiones Selectae* (Leipsic, 1903-1905), vol. i. pp. 482 *sqq.* No. 315. For more evidence of inscriptions see H.

Hepding, *Attis*, p. 79 ; Rapp, *s.v.* " Attis," in W. H. Roscher's *Lexikon der griech. und röm. Mythologie*, i. 724. See also Polybius, xxii. 18 (20), (ed. L. Dindorf), who mentions a priest of the Mother of the Gods named Attis at Pessinus.

[2] The conjecture is that of Henzen, in *Annal. d. Inst.* 1856, p. 110, referred to by Rapp, *l.c.*

[3] *The Magic Art and the Evolution of Kings*, ii. 75 *sq.* ; *The Dying God*, pp. 151 *sq.*, 209.

death in
the char-
acter of
the god.

of opinion that at these Phrygian ceremonies "the representative of the god was probably slain each year by a cruel
death, just as the god himself died."[1]   We know from
Strabo[2] that the priests of Pessinus were at one time
potentates as well as priests; they may, therefore, have
belonged to that class of divine kings or popes whose duty
it was to die each year for their people and the world.

The name
of Attis in
the royal
families of
Phrygia
and Lydia.

The name of Attis, it is true, does not occur among the
names of the old kings of Phrygia, who seem to have borne
the names of Midas and Gordias in alternate generations;
but a very ancient inscription carved in the rock above a
famous Phrygian monument, which is known as the Tomb
of Midas, records that the monument was made for, or
dedicated to, King Midas by a certain Ates, whose name
is doubtless identical with Attis, and who, if not a king
himself, may have been one of the royal family.[3]   It is
worthy of note also that the name Atys, which, again,
appears to be only another form of Attis, is recorded as
that of an early king of Lydia;[4] and that a son of Croesus,
king of Lydia, not only bore the name Atys but was said
to have been killed, while he was hunting a boar, by a
member of the royal Phrygian family, who traced his lineage
to King Midas and had fled to the court of Croesus because
he had unwittingly slain his own brother.[5]   Scholars have
recognized in this story of the death of Atys, son of Croesus,
a mere double of the myth of Attis;[6] and in view of the
facts which have come before us in the present inquiry[7] it

---

[1] Article "Phrygia," in *Encyclopaedia Britannica*, 9th ed. xviii. (1885) p. 853. Elsewhere, speaking of the religions of Asia Minor in general, the same writer says: "The highest priests and priest-esses played the parts of the great gods in the mystic ritual, wore their dress, and bore their names" (*Cities and Bishoprics of Phrygia*, i. 101).

[2] Strabo, xii. 5. 3, p. 567.

[3] (Sir) W. M. Ramsay, "A Study of Phrygian Art," *Journal of Hellenic Studies*, ix. (1888) pp. 379 *sqq.*; *id.*, "A Study of Phrygian Art," *Journal of Hellenic Studies*, x. (1889) pp. 156 *sqq.*; G. Perrot et Ch. Chipiez, *Histoire de l'Art dans l'Antiquité*, v. 82 *sqq.*

[4] Herodotus, i. 94. According to

Sir W. M. Ramsay, the conquering and ruling caste in Lydia belonged to the Phrygian stock (*Journal of Hellenic Studies*, ix. (1888) p. 351).

[5] Herodotus, i. 34-45. The tradi-tion that Croesus would allow no iron weapon to come near Atys suggests that a similar taboo may have been imposed on the Phrygian priests named Attis. For taboos of this sort see *Taboo and the Perils of the Soul*, pp. 225 *sqq.*

[6] H. Stein on Herodotus, i. 43; Ed. Meyer, *s.v.* "Atys," in Pauly-Wissowa's *Real-Encyclopädie der clas-sischen Altertumswissenschaft*, ii. 2 col. 2262.

[7] See above, pp. 13, 16 *sq.*, 48 *sqq.*

is a remarkable circumstance that the myth of a slain god should be told of a king's son. May we conjecture that the Phrygian priests who bore the name of Attis and represented the god of that name were themselves members, perhaps the eldest sons, of the royal house, to whom their fathers, uncles, brothers, or other kinsmen deputed the honour of dying a violent death in the character of gods, while they reserved to themselves the duty of living, as long as nature allowed them, in the humbler character of kings ? If this were so, the Phrygian dynasty of Midas may have presented a close parallel to the Greek dynasty of Athamas, in which the eldest sons seem to have been regularly destined to the altar.[1] But it is also possible that the divine priests who bore the name of Attis may have belonged to that indigenous race which the Phrygians, on their irruption into Asia from Europe, appear to have found and conquered in the land afterwards known as Phrygia.[2] On the latter hypothesis the priests may have represented an older and higher civilization than that of their barbarous conquerors. Be that as it may, the god they personated was a deity of vegetation whose divine life manifested itself especially in the pine-tree and the violets of spring ; and if they died in the character of that divinity, they corresponded to the mummers who are still slain in mimicry by European peasants in spring, and to the priest who was slain long ago in grim earnest on the wooded shore of the Lake of Nemi.

The Phrygian Attis may have been members of the royal family.

[1] *The Dying God*, pp. 161 *sqq.*

[2] See (Sir) W. M. Ramsay, *s.v.* "Phrygia," *Encyclopaedia Britannica*, 9th ed. xviii. 849 *sq.* ; *id.*, "A Study of Phrygian Art," *Journal of Hellenic Studies*, ix. (1888)

pp. 350 *sq.* Prof. P. Kretschmer holds that both Cybele and Attis were gods of the indigenous Asiatic population, not of the Phrygian invaders (*Einleitung in die Geschichte der griechischen Sprache*, Göttingen, 1896, pp. 194 *sq.*).

CHAPTER V

THE HANGED GOD

The way in which the representatives of Attis were put to death is perhaps shown by the legend of Marsyas, who was hung on a pine-tree and flayed by Apollo. A REMINISCENCE of the manner in which these old representatives of the deity were put to death is perhaps preserved in the famous story of Marsyas. He was said to be a Phrygian satyr or Silenus, according to others a shepherd or herdsman, who played sweetly on the flute. A friend of Cybele, he roamed the country with the disconsolate goddess to soothe her grief for the death of Attis.[1] The composition of the Mother's Air, a tune played on the flute in honour of the Great Mother Goddess, was attributed to him by the people of Celaenae in Phrygia.[2] Vain of his skill, he challenged Apollo to a musical contest, he to play on the flute and Apollo on the lyre. Being vanquished, Marsyas was tied up to a pine-tree and flayed or cut limb from limb either by the victorious Apollo or by a Scythian slave.[3] His skin was shown at Celaenae in historical times. It

---

[1] Diodorus Siculus, iii. 58 sq. As to Marsyas in the character of a shepherd or herdsman see Hyginus, Fab. 165 ; Nonnus, Dionys. i. 41 sqq. He is called a Silenus by Pausanias (i. 24. 1).

[2] Pausanias, x. 30. 9.

[3] Apollodorus, Bibliotheca, i. 4. 2 ; Hyginus, Fab. 165. Many ancient writers mention that the tree on which Marsyas suffered death was a pine. See Apollodorus, l.c. ; Nicander, Alexipharmaca, 301 sq., with the Scholiast's note ; Lucian, Tragodopodagra, 314 sq. ; Archias Mitylenaeus, in Anthologia Palatina, vii. 696 ; Philostratus, Junior, Imagines, i. 3 ; Longus, Pastor. iv. 8 ; Zen-

obius, Cent. iv. 81 ; J. Tzetzes, Chiliades, i. 353 sqq. Pliny alone declares the tree to have been a plane, which according to him was still shown at Aulocrene on the way from Apamea to Phrygia (Nat. Hist. xvi. 240). On a candelabra in the Vatican the defeated Marsyas is represented hanging on a pine-tree (W. Helbig, Führer,² i. 225 sq.) ; but the monumental evidence is not consistent on this point (Jessen, s.v. "Marsyas," in W. H. Roscher's Lexikon der griech. und röm. Mythologie, ii. 2442). The position which the pine held in the myth and ritual of Cybele supports the preponderance of ancient testimony in favour of that tree.

hung at the foot of the citadel in a cave from which the river Marsyas rushed with an impetuous and noisy tide to join the Maeander.[1] So the Adonis bursts full-born from the precipices of the Lebanon; so the blue river of Ibreez leaps in a crystal jet from the red rocks of the Taurus; so the stream, which now rumbles deep underground, used to gleam for a moment on its passage from darkness to darkness in the dim light of the Corycian cave. In all these copious fountains, with their glad promise of fertility and life, men of old saw the hand of God and worshipped him beside the rushing river with the music of its tumbling waters in their ears. At Celaenae, if we can trust tradition, the piper Marsyas, hanging in his cave, had a soul for harmony even in death; for it is said that at the sound of his native Phrygian melodies the skin of the dead satyr used to thrill, but that if the musician struck up an air in praise of Apollo it remained deaf and motionless.[2]

In this Phrygian satyr, shepherd, or herdsman who enjoyed the friendship of Cybele, practised the music so characteristic of her rites,[3] and died a violent death on her sacred tree, the pine, may we not detect a close resemblance to Attis, the favourite shepherd or herdsman of the goddess, who is himself described as a piper,[4] is said to have perished under a pine-tree, and was annually represented by an effigy hung, like Marsyas, upon a pine? We may conjecture that in old days the priest who bore the name and played the part of Attis at the spring festival of Cybele was regularly hanged or otherwise slain upon the sacred tree, and that this barbarous custom was afterwards mitigated into the form in which it is known to us in later times, when the priest merely drew blood from his body under the tree and attached an effigy instead of himself to its trunk. In the holy grove at Upsala men and animals were sacrificed by

(marginal note: Marsyas apparently a double of Attis.*)*

---

[1] Herodotus, vii. 26; Xenophon, *Anabasis*, i. 2. 8; Livy, xxxviii. 13. 6: Quintus Curtius, iii. 1. 1-5; Pliny, *Nat. Hist.* v. 106. Herodotus calls the river the Catarrhactes.

[2] Aelian, *Var. Hist.* xiii. 21.

[3] Catullus, lxiii. 22; Lucretius, ii. 620; Ovid, *Fasti*, iv. 181 *sq.*,

341; Polyaenus, *Stratagem.* viii. 53. 4. Flutes or pipes often appear on her monuments. See H. Dessau, *Inscriptiones Latinae Selectae*, Nos. 4100, 4143, 4145, 4152, 4153.

[4] Hippolytus, *Refutatio omnium haeresium*, v. 9, p. 168, ed. Duncker and Schneidewin.

The
hanging
and spear-
ing of Odin
and his
human
victims on
sacred
trees.

being hanged upon the sacred trees.[1]   The human victims
dedicated to Odin were regularly put to death by hanging
or by a combination of hanging and stabbing, the man
being strung up to a tree or a gallows and then wounded
with a spear.   Hence Odin was called the Lord of the
Gallows or the God of the Hanged, and he is represented
sitting under a gallows tree.[2]   Indeed he is said to have
been sacrificed to himself in the ordinary way, as we learn
from the weird verses of the *Havamal*, in which the god
describes how he acquired his divine power by learning the
magic runes :

> "*I know that I hung on the windy tree*
> *For nine whole nights,*
> *Wounded with the spear, dedicated to Odin,*
> *Myself to myself.*"[3]

The hang-
ing and
spearing

The Bagobos of Mindanao, one of the Philippine Islands,
used annually to sacrifice human victims for the good of
the crops in a similar way.   Early in December, when the

---

[1] Adam of Bremen, *Descriptio insularum Aquilonis*, 27 (Migne's *Patrologia Latina*, cxlvi. 643).

[2] S. Bugge, *Studien über die Entstehung der nördischen Götter- und Heldensagen* (Munich, 1889), pp. 339 *sqq.*; K. Simrock, *Die Edda*[8] (Stuttgart, 1882), p. 382; K. Müllenhoff, *Deutsche Altertumskunde* (Berlin, 1870–1900), iv. 244 *sq.*; H. M. Chadwick, *The Cult of Othin* (London, 1899), pp. 3-20.   The old English custom of hanging and disembowelling traitors was probably derived from a practice of thus sacrificing them to Odin ; for among many races, including the Teutonic and Latin peoples, capital punishment appears to have been originally a religious rite, a sacrifice or consecration of the criminal to the god whom he had offended.   See F. Liebrecht, *Zur Volkskunde* (Heilbronn, 1879), pp. 8 *sq.* ; K. von Amira, in H. Paul's *Grundriss der germanischen Philologie*,[2] iii. (Strasburg, 1900) pp. 197 *sq.* ; G. Vigfusson and F. York Powell, *Corpus Poeticum Boreale* (Oxford, 1883), i. 410 ; W. Golther, *Handbuch der germanischen Mythologie* (Leipsic,

1895), pp. 548 *sq.* ; Th. Mommsen, *Roman History*, bk. i. ch. 12 (vol. i. p. 192, ed. 1868) ; *id.*, *Römisches Strafrecht* (Leipsic, 1899), pp. 900 *sqq.* ; F. Granger, *The Worship of the Romans* (London, 1895), p. 259 *sqq.* ; E. Westermarck, *The Origin and Development of the Moral Ideas*, i. (London, 1906) pp. 439 *sq.* So, too, among barbarous peoples the slaughter of prisoners in war is often a sacrifice offered by the victors to the gods to whose aid they ascribe the victory.   See A. B. Ellis, *The Tshi-speaking Peoples of the Gold Coast* (London, 1887), pp. 169 *sq.* ; W. Ellis, *Polynesian Researches*[2] (London, 1832–1836), i. 289 ; Diodorus Siculus, xx. 65 ; Strabo, vii. 2. 3, p. 294 ; Caesar, *De bello Gallico*, vi. 17 ; Tacitus, *Annals*, i. 61, xiii. 57 ; Procopius, *De bello Gothico*, ii. 15. 24, ii. 25. 9 ; Jornandes, *Getica*, vi. 41 ; J. Grimm, *Deutsche Mythologie*[4] (Berlin, 1875–1878), i. 36 *sq.* ; Fr. Schwally, *Semitische Kriegsaltertümer* (Leipsic, 1901), pp. 29 *sqq.*

[3] *Havamal*, 139 *sqq.* (K. Simrock, *Die Edda*,[8] p. 55 ; K. Müllenhoff, *Deutsche Altertumskunde*, v. 270 *sq.*).

constellation Orion appeared at seven o'clock in the evening, of human
the people knew that the time had come to clear their fields victims
among the
for sowing and to sacrifice a slave. The sacrifice was Bagobos.
presented to certain powerful spirits as payment for the good
year which the people had enjoyed, and to ensure the
favour of the spirits for the coming season. The victim was
led to a great tree in the forest; there he was tied with
his back to the tree and his arms stretched high above his
head, in the attitude in which ancient artists portrayed
Marsyas hanging on the fatal tree. While he thus hung
by the arms, he was slain by a spear thrust through his
body at the level of the armpits. Afterwards the body was
cut clean through the middle at the waist, and the upper
part was apparently allowed to dangle for a little from the
tree, while the under part wallowed in blood on the ground.
The two portions were finally cast into a shallow trench
beside the tree. Before this was done, anybody who wished
might cut off a piece of flesh or a lock of hair from the
corpse and carry it to the grave of some relation whose
body was being consumed by a ghoul. Attracted by the fresh
corpse, the ghoul would leave the mouldering old body in
peace. These sacrifices have been offered by men now living.[1]

In Greece the great goddess Artemis herself appears The
to have been annually hanged in effigy in her sacred grove hanging of
Artemis.
of Condylea among the Arcadian hills, and there accordingly
she went by the name of the Hanged One.[2] Indeed a trace
of a similar rite may perhaps be detected even at Ephesus,
the most famous of her sanctuaries, in the legend of a woman
who hanged herself and was thereupon dressed by the com-
passionate goddess in her own divine garb and called by the
name of Hecate.[3] Similarly, at Melite in Phthia, a story

---

[1] Fay-Cooper Cole, *The Wild Tribes
of Davao District, Mindanao* (Chicago,
1913), pp. 114 *sqq.* (*Field Museum
of Natural History, Publication* 170).

[2] Pausanias, viii. 23. 6 *sq.* The
story, mentioned by Pausanias, that
some children tied a rope round the
neck of the image of Artemis was
probably invented to explain a ritual
practice of the same sort, as scholars
have rightly perceived. See L. Preller,

Griechische Mythologie, i.[4] 305, note [2];
L. R. Farnell, *The Cults of the Greek
States* (Oxford, 1896–1909), ii. 428 *sq.*;
M. P. Nilsson, *Griechische Feste*
(Leipsic, 1906), pp. 232 *sqq.* The
Arcadian worship of the Hanged
Artemis was noticed by Callimachus.
See Clement of Alexandria, *Protrept.*
ii. 38, p. 32, ed. Potter.

[3] Eustathius on Homer, *Od.* xii. 85,
p. 1714; I. Bekker, *Anecdota Graeca*

was told of a girl named Aspalis who hanged herself, but who appears to have been merely a form of Artemis. For after her death her body could not be found, but an image of her was discovered standing beside the image of Artemis, and the people bestowed on it the title of Hecaerge or Far-shooter, one of the regular epithets of the goddess. Every year the virgins sacrificed a young goat to the image by hanging it, because Astypalis was said to have hanged herself.[1] The sacrifice may have been a substitute for hang-

The hanging of Helen.

ing an image or a human representative of Artemis. Again, in Rhodes the fair Helen was worshipped under the title of Helen of the Tree, because the queen of the island had caused her handmaids, disguised as Furies, to string her up to a bough.[2] That the Asiatic Greeks sacrificed animals in

The hanging of animal victims.

this fashion is proved by coins of Ilium, which represent an ox or cow hanging on a tree and stabbed with a knife by a man, who sits among the branches or on the animal's back.[3] At Hierapolis also the victims were hung on trees before they were burnt.[4] With these Greek and Scandinavian parallels before us we can hardly dismiss as wholly improb-

---

(Berlin, 1814–1821), i. 336 *sq.*, *s.v.* Ἄγαλμα Ἑκάτης. The goddess Hecate was sometimes identified with Artemis, though in origin probably she was quite distinct. See L. R. Farnell, *The Cults of the Greek States*, ii. 499 *sqq.*

[1] Antoninus Liberalis, *Transform.* xiii.

[2] Pausanias, iii. 19. 9 *sq.*

[3] H. von Fritze, "Zum griechischen Opferritual," *Jahrbuch des kaiser. deutsch. Archäologischen Instituts*, xviii. (1903) pp. 58-67. In the ritual of Eleusis the sacrificial oxen were sometimes lifted up by young men from the ground. See G. Dittenberger, *Sylloge Inscriptionum Graecarum*,[2] vol. ii. pp. 166 *sq.* No. 521 (ἤραντο δὲ καὶ τοῖς μυστηρίοις τοὺς βοῦς ἐν Ἐλευσῖνι τῇ θυσίαι, κτλ.); E. S. Roberts and E. A. Gardner, *Introduction to Greek Epigraphy*, ii. (Cambridge, 1905) pp. 176 *sq.*, No. 65. In this inscription the word ἤραντο is differently interpreted by P. Stengel, who supposes that it refers merely to

turning backwards and upwards the head of the victim. See P. Stengel, "Zum griechischen Opferritual," *Jahrbuch des kaiser. deutsch. Archäologischen Instituts*, xviii. (1903) pp. 113-123. But it seems highly improbable that so trivial an act should be solemnly commemorated in an inscription among the exploits of the young men (*epheboi*) who performed it. On the other hand, we know that at Nysa the young men did lift and carry the sacrificial bull, and that the act was deemed worthy of commemoration on the coins. See above, p. 206. The Wajagga of East Africa dread the ghosts of suicides; so when a man has hanged himself they take the rope from his neck and hang a goat in the fatal noose, after which they slay the animal. This is supposed to appease the ghost and prevent him from tempting human beings to follow his bad example. See B. Gutmann, "Trauer und Begrabnissitten der Wadschagga," *Globus*, lxxxix. (1906) p. 200.

[4] See above, p. 146.

able the conjecture that in Phrygia a man-god may have hung year by year on the sacred but fatal tree.

The tradition that Marsyas was flayed and that his skin was exhibited at Celaenae down to historical times may well reflect a ritual practice of flaying the dead god and hanging his skin upon the pine as a means of effecting his resurrection, and with it the revival of vegetation in spring. Similarly, in ancient Mexico the human victims who personated gods were often flayed and their bloody skins worn by men who appear to have represented the dead deities come to life again.[1] When a Scythian king died, he was buried in a grave along with one of his concubines, his cup-bearer, cook, groom, lacquey, and messenger, who were all killed for the purpose, and a great barrow was heaped up over the grave. A year afterwards fifty of his servants and fifty of his best horses were strangled ; and their bodies, having been disembowelled and cleaned out, were stuffed with chaff, sewn up, and set on scaffolds round about the barrow, every dead man bestriding a dead horse, which was bitted and bridled as in life.[2] These strange horsemen were no doubt supposed to mount guard over the king. The setting up of their stuffed skins might be thought to ensure their ghostly resurrection.

That some such notion was entertained by the Scythians is made probable by the account which the mediaeval traveller de Plano Carpini gives of the funeral customs of the Mongols. The traveller tells us that when a noble Mongol died, the custom was to bury him seated in the middle of a tent, along with a horse saddled and bridled, and a mare and her foal. Also they used to eat another horse, stuff the carcase with straw, and set it up on poles. All this they did in order that in the other world the dead man might have a tent to live in, a mare to yield milk, and a steed to ride, and that he might be able to breed horses. Moreover, the bones of the horse which they ate were burned for the good of his soul.[3] When the Arab traveller Ibn Batuta visited Peking in the fourteenth century,

Use of the skins of human victims to effect their resurrection.

Skins of men and horses stuffed and set up at graves.

---

[1] *The Scapegoat*, pp. 294 *sqq.*

[2] Herodotus, iv. 71 *sq.*

[3] Jean du Plan de Carpin, *Historia Mongalorum*, ed. D'Avezac (Paris, 1838), cap. iii. § iii.

he witnessed the funeral of an emperor of China who had been killed in battle.   The dead sovereign was buried along with four young female slaves and six guards in a vault, and an immense mound like a hill was piled over him. Four horses were then made to run round the hillock till they could run no longer, after which they were killed, impaled, and set up beside the tomb.[1]   When an Indian of Patagonia dies, he is buried in a pit along with some of his property.   Afterwards his favourite horse, having been killed, skinned, and stuffed, is propped up on sticks with its head turned towards the grave.   At the funeral of a chief four horses are sacrificed, and one is set up at each corner of the burial-place.   The clothes and other effects of the deceased are burned ; and to conclude all, a feast is made of the horses' flesh.[2]   The Scythians certainly believed in the existence of the soul after death and in the possibility of turning it to account.   This is proved by the practice of one of their tribes, the Taurians of the Crimea, who used to cut off the heads of their prisoners and set them on poles over their houses, especially over the chimneys, in order that the spirits of the slain men might guard the dwellings.[3]

Some tribes of Borneo use the skulls of their enemies to

Some of the savages of Borneo allege a similar reason for their favourite custom of taking human heads. " The custom," said a Kayan chief, " is not horrible.   It is an ancient custom, a good, beneficent custom, bequeathed to us

[1] *Voyages d'Ibn Batoutah, texte Arabe accompagné d'une traduction,* par C. Défrémery et B. R. Sanguinetti (Paris, 1853–1858), iv. 300 *sq.* For more evidence of similar customs, observed by Turanian peoples, see K. Neumann, *Die Hellenen im Skythenlande* (Berlin, 1855), pp. 237-239.

[2] Captain R. Fitz-roy, *Narrative of the Surveying Voyages of His Majesty's Ships " Adventure" and " Beagle"* (London, 1839), ii. 155 *sq.*

[3] Herodotus, iv. 103.   Many Scythians flayed their dead enemies, and, stretching the skin on a wooden framework, carried it about with them on horseback (Herodotus, iv. 64).   The souls of the dead may have been thought to attend on and serve the man who thus bore their remains about with him.   It is also possible that

the custom was nothing more than a barbarous mode of wreaking vengeance on the dead.   Thus a Persian king has been known to flay an enemy, stuff the skin with chaff, and hang it on a high tree (Procopius, *De bello Persico,* i. 5. 28).   This was the treatment which the arch-heretic Manichaeus is said to have received at the hands of the Persian king whose son he failed to cure (Socrates, *Historia Ecclesiastica,* i. 22 ; Migne's *Patrologia Graeca,* lxvii. 137, 139).   Still such a punishment may have been suggested by a religious rite.   The idea of crucifying their human victims appears to have been suggested to the negroes of Benin by the crucifixes of the early Portuguese missionaries. See H. Ling Roth, *Great Benin* (Halifax, 1903), pp. 14 *sq.*

by our fathers and our fathers' fathers ; it brings us blessings, plentiful harvests, and keeps off sickness and pains.   Those who were once our enemies, hereby become our guardians, our friends, our benefactors." [1]   Thus to convert dead foes into friends and allies all that is necessary is to feed and other- wise propitiate their skulls at a festival when they are brought into the village.   " An offering of food is made to the heads, and their spirits, being thus appeased, cease to entertain malice against, or to seek to inflict injury upon, those who have got possession of the skull which formerly adorned the now forsaken body." [2]   When the Sea Dyaks of Sarawak return home successful from a head-hunting expedition, they bring the head ashore with much ceremony, wrapt in palm leaves.   " On shore and in the village, the head, for months after its arrival, is treated with the greatest consideration, and all the names and terms of endearment of which their language is capable are abundantly lavished on it ; the most dainty morsels, culled from their abundant though inelegant repast, are thrust into its mouth, and it is instructed to hate its former friends, and that, having been now adopted into the tribe of its captors, its spirit must be always with them ; sirih leaves and betel-nut are given to it, and finally a cigar is frequently placed between its ghastly and pallid lips.   None of this disgusting mockery is performed with the intention of ridicule, but all to propitiate the spirit by kindness, and to procure its good wishes for the tribe, of whom it is now supposed to have become a member." [3] Amongst these Dyaks the " Head-Feast," which has been just described, is supposed to be the most beneficial in its

[1] W. H. Furness, *Home-Life of Borneo Head-Hunters* (Philadelphia, 1902), p. 59. According to Messrs. Hose and McDougall, the spirits which animate the skulls appear not to be those of the persons from whose shoulders the heads were taken. How- ever, the spirits (called *Toh*) reside in or about the heads, and "it is held that in some way their presence in the house brings prosperity to it, especially in the form of good crops ; and so essential to the welfare of the house are the heads held to be that, if through fire a house has lost its heads and has no occasion for war, the people will beg a head, or even a fragment of one, from some friendly house, and will instal it in their own with the usual ceremonies." See Ch. Hose and W. McDougall, *The Pagan Tribes of Borneo* (London, 1912), ii. 20, 23.

[2] Spenser St. John, *Life in the Forests of the Far East* [2] (London, 1863), i. 197.

[3] Hugh Low, *Sarawak* (London, 1848), pp. 206 *sq.* In quoting this passage I have taken the liberty to correct a grammatical slip.

influence of all their feasts and ceremonies. "The object of them all is to make their rice grow well, to cause the forest to abound with wild animals, to enable their dogs and snares to be successful in securing game, to have the streams swarm with fish, to give health and activity to the people themselves, and to ensure fertility to their women. All these blessings, the possessing and feasting of a fresh head are supposed to be the most efficient means of securing. The very ground itself is believed to be benefited and rendered fertile, more fertile even than when the water in which fragments of gold presented by the Rajah have been washed, has been sprinkled over it." [1]

In like manner, if my conjecture is right, the man who represented the father-god of Phrygia used to be slain and his stuffed skin hung on the sacred pine in order that his spirit might work for the growth of the crops, the multiplication of animals, and the fertility of women. So at Athens an ox, which appears to have embodied the corn-spirit, was killed at an annual sacrifice, and its hide, stuffed with straw and sewn up, was afterwards set on its feet and yoked to a plough as if it were ploughing, apparently in order to represent, or rather to promote, the resurrection of the slain

The stuffed skin of the human representative of the Phrygian god may have been used for like purposes.

---

[1] Spenser St. John, *op. cit.* i. 204. See further G. A. Wilken, "Iets over de schedelvereereing," *Bijdragen tot de Taal- Land- en Volkenkunde van Nederlandsch-Indië*, xxxviii. (1889) pp. 89-129; *id.*, *Verspreide Geschriften* (The Hague, 1912), iv. 37-81. A different view of the purpose of head-hunting is maintained by Mr. A. C. Kruyt, in his essay, "Het koppensnellen der Toradja's van Midden-Celebes, en zijne Beteekenis," *Verslagen en Mede-deelingen der koninklijke Akademie van Wetenschappen*, Afdeeling Letterkunde, Vierde Reeks, iii. 2 (Amsterdam, 1899), pp. 147 *sqq.*

The natives of Nias, an island to the west of Sumatra, think it necessary to obtain the heads of their enemies for the purpose of celebrating the final obsequies of a dead chief. Their notion seems to be that the ghost of the deceased ruler demands this sacrifice in his honour, and will punish the omission of it by sending sickness or other misfortunes on the survivors. Thus among these people the custom of head-hunting is based on their belief in human immortality and on their conception of the exacting demands which the dead make upon the living. When the skulls have been presented to a dead chief, the priest prays to him for his blessing on the sowing and harvesting of the rice, on the fruit-fulness of women, and so forth. See C. Fries, "Das 'Koppensnellen' auf Nias," *Allgemeine Missions-Zeitschrift*, February, 1908, pp. 73-88. From this account it would seem that it is not the spirits of the slain men, but the ghost of the dead chief from whom the blessings of fertility and so forth are supposed to emanate. Compare Th. C. Rappard, "Het eiland Nias en zijne bewoners," *Bijdragen tot de Taal- Land- en Volkenkunde van Nederlandsch-Indië*, lxii. (1909) pp. 609-611.

corn-spirit at the end of the threshing.[1]   This employment
of the skins of divine animals for the purpose of ensuring
the revival of the slaughtered divinity might be illustrated by
other examples.[2]   Perhaps the hide of the bull which was
killed to furnish the regenerating bath of blood in the rites
of Attis may have been put to a similar use.

[1] *Spirits of the Corn and of the Wild*, ii. 4-7.

[2] *Spirits of the Corn and of the Wild*, ii. 169 *sqq.*

Popularity of the worship of Cybele and Attis in the Roman Empire. THE worship of the Great Mother of the Gods and her lover or son was very popular under the Roman Empire. Inscriptions prove that the two received divine honours, separately or conjointly, not only in Italy, and especially at Rome, but also in the provinces, particularly in Africa, Spain, Portugal, France, Germany, and Bulgaria.[1] Their worship survived the establishment of Christianity by Constantine ; for Symmachus records the recurrence of the festival of the Great Mother,[2] and in the days of Augustine her effeminate priests still paraded the streets and squares of Carthage with whitened faces, scented hair, and mincing gait, while, like the mendicant friars of the Middle Ages, they begged alms from the passers-by.[3] In Greece, on the other hand, the bloody orgies of the Asiatic goddess and her consort appear to have found little favour.[4] The barbarous and cruel character of the worship, with its frantic excesses, was doubtless repugnant to the good taste and humanity of the Greeks, who seem to have preferred the kindred but gentler rites of Adonis. Yet the same features which shocked and repelled the Greeks may have positively

---

[1] H. Dessau, *Inscriptiones Latinae Selectae*, Nos. 4099, 4100, 4103, 4105, 4106, 4116, 4117, 4119, 4120, 4121, 4123, 4124, 4127, 4128, 4131, 4136, 4139, 4140, 4142, 4156, 4163, 4167 ; H. Hepding, *Attis*, pp. 85, 86, 93, 94, 95, Inscr. Nos. 21-24, 26, 50, 51, 52, 61, 62, 63. See further, J. Toutain, *Les Cultes Païens dans l'Empire Romain* (Paris, 1911), pp. 73 *sqq.*, 103 *sqq.*

[2] S. Dill, *Roman Society in the Last Century of the Western Empire* [2] (London, 1899), p. 16.

[3] Augustine, *De civitate Dei*, vii. 26.

[4] But the two were publicly worshipped at Dyme and Patrae in Achaia (Pausanias, vii. 17. 9, vii. 20. 3), and there was an association for their worship at Piraeus. See P. Foucart, *Des Associations Religieuses chez les Grecs* (Paris, 1873), pp. 85 *sqq.*, 196 ; Ch. Michel, *Recueil d'Inscriptions Grecques*, p. 772, No. 982.

attracted the less refined Romans and barbarians of the West. The ecstatic frenzies, which were mistaken for divine inspiration,[1] the mangling of the body, the theory of a new birth and the remission of sins through the shedding of blood, have all their origin in savagery,[2] and they naturally appealed to peoples in whom the savage instincts were still strong. Their true character was indeed often disguised under a decent veil of allegorical or philosophical interpretation,[3] which probably sufficed to impose upon the rapt and enthusiastic worshippers, reconciling even the more cultivated of them to things which otherwise must have filled them with horror and disgust.

The religion of the Great Mother, with its curious blending of crude savagery with spiritual aspirations, was only one of a multitude of similar Oriental faiths which in the later days of paganism spread over the Roman Empire, and by saturating the European peoples with alien ideals of

The spread of Oriental faiths over the Roman Empire contributed to under-

---

[1] Rapp, *s.v.* "Kybele," in W. H. Roscher's *Lexikon der griech. und röm. Mythologie*, ii. 1656.

[2] As to the savage theory of inspiration or possession by a deity see (Sir) Edward B. Tylor, *Primitive Culture*,[2] ii. 131 *sqq.* As to the savage theory of a new birth see *Balder the Beautiful*, ii. 251 *sqq.* As to the use of blood to wash away sins see *The Magic Art and the Evolution of Kings*, ii. 107 *sqq.* ; *Psyche's Task*, Second Edition, pp. 44 *sq.*, 47 *sqq.*, 116 *sq.* Among the Cameroon negroes accidental homicide can be expiated by the blood of an animal. The relations of the slayer and of the slain assemble. An animal is killed and every person present is smeared with its blood on his face and breast. They think that the guilt of manslaughter is thus atoned for, and that no punishment will overtake the homicide. See Missionary Autenrieth, "Zur Religion der Kamerun-Neger," in *Mitteilungen der geographischen Gesellschaft zu Jena*, xii. (1893) pp. 93 *sq.* In Car Nicobar a man possessed by devils is cleansed of them by being rubbed all over with pig's blood and beaten with leaves.

The devils are thus transferred to the leaves, which are thrown into the sea before daybreak. See V. Solomon, "Extracts from diaries kept in Car Nicobar," in *Journal of the Anthropological Institute*, xxxii. (1902) p. 227. Similarly the ancient Greeks purified a homicide by means of pig's blood and laurel leaves. See my note on Pausanias, ii. 31. 8 (vol. iii. pp. 276-279). The original idea of thus purging a manslayer was probably to rid him of the angry ghost of his victim, just as in Car Nicobar a man is rid of devils in the same manner. The purgative virtue ascribed to the blood in these ceremonies may be based on the notion that the offended spirit accepts it as a substitute for the blood of the guilty person. This was the view of C. Meiners (*Geschichte der Religionen*, Hanover, 1806–1807, ii. 137 *sq.*) and of E. Rohde (*Psyche*,[3] Tübingen and Leipsic, 1903, ii. 77 *sq.*).

[3] A good instance of such an attempt to dress up savagery in the garb of philosophy is the fifth speech of the emperor Julian, "On the Mother of the Gods" (pp. 206 *sqq.* ed. F. C. Hertlein, Leipsic, 1875–1876).

mine the
fabric of
Greek and
Roman
civilization
by inculcat-
ing the
salvation
of the
individual
soul as the
supreme
aim of life.

life gradually undermined the whole fabric of ancient
civilization.[1] Greek and Roman society was built on the
conception of the subordination of the individual to the
community, of the citizen to the state ; it set the safety of
the commonwealth, as the supreme aim of conduct, above
the safety of the individual whether in this world or in a
world to come.   Trained from infancy in this unselfish
ideal, the citizens devoted their lives to the public service
and were ready to lay them down for the common good ;
or if they shrank from the supreme sacrifice, it never
occurred to them that they acted otherwise than basely in
preferring their personal existence to the interests of their
country.   All this was changed by the spread of Oriental
religions which inculcated the communion of the soul
with God and its eternal salvation as the only objects
worth living for, objects in comparison with which the
prosperity and even the existence of the state sank into
insignificance.   The inevitable result of this selfish and
immoral doctrine was to withdraw the devotee more
and more from the public service, to concentrate his
thoughts on his own spiritual emotions, and to breed in
him a contempt for the present life which he regarded
merely as a probation for a better and an eternal.   The
saint and the recluse, disdainful of earth and rapt in ecstatic
contemplation of heaven, became in popular opinion the
highest ideal of humanity, displacing the old ideal of the
patriot and hero who, forgetful of self, lives and is ready to
die for the good of his country.   The earthly city seemed
poor and contemptible to men whose eyes beheld the City
of God coming in the clouds of heaven.   Thus the centre
of gravity, so to say, was shifted from the present to a
future life, and however much the other world may have
gained, there can be little doubt that this one lost heavily
by the change.   A general disintegration of the body
politic set in.   The ties of the state and the family were
loosened : the structure of society tended to resolve itself

[1] As to the diffusion of Oriental
religions in the Roman Empire see
G. Boissier, *La Religion Romaine
d'Auguste aux Antonins*[5] (Paris, 1900),
i. 349 *sqq.* ; J. Reville, *La Religion à*

Rome sous les Sévères (Paris, 1886), pp.
47 *sqq.* ; S. Dill, *Roman Society in the
Last Century of the Western Empire*[2]
(London, 1899), pp. 76 *sqq.*

into its individual elements and thereby to relapse into barbarism ; for civilization is only possible through the active co-operation of the citizens and their willingness to subordinate their private interests to the common good. Men refused to defend their country and even to continue their kind.[1] In their anxiety to save their own souls and the souls of others, they were content to leave the material world, which they identified with the principle of evil, to perish around them.   This obsession lasted for a thousand years.   The revival of Roman law, of the Aristotelian philosophy, of ancient art and literature at the close of the Middle Ages, marked the return of Europe to native ideals of life and conduct, to saner, manlier views of the world. The long halt in the march of civilization was over.   The tide of Oriental invasion had turned at last.   It is ebbing still.[2]

Among the gods of eastern origin who in the decline of the ancient world competed against each other for the allegiance of the West was the old Persian deity Mithra.

Popularity of the worship of Mithra :

[1] Compare Servius on Virgil, *Aen.* ii. 604, vi. 661 ; Origen, *Contra Celsum*, viii. 73 (Migne's *Patrologia Graeca*, xi. 1628) ; G. Boissier, *La Religion Romaine d'Auguste aux Antonins*[5] (Paris, 1900), i. 357 *sq.* ; E. Westermarck, *The Origin and Development of the Moral Ideas* (London, 1906–1908), i. 345 *sq.* ; H. H. Milman, *History of Latin Christianity*,[4] i. 150-153, ii. 90.   In the passage just cited Origen tells us that the Christians refused to follow the Emperor to the field of battle even when he ordered them to do so ; but he adds that they gave the emperor the benefit of their prayers and thus did him more real service than if they had fought for him with the sword. On the decline of the civic virtues under the influence of Christian asceticism see W. E. H. Lecky, *History of European Morals from Augustus to Charlemagne*[3] (London, 1877), ii. 139 *sqq.*

[2] To prevent misapprehension I will add that the spread of Oriental religions was only one of many causes which contributed to the downfall of ancient civilization.   Among these contributory causes a friend, for whose judgment and learning I entertain the highest respect, counts bad government and a ruinous fiscal system, two of the most powerful agents to blast the prosperity of nations, as may be seen in our own day by the blight which has struck the Turkish empire.   It is probable, too, as my friend thinks, that the rapid diffusion of alien faiths was as much an effect as a cause of widespread intellectual decay.   Such unwholesome growths could hardly have fastened upon the Graeco-Roman mind in the days of its full vigour.   We may remember the energy with which the Roman Government combated the first outbreak of the Bacchic plague (Th. Mommsen, *Roman History*, iii. 115 *sq.*, ed. 1894).   The disastrous effects of Roman financial oppression on the industries and population of the empire, particularly of Greece, are described by George Finlay (*Greece under the Romans*,[2] Edinburgh and London, 1857, pp. 47 *sqq.*).

The immense popularity of his worship is attested by the monuments illustrative of it which have been found scattered in profusion all over the Roman Empire.[1] In respect both of doctrines and of rites the cult of Mithra appears to have presented many points of resemblance not only to the religion of the Mother of the Gods[2] but also to Christianity.[3] The similarity struck the Christian doctors themselves and was explained by them as a work of the devil, who sought to seduce the souls of men from the true faith by a false and insidious imitation of it.[4] So to the Spanish conquerors of Mexico and Peru many of the native heathen rites appeared to be diabolical counterfeits of the Christian sacraments.[5] With more probability the modern student of comparative religion traces such resemblances to the similar and independent workings of the mind of man in his sincere, if crude, attempts to fathom the secret of the universe, and to adjust his little life to its awful mysteries. However that may be, there can be no doubt that the Mithraic religion proved a formidable rival to Christianity, combining as it did a solemn ritual with aspirations after moral purity and a hope of immortality.[6] Indeed the issue of the conflict between the two faiths appears for a time to have hung in the balance.[7] An instructive relic of the long

---

[1] See Fr. Cumont, *Textes et Monuments figurés relatifs aux Mystères de Mithra* (Brussels, 1896–1899); *id.*, *s.v.* "Mithras," in W. H. Roscher's *Lexikon der griech. und röm. Mythologie*, ii. 3028 *sqq.* Compare *id.*, *Les Religions Orientales dans le Paganisme Romain*[2] (Paris, 1909), pp. 207 *sqq.*

[2] Fr. Cumont, *Textes et Monuments*, i. 333 *sqq.*

[3] E. Renan, *Marc-Aurèle et la Fin du Monde Antique* (Paris, 1882), pp. 576 *sqq.*; Fr. Cumont, *Textes et Monuments*, i. 339 *sqq.*

[4] Tertullian, *De corona*, 15; *id.*, *De praescriptione haereticorum*, 40; Justin Martyr, *Apologia*, i. 66; *id.*, *Dialogus cum Tryphone*, 78 (Migne's *Patrologia Graeca*, vi. 429, 660). Tertullian explained in like manner the resemblance of the fasts of Isis and Cybele to the fasts of Christianity (*De jejunio*, 16). Justin Martyr thought that by

listening to the words of the inspired prophets the devils discovered the divine intentions and anticipated them by a series of profane and blasphemous imitations. Among these travesties of Christian truth he enumerates the death, resurrection, and ascension of Dionysus, the virgin birth of Perseus, and Bellerophon mounted on Pegasus, whom he regards as a parody of Christ riding on an ass. See Justin Martyr, *Apology*, i. 54.

[5] J. de Acosta, *Natural and Moral History of the Indies*, translated by E. Grimston (London, 1880), bk. v. chs. 11, 16, 17, 18, 24-28, vol. ii. pp. 324 *sq.*, 334 *sqq.*, 356 *sqq.*

[6] Compare S. Dill, *Roman Society in the Last Century of the Western Empire*[2] (London, 1899), pp. 80 *sqq.*; *id.*, *Roman Society from Nero to Marcus Aurelius* (London, 1904), pp. 619 *sqq.*

[7] E. Renan, *Marc-Aurèle et la Fin*

struggle is preserved in our festival of Christmas, which the The festival of Christmas borrowed by the Church from the religion of Mithra. Church seems to have borrowed directly from its heathen rival. In the Julian calendar the twenty-fifth of December was reckoned the winter solstice,[1] and it was regarded as the Nativity of the Sun, because the day begins to lengthen and the power of the sun to increase from that turning-point of the year.[2]   The ritual of the nativity, as it appears to have been celebrated in Syria and Egypt, was remarkable. The celebrants retired into certain inner shrines, from which at midnight they issued with a loud cry, " The Virgin has brought forth! The light is waxing!"[3]   The Egyptians even represented the new-born sun by the image of an infant which on his birthday, the winter solstice, they brought forth and exhibited to his worshippers.[4]   No doubt the Virgin who thus conceived and bore a son on the twenty-fifth of December was the great Oriental goddess whom the Semites called the Heavenly Virgin or simply the Heavenly Goddess; in Semitic lands she was a form of Astarte.[5]   Now

---

du Monde Antique (Paris, 1882), pp. 579 *sq.* ; Fr. Cumont, *Textes et Monuments*, i. 338.

[1] Pliny, *Nat. Hist.* xviii. 221 ; Columella, *De re rustica*, ix. 14. 12 ; L. Ideler, *Handbuch der mathematischen und technischen Chronologie* (Berlin, 1825–1826), ii. 124 ; G. F. Unger, in Iwan Müller's *Handbuch der klassischen Altertumswissenschaft*, i.[1] (Nördlingen, 1886) p. 649.

[2] In the calendar of Philocalus the twenty-fifth of December is marked *N. Invicti*, that is, *Natalis Solis Invicti*. See *Corpus Inscriptionum Latinarum*, i.[2] Pars prior (Berlin, 1893), p. 278, with Th. Mommsen's commentary, pp. 338 *sq.*

[3] Cosmas Hierosolymitanus, *Com-. mentarii in Sancti Gregorii Nazianzeni Carmina* (Migne's *Patrologia Graeca*, xxxviii. 464): ταύτην [Christmas] ἦγον ἔκπαλαι δὲ τὴν ἡμέραν ἑορτὴν Ἕλληνες, καθ' ἣν ἐτελοῦντο κατὰ τὸ μεσονύκτιον, ἐν ἀδύτοις τισὶν ὑπεισερχόμενοι, ὅθεν ἐξιόντες ἔκραζον· "'Η παρθένος ἔτεκεν, αὔξει φῶς." ταύτην 'Επιφάνιος ὁ μέγας τῆς Κυπρίων ἱερεύς φησι τὴν ἑορτὴν καὶ Σαρρακηνοὺς ἄγειν τῇ παρ' αὐτῶν σεβομένῃ

'Αφροδίτῃ, ἣν δὴ Χαμαρᾷ τῇ αὐτῶν προσαγορεύουσι γλώττῃ. The passage is quoted, with some verbal variations, by Ch. Aug. Lobeck, *Aglaophamus* (Königsberg, 1829), ii. 1227 note[2]. See Franz Cumont, " Le Natalis Invicti," *Comptes Rendus de l'Académie des Inscriptions et Belles-Lettres, 1911* (Paris, 1911), pp. 292-298, whose learned elucidations I follow in the text.   That the festival of the Nativity of the Sun was similarly celebrated in Egypt may be inferred from a Greek calendar drawn up by the astrologer Antiochus in Lower Egypt at the end of the second or the beginning of the third century A.D. ; for under the 25th December the calendar has the entry, " Birthday of the Sun, the light waxes " ('Ηλίου γενέθλιον· αὔξει φῶς). See F. Cumont, *op. cit.* p. 294.

[4] Macrobius, *Saturnalia*, i. 18. 10.

[5] F. Cumont, *s.v.* " Caelestis," in Pauly - Wissowa's *Real - Encyclopädie der classischen Altertumswissenschaft*, v. i. 1247 *sqq.* She was called the Queen of Heaven (Jeremiah vii. 18, xliv. 18), the Heavenly Goddess (Herodotus, iii. 8 ; Pausanias, i. 14.

Mithra was regularly identified by his worshippers with the Sun, the Unconquered Sun, as they called him;[1] hence his nativity also fell on the twenty-fifth of December.[2] The Gospels say nothing as to the day of Christ's birth, and accordingly the early Church did not celebrate it. In time, however, the Christians of Egypt came to regard the sixth of January as the date of the Nativity, and the custom of commemorating the birth of the Saviour on that day gradually spread until by the fourth century it was universally established in the East. But at the end of the third or the beginning of the fourth century the Western Church, which had never recognized the sixth of January as the day of the Nativity, adopted the twenty-fifth of December as the true date, and in time its decision was accepted also by the Eastern Church. At Antioch the change was not introduced till about the year 375 A.D.[3]

Motives for the institution of Christmas. What considerations led the ecclesiastical authorities to institute the festival of Christmas? The motives for the innovation are stated with great frankness by a Syrian writer, himself a Christian. "The reason," he tells us, "why the fathers transferred the celebration of the sixth of January to the twenty-fifth of December was this. It was a custom of the heathen to celebrate on the same twenty-fifth of December the birthday of the Sun, at which they kindled

---

7), or the Heavenly Virgin (Tertullian, *Apologeticus*, 23; Augustine, *De civitate Dei*, ii. 4). The Greeks spoke of her as the Heavenly Aphrodite (Herodotus, i. 105; Pausanias, i. 14. 7). A Greek inscription found in Delos contains a dedication to Astarte Aphrodite; and another found in the same island couples Palestinian Astarte and Heavenly Aphrodite. See G. Dittenberger, *Sylloge Inscriptionum Graecorum*,[2] vol. ii. pp. 619 *sq.*, No. 764; R. A. Stewart Macalister, *The Philistines, their History and Civilization* (London, 1913), p. 94.

[1] Dedications to Mithra the Unconquered Sun (*Soli invicto Mithrae*) have been found in abundance. See Fr. Cumont, *Textes et Monuments*, ii. 99 *sqq.* As to the worship of the Unconquered Sun (*Sol Invictus*) see

H. Usener, *Das Weihnachtsfest*[2] (Bonn, 1911), pp. 348 *sqq.*

[2] Fr. Cumont, *op. cit.* i. 325 *sq.*, 339.

[3] J. Bingham, *The Antiquities of the Christian Church*, bk. xx. ch. iv. (Bingham's *Works*, vol. vii. pp. 279 *sqq.*, Oxford, 1855); C. A. Credner, "De natalitiorum Christi origine," *Zeitschrift für die historische Theologie*, iii. 2 (1833), pp. 236 *sqq.*; Mgr. L. Duchesne, *Origines du Culte Chrétien*[3] (Paris, 1903), pp. 257 *sqq.*; Th. Mommsen, in *Corpus Inscriptionum Latinarum*, i.[2] Pars prior, p. 338. The earliest mention of the festival of Christmas is in the calendar of Philocalus, which was drawn up at Rome in 336 A.D. The words are *VIII. kal. jan.*, *natus Christus in Betleem Judee* (L. Duchesne, *op. cit.* p. 258).

lights in token of festivity.   In these solemnities and festivities the Christians also took part.   Accordingly when the doctors of the Church perceived that the Christians had a leaning to this festival, they took counsel and resolved that the true Nativity should be solemnized on that day and the festival of the Epiphany on the sixth of January. Accordingly, along with this custom, the practice has prevailed of kindling fires till the sixth." [1]   The heathen origin of Christmas is plainly hinted at, if not tacitly admitted, by Augustine when he exhorts his Christian brethren not to celebrate that solemn day like the heathen on account of the sun, but on account of him who made the sun.[2]   In like manner Leo the Great rebuked the pestilent belief that Christmas was solemnized because of the birth of the new sun, as it was called, and not because of the nativity of Christ.[3]

Thus it appears that the Christian Church chose to celebrate the birthday of its Founder on the twenty-fifth of December in order to transfer the devotion of the heathen from the Sun to him who was called the Sun of Righteousness.[4]   If that was so, there can be no intrinsic improba-

The Easter celebration of the death and resurrection of Christ

---

[1] Quoted by C. A. Credner, *op. cit.* p. 239, note [46]; by Th. Mommsen, *Corpus Inscriptionum Latinarum*, i.[2] Pars prior, pp. 338 *sq.*; and by H. Usener, *Das Weihnachtsfest*[2] (Bonn, 1911), pp. 349 *sq.*

[2] Augustine, *Serm.* cxc. 1 (Migne's *Patrologia Latina*, xxxviii. 1007).

[3] Leo the Great, *Serm.* xxii. (*al.* xxi.) 6 (Migne's *Patrologia Latina*, liv. 198).   Compare St. Ambrose, *Serm.* vi. 1 (Migne's *Patrologia Latina*, xvii. 614).

[4] A. Credner, *op. cit.* pp. 236 *sqq.*; E. B. Tylor, *Primitive Culture*,[2] ii. 297 *sq.*; Fr. Cumont, *Textes et Monuments*, i. 342, 355 *sq.*; Th. Mommsen, in *Corpus Inscriptionum Latinarum*, i.[2] Pars prior, pp. 338 *sq.*; H. Usener, *Das Weihnachtsfest*[2] (Bonn, 1911), pp. 348 *sqq.* A different explanation of Christmas has been put forward by Mgr. Duchesne.   He shows that among the early Christians the death of Christ was commonly supposed to have fallen on the twenty-fifth of March, that day

having been "chosen arbitrarily, or rather suggested by its coincidence with the official equinox of spring." It would be natural to assume that Christ had lived an exact number of years on earth, and therefore that his incarnation as well as his death took place on the twenty-fifth of March.   In point of fact the Church has placed the Annunciation and with it the beginning of his mother's pregnancy on that very day.   If that were so, his birth would in the course of nature have occurred nine months later, that is, on the twenty-fifth of December.   Thus on Mgr. Duchesne's theory the date of the Nativity was obtained by inference from the date of the Crucifixion, which in its turn was chosen because it coincided with the official equinox of spring. Mgr. Duchesne does not notice the coincidence of the vernal equinox with the festival of Attis.   See his work, *Origines du Culte Chrétien*[3] (Paris, 1903), pp. 261-265, 272.   The tradition that both the conception and the

appears to
have been
assimilated
to the
celebration
of the
death and
resurrec-
tion of
Attis,
which was
held at
Rome at
the same
season.

bility in the conjecture that motives of the same sort may
have led the ecclesiastical authorities to assimilate the
Easter festival of the death and resurrection of their Lord
to the festival of the death and resurrection of another
Asiatic god which fell at the same season.   Now the Easter
rites still observed in Greece, Sicily, and Southern Italy bear
in some respects a striking resemblance to the rites of
Adonis, and I have suggested that the Church may have
consciously adapted the new festival to its heathen predecessor for the sake of winning souls to Christ.[1]   But this
adaptation probably took place in the Greek-speaking
rather than in the Latin-speaking parts of the ancient
world ; for the worship of Adonis, while it flourished among
the Greeks, appears to have made little impression on Rome
and the West.[2]   Certainly it never formed part of the official
Roman religion.   The place which it might have taken in
the affections of the vulgar was already occupied by the
similar but more barbarous worship of Attis and the Great
Mother.   Now the death and resurrection of Attis were
officially celebrated at Rome on the twenty-fourth and
twenty-fifth of March,[3] the latter being regarded as the
spring equinox,[4] and therefore as the most appropriate day
for the revival of a god of vegetation who had been dead
or sleeping throughout the winter.   But according to an
ancient and widespread tradition Christ suffered on the
twenty-fifth of March, and accordingly some Christians
regularly celebrated the Crucifixion on that day without
any regard to the state of the moon.   This custom was
certainly observed in Phrygia, Cappadocia, and Gaul, and
there seem to be grounds for thinking that at one time it
was followed also in Rome.[5]   Thus the tradition which

---

death of Christ fell on the twenty-fifth
of March is mentioned and apparently
accepted by Augustine (*De Trinitate*,
iv. 9, Migne's *Patrologia Latina*, xlii.
894).

[1] See above, pp. 253 *sqq.*

[2] However, the lament for Adonis
is mentioned by Ovid (*Ars Amat.* i.
75 *sq.*) along with the Jewish observance of the Sabbath.

[3] See above, pp. 268 *sqq.*

[4] Columella, *De re rustica*, ix. 14. 1 ;
Pliny, *Nat. Hist.* xviii. 246 ; Macrobius, *Saturn.* i. 21. 10 ; L. Ideler,
*Handbuch der mathematischen und
technischen Chronologie*, ii. 124.

[5] Mgr. L. Duchesne, *Origines du
Culte Chrétien*,[3] pp. 262 *sq.*   That
Christ was crucified on the twenty-
fifth of March in the year 29 is ex-
pressly affirmed by Tertullian (*Adversus
Judaeos*, 8, vol. ii. p. 719, ed. F.

placed the death of Christ on the twenty-fifth of March was ancient and deeply rooted. It is all the more remarkable because astronomical considerations prove that it can have had no historical foundation.[1] The inference appears to be inevitable that the passion of Christ must have been arbitrarily referred to that date in order to harmonize with an older festival of the spring equinox. This is the view of the learned ecclesiastical historian Mgr. Duchesne, who points out that the death of the Saviour was thus made to fall upon the very day on which, according to a widespread belief, the world had been created.[2] But the resur-

Oehler), Hippolytus (*Commentary on Daniel*, iv. 23, vol. i. p. 242, ed. Bonwetsch and Achelis), and Augustine (*De civitate Dei*, xviii. 54; *id.*, *De Trinitate*, iv. 9). See also *Thesaurus Linguae Latinae*, iv. (Leipsic, 1906–1909) col. 1222, *s.v.* "Crucimissio": "*POL. SILV. fast. Mart* 25 *aequinoctium. principium veris. crucimissio gentilium. Christus passus hoc die.*" From this last testimony we learn that there was a gentile as well as a Christian crucifixion at the spring equinox. The gentile crucifixion was probably the affixing of the effigy of Attis to the tree, though at Rome that ceremony appears to have taken place on the twenty-second rather than on the twenty-fifth of March. See above, p. 267. The Quartodecimans of Phrygia celebrated the twenty-fifth of March as the day of Christ's death, quoting as their authority certain acts of Pilate; in Cappadocia the adherents of this sect were divided between the twenty-fifth of March and the fourteenth of the moon. See Epiphanius, *Adversus Haeres.* l. 1 (vol. ii. p. 447, ed. G. Dindorf; Migne's *Patrologia Graeca*, xli. 884 *sq.*). In Gaul the death and resurrection of Christ were regularly celebrated on the twenty-fifth and twenty-seventh of March as late as the sixth century. See Gregory of Tours, *Historia Francorum*, viii. 31. 6 (Migne's *Patrologia Latina*, lxxi. 566); S. Martinus Dumiensis (bishop of Braga), *De Pascha*, 1 (Migne's *Patrologia Latina*, lxxii. 50), who says: "*A plerisque Gallicanis episcopis usque*

ante non multum tempus custoditum est, ut semper VIII. Kal. April. diem Paschae celebrent, in quo facta Christi resurrectio traditur." According to this last testimony, it was the resurrection, not the crucifixion, of Christ that was celebrated on the twenty-fifth of March; but Mgr. Duchesne attributes the statement to a mistake of the writer. With regard to the Roman practice the twenty-fifth and twenty-seventh of March are marked in ancient Martyrologies as the dates of the Crucifixion and Resurrection. See *Vetustius Occidentalis Ecclesiae Martyrologium*, ed. Franciscus Maria Florentinus (Lucca, 1667), pp. 396 *sq.*, 405 *sq.* On this subject Mgr. Duchesne observes: "Hippolytus, in his Paschal Table, marks the Passion of Christ in a year in which the fourteenth of Nisan falls on Friday twenty-fifth March. In his commentary on Daniel he expressly indicates Friday the twenty-fifth of March and the consulship of the two Gemini. The Philocalien Catalogue of the Popes gives the same date as to day and year. It is to be noted that the cycle of Hippolytus and the Philocalien Catalogue are derived from official documents, and may be cited as evidence of the Roman ecclesiastical usage" (*Origines du Culte Chrétien*,[3] p. 262).

[1] Mgr. L. Duchesne, *op. cit.* p. 263.
[2] Mgr. L. Duchesne, *l.c.* A sect of the Montanists held that the world began and that the sun and moon were created at the spring equinox, which, however, they dated on the twenty-

rection of Attis, who combined in himself the characters
of the divine Father and the divine Son,[1] was officially
celebrated at Rome on the same day.   When we remember
that the festival of St. George in April has replaced the
ancient pagan festival of the Parilia;[2] that the festival of
St. John the Baptist in June has succeeded to a heathen
Midsummer festival of water;[3] that the festival of the
Assumption of the Virgin in August has ousted the festival
of Diana;[4] that the feast of All Souls in November is a
continuation of an old heathen feast of the dead;[5] and
that the Nativity of Christ himself was assigned to the
winter solstice in December because that day was deemed
the Nativity of the Sun;[6] we can hardly be thought rash
or unreasonable in conjecturing that the other cardinal
festival of the Christian church — the solemnization of
Easter—may have been in like manner, and from like
motives of edification, adapted to a similar celebration of
the Phrygian god Attis at the vernal equinox.[7]

Coinci-
dence be-
tween the
pagan
and the
Christian
festivals of
the divine
death and
resurrec-
tion.

At least it is a remarkable coincidence, if it is nothing
more, that the Christian and the heathen festivals of the
divine death and resurrection should have been solemnized
at the same season and in the same places.   For the places
which celebrated the death of Christ at the spring equinox
were Phrygia, Gaul, and apparently Rome, that is, the very
regions in which the worship of Attis either originated or

---

fourth of March (Sozomenus, *Historia
Ecclesiastica*, vii. 18).   At Henen-Su in
Egypt there was celebrated a festival
of the "hanging out of the heavens,"
that is, the supposed reconstituting of
the heavens each year in the spring
(E. A. Wallis Budge, *The Gods of the
Egyptians*, ii. 63).   But the Egyptians
thought that the creation of the world
took place at the rising of Sirius
(Porphyry, *De antro nympharum*, 24;
Solinus, xxxii. 13), which in antiquity
fell on the twentieth of July (L. Ideler,
*Handbuch der mathematischen und
technischen Chronologie*, i. 127 *sqq.*).

[1] See above, pp. 263, 281 *sqq.*
[2] *The Magic Art and the Evolution
of Kings*, ii. 324 *sqq.*
[3] Above, pp. 246 *sqq.*
[4] *The Magic Art and the Evolution*

of Kings, i. 14 *sqq.*
[5] See below, vol. ii. pp. 81 *sqq.*
[6] Above, pp. 302 *sqq.*
[7] Another instance of the substitution of a Christian for a pagan festival
may be mentioned.   On the first of
August the people of Alexandria used
to commemorate the defeat of Mark
Antony by Augustus and the entrance
of the victor into their city.   The
heathen pomp of the festival offended
Eudoxia, wife of Theodosius the
Younger, and she decreed that on that
day the Alexandrians should thenceforth celebrate the deliverance of St.
Peter from prison instead of the deliverance of their city from the yoke of
Antony and Cleopatra. See L. Ideler,
*Handbuch der mathematischen und
technischen Chronologie*, i. 154.

struck deepest root. It is difficult to regard the coincidence as purely accidental. If the vernal equinox, the season at which in the temperate regions the whole face of nature testifies to a fresh outburst of vital energy, had been viewed from of old as the time when the world was annually created afresh in the resurrection of a god, nothing could be more natural than to place the resurrection of the new deity at the same cardinal point of the year. Only it is to be observed that if the death of Christ was dated on the twenty-fifth of March, his resurrection, according to Christian tradition, must have happened on the twenty-seventh of March, which is just two days later than the vernal equinox of the Julian calendar and the resurrection of Attis. A similar displacement of two days in the adjustment of Christian to heathen celebrations occurs in the festivals of St. George and the Assumption of the Virgin. However, another Christian tradition, followed by Lactantius and perhaps by the practice of the Church in Gaul, placed the death of Christ on the twenty-third and his resurrection on the twenty-fifth of March.[1] If that was so, his resurrection coincided exactly with the resurrection of Attis.

In point of fact it appears from the testimony of an anonymous Christian, who wrote in the fourth century of our era, that Christians and pagans alike were struck by the remarkable coincidence between the death and resurrection of their respective deities, and that the coincidence formed a theme of bitter controversy between the adherents of the rival religions, the pagans contending that the resurrection of Christ was a spurious imitation of the resurrection of Attis, and the Christians asserting with equal warmth that the resurrection of Attis was a diabolical counterfeit of the resurrection of Christ. In these unseemly bickerings the heathen took what to a superficial observer might seem strong ground by arguing that their god was the older and therefore presumably the original, not the counterfeit, since as a general rule an original is older than its copy. This feeble argument the Christians easily rebutted. They

Different theories by which pagans and Christians explained the coincidence.

---

[1] Lactantius, *De mortibus persecutorum*, 2 ; *id.*, *Divin. Institut.* iv. 10. 18. As to the evidence of the Gallic usage see S. Martinus Dumiensis, quoted above, p. 307 note.

admitted, indeed, that in point of time Christ was the junior deity, but they triumphantly demonstrated his real seniority by falling back on the subtlety of Satan, who on so important an occasion had surpassed himself by inverting the usual order of nature.[1]

Com-
promise of
Christi-
anity with
paganism.

Taken altogether, the coincidences of the Christian with the heathen festivals are too close and too numerous to be accidental. They mark the compromise which the Church in the hour of its triumph was compelled to make with its vanquished yet still dangerous rivals. The inflexible Protestantism of the primitive missionaries, with their fiery denunciations of heathendom, had been exchanged for the supple policy, the easy tolerance, the comprehensive charity of shrewd ecclesiastics, who clearly perceived that if Christianity was to conquer the world it could do so only by relaxing the too rigid principles of its Founder, by widening a little the narrow gate which leads to salvation. In this respect an instructive parallel might be drawn between the history of Christianity and the

Parallel
with
Buddhism.

---

[1] The passage occurs in the 84th of the *Quaestiones Veteris et Novi Testamenti* (Migne's *Patrologia Latina*, xxxv. 2279), which are printed in the works of Augustine, though internal evidence is said to shew that they cannot be by that Father, and that they were written three hundred years after the destruction of Jerusalem. The writer's words are as follows: "*Diabolus autem, qui est satanas, ut fallaciae suae auctoritatem aliquam possit adhibere, et mendacia sua commentitia veritate colorare, primo mense quo sacramenta dominica scit celebranda, quia non mediocris potentiae est, Paganis quae observarent instituit mysteria, ut animas eorum duabus ex causis in errore detineret: ut quia praevenit veritatem fallacia, melius quiddam fallacia videretur, quasi antiquitate praejudicans veritati. Et quia in primo mense, in quo aequinoctium habent Romani, sicut et nos, ea ipsa observatio ab his custoditur; ita etiam per sanguinem dicant expiationem fieri, sicut et nos per crucem: hac versutia Paganos detinet in errore, ut putent*

veritatem nostram imitationem potius videri quam veritatem, quasi per aemulationem superstitione quadam inventam. Nec enim verum potest, inquiunt, aestimari quod postea est inventum. Sed quia apud nos pro certo veritas est, et ab initio haec est, virtutum atque prodigiorum signa perhibent testimonium, ut, teste virtute, diaboli improbitas innotescat." I have to thank my learned friend Professor Franz Cumont for pointing out this passage to me. He had previously indicated and discussed it ("La Polémique de l'Ambrosiaster contre les Païens," *Revue d'Histoire et de Littérature religieuses*, viii. (1903) pp. 419 sqq.). Though the name of Attis is not mentioned in the passage, I agree with Prof. Cumont in holding that the bloody expiatory rites at the spring equinox, to which the writer refers, can only be those of the Day of Blood which formed part of the great aequinoctial festival of Attis. Compare F. Cumont, *Les Religions Orientales dans le Paganisme Romain*[2] (Paris, 1909), pp. 106 *sq.*, 333 *sq.*

history of Buddhism.[1]   Both systems were in their origin
essentially ethical reforms born of the generous ardour,
the lofty aspirations, the tender compassion of their noble
Founders, two of those beautiful spirits who appear at
rare intervals on earth like beings come from a better
world to support and guide our weak and erring nature.[2]
Both preached moral virtue as the means of accomplishing
what they regarded as the supreme object of life, the
eternal salvation of the individual soul, though by a curious
antithesis the one sought that salvation in a blissful eternity,
the other in a final release from suffering, in annihilation.
But the austere ideals of sanctity which they inculcated
were too deeply opposed not only to the frailties but to
the natural instincts of humanity ever to be carried out in
practice by more than a small number of disciples, who
consistently renounced the ties of the family and the state
in order to work out their own salvation in the still
seclusion of the cloister.   If such faiths were to be
nominally accepted by whole nations or even by the
world, it was essential that they should first be modified
or transformed so as to accord in some measure with the
prejudices, the passions, the superstitions of the vulgar.
This process of accommodation was carried out in after
ages by followers who, made of less ethereal stuff than
their masters, were for that reason the better fitted to
mediate between them and the common herd.   Thus as
time went on, the two religions, in exact proportion to
their growing popularity, absorbed more and more of those
baser elements which they had been instituted for the very
purpose of suppressing.   Such spiritual decadences are

---

[1] On the decadence of Buddhism
and its gradual assimilation to those
popular Oriental superstitions against
which it was at first directed, see
Monier Williams, *Buddhism* [2] (London,
1890), pp. 147 *sqq.*

[2] The historical reality both of
Buddha and of Christ has sometimes
been doubted or denied.   It would
be just as reasonable to question the
historical existence of Alexander the
Great and Charlemagne on account

of the legends which have gathered
round them.   The great religious
movements which have stirred humanity
to its depths and altered the beliefs
of nations spring ultimately from the
conscious and deliberate efforts of extraordinary minds, not from the blind un-
conscious co-operation of the multitude.
The attempt to explain history without
the influence of great men may flatter
the vanity of the vulgar, but it will
find no favour with the philosophic
historian.

inevitable. The world cannot live at the level of its great men. Yet it would be unfair to the generality of our kind to ascribe wholly to their intellectual and moral weakness the gradual divergence of Buddhism and Christianity from their primitive patterns. For it should never be forgotten that by their glorification of poverty and celibacy both these religions struck straight at the root not merely of civil society but of human existence. The blow was parried by the wisdom or the folly of the vast majority of mankind, who refused to purchase a chance of saving their souls with the certainty of extinguishing the species.

CHAPTER VII

HYACINTH

ANOTHER mythical being who has been supposed to belong to the class of gods here discussed is Hyacinth. He too has been interpreted as the vegetation which blooms in spring and withers under the scorching heat of the summer sun.[1] Though he belongs to Greek, not to Oriental mythology, some account of him may not be out of place in the present discussion. According to the legend, Hyacinth was the youngest and handsomest son of the ancient king Amyclas, who had his capital at Amyclae in the beautiful vale of Sparta. One day playing at quoits with Apollo, he was accidentally killed by a blow of the god's quoit. Bitterly the god lamented the death of his friend. The hyacinth—" that sanguine flower inscribed with woe "— sprang from the blood of the hapless youth, as anemones and roses from the blood of Adonis, and violets from the blood of Attis:[2] like these vernal flowers it heralded the advent of another spring and gladdened the hearts of men with the promise of a joyful resurrection. The flower is usually supposed to be not what we call a hyacinth, but a little purple iris with the letters of lamentation (AI, which in

The Greek Hyacinth interpreted as the vegetation which blooms and withers away.

[1] G. F. Schömann, *Griechische Alterthümer*[4] (Berlin, 1897–1902), ii. 473; L. Preller, *Griechische Mythologie*, i.[4] (Berlin, 1894) pp. 248 *sq.*; Greve, *s.v.* "Hyakinthos," in W. H. Roscher's *Lexikon der griech. und röm. Mythologie*, i. 2763 *sq.* Other views of Hyacinth have been expressed by G. F. Welcker (*Griechische Götterlehre*, Göttingen, 1857–1862, i. 472), G. F. Unger ("Der Isthmientag und die Hyakin-thien," *Philologus*, xxxvii. (1877) pp. 20 *sqq.*), E. Rohde (*Psyche*,[3] i. 137 *sqq.*) and S. Wide (*Lakonische Kulte*, Leipsic, 1893, p. 290).

[2] Apollodorus, *Bibliotheca*, i. 3. 3, iii. 10. 3; Nicander, *Ther.* 901 *sqq.*, with the Scholiast's note; Lucian, *De saltatione*, 45; Pausanias, iii. 1. 3, iii. 19. 5; J. Tzetzes, *Chiliades*, i. 241 *sqq.*; Ovid, *Metam.* x. 161-219; Pliny, *Nat. Hist.* xxi. 66.

Greek means "alas") clearly inscribed in black on its petals. In Greece it blooms in spring after the early violets but before the roses.[1]　One spring, when the hyacinths were in bloom, it happened that the red-coated Spartan regiments lay encamped under the walls of Corinth. Their com-mander gave the Amyclean battalion leave to go home and celebrate as usual the festival of Hyacinth in their native town. But the sad flower was to be to these men an omen of death ; for they had not gone far before they were enveloped by clouds of light-armed foes and cut to pieces.[2]

The tomb and the festival of Hyacinth at Amyclae.

The tomb of Hyacinth was at Amyclae under a massive altar-like pedestal, which supported an archaic bronze image of Apollo. In the left side of the pedestal was a bronze door, and through it offerings were passed to Hyacinth, as to a hero or a dead man, not as to a god, before sacrifices were offered to Apollo at the annual Hyacinthian festival. Bas-reliefs carved on the pedestal represented Hyacinth and his maiden sister Polyboea caught up to heaven by a company of goddesses.[3]　The annual festival of the Hyacinthia was held in the month of Hecatombeus, which seems to have corresponded to May.[4]　The ceremonies occupied three days. On the first the people mourned for

---

[1] Theophrastus, *Histor. Plant.* vi. 8. 1 *sq.* That the hyacinth was a spring flower is plainly indicated also by Philostratus (*Imag.* i. 23. 1) and Ovid (*Metam.* x. 162-166). See further Greve, *s.v.* "Hyakinthos," in W. H. Roscher's *Lexikon der griech. und röm. Mythologie*, i. 2764 ; J. Murr, *Die Pflanzenwelt in der griechi-schen Mythologie* (Innsbruck, 1890), pp. 257 *sqq.* ; O. Schrader, *Reallexi-kon der Indogermanischen Altertums-kunde* (Strasburg, 1901), pp. 383 *sq.* Miss J. E. Harrison was so kind as to present me with two specimens of the flower (*Delphinium Ajacis*) on which the woful letters were plainly visible. A flower similarly marked, of a colour between white and red, was associated with the death of Ajax (Pausanias, i. 35. 4). But usually the two flowers were thought to be the same (Ovid, *Metam.* xiii. 394 *sqq.* ; Scholiast on

Theocritus, x. 28 ; Pliny, *Nat. Hist.* xxi. 66 ; Eustathius on Homer, *Iliad*, ii. 557, p. 285).

[2] Xenophon, *Hellenica*, iv. 5. 7-17 ; Pausanias, iii. 10. 1.

[3] Pausanias, iii. 1. 3, iii. 19. 1-5.

[4] Hesychius, *s.v.* Ἑκατομβεύς ; G. F. Unger in *Philologus*, xxxvii. (1877) pp. 13-33 ; Greve, *s.v.* "Hyakinthos," in W. H. Roscher's *Lexikon der griech. und röm. Mythologie*, i. 2762 ; W. Smith, *Dictionary of Greek and Roman Antiquities*,[3] i. 339. From Xenophon (*Hellenica*, iv. 5) we learn that in 390 B.C. the Hyacinthian followed soon after the Isthmian festival, which that year fell in spring. Others, however, identifying Hecatom-beus with the Attic month Hecatom-baeon, would place the Hyacinthia in July (K. O. Müller, *Dorier*,[2] Breslau, 1844, i. 358). In Rhodes, Cos, and other Greek states there was a month

Hyacinth, wearing no wreaths, singing no paeans, eating no bread, and behaving with great gravity. It was on this day probably that the offerings were made at Hyacinth's tomb. Next day the scene was changed. All was joy and bustle. The capital was emptied of its inhabitants, who poured out in their thousands to witness and share the festivities at Amyclae. Boys in high-girt tunics sang hymns in honour of the god to the accompaniment of flutes and lyres. Others, splendidly attired, paraded on horseback in the theatre: choirs of youths chanted their native ditties: dancers danced: maidens rode in wicker carriages or went in procession to witness the chariot races: sacrifices were offered in profusion: the citizens feasted their friends and even their slaves.[1] This outburst of gaiety may be supposed to have celebrated the resurrection of Hyacinth and perhaps also his ascension to heaven, which, as we have seen, was represented on his tomb. However, it may be that the ascension took place on the third day of the festival; but as to that we know nothing. The sister who went to heaven with him was by some identified with Artemis or Persephone.[2]

It is highly probable, as Erwin Rohde perceived,[3] that Hyacinth was an old aboriginal deity of the underworld who had been worshipped at Amyclae long before the Dorians invaded and conquered the country. If that was so, the story of his relation to Apollo must have been a comparatively late invention, an attempt of the newcomers to fit the ancient god of the land into their own mythical system, in order that he might extend his protection to them. On this theory it may not be without significance

[marginal note:] Hyacinth an aboriginal god, perhaps a king, who was worshipped in Laconia before the invasion of the Dorians.

---

called Hyacinthius, which probably took its name from the Hyacinthian festival. The month is thought to correspond to the Athenian Scirophorion and therefore to June. See E. Bischof, "De fastis Graecorum antiquioribus," *Leipziger Studien für classische Philologie*, vii. (1884) pp. 369 *sq.*, 381, 384, 410, 414 *sq.*; G. Dittenberger, *Sylloge Inscriptionum Graecarum*,[2] vol. i. pp. 396, 607, Nos. 614, note [3], 744, note [1]. If this latter identification of

the month is correct, it would furnish an argument for dating the Spartan festival of Hyacinth in June also. The question is too intricate to be discussed here.

[1] Athenaeus, iv. 17, pp. 139 *sq.* Strabo speaks (vi. 3. 2, p. 278) of a contest at the Hyacinthian festival. It may have been the chariot races mentioned by Athenaeus.

[2] Hesychius, *s.v.* Πολύβοια.

[3] E. Rohde, *Psyche*,[3] i. 137 *sqq.*

that sacrifices at the festival were offered to Hyacinth, as to a hero, before they were offered to Apollo.[1] Further, on the analogy of similar deities elsewhere, we should expect to find Hyacinth coupled, not with a male friend, but with a female consort. That consort may perhaps be detected in his sister Polyboea, who ascended to heaven with him. The new myth, if new it was. of the love of Apollo for Hyacinth would involve a changed conception of the aboriginal god, which in its turn must have affected that of his spouse. For when Hyacinth came to be thought of as young and unmarried there was no longer room in his story for a wife, and she would have to be disposed of in some other way. What was easier for the myth-maker than to turn her into his unmarried sister? However we may explain it, a change seems certainly to have come over the popular idea of Hyacinth; for whereas on his tomb he was portrayed as a bearded man, later art represented him as the pink of youthful beauty.[2] But it is perhaps needless to suppose that the sisterly relation of Polyboea to him was a late modification of the myth. The stories of Cronus and Rhea, of Zeus and Hera, of Osiris and Isis, remind us that in old days gods, like kings, often married their sisters, and probably for the same reason, namely, to ensure their own title to the throne under a rule of female kinship which treated women and not men as the channel in which the blood royal flowed.[3] It is not impossible that Hyacinth may have been a divine king who actually reigned in his lifetime at Amyclae and was afterwards worshipped at his tomb. The representation of his triumphal ascent to heaven in company with his sister suggests that, like Adonis and Persephone, he may have been supposed to spend one part of the year in the

His sister Polyboea may perhaps have been his spouse.

---

[1] Pausanias, iii. 19. 3. The Greek word here used for sacrifice (ἐναγίζειν) properly denotes sacrifices offered to the heroic or worshipful dead ; another word (θύειν) was employed for sacrifices offered to gods. The two terms are distinguished by Pausanias here and elsewhere (ii. 10. 1, ii. 11. 7). Compare Herodotus, ii. 44. Sacrifices to the worshipful dead were often annual. See Pausanias, iii. 1. 8, vii. 19. 10, vii. 20. 9, viii. 14. 11, viii. 41. 1, ix. 38. 5, x. 24. 6. It has been observed by E. Rohde (*Psyche*,[3] i. 139, note [2]) that sacrifices were frequently offered to a hero before a god, and he suggests with much probability that in these cases the worship of the hero was older than that of the deity.

[2] Pausanias, iii. 19. 14.

[3] See above, p. 44 ; and below, vol. ii. pp. 213 *sqq.*

under-world of darkness and death, and another part in the upper-world of light and life. And as the anemones and the sprouting corn marked the return of Adonis and Persephone, so the flowers to which he gave his name may have heralded the ascension of Hyacinth.

END OF VOL. I

Printed by R. & R. CLARK, LIMITED, Edinburgh.

Works by J. G. FRAZER, D.C.L., LL.D., Litt.D.

THE GOLDEN BOUGH

A STUDY IN MAGIC AND RELIGION

Third Edition, revised and enlarged. 8vo.

Part I. THE MAGIC ART AND THE EVOLUTION OF KINGS. Two volumes. Second Impression. 20s. net.

II. TABOO AND THE PERILS OF THE SOUL. One volume. Second Impression. 10s. net.

III. THE DYING GOD. One volume. Second Impression. 10s. net.

IV. ADONIS, ATTIS, OSIRIS. Two volumes. Third Edition. 20s. net.

V. SPIRITS OF THE CORN AND OF THE WILD. Two volumes. 20s. net.

VI. THE SCAPEGOAT. One volume. 10s. net.

VII. BALDER THE BEAUTIFUL : THE FIRE-FESTIVALS OF EUROPE AND THE DOCTRINE OF THE EXTERNAL SOUL. Two volumes. 20s. net.

Vol. XII. GENERAL INDEX AND BIBLIOGRAPHY. [*In the Press.*

TIMES.—"The verdict of posterity will probably be that *The Golden Bough* has influenced the attitude of the human mind towards supernatural beliefs and symbolical rituals more profoundly than any other books published in the nineteenth century except those of Darwin and Herbert Spencer."

TOTEMISM AND EXOGAMY. A Treatise on Certain Early Forms of Superstition and Society. With Maps. Four vols. 8vo. 50s. net.

MR. A. E. CRAWLEY in *NATURE.*—"That portion of the book which is concerned with totemism (if we may express our own belief at the risk of offending Prof. Frazer's characteristic modesty) is actually 'The Complete History of Totemism, its Practice and its Theory, its Origin and its End.' . . . Nearly two thousand pages are occupied with an ethnographical survey of totemism, an invaluable compilation. The maps, including that of the distribution of totemic peoples, are a new and useful feature."

LECTURES ON THE EARLY HISTORY OF THE KINGSHIP. 8vo. 8s. 6d. net.

ATHENÆUM.—"It is the effect of a good book not only to teach, but also to stimulate and to suggest, and we think this the best and highest quality, and one that will recommend these lectures to all intelligent readers, as well as to the learned."

PSYCHE'S TASK. A Discourse concerning the Influence of Superstition on the Growth of Institutions. Second Edition, revised and enlarged. To which is added " The Scope of Social Anthropology." 8vo. 5s. net.

OUTLOOK.—"Whether we disagree or agree with Dr. Frazer's general conclusions, he has provided us with a veritable storehouse of correlated facts, for which, and for the learning that has gone to their collection, and for the intellectual brilliance that has gone to their arrangement, we can never be sufficiently grateful."

MACMILLAN AND CO., LTD., LONDON.

Lightning Source UK Ltd.
Milton Keynes UK
UKHW011844160620
364869UK00001B/19

9 781108 047340